Race and Modern Architecture

Culture, Politics, and the Built Environment

Dianne Harris, Editor

RACE AND MODERN ARCHITECTURE

A Critical History from the Enlightenment to the Present

Edited by **IRENE CHENG**
CHARLES L. DAVIS II
MABEL O. WILSON

University of Pittsburgh Press

Graham Foundation

This publication has been supported by a grant from the Graham Foundation for Advanced Studies in the Fine Arts.

Published by the University of Pittsburgh Press, Pittsburgh, Pa., 15260

Copyright © 2020, University of Pittsburgh Press

All rights reserved

This paperback edition, 2020

Manufactured in the United States of America

Printed on acid-free paper

10 9 8 7 6 5 4 3 2 1

Cataloging-in-Publication data is available from the Library of Congress

ISBN 13: 978-0-8229-6659-3

ISBN 10: 0-8229-6659-X

Book and cover design by Joel W. Coggins

Contents

Acknowledgments

In the fall of 2015, the editors of this book organized an interdisciplinary research group, the Race and Modern Architecture Project (R+MAP), to begin investigating the ways that race has been integral in shaping modern architectural discourse from the Enlightenment to the present. To begin our study, we assembled a bibliography of primary and secondary readings on general race theory, the history of slavery and colonialism in the West, primary texts in architecture that exemplified those themes, and publications from contemporary scholars pioneering new readings and interpretations. This initial bibliography provided a common foundation and set of references for the work of the research group. After a call for papers, we convened a symposium in the spring of 2016 at Columbia University's Graduate School of Architecture, Planning and Preservation that opened with the round-table "Critical Dialogues on Race and Modern Architecture" before turning to a series of paper presentations. These presentations served as the foundations for the chapters of this book. We believe that the resulting work will bring much needed visibility and momentum to the study of race in architecture, as well as provide architectural historians and allied scholars with the critical tools necessary to articulate the latent cultural underpinnings of our discipline.

This book was generously supported by a publication grant from the Graham Foundation for Advanced Studies in the Fine Arts. Additional support during various stages of the project came from Columbia University's Graduate School of Architecture, Planning and Preservation, with special thanks to Dean Amale Andraos and Associate Dean David Hinkle. Saidiya Hartman also provided reflective insights very early in the process.

This book is all the better thanks to all of the talented people at the University of Pittsburgh Press, including the series editor, Dianne Harris, and the acquisitions editor, Abby Collier. It also benefited from two anonymous peer reviewers and several colleagues and students who assisted in the manuscript's development, including Caitlin Blanchfield, Emma Macdonald, Addison Godel, Fangying Zhu, and Lina Kudinar. We are grateful for the patience, enthusiasm, and intelligence of the many collaborators who helped bring this book to fruition.

Race and Modern Architecture

Introduction

Irene Cheng, Charles L. Davis II, and Mabel O. Wilson

Architectural historians have traditionally avoided the topic of race.[1] When they do acknowledge the subject, they often quickly dismiss its significance, or cast it outside the proper boundaries of the discipline. Hanno-Walter Kruft's treatment of Eugène-Emmanuel Viollet-le-Duc's reliance on the racial theories of Arthur de Gobineau is typical. Such views, Kruft writes, "are not calculated to arouse our admiration today; however, they are only later accretions to his work."[2] Other scholars have danced around the topic of race by tackling architecture's engagement with related but more neutral historical formations, such as nationalism, ethnography, and evolution, while somehow downplaying the entanglement of each of these with racial theories.[3] These silences and avoidances stand in contrast to the approach taken in fields like history, law, anthropology, geography, political science, cultural studies, and literature, which have given birth to important interdisciplines like colonial studies, postcolonial theory, critical race studies, and whiteness studies. Scholars in these fields have revealed the modern Western episteme to be deeply racialized—a product of Europe's deployment of ethnographic, aesthetic, scientific, and philosophical concepts of human difference to universalize its ideologies and practices while ignoring and destroying other ways of knowing and being.[4] Modern architecture entailed spatial practices like classifying, mapping, planning, and building that were integral to the erection of this racialized epistemology, and to the development of European colonialism and capitalism. Yet architectural history has produced only a limited body of knowledge about the influence of racial thought on the discipline of architecture.

In response to this reticence, *Race and Modern Architecture: A Critical History from the Enlightenment to the Present* investigates how modern architectural discourse and practice from the Enlightenment to the present have been influenced by race—a concept of human difference that established hierarchies of power and domination between Europe and Europe's "others," by classifying human subjects into modern/non-modern, civilized/primitive, white/nonwhite, and human/less than human binaries. It must be acknowledged from the outset that the primary focus of the book is on European and American architecture and theory. While the chapters in the book gesture toward the global range and diversity of racial discourses, encompassing locales from Mexico to Nigeria, our focus is on the constructions of race created by the movement of ideas, people, goods, and capital between Europe/North America and the non-Western territories pulled into this orbit by the transatlantic slave trade, colonialism, imperialism, and capitalist globalization. These historical forces contributed to creating European-American hegemony in the political, economic, and cultural spheres, and to producing a canon of architectural history that was largely white, male, and geographically limited yet imagined to be universal. *Race and Modern Architecture* therefore complements, but is distinct from, the equally important work of scholars who write about the creative work of subaltern, non-Western designers and people of color. This book contends that to understand the imbrication of race in modern architectural history, we must not only incorporate previously excluded building practices, but we must also look to the heart of the canon, deconstructing that which appears universal, modern, and transparent. In other words, race can be read as much within the canon as outside of it.

Race and Modern Architecture, which grows out of a four-year interdisciplinary research project, represents both an attempt to collect current scholarship and a call for further research to write race back into architectural history. Collectively, the authors explore how racial thinking has influenced some of the key concepts of modern architecture and culture—including freedom, revolution, character, national and indigenous styles, progress, hybridity, climate, and representation. They do this by offering close readings of a series of historical cases that exemplify how modern architecture has been intimately shaped by the histories of slavery, colonialism, and racial inequality—from eighteenth-century neoclassical governmental buildings that purported to embody freedom, to very recent housing projects for immigrants that address the rights of noncitizens. Several of the chapters

Irene Cheng, Charles L. Davis II, and Mabel O. Wilson

explore how race, in its varied formations and formulations, influenced architectural theoretical tropes once conceived of as "race-neutral," such as the nineteenth-century discourse of style, or the idea of the "modern" itself. Other chapters examine the range and racial identities of the subjects interpellated by modern architecture, including its occupants, the communities it claims to represent, and the laborers who built it. Altogether, *Race and Modern Architecture* presents a critical, concerted effort to revise one of the core narratives of modern architecture—its association with universal emancipation and progress—by uncovering modernism's long entanglement with racial thought.

Race, Modernity, Modernism

Recent revisionist histories have shown modernity to be a product of the intertwined forces of capitalism, slavery, and empire.[5] European colonial expansion and the subsequent development of racial slavery, mercantilism, and industrial capitalism depended indispensably on the creation of ideologies of human difference and inequality. Walter Mignolo has described "coloniality" as the "reverse and unavoidable side of 'modernity'—its darker side, like the part of the moon we do not see when we observe it from earth."[6] Thus, to understand architecture's role within global modernity requires not just incorporating objects, buildings, and designers from an expanded geographical range (as in some versions of "global architectural history") but also grappling with the constitutive importance of race. It requires uncovering how colonial violence and slavery were inextricably entangled with cultural narratives and forms embodying reason and progress.

Although the rapprochement of race and architectural theory can be traced to at least the sixteenth century (for example in the Law of the Indies), *Race and Modern Architecture* takes the eighteenth century as a constitutive moment when European Americans began to develop systematic and self-conscious theories of race and modern architecture. As colonial expansion intensified European contacts with a wide array of peoples and cultures in Asia, Africa, and the Americas, disciplines such as philology, anthropology, archaeology, and art history emerged to order and make sense of the growing diversity of languages, peoples, and artifacts that populated the European imagination. These disciplines produced rationalized hierarchical classifications of racial difference that in turn bolstered and justified European and American conquest and rule over peoples and cultures labeled as primitive or autochthonous. Architectural thought was implicated in and shaped by this imperial and scientific-intellectual milieu, both directly and indirectly. Architectural writers in this period developed some of the first polygenetic theories of architecture, which contradicted the image of neoclassicism as an eternal, universal idiom. The limitations and paradoxes in neoclassicism's capacity to embody human reason and freedom vis-à-vis race can be seen in its deployment in the eighteenth-century capitols of the United States, a society dependent on chattel slavery. Over the course of the nineteenth century, architectural thought shifted from an Enlightenment-era approach to human and architectural variety that emphasized differences across geographical space—ordered through typological classification—to a historicist framework that stressed development in time—figured in hierarchical linear chronologies that placed nonwhite contemporary human groups at an earlier, lower stage of cultural development, while representing white European and American populations and their cultural outputs as the most advanced edge of civilizational progress. The definition of what was "modern" architecture entailed constructing other building traditions as "non-modern," "vernacular," or "primitive," depending on context and proximity. Racial thought persisted in twentieth-century architectural modernism in concepts such as evolution, progress, climatic determination, and regionalism, even as these became separated from their origins in racial discourse and subsumed in the broader ideology of internationalism and color-blindness embodied by modernism's white walls. "Modernism"—a philosophical, technical, stylistic, and aesthetic movement promoted through educational and professional institutions—became an effective agent of modernization: policies and programs aimed at the improvement of places and people. While modern architects envisioned society's members inhabiting orderly standardized social housing, schools, railroad stations, government buildings, factories, and private homes in the "first world," those on the dark side of modernity, rationalized as racial inferiors, continued to dwell in substandard spaces formed from the expropriation of labor, land, and resources. Racial inequalities have continued to plague modern architecture up to the present day, for example in urban renewal discourses that deem certain parts of the city as "blighted"—discourses which are paralleled in art historical designations of certain works as "junk art."

Calling out race as a distinct concept within the development of architectural thought helps prevent the bare violence and inequity of modern architecture's historical formation from being sublimated and erased. *Race and Modern Architecture* argues that processes of racialization shaped the very definition of what it means to be modern. Architectural historians must contend with these racialized histories, as well as how the disciplines of art and architectural history themselves emerged from racial-nationalist logics.

Writing Race, Writing History

Within the discipline of architecture, race and style operated as empirical proofs of the universal principles of order that seemingly regulated cultural history. The influence of race thinking on architectural history can be seen in the epistemic logic of foundational texts in architectural education: architectural history surveys.

Irene Cheng, Charles L. Davis II, and Mabel O. Wilson

Concepts of race have figured prominently in the writing of architectural history, from late-eighteenth-century developmental narratives of human physiognomy to nineteenth-century historical narratives of the evolution of architectural styles. In eighteenth-century surveys, scholars adopted the comparative method, examining the essential traits of ancient and modern buildings around the European continent in relation to buildings in other regions of the world. Early comparative methods drew from theories of climate and geography developed by Johann Joachim Winckelmann in the *History of Ancient Art* (1764). The German art historian argued that the ancient arts and architecture of Greece flourished, achieving the pinnacle of aesthetic perfection, precisely because the country's temperate climate and geographical location produced the most beautiful bodies and character.[7] He laid out a developmental trajectory of the arts (and architecture) that stemmed from basic needs, developed through aesthetic refinement, and eventually decayed due to political decline.[8] Though Winckelmann did not suggest that the Greeks were racially superior (he saw them as a nation not a race), physiognomists like Johann Casper Lavater and Pieter Camper would eventually draw upon his work to forge a link between racial physiognomy, aesthetic beauty, and moral advancement. Their rationales elevated the physique of European Man and his cultural productions as the universal ideal, which provided an aesthetic criterion for treating race and style as visual proxies of one another in architectural discourse.[9]

The developmental and universalist framework of the comparative method continued to hold sway among scholars writing architecture history surveys in the nineteenth century. In *A History of Architecture* (1849), for example, British-born E. A. Freeman traced the "successive development" of architecture in order to make the Gothic style of "Teutonic Christendom" comparable to Greek classicism.[10] Freeman's architectural history was part of a larger historiographic, linguistic, and political project to invent a superior Anglo-Saxon and Aryan racial tradition supporting British nationalism.[11] Indebted to Freeman, Banister Fletcher, in his comprehensive global survey *A History of Architecture on the Comparative Method* (1896), cited geography, geology, climate, religion, history, and sociopolitical factors in the development of architecture around the world.[12] To visualize the evolution of architectural styles, Fletcher conceived his "Tree of Architecture" diagram (figure I.1). On the upper boughs Fletcher placed the national architectures and historical styles of Europe, representing these as the highest outgrowth of a linear trunk leading from the Greek to the Roman and Romanesque, while the lower boughs of Chinese, Indian, Saracenic, and other styles of architecture are shown terminating without further development.[13] Even in cases where theories of stylistic difference were not explicitly based on the racialist frameworks of modern ethnography, race and style became isomorphic terms for explaining cul-

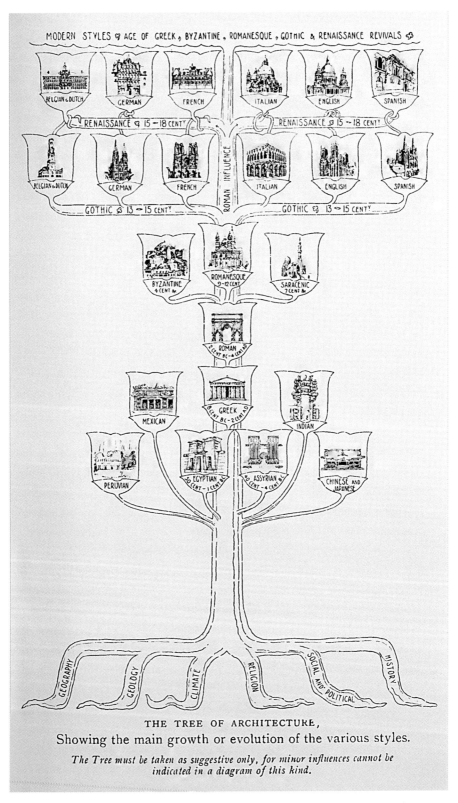

Fig. I.1 "Tree of Architecture" diagram from Banister Fletcher's *A History of Architecture on the Comparative Method*, 1905 edition.

tural differences that legitimized the broader scientific aspirations of the discipline and the politics of empire.

These racialized comparative methods continued to inform the writing of architectural surveys well into the twentieth century. In outlining the importance of character as a determinant in the emerging style of American colonial architecture, historian William H. Pierson Jr., in the first volume of his survey *American Buildings and their Architects* (1970), turned to the formal traits of race types as an analogy for interpreting architectural style:

> Each man, in spite of his uniqueness, is endowed with certain physical traits which relate him at once to a number of other human beings. Different races of man, for example, can be distinguished by the color of the skin. We recognize this as a major racial classification. By observing and relating other identifying features, however, such as the color of the hair and eyes, the shape, size and proportion of the body, and the manner of speech and movement, subgroups can be determined; and through this method, for one purpose or another, mankind can be divided into an infinite variety of types, or "styles."[14]

For Pierson observation of the characteristics of architectural styles directly correlated to analysis of the phenotypical characteristics of racial types. Thus, even by the 1970s, the methodology of some architectural historians still paralleled the work of nineteenth-century racial scientists. An echo of this thinking is still latent in the contemporary essentializing of vernacular building types as signs of static primitive identity or the notion that Western architecture can only advance by producing a formal idiom that summarizes the advances of contemporary technology. Both of these myths continue to haunt architectural education through the publication of surveys that have not properly excised racialist models of interpreting the past.

Archives and Methods

Race and Modern Architecture begins the work of exhuming the racial logics embedded in our most canonical histories, uncovering missing histories, and writing race back into our understanding of modern architecture. This task requires asking a number of questions about methodology: What extra- and intra-disciplinary strategies should be mobilized for writing the racial history of modernism? What new tools of analysis must be created? How might historians question the neutrality of their critical tools of investigation—including long held assumptions about archives, evidence, and hermeneutical methods?

One of the challenges to uncovering the operations of race within architecture is the mutability of the concept of racial difference over time. In the eighteenth and nineteenth centuries, architectural thinkers associated race not only with phenotypical traits such as skin color, but also with cultural attributes such as language and food, elements of material culture, and even the structural systems of vernacular architectures, not to mention environmental determinants like climate. Attention to the historical transformations of these associations is required for a historian to detect the lingering racial subtext of contemporary discourses such as climatic architecture, to cite just one example. While earlier writers tended to be more transparent and explicit in their discussions of race, the rising taboo surrounding the use of racist language after World War II, seen as an advancement of racial equality, has paradoxically led to the masking of racial thinking in postwar and contemporary architecture. The contemporary rhetoric of color-blindness and universal condemnation of racism have also perhaps prevented scholars from acknowledging the centrality of race in the work of historic architects—out of a misguided fear that calling attention to an architect's racial beliefs will distort appreciation of his or her oeuvre.

To write a critical history of race in modern architecture therefore requires several transformations in architectural historical methodology as well as institutional practice. First, and most obviously, historians must expand the range of figures and objects we study to include the work of nonwhite subjects—including peoples previously deemed "outside history," whose records were seen as not worthy of preservation. This requires consulting a wider range of archives and being inventive about what can constitute historical evidence. We must go beyond architects' archives or buildings (the fodder of classic monographic studies). But as we suggest above, the task is not merely to enlarge the canon, but also to question and make visible how race affects the institutional processes of historical collection, valorization, and narrativization.

We can cite several important models of how the expansion of the historical archive has led to the writing of new architectural histories attentive to race. Beginning in the 1980s, historians of "folk" and "vernacular" architecture did much to recover the material records of minority subjects, including the enslaved builders and inhabitants of southern American plantations. Scholars such as Dell Upton and John Michael Vlach applied techniques of architectural historical documentation and analysis to buildings previously regarded as not meriting scholarly attention, such as slave quarters, overseers' dwellings, and smokehouses.[15] Beyond exploring new objects of study, these researchers confronted a methodological challenge in reconstructing historical narratives out of both extant written evidence and meticulous analysis of absences and silences in the historical record. Archaeological records and oral histories supplemented the kinds of drawings and documents more commonly utilized by modern architectural historians. These approaches challenge the supremacy of material archives that prioritize architects' records and intentions, seeking instead to construct a comprehensive account of how the built environment is coauthored by a diverse range of constituents, including nonwhite and female builders and inhabitants. Another important body of work that has revealed the racial construction of modernity comprises studies of European and American colonial architecture and planning, as well as international, colonial, and national exhibitions. For example, Zeynep Çelik, Mark Crinson, Patricia Morton, and others have uncovered how ideas about race, modernity, and progress were mutually constructed through social, political, spatial, and architectural means in colonial buildings and at world's fairs from the 1850s through the late twentieth century.[16] This scholarship is part of a growing body of critical studies of colonial and postcolonial architecture.[17] Together, the work on world exhibitions and colonial architecture has pushed sites that had previously seemed marginal to the center, and asked how periphery and core were coproduced—how the ethnographic village was crucial to the Eiffel Tower, how Casablanca enabled postwar Paris.

Second, beyond expanding the canon and the archive, architectural historians must develop, or adapt from other disciplines, critical hermeneutical methods for uncovering the role of racial thought in familiar objects and narratives, including those in which race does not appear at first glance to be operative. This entails looking both microscopically and macroscopically, employing new methods of close reading and visual analysis, as well as expanding the kind of contextual histories we read and imagine to be relevant to architectural study. Martin A. Berger has written about the necessity of combining close analysis of the visible evidence in artworks with an explication of the tacit, "unseen" discourses and structures that guide and delimit the meanings of the work. In his book *Sight Unseen: Whiteness and American Visual Culture*, he reveals racialized perspectives in artworks and buildings that ostensibly have nothing to do with race.[18] Race is there, even when we think it is not. And sometimes it was there all along, but we did not know how to "see" it. Some scholars have compared the process to an exhumation: Simon Gikandi, in his study of the relationship between slavery and the eighteenth-century English cultures of taste, describes his method as "reading what lies buried in the crypt, what survives in the 'secret tomb' of modern subjectivity."[19] Others, like the literary scholar Anne Anlin Cheng, have argued for surface reading that eschews the hermeneutics of suspicion. In her study of racial themes in Adolf Loos's work, she writes, "Sometimes it is not a question of what the visible hides but how it is that we have failed to see certain things on the surface."[20]

A number of examples can be cited that start to recover the repressed racial formations of modern architecture: In contrast to Kruft's earlier-cited dismissal of racial themes in Viollet-le-Duc's work, recent studies have shown that race was much more central to the French architect's seminal ideas about style than previously thought.[21] Dianne Harris, a contributor to this book, provides another model of how historians might relate architecture to larger contexts of cultural values and beliefs. In her book *Little White Houses*, she utilizes analytical methods from the fields of whiteness studies, cultural studies, and visual studies to show how 1950s advertisements and magazine layouts depicting postwar American suburban homes projected a cultural ideal of white identity associated with cleanliness, order, property, and the nuclear family.[22] Lastly, theorists like Darell Fields have incorporated methods drawn from literary deconstruction and critical race studies to uncover the racial logics behind Hegelian universal history and postmodern aesthetics, as well as a racial model of dialectics fundamental to architectural discourse.[23] This diverse scholarship has employed a range of new and borrowed analytical methods to uncover the racial subtexts embedded in modern architectural discourse. These approaches call into question the neutrality of the historian's task and critical tools of investigation, as well as the hierarchies that those tools help to maintain.

Critical Approaches to Race

Race and Modern Architecture includes contributions that model diverse strategies for integrating the study of race into architectural history. The field of race studies encompasses a wide range of academic disciplines and expertise that can be grouped into three overlapping rubrics since the postwar period: American studies, colonial/postcolonial studies, and global approaches. The first rubric originated with scholars focusing on race in North America and the Atlantic world, who produced an in-depth critique of the Western canons that privileged white, Euro-American narratives for North American and transatlantic history. This challenge has prompted a reconsideration of the hegemonic role of canonicity in several fields of study. In philosophy, the fields of African American philosophy and black existentialism displaced the Enlightenment myth of a universal subjectivity by examining the social realities and traumas specific to marginalized nonwhite subjects.[24] Literary critics such as Henry Louis Gates Jr. and Houston A. Baker Jr. have demonstrated the rich contributions of African American literature to the American canon by tracing black writers' syncretic transformations of transatlantic religious, poetic, and musical traditions in the United States.[25] Toni Morrison's groundbreaking *Playing in the Dark* showed how canonical novelists evoked a metaphorical blackness to complicate representations of whiteness and white identity in seminal works of American literature.[26] And in legal studies, Derrick Bell, Patricia Williams, Kimberlé Crenshaw, Kendall Thomas, and Mari Matsuda's interrogation of the legal basis of white supremacy in the United States fostered the creation of critical race theory.[27] While this body of work was heavily influenced by a desire to combat antiblack racism in the United States, it has provided a robust model of analysis for identifying and critiquing the function of whiteness in realms beyond the law. Originating in the field of sociology, Michael Omi and Howard Winant's theory of racial formation has also been beneficial in identifying the structural role of race in shaping U.S. political and social institutions.[28] Several contributors to this volume draw on the rich tradition of American critical race studies, for example by exposing the structural role of whiteness in shaping modern architectural debates, or pointing to architecture's role in perpetuating structural violence and inequality in society.

A second wave of scholars studying race focused on the cultural politics of European colonialism and the long-term effects of these ideologies on postcolonial societies. Edward Said's postwar critique of Orientalism was influential in exposing the Western world's simultaneous fetishizing and stigmatizing of Middle Eastern cultures—practices that perpetually designated these cultures as exotic and other, but still necessary in defining European modernity, particularly metropolitan culture.[29] Said's research inspired figures such as Gayatri Chakravorty Spivak and Homi Bhabha to consider the independence and agency of subaltern voices in the social construction of colonial spaces, even when these sites seem to be fully defined by the oppressive politics of European colonizers.[30] Several chapters of this volume demonstrate the manner in which the racial discourses in western Europe and the United States continued to flourish in colonial territories of the nineteenth century and in neocolonial relations of the twentieth and twenty-first centuries. More recently, the analysis of social inequalities and genocidal practices of European colonies when linked to the institutional patterns of North American imperialism has inspired a rich body of scholarship on the imperialist discourses that enabled U.S. expansion beyond the North American continent, the rise of American protectorates in the Pacific, and the increased role of American military power and cultural influence abroad during the interwar and Cold War periods.[31]

A third wave of scholars shifted their focus to the influence of racial discourses on global networks of power that extend beyond the geographical limits of preexisting national and international boundaries. Several major themes of the most contemporary writings on this subject have influenced the contributions to this volume. In their critical project to decolonize the Western episteme, Dipesh Chakrabarty, Walter D. Mignolo, Aníbal Quijano, and Sylvia Wynter have vigorously challenged Enlightenment representations of history and humanism as primary agents of racialization in service of capitalist expansion in the colonial context. Denise Ferreira da Silva's writings moved beyond a critique of the exclusionary logic of Enlightenment ideas on race and representation by proposing that racial discourses are more constitutive of the material logic of Euro-American modernity than current studies suggest.[32] Her analysis of the mutual structural positions of racial minorities around the globe suggests that there is an ontological and operative logic to modern cultural differences that still remains latent in aesthetic critiques of modern architecture. Jodi Melamed's writings on race and globalism critique the apparent flaws of the liberal doctrine of American antiracism that has become a pervasive institutional force in multinational institutions and liberal democracies around the world.[33] Her study of the mutual effects of racial politics at home and abroad introduces new comparative modes of analyzing the global politics of modern architectural debates. Linda Martín Alcoff and Sara Ahmed's studies of the ontology of racial identities suggest that race has phenomenological effects on how bodies inhabit space, which can be measured in the social experiences of particular groups.[34] This phenomenological orientation toward race holds potential for influencing future studies of race and place that extend beyond the visual aspects of architecture. Fred Moten, Saidiya Hartman, Hortense Spillers, and others have considered the psychic and material spaces of black life in the wake of the transatlantic slave trade's brutal colonialism and racism.[35] Their robust critiques have asked for what Spillers has called a new "American grammar" to account for how white supremacy dehumanized the racialized (and gendered) subject, thus providing a lexicon for historians in this volume to unpack urban terms like "the ghetto" and "blight." This body of work helps us see historical linkages across global urban geographies formed in the wake of colonialism and imperialism.

Modern Architecture's Imbrications with Racial Subjects

Race and Modern Architecture's chapters are organized into thematic and chronological sections, each addressing the relation of race to a key concept in architectural history and theory: Enlightenment, organicism, nationalism, representation, colonialism, and urbanism.

The first section, "Race and the Enlightenment," explores the integral relationship of race and slavery to the formation of the eighteenth-century European and American ideals of reason, freedom, and citizenship, and how this relationship was manifested in architecture. Two capitols built in the early United States, a slave society self-consciously and contradictorily dedicated to promoting the principle of liberty, offer exemplary cases to understand this dialectical relationship of liberty and slavery. Mabel O. Wilson illuminates Thomas Jefferson's design of the Virginia Statehouse, a neoclassical temple to democracy constructed in part by enslaved black workers, in parallel with his contemporaneously written text *Notes on the State of Virginia*, in which he asserted the inherent inferiority of black peoples. Peter Minosh focuses on the U.S. Capitol building, designed just a few years after Jefferson's statehouse by William Thornton, a slaveholding abolitionist enmeshed in the networks of the Atlantic world. Both Jefferson and Thornton used neoclassical architecture to obfuscate the violence of slavery behind an architectural facade of reason and democracy. Each essays shows how slavery was not an extrinsic blemish on the ideals of American democracy and republican citizenship but rather integral to their founding premises. Reinhold Martin also takes up Jefferson as a paradigmatic figure, focusing on a series of spatio-technical devices—dumbwaiters, copying machines, and libraries—that were instrumental to producing a model enlightened citizen, a model predicated on the literal silencing and exclusion of black slaves. Martin describes the afterlife of this racialized Enlightenment ideal in early twentieth-century debates about architecture and "civilization" carried out by Lewis Mumford and W. E. B. Du Bois. If freedom and slavery were inextricably intertwined in the American context, then so too in England and Europe, Enlightenment knowledge and empire were inseparable. Addison Godel's chapter traces evolving European attitudes towards the Chinese garden to elucidate the intensification of racial thinking, paralleling the growth of imperialism, over the course of the eighteenth and nineteenth centuries. The garden's course from object of curious fascination to target of armed destruction illustrates the rise of racialism as an ideology justifying European empire.

The second section of the book, "Race and Organicism," focuses on the role of race in constructing some of the leading concepts of nineteenth-century architecture, including progress, style, and organicism or naturalism—the idea that architecture should derive legitimacy and authority from its mirroring of natural laws. The chapters by Charles L. Davis II, Joanna Merwood-Salisbury, and Irene Cheng all testify to the pervasive and profound influence of racial thought in Europe and America by the mid-nineteenth century. Writing about the American context, Davis and Merwood-Salisbury present revealing revisionist readings of familiar figures and movements: Davis positions the architecture of Henry Van Brunt in relation to the mythology of manifest destiny, which idealized white settler culture as the source for the evolution of American culture. Van Brunt's architecture, like the midwestern cities in which his buildings were located, were imagined to mediate between the primitive and the advanced, between nature and technology, and thus relied on techniques of racial conquest, erasure, and romanticization. Merwood-Salisbury elucidates how the Gothic Revival, as epitomized in Peter Wight's National Academy of Design, relied on ideas about "free labor" that were inextricable from contemporaneous debates about white workers and slavery. As Merwood-Salisbury's previous research has shown, Van Brunt, Wight, and many other American architects in this period were significantly influenced by European architectural theory that linked the possibility of a new modern architectural style to racial evolution—specifically the emergence (or resurgence) of a Germanic or Anglo-Saxon race. The development of these European ideas about race, style, history, and modernity are traced in Irene Cheng's chapter, which shows how racial thought became assimilated by some of the most influential nineteenth-century architectural thinkers and historians, including James Fergusson, Owen Jones, and Eugène-Emmanuel Viollet-le-Duc. Their ideas about race and stylistic evolution would eventually be absorbed by modernism, though shorn of its racial underpinnings.

Section three, "Race and Nationalism," investigates parallel discourses of race, nation, and architecture in three national and transnational early twentieth-century contexts: postrevolutionary Mexico, fascist Italy, and imperial Germany. Luis E. Carranza's chapter examines the deployment of hybridization as a theme in the nationalist rhetoric and architectural traditions of postrevolutionary Mexican governments from the 1910s to the 1930s. In this dynamic political context, "race" no longer operated as a fixed biological category but became a meta-category for drawing individuals together under a common ethnic-national tradition. Carranza identifies two competing notions of the body politic that influenced architecture: Federico Mariscal, Jesus Acevedo, and José Vasconcelos's postcolonial theories of a Mestizo identity that hybridized pre-Columbian and Spanish colonial architectures, and Manuel Amábilis's conception of a precolonial Mexican race as pure and indigenous, and thus unregulated by any contact with European aesthetic standards. Both approaches attempted to transform race into a unifying political ethos, or what Étienne Balibar has called "fictional ethnicity." Brian L. McLaren's chapter examines the critical relationships between political ideologies of racial purity in Fascist Italy and Mario De Renzi and Gino Pollini's design of the Piazza e gli edifici delle Forze Armate for the Esposizione Universale di Roma. McLaren demonstrates the ways that social fears of Jewish racial characteristics motivated the restrictive material and aesthetic shaping of university buildings and spaces—a shaping that mirrors the ideologies of racial refinement expressed in the scientific paradigm of eugenics. In a related analysis of race and nation, Kenny Cupers questions the racial politics behind imperial Germans' deployment of the concept of "indigenous architecture," which they believed transparently reflected the racial and ethnic traits of specific populations. Cupers's chapter outlines how architectural images of premodern German life were purposefully manufactured to legitimize a politicized notion of *Heimat* or homeland culture that was deployed in European and colonial settings alike. The regressive politics of this historical style should provide a necessary corrective for the modern architect's naive faith in the authenticity of vernacular styles of building.

The fourth section, "Race and Representation," gathers two case studies, both exploring how print and photography constructed the racial discourses of architecture in the early to mid-twentieth century. Adrienne Brown attends to the visual construction of modern architecture by focusing on the historical erasures that were necessary to elevate the primacy of the designer's intentions in modernist discourses. Examining the language that William Starrett uses in *Skyscrapers*

Irene Cheng, Charles L. Davis II, and Mabel O. Wilson

and the Men Who Build Them to aggrandize his own role in the erection of modern skyscrapers, Brown traces the rhetorical alignment of the skills of the licensed architect with those of the building contractor. The conceptual alignment of these administrative forces renders the physical labor of the workmen, many of whom were racialized in the popular press, as a material exponent of more invisible technological forces and design ideas. Dianne Harris invites her readers to discover the latent institutional structures that connect two seemingly disparate photographic portraits of postwar life—that of black Americans in the disfigured body of Emmett Till and that of white Americans in mundane images of modern suburban homes. Harris peers beneath the seemingly distinct geographies of each image to reveal the segregationist politics that subtend these contexts: for it was the violent abuse of the black body that made exclusively white spaces socially possible and economically profitable. By tracing the dissemination of research photos of model housing completed by the U.S. Gypsum company into advertisements for local housing associations and lifestyle magazines, she recovers the visual construction of whiteness that was an important institutional element of white suburban life.

The chapters in the fifth section, "Race and Colonialism," offer comparative perspectives on the racialization of architecture in the nineteenth- and twentieth-century colonial contexts of Africa and Southeast Asia. The essays by Jiat-Hwee Chang and Mark Crinson explore how the racialized discourses of modern architecture emerged from British imperial urban planning and design practices for managing colonial populations. Through a study of the key texts of tropical architecture produced by British architects and the pedagogy of the Architectural Association's influential Department of Tropical Studies, Chang traces the connections between tropical architecture in the mid-twentieth century and earlier ideas about race, climate, health, and civilization. Chang explores the subsequent appropriation of British tropical architecture discourses in 1960s Malaysia and Singapore, illuminating how the underlying racial thinking was translated by "indigenous" architects in these new multiethnic, postcolonial nations. Frantz Fanon's idea of colonialism as a "compartmentalized world" provides a starting point for Mark Crinson's examination of the separations but also the entanglements of the building world in Kenya at a time of colonial crisis in the mid-twentieth century. Crinson charts the influence of "ethnopsychiatry" on "villagization," policies that drew upon ideas of the pastoral and vernacular in East Africa. His account forcefully argues that through discourses on race, population control was connected to many other facets of the production of space in colonialism: from the "high" architecture of the state to ideal planning schemes to modernist housing in Kenya. Adedoyin Teriba's probing chapter explores the complex overlay of racial and architectural identities at the turn of the twentieth century in Lagos, Nigeria—a city with a diverse population that included migrants of African descent from Brazil, the Caribbean, Sierra Leone, and England. Teriba focuses on the Shitta-Bey Mosque, constructed by the Portuguese, the English, and biracial Brazilians whom the locals called *òyìnbó dúdú*, meaning "white-black" in Yorùbá.

The sixth section, "Race and Urbanism," explores how racial thinking influenced approaches to the challenges of the late twentieth-century city. By sifting through urban, artistic, and architectural responses to modern urban conditions in Detroit, Los Angeles, and Berlin, the essays by Andrew Herscher, Lisa Uddin, and Esra Ackan expertly mine the racialized conceptual substrates of modernism and urbanism. The racialized discourse in postindustrial urban America of "blight"— one of a taxonomy of terms drawn from agriculture, biology, and ecology applied to urban science—is the focus of Andrew Herscher's illuminating chapter on Detroit's uneven urban development. Herscher analyzes the use of nonwhite identity as an explicit early indicator of blight and the implicit effects of racial prejudice and white supremacy in contemporary blight studies and municipal actions to counter blight. Uddin, like Herscher, also examines the American postindustrial landscape, focusing on the artist and designer Noah Purifoy. Purifoy's poetic "junk modernism" responded to the policies and conditions of racially segregated Los Angeles in the 1960s and 1970s. As Uddin argues, the otherworldly forms of Purifoy's assemblages, which incorporated debris from the 1968 Watts uprising and detritus from the incremental disinvestment in black communities, posited a radical black humanity that challenged the racialized biopolitics of modern urban planning discourse. In her essay on the immigrant Berlin neighborhood of Kreuzberg, also known as the "German Harlem," Esra Akcan studies how housing design exacerbated the tensions between the ethnic identity of immigrants (ethnicity here serving as a sanitized proxy for racial and religious differences) and the dominant white Christian imaginary of German citizenship. Akcan documents how Berlin's noncitizen housing laws, such as a "ban on entry and settlement" and the "desegregation regulation," were transposed into the new buildings' functional programs. In response to these housing laws, the IBA 1984/87's architects offered a range of responses to immigrant communities, which support her theory of "open architecture," defined as the translation of a new ethics of hospitality into architecture, the welcoming of the noncitizen into architectural design.

While the chapters are clustered by theme, time period, and geography, we are cognizant that this organization mirrors how Western epistemology has structured the modern world—that is, into temporal periods arranged from the past to the present, from the "primitive" to the "modern," and geographic territories ranged according to national/cultural affinities. These concerns are counterbalanced by a belief that this organizational strategy will enable readers to detect the

Irene Cheng, Charles L. Davis II, and Mabel O. Wilson

long-term effects of race theory in modern architectural debates from the Enlightenment forward, as well as to easily compare and contrast its use during distinct periods and in discrete geographies. In this manner, the book reveals how racial discourses have been deployed to organize and conceptualize the spaces of modernity, from the individual building to the city to the nation to the planet.

•   •   •

Race and Modern Architecture insists upon seeing race in every context, not just in the typical sites examined by architectural historians. In practical terms, this means countering the expectation that race is only operative in nonwhite or subaltern spaces. Instead, we hold that race operates in the construction of both the statehouse and the outhouse. *Race and Modern Architecture* contends that architectural historians must take account of the whiteness central to the universal mythologies of Enlightenment discourses and how these have relied on the suppression of particularity and difference. The book's goal is to demonstrate that attention to race is no longer optional in the study of modern architectural history. Instead, the racial animus of Euro-American cultural politics has to be accounted for in any future analysis of modern buildings and territories. At the very least, this means acknowledging the white cultural nationalism that lies at the heart of the Enlightenment project and its attendant processes of canon formation. This collection opens up new methodologies for exploring architecture's role in the social processes of subjection. If the methodological approaches of critical race theorists and postcolonial scholars already teach us to identify the underlying discourses that structure the gaze of the architect or designer, then the book's chapters identify what tools are still necessary to relate the built environment to these broader cultural processes. Its research analyzes how the construction of race within the modernist project affected the diverse communities under these regimes, not only by producing material hierarchies of power, but also by interpellating subjects into various racially defined roles—whether as designers, laborers, muses, or inhabitants of modern buildings.

As mentioned earlier, we see this book as instigating a beginning rather than assembling the summation of a body of work. As the editors and contributors to *Race and Modern Architecture*, we are keenly attuned to the fact that this volume is an outcome of our own subject positions, intellectual genealogies, academic training, and current institutional appointments in North American universities. We hope that this book is not the definitive volume on the topic, but merely the initiation of a much needed dialogue and a critical historiographic project that we anticipate will be vigorously debated and enthusiastically expanded. While the essays foreground race as a grossly understudied social formation, we also want to acknowledge that race is entangled with other social constructions that built the modern world, including gender, sexuality, class, and disability, which also are in need of further study for their impact on modern architectural discourse. We have compiled this volume in solidarity with Donna Haraway's argument for a "politics and epistemologies of location, positioning, and situating, where partiality and not universality is the condition of being heard to make rational knowledge claims."[36] The modern Western episteme's embrace of universal history, particularly after Hegel, compelled the gaze of the architectural historian to incorporate practices of buildings from around the world—the putatively primitive, Egyptian, Persian, Chinese, and so forth—under the rubric of "architecture," the European term for the art of building. Simultaneously with these processes of engulfment, modernity and modern rationality also defended and excluded difference, which are precisely the logics of how race forms hierarchies of power.[37] *Race and Modern Architecture* does not argue that uncovering the formative role of racial discourses in modern architectural debates can lead to a transparent, "truthful" history. Instead, the book's chapters seek to provoke architectural historians, students, architects, and scholars to become more self-aware of the limits and potentials associated with uncovering the critical function of race in modern architectural debates.

Irene Cheng, Charles L. Davis II, and Mabel O. Wilson

PART I

RACE AND THE ENLIGHTENMENT

1
___

Notes on the Virginia Capitol

Nation, Race, and Slavery in Jefferson's America

Mabel O. Wilson

While visiting Richmond, Virginia, in 1796, newly immigrated British architect Benjamin Henry Latrobe painted two watercolors of the state's new capitol building. In translucent hues, one of the watercolors depicted the stately white temple in the distance, sitting nobly atop Shockoe Hill, overlooking the town's sparsely populated pastoral landscape (figure 1.1). One of the earliest examples of American civic architecture, the capitol building, which had been completed in 1788, was designed by statesman, architect, planter, and slave owner Thomas Jefferson and modeled in part on the Maison Carrée, a first-century Roman temple in Nimês, France. In 1776, twenty years before Latrobe's visit, Virginia had drafted and ratified its state constitution, of which Jefferson had been a key author; the document established a separation of powers that would go on to become a model for the organization of the federal government. The new building Jefferson envisioned in 1776 to house Virginia's governmental functions needed both to symbolize and to enable the power of "the people" to govern and adjudicate the laws of the new state. The self-trained architect also intended the neoclassical state capitol to serve as a model for civic architecture throughout the thirteen states, as well as in the yet-to-be determined seat of the federal government.

Fig. 1.1 *View of the City of Richmond from the Bank of the James River* (1798) by Benjamin Henry Latrobe. Courtesy of Maryland Historical Society.

It is critical that we understand how "the people" of Virginia—and by extension "the people" of the United States of America—were identified and defined during this period of revolutionary action and postrevolutionary planning; it is important to trace the various rationales conceived to identify who made up "the people" of Virginia, and by extension "the people" of the United States of America. In other words, who were Virginians or American citizens, endowed with constitutional rights, and who were not? A survey of the population of the port town of Richmond reveals the racial contours of this division. The city's white residents, who were America's newly minted citizenry, staffed and served in its government seat; patronized its taverns, shops, stables, and inns; profited from its docks along the James River and from its warehouses trading in tobacco and slaves; and lived in the wood-framed houses shown in the foreground of Latrobe's watercolor. Among the several thousand white Americans living in Virginia in the late eighteenth century labored an almost equally numerous population of noncitizens—free and enslaved African men, women, and children. The enslaved served their masters and mistresses to produce the region's great wealth. A depiction of this slave economy can be found among a later series of watercolors Latrobe produced during travels north to Fredericksburg, Virginia. One scene documents a white overseer keeping

Mabel O. Wilson

Fig. 1.2 *An Overseer Doing His Duty near Fredericksburg, Virginia* (1798), by Benjamin Henry Latrobe. Courtesy of Maryland Historical Society.

dutiful watch over two enslaved women who, with hoes raised in midair, cleared the burnt remains of a forest for either cultivation or new construction (figure 1.2). Chattel slavery—believed by some to be a necessary evil—buttressed America's civilized values of freedom, liberty, and equality.

It is critical to consider that enslaved black people, humans classified as property, built several of the nation's most important civic buildings: the Virginia State Capitol, the White House, and the U.S. Capitol. Designed by white architects, these edifices stand as the Enlightenment's monuments to the power of reason and the virtues of equality, justice, and freedom. One astute deliberation on the moral peril of slavery, still tempered by belief in the natural inferiority of the Negro's mind and body, can be found in Jefferson's *Notes on the State of Virginia* (1785), a lengthy compendium of the state's geography, geology, wildlife, human inhabitants, and political economy. Jefferson wrote and revised *Notes on the State of Virginia* during the same years that he designed Virginia's capitol building. If the capitol were to physically represent the institution of state governance, *Notes on the State of Virginia* was a kind of philosophical natural history addressed in part to a European audience and attesting to the geographic and political fitness of the region.

Born into the wealthy European planter class of colonial Virginia, Jefferson epitomized the consummate humanist polymath. Because his oeuvre encompasses the aesthetic and technical domain of architecture, the political realm of government, and the rational sphere of natural philosophy and history, his works offer an ideal lens through which to understand the intersections of the emerging discourses of architecture, nationalism, and racial difference as they coalesced in the late eighteenth century. Analyzing Jefferson's architecture and his writings, together with correspondence from this period, broadens our understanding of the social, economic, cultural, and political context in which the first work of American civic architecture—the Virginia State Capitol—was conceived and realized. By expanding the types of archival materials accessed to not only include architectural drawings, but also letters and scientific treatises, I analyze the productive relationship between democratic ideals and racial difference. I explore how the ontological and epistemological ground for the racialized citizen/noncitizen dynamic is one structured conceptually, physically, and spatially by the earliest American civic buildings and the contexts in which they were built.

Race, Reason, and Architecture

Scholars who have written about Jefferson's designs for the Virginia State Capitol—including the architectural historians Fiske Kimball and Frederick D. Nichols—have failed to examine in depth chattel slavery's connection to the building's conception, construction, or context. Slavery was not simply an odious institution rooted in the remote confines of southern backwoods plantations. In truth it was integral to the formation of the economy, government, and national character of the United States. To be sure, many people recognized the enslavement of "Negroes," to use a term common during the period, to be undeniably contrary to the nation's founding creed: the "self-evident" truth that "all men are created equal." That equality originated in nature and that equality was necessary for liberty were moral principles Jefferson enshrined in the Declaration of Independence (1776). There is, however, an inherent contradiction—some might argue a disavowal—in how the founding fathers constituted a new nation that ensured liberalism's "unalienable rights" to "Life, Liberty and the pursuit of Happiness," while continuing to violently enslave other human beings for personal gain.

With nationalism growing in the West in the closing decades of the eighteenth century, Europeans continued to conceptualize the racial paradigm of human difference that had emerged from centuries of contact with and colonial expansion into Asia, Africa, and the New World. During the Revolutionary period and shortly thereafter, "race" had not yet been categorized in the hierarchical terms of biological variations and evolution as would happen under the disciplines of modern science in the mid-nineteenth century. Natural philosophers and historians of this period, among them Immanuel Kant, Johann Gottfried Herder, Comte de Buffon, and Thomas Jefferson, debated the meaning of the human species's observable physiognomic variations (outer character) and perceived mental distinctions, such as temperaments and humors (inner character). Their observations and experimentations sought to uncover the laws—climatic or geographic—that governed differentiation in the human species across the globe. In *Observations on the Feeling of the Beautiful and the Sublime* (1764), Kant, for example, scrutinized the "national character" to be observed in the Negro:

> The Negroes of Africa have by nature no feeling that rises above the trifling. Mr. Hume challenges anyone to cite a single example in which a Negro has shown talents, and asserts that among the hundreds of thousands of blacks who are transported elsewhere from their countries, although many of them have even been set free, still not a single one was ever found who presented anything great in art or science or any other praiseworthy quality, even though among the whites some continually rise aloft from the lowest rabble, and through superior gifts earn respect in the world.[1]

Kant and other such men of letters placed European "man" in a position of superiority above the other races, by virtue of the aesthetic perfection of white skin and the capacity to reason, evident in the ability to comprehend the law and to appreciate beauty.[2]

For theorist Sylvia Wynter this overdetermined European mode of being human, "man," evolved in two phases. The first period, from the fourteenth to the eighteenth century, charted the decline of belief in divine and magical causation and witnessed the rise of the physical sciences that sought to understand the natural forces that animated the world, replacing the belief that the biblical curse of Ham, for example, had colored Africans black. During the second period, from the eighteenth century onward, the biological sciences developed; these demonstrated that nature's own laws were behind natural forces. It was through this rational framework that race came to be considered as biologically determined.[3] This invented "man" was for Wynter "made possible only on the basis of the dynamics of a colonizer/colonized relation that the West was to discursively constitute and empirically institutionalize on the islands of the Caribbean and, later, on the mainland of the Americas."[4] The resulting forms of racial patriarchy nominated white males as the bearers of power and the symbolic subjects of modernity, while simultaneously dismissing other epistemological frameworks as archaic and devaluing other ways of being human. Europe, as Wynter and others have written, invented race as an instrument of domination.[5]

As the West shifted from a Judeo-Christian cosmology of heavens and the earth to a humanist worldview, philosophers deployed universal reason to imagine a self-determined and self-conscious moral subject—political man—who perceived and conceived "the nature of things," including his social relations.[6] Natural rights became foundational for new social formations—nation states—whose governments, guided by historically derived ideas of democracy, ensured freedom for their citizens. At the same time, Europeans also invented the category "Others of Europe," to borrow Denise Ferreira da Silva's term, to describe those who were not modern, not rational, not free, not white, and not citizens. These subhumans, often feminized as weak and submissive, labored in the colonies and dwelled in yet-to-be-charted territories.[7] Europeans consigned nonwhite people, with their supposedly tenuous moral and physical character, to the bottom of the repurposed Great Chain of Being. Natural historians and scientists developed representations of time and space in the emerging discourses of history and science that placed nonwhite people in prehistory and in regions unexplored on colonial maps. The rendering of nonwhite people as primitive and uncivilized in turn rationalized the conquest of their territories, the expropriation of their land and labor, and the elimination of their lives by war or disease. The "Others of Europe's" racial inferiority, particularly their lack of culture in white European eyes, dialectically elevated and affirmed the universal man and whiteness as the ideal representations of the human in the West's own imagination.[8]

It is important to keep in mind that from the fifteenth century onward, secular reason also had an impact on European "arts of building," on building's transformation from a medieval trade guild to the modern discipline of architecture.[9] With the rise of academies and learned societies, architectural treatises circulated debates on the appropriate use of architecture, proportions of classical elements, and the ideal configuration of different building types. New techniques of geometry and cartography influenced modes of architectural representation. A growing interest in mechanics, documented at length in dictionaries and encyclopedias, advanced new construction methods that separated architecture from engineering. In other arenas, natural philosophers explored man's capacity for aesthetic judgment to assess which ideal forms were visually pleasing. The taxonomic methods used by natural historians to discern speciation, in particular racial differences, were applied to the study of the historical transformation of buildings to determine character and organization. To begin to chart a history of architecture, scholars made comparative archeological, ethnographic, and aesthetic evaluations of how far Europe's architecture had advanced beyond the rest of the world's ancient and primitive building practices.

These technical and aesthetic developments gave rise to the figure of the modern architect. At first self-taught elites like Jefferson, but eventually European apprentice-trained architects like Latrobe, were employed by the state and private citizens to design the government buildings, offices, banks, customhouses, storehouses, libraries, museums, prisons, great houses, and plantations that symbolized regimes of power and organized the territorial dynamic between the metropole and colony. Jefferson's designs for the Virginia State Capitol reveal the mutually constitutive relationship between race, reason, and architecture.

A Perfect Morsel of Good Taste

In 1776, Jefferson proposed a bill to the Virginia House of Delegates to move its state capital from Williamsburg, the colonial seat since 1699, to Richmond, a fledgling settlement farther up the James River. The bill was passed by the House of Delegates in 1779 shortly before Jefferson became governor of Virginia, a post he held for two years.[10] Richmond would be more centrally accessible to the state's citizens and representatives, safe from enemy incursion, and navigable by waterway.[11]

Home to a wealthy planter class who eagerly sought independence in steward-ing their own affairs, Virginia was one of the most powerful and prosperous of the thirteen colonies. The growing ranks of landed English farmers began assembling larger tracts of fertile territory in the late 1600s for the cultivation of the colony's main cash crop and export, tobacco. This territorial expansion, a system of land privatization enabled by patents and headrights awarded by the crown, further encroached upon the lands of indigenous peoples—the tribes of the Powhatan confederacy—and pushed them westward into the lands of the Monacan and Manahoac peoples. By the time the Second Continental Congress met in Philadelphia to declare independence from the Great Britain in July 1776, Virginia's free white population had grown substantially, along with its population of enslaved black workers. The latter had been purchased and imported as a labor force to tend the tobacco fields, and unlike indentured European laborers, could be held in perpetuity.

The bill to move the capital from Williamsburg to Richmond laid out a plan for the new seat of government. Jefferson's scheme for the civic district of Richmond subdivided blocks into plots, which were sold at auction. Jefferson drew up the first designs for the Virginia State Capitol in 1776, the same year that he drafted the state constitution, and revised them from 1779 to 1780.[12] In Jefferson's estimation, to adequately house Virginia's growing white constituency and gov-ernment, construction practices needed to evolve beyond the production of the crude, ugly wooden structures and awkwardly proportioned brick buildings that were found in Williamsburg. "Architecture," he lamented, "seems to have shed its maledictions over this land."[13] Brick and stone were proper materials for building because of their longevity, he rationalized. However, Virginia lacked craftsmen and workmen trained to draw and execute correctly the classical orders of entablatures, pediments, and columns. This lack of skilled labor was perhaps an outcome of the fact that one segment of the construction workforce was enslaved. Literacy, especially the ability to write, was discouraged among the enslaved in order to maintain subjugation and suppress revolt.

All the components of the new republic—executive, legislative, judicial—were accounted for in Jefferson's bill and in his initial drawings of the state capitol that placed each branch in its own building on Shockoe Hill. Jefferson possessed several key folios of Palladio and other volumes on Greek and Roman antiquities. He had experimented with Palladian neoclassicism at Monticello, his plantation house under construction in the Piedmont, and in unbuilt designs for his alma mater, the College of William and Mary.[14] For the state capitol, Jefferson placed the House of Delegates and other offices on the lower level. The senate chambers, associated clerks, and other legislative functions were located on the upper level.[15] Astutely aware of architecture's ability to project the longevity and stability of the state, Jefferson believed that the new capitol and courthouse buildings should be "built in a handsome manner with walls of Brick, or stone and Porticos."[16] A neoclassical exterior that echoed the architecture and ideals of Roman republicanism and Athenian democracy would best speak to the new country's values of liberty and justice.

In 1784, Jefferson succeeded Benjamin Franklin as the minister plenipotentiary to France, a post he held for five years. During his diplomatic assignment in Paris, where he lived with his two daughters, along with several enslaved Africans he had brought along to tend to their needs, Jefferson was charged with finally completing the plans for the Virginia capitol once the land on Shockoe Hill had been claimed by eminent domain.[17] In summer of 1785, two of the state government's directors of public buildings—James Buchanan and William Hay—sent revised plans of the capitol's foundations to Jefferson to review as a means of quelling discontent in the state legislature over the choice of the building's site. Buchanan and Hay's pragmatic scheme—a series of rooms divided by a long central hallway—lacked the aesthetic vision of Jefferson's skillful plans. Governor Patrick Henry wrote to Jefferson in the late summer of 1785 that a cornerstone had been laid and that foundations of brick, their construction overseen by Hay and Buchanan, were out of the ground, based on Jefferson's earlier drawings (figures 1.3 and 1.4).[18]

With construction commencing, Jefferson needed to act quickly to refine and complete his designs. To assist with the preparation of drawings and a model, he recruited French architect Charles-Louis Clérisseau, a skilled draftsman and archaeologist. Jefferson had reviewed drawings of the perfectly preserved Maison Carrée in books and greatly admired Clérisseau's publication *Antiquités de la France, Première Parti: Monumens de Nîmes* (1778), which he eventually purchased from Clérisseau while in Paris.[19] Clérisseau's meticulous orthographic documentation of the temple's details, proportions, and layout suited Jefferson, who

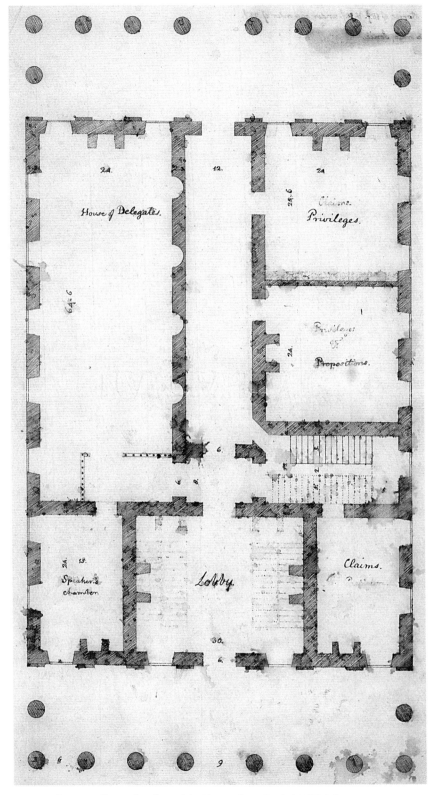

Fig. 1.3 Thomas Jefferson, first floor of the Virginia State Capitol, 1780. Ink on paper. CSmH9372, courtesy of Huntington Library, San Marino, California.

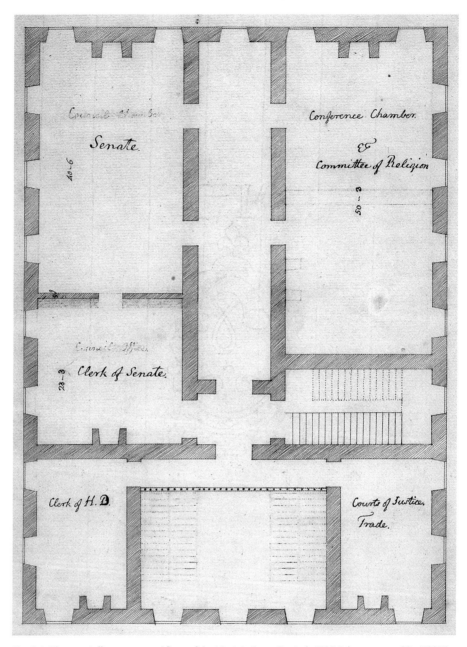

Fig. 1.4 Thomas Jefferson, second floor of the Virginia State Capitol, 1780. Ink on paper. CSmH9372, courtesy of Huntington Library, San Marino, California.

possessed not only the eye of an architect, but also the fastidious gaze of a naturalist.

Because the legislators desired to conduct all of the state's business in one structure, Jefferson with Clérisseau revised the earlier plans and placed the General Court on the first floor, across from the state's lower chamber, the House of Delegates. At the center of the elegantly proportioned two-story atrium that con-

Mabel O. Wilson

nected the two chambers with other functions in the building, Virginians planned to erect a statue to General George Washington, a former member of the House of Burgesses; the statue would aesthetically enhance and elevate the environment for civil debate.[20] The second floor housed the senate chambers and auxiliary spaces for clerks. The new design took advantage of the basilica form, so that the protocols of assembly, deliberation, and adjudication, adapted from the colonial government, would operate smoothly in the space.

In a letter to James Madison, Jefferson expressed his desire that Virginia's new capitol building would become a model of architecture worth emulating throughout the new nation: "How is a taste in this beautiful art to be formed in our countrymen, unless we avail ourselves of every occasion when public buildings are to be erected, of presenting to them models for their study and imitation?"[21] Jefferson apprised his friend that for many people the Maison Carrée was "one of the most beautiful, if not the most beautiful and precious morsel of architecture left us by antiquity."[22] The monuments of antiquity offered Americans perfectly preserved examples of Greco-Roman classicism, an architecture emblematic of truth, justice, and democracy, one that for Jefferson had not been corrupted by capricious flourishes of the late baroque's rococo period that suited the tastes of the French aristocracy. He commissioned model maker Jean-Pierre Fouquet to complete a plaster maquette of the design. In June 1786, he shipped the model along with Clérisseau's drawings to Hay and Buchanan in Richmond.[23]

The didactic purpose of this novel design for the capitol building, Jefferson wrote to Madison, was heuristic: "Its object is to improve the taste of my countrymen, to increase their reputation, to reconcile to them the respect of the world and procure them it's [sic] praise."[24] In return for erecting a beautiful work of civic architecture, Americans would gain the regard of the world, which for Jefferson meant the new nation would win the admiration of Europeans. The rationale for replicating historical buildings held in high regard was that the design for such buildings was "very simple, but it is noble beyond expression, and would have done honour to our country as presenting to travellers a morsel of taste in our infancy promising much for our maturer age."[25] What Jefferson feared most was the prospect of erecting a tasteless "monument to our Barbarism."[26] Jefferson hoped that the new capitol building would be a transformative exercise that would seed a new culture and society in the New World, yielding a ripe American civilization. His proposed designs for the Virginia State Capitol would offer an invaluable public primer on how architecture could represent the virtues of durability, utility, and beauty (figure 1.5).

One challenge faced by Virginians—and the new union of thirteen states—was how to cultivate the character of its new political subjects, "the people." In eighteenth-century Europe and its colonies, refined taste in art, dress, architecture,

Fig. 1.5 Front view of Virginia State Capitol, Richmond, Virginia, 1865. Courtesy of Library of Congress, LC-DIG-cwpb-02891.

and food (fueled by the growing appetite for sugar, coffee, and tobacco) became a marker of elevated intellectual and economic status. But this "culture of taste," writes Simon Gikandi, also harbored "repressive tendencies—namely, the attempt to use *culture* to conceal the intimate connection between modern subjectivity and the political economy of slavery."[27] This interdependence between the formation of a new white American culture, one that included the arts of building, and the enslavement of African peoples, justified by their presumed innate mental and physical inferiority, can be found in *Notes on the State of Virginia*, which Jefferson wrote in the same period in which he conceived the designs for Virginia's capitol building.

The State of Virginia

An esteemed member of the American Philosophical Society and deeply invested in the philosophical tenets and methods of the period, Jefferson took great interest in scientific principles drawn from the careful observation of facts and by the meticulous study of things and phenomena. His command of natural history and natural philosophy birthed *Notes on the State of Virginia*, Jefferson's only published book. He printed a private edition in 1785 that he gave to friends. A public edition was printed in London two years later.

Notes on the State of Virginia originated as a report prepared in response to twenty-three queries sent to Jefferson in 1780 by a French diplomat, François Barbé-Marbois, who had created the survey to gain a better understanding of the geographic and historic character of the newly formed United States. In *Notes on the State of Virginia* Jefferson took stock of the state's natural features and human inhabitants. In the first part, his taxonomic assessment of plants, animals, minerals, climate, rivers, mountains, and caves highlighted the state's bountiful resources. He noted that natural laws also governed the human species residing within the state's boundaries and divided them into the racial taxonomies of Europeans, Aboriginals, and Africans. The book also reviewed the state's systems and institutions that organized its society, namely its commerce, manufacturing, government, religion, and civil society. Intimately familiar with Virginia's constitution, Jefferson outlined the government's branches and duties, noting in detail the rights and laws that adjudicated the legal status and relationships, albeit unequally, between the aforementioned races.

Jefferson divided *Notes on the State of Virginia* into sections according to Barbé-Marbois's original queries in order to incrementally introduce his reader to the varied geography, species, and political sphere of Virginia. Throughout the book, Jefferson's sketch of New World ecology emphasizes the symbiotic relationship between soil, climate, and speciation. What he labeled as "nutritive juices" sustained the life force of various species, including humans.[28] Naturalists in this period were keen on observing the forces that affected how species of plants and animals developed over time. Jefferson noted in his answer to Query 6, for example, that "the difference of increment" in the minerals, flora, fauna, and species depended "on circumstances unsearchable to beings with our capacities." "Every race of animals," he added, "seems to have received from their Maker certain laws of extension at the time of their formation."[29] For many natural historians in Jefferson's era, divine forces were considered to be the regulators of the laws of nature; nature had not yet been determined to have its own laws. This logic extended to the observable differences in the physical and mental characteristics of the human species. Secular rationalism promoted a logical framework of historical succession, but scientists believed these measurable innate forces were outside the control of man.

Elsewhere in his response to Query 6 Jefferson refutes at length the hypotheses of French naturalist Georges-Louis Leclerc, the Comte de Buffon, taking aim at the Frenchman's claim that "the animals common both to the old and new world, are smaller in the latter," in part due to greater heat and humidity of the Americas.[30] Through an analysis of different animal and vegetable species as they related to the climatic and geographic conditions of Virginia, Jefferson countered Buffon, showing that there had been neither a reduction of stature nor diminished diversity in any American species. This was critical for Jefferson because Buffon had also applied his theory of degeneration to humans, in particular American Indians, the "aboriginal" human in the Americas. Fearing that Buffon's assertions would suggest future degradation in Europeans who had migrated to North America, Jefferson endeavored to disprove the naturalist's claims regarding physical and mental degeneration, arguing that the species "*Homo sapiens Europaeus*" had for three centuries dwelled in the same temperate zones, nourished by the same plants and animals as the Indian of North America.[31]

One central tenet of Enlightenment natural philosophy was that in nature all races of the human species had been born equal, a view cherished by natural rights advocates such as John Locke and Charles Montesquieu, and the nation's founding patriarchs, who had formed a new nation according to principles of equality. What mattered most, however, was the difference in how far each race had advanced to become liberal subjects capable of self-governance, a state of enlightenment dependent upon innate faculties of mind and body. Thus "before we condemn the Indians of this continent as wanting genius," Jefferson countered Europeans like Buffon, "we must consider that letters have not been introduced among them." In other words, American Indians had not yet evolved to a rationalized state of civilization.[32] Regardless, almost all philosophers agreed that white Europeans were by far the superior race. They did not agree, however, on Jefferson's rationale that indigenous Americans were superior to enslaved Africans.

Jefferson advanced the logic of his observation in Query 6 by defending European colonists. He shielded them from Buffon's caustic judgments that "belittle her productions on this side of the Atlantic."[33] Jefferson provided evidence in philosophy, war, government, oratory, painting, and the plastic arts to show that "America, though but a child of yesterday, has already given hopeful proofs of genius."[34] America—its politics and culture, as Jefferson had also assessed in his letter to Madison—was still in its infancy. He was confident the United States would evolve to rival if not surpass Europe, if the minds and tastes of its white citizenry were properly nurtured, for instance, by exposure to tasteful, aesthetically pleasing architecture of the kind exemplified by the Virginia capitol building. Even though he sought to sever ties with what he believed to be a calcifying European aristocratic culture, Jefferson nonetheless preserved its aesthetic values as a visible register of white American culture.

The transatlantic slave trade had transported another race to the Americas—*Homo Sapiens Afer*, Africans or Negroes. For Jefferson, Negroes, because of their naturally inferior faculties, could not be incorporated into the new nation state as citizens. In his response to Query 14, "The Administration of Justice and the Description of the Laws," Jefferson sought a political solution to the problem of what to do with the Negro population living in Virginia, the majority of which was enslaved. On several occasions in state legislation and in early drafts of the Declaration of Independence, Jefferson had proposed language that terminated the importation of slaves into Virginia and the United States. (During his presidency he would succeed in 1808 in abolishing the international slave trade, but not its lucrative domestic market.)

Along with political concerns, Jefferson held "physical and moral objections" to Negroes based on a lifetime of observations of what he considered to be their comportment and character.[35] Because universal reason relied upon experimentation and observation for the validation of truth, Jefferson's conceptualization of the racial paradigm of human difference found one promising register in skin color. He rationalized that what counted as beautiful could be applied to the breeding of animals and therefore also to the human species—where variations in physiognomy, hair texture, and skin color were visible. Out of all these markers, skin color was the most obvious indicator of racial difference. The origins of the skin's coloration for Jefferson, however, could not be discerned by dissection of the epidermal layers or a chemical analysis of blood or bile. He determined skin color then as "fixed in nature," and therefore of divine causation. The aesthetics of blackness was part of a rationalization of the variations in the human species that divided peoples living on the continents of Europe, Asia, Africa, and the Americas and affirmed the superiority of Europeans and their whiteness.

Under Jefferson's probing gaze, the features of the black body were seen as less beautiful in comparison to the symmetry and flowing hair of white physiognomy. The overall lack of beauty in blackness visually and viscerally appalled Jefferson. He verified this by suggesting that even Native Americans found whites preferable, just as "the preference of the Oranootan [sic] [is] for the black women [sic] over those of his own species."[36] To posit black women as subhuman, closer to primates, was based on a theory of polygenesis in natural history, which maintained that each race was a different species. This degrading concept had circulated ten years earlier in Edward Long's epic *History of Jamaica*. As Fred Moten writes, "The pathologization of blacks and blackness in the discourse of human and natural sciences and in the corollary emergence of expertise [serves] as the defining epistemological register of the modern subject."[37] Blackness signified the Negro's sub-humanity and validated her ruthless exploitation.

The Negroes' supposed inability to appreciate beauty, except in the most sensual manner, or to create works of true aesthetic value, except out of mimicry, also provided Jefferson with additional evidence of their natural mental inferiority. In Query 14 Jefferson surmised that in their ability to remember, blacks were equal to whites, but in their ability to reason and to comprehend mathematics and sciences, they were certainly inferior. "In their imagination," he wrote, blacks were "dull, tasteless, and anomalous."[38] To affirm the truth of his observations, Jefferson offered the examples of composer/writer Ignatius Sancho and poet Phillis Wheatley.

Jefferson held nothing but contempt for Ignatius Sancho, whose "letters do more to honour the heart than the head."[39] Sancho was born on a slave ship en route to the Caribbean and at age two migrated to England with his master. There he cleverly escaped enslavement by entering into domestic service in the households of several aristocratic families. Self-educated, he advocated for the abolition of slavery in a series of letters exchanged with a highly regarded abolitionist that brought him praise. Sancho leveraged his fame to become a well-known actor, playwright, and composer and an acquaintance to many of Europe's political and aristocratic elites. A celebrity in his right, Sancho sat for a portrait by the great painter Thomas Gainsborough. But in Query 14, Jefferson ranked Sancho, who was the first black person to vote in a British election, at the bottom in comparison to contemporary white men of letters. Jefferson suggested that if Sancho's works had any merit at all it was most likely attributable to a white collaborator rather than Sancho's own genius.

In Jefferson's mind, poet Phillis Wheatley possessed the inferior traits of both her race and gender. Wheatley was enslaved to a Boston family at age eight. Her owners named her Phillis, after the slave ship that had transported her from Senegambia to the port of Boston. Yet despite her appalling plight as an enslaved servant, she like Sancho learned to read and write at a young age. She was well read in ancient history and, inspired by the verses of Homer and John Milton, began to write poetry, publishing a collection in 1773 (figure 1.6). One of the few eighteenth-century American women to have been published, Wheatley used her public stature to advocate for American independence and for the natural rights of slaves. She was eventually freed by her owners after her first and only volume was published. Despite Wheatley's remarkable achievements under the harshest of circumstances, Jefferson believed her incapable of writing poetry, since love for the Negro could only stimulate the senses but not the imagination. He wrote that her poems were "below the dignity of criticism."[40]

Mabel O. Wilson

Fig. 1.6 Engraving after Scipio Moorhead. Frontispiece, *Poems on Various Subjects, Religious and Moral*, by Phillis Wheatley (London: A. Bell, 1773). Courtesy of Library of Congress, LC-DIG-ppmsca-02947.

"Deep Rooted Prejudices," "Ten Thousand Recollections"

Did the Negro, whether enslaved or freed, have a place in America? Jefferson put forward an emancipation scheme in his response to Query 14. He proposed that enslaved children "should continue with their parents to a certain age, then be brought up, at the public expence [*sic*], to tillage, arts or sciences, according to their geniusses [*sic*]."[41] Once adults, women age eighteen and men age twenty-three should be colonized to African, Caribbean, or western U.S. territories and supported until they grew in strength.[42] To replace the now-absent labor Jefferson proposed to send "vessels at the same time to other parts of the world for an equal number of white inhabitants."[43] The arrival of European immigrants would realize Jefferson's vision of a nation composed of white freeholders whose homesteads would expand the nation's boundaries westward.

Pragmatically, Jefferson believed that Virginia's history of chattel slavery would prevent black and white races from living together peacefully in the same place, citing those "deep rooted prejudices entertained by whites; ten thousand recollections, by the blacks, of the injuries they sustained."[44] Emancipation and citizenship for freed blacks could only result in "convulsions which will probably never end but in the extermination of one or the other race."[45] American civilization, therefore, could not thrive with a free black population. The undesirability of blackness, the "unfortunate difference of color, and perhaps faculty, is a powerful obstacle to emancipation of their people," argued Jefferson.[46]

Once enslaved blacks were freed, Jefferson required them to be "removed beyond the reach of mixture."[47] Thus not only did revenge by blacks pose a threat to the new nation in Jefferson's eyes, but he also feared miscegenation.[48] These sentiments on the abolition of slavery and the slave trade, as well as on the resettlement of freed Africans, were beginning to circulate widely, including among some abolitionist circles. Colonization societies were established on both sides of the Atlantic, eventually leading to the founding of Sierra Leone (1808) and Liberia (1822). The conservation of whiteness—symbolically and biologically—was paramount to the formation the United States' cultural identity.

While emancipation might have been desirable for political and moral reasons, the economic realities of how chattel slavery fueled the wealth and maintained the well-being of white Americans made it difficult to terminate an already two-century-long reliance on slave labor. The enlightened white men who "liberated" the nation espoused the humanistic values of natural rights, Lockean "life and liberty," yet many were unwilling to part with their human property. Some of Jefferson's generation did manumit their slaves either during their lifetime or upon death, as did George Washington and his heirs. However, Jefferson, who owned up to two hundred slaves at one time, more than six hundred over his lifetime, freed only seven slaves—two during his lifetime and five upon his death.[49]

In later editions of *Notes on the State of Virginia*, Jefferson records that by 1792 there was almost an equal number of enslaved blacks and free whites living in Virginia. The population of free blacks had grown substantially as slaveholders liberated slaves after the Revolutionary War. But those manumissions began to taper off as the value of slaves increased. The domestic slave trade began prospering as new states and territories opened up to the west due to demand for vast swathes of land for large plantation operations. Slave labor was indispensable for cultivat-

Mabel O. Wilson

ing crops like wheat and cotton, which were becoming more popular as tobacco farming had exhausted the soil in the mid-Atlantic. Slave owners profited from hiring out enslaved blacks to other plantations or as unskilled and skilled workers in towns and cities. Places like Alexandria and Richmond, where the capitol was under construction, teemed with enslaved and free black artisans and laborers.[50]

In 1785, Jefferson wrote from Paris to Hay and Buchanan that given the scarcity of talented craftsmen in Virginia it might be wise to hire European craftsmen well versed in wood-, stone-, and plaster-construction techniques. Securing the services of a skillful stonecutter, for example, was desirable, because, according to Jefferson, "under his [the stonecutter's] direction, negroes who never saw a tool, will be able to prepare the work for him to finish."[51]

Once construction of the capitol building was under way, enslaved laborers joined the teams of workers that cleared the land, dug foundations, hauled wood, cut lumber, molded and fired bricks, transported stone, painted walls and trim, and removed the waste from Shockoe Hill. While members of Virginia's planter class like Jefferson possessed hundreds of slaves to work their agricultural holdings and small-scale industries such as nail manufacturing, it was also common for free white Virginians engaged in business and trade, including construction, to possess a small number of enslaved Africans. William Hay, the director of public buildings in Richmond, for example, owned six slaves over the age of sixteen (tax records only make note of those who were taxable, so there could have been others under age twelve).[52] Samuel Dobie, a skilled Richmond builder who executed Jefferson's neoclassical designs, though not always faithfully to the statesman's intent, owned two adult slaves during the time of construction.[53]

Many of the tradesmen—plasterers, plumbers, and painters—who worked on the Virginia capitol owned several slaves. Edward Voss of Culpeper, a subcontractor and the supplier of the four hundred thousand bricks for the building's foundations, owned seven slaves. In October 1788 Voss sent an invoice to the directors to pay Robert Goode "the sum of ten pounds 20 shillings for the hire of Negroes to oblige."[54] To perform numerous rough carpentry and woodworking tasks for several years through 1795, Dobie subcontracted Dabney Minor, who lived on a farm in Woodlawn, in nearby Orange, Virginia, where he owned seven slaves; Minor kept ten slaves in Richmond.[55] Minor's arrangement exemplifies the connection between rural regions where raw materials were cultivated and towns where commodities and goods, including slaves, circulated in and out of markets. During the busy year of 1789, Minor's workers erected the interior framing of the courtroom and doorways, laid tongue-and-groove flooring in the courtroom, mounted scaffolding for workers to install pediments and cornices, moved bricks, and cut the wooden templates Voss used to erect the exterior columns—all part of a long list of tasks for which Minor was paid £154 (in 1788 Minor earned £1,004 for work on the site).[56] An advertisement Minor placed in Richmond and Hanover newspapers in 1794 explained that runaway slave Lewis or Lewy had been "employed at the whip-saw, and in rough plaining [*sic*]," which shows how Minor deployed enslaved workers in the various facets of his construction business.[57]

Because Richmond was a port town, freed black men also worked on the capitol building. A laborer named Fortune, who was known to Hay and Dobie, worked on the construction site for several months in 1788. His tasks included clearing away timber, planks, and rubbish from the yard. Fortune was paid directly, indicating that he might be either a freedman or an enslaved laborer who had some modicum of control over his time.[58] It is unclear from records whether enslaved Africans were rented for long periods of time and hence lived onsite. But given that Richmond was already a busy port town, the enslaved population, including women and children, provided a range of services from cooking to laundering to stabling. Enslaved blacks provided a significant portion of the labor necessary to erect Jefferson's monument to American civic life.

"Immovable Veil of Black"

The second of Latrobe's watercolors of the Virginia State Capitol, whose perspective is taken from across the James River, depicts the civic temple dominating the rustic landscape, much in the way that Jefferson's Monticello and the University of Virginia, which he also designed, commanded their respective sites. In these two other designs, the high ground, both natural and man-made, provided Jefferson the opportunity to architecturally reconcile the paradox between freedom and slavery by placing some of the slave dependencies beneath the main living spaces in rooms and passages hidden from view. This way, the white-columned neoclassical buildings appeared to visitors as idyllic beacons of democratic values overlooking sublime nature unsullied by the presence of those spaces in which unsightly slaves toiled to make the land fertile and the lives of white citizens comfortable.

Blackness was a sublime "eternal monotony," an "immovable veil of black which covers all the emotions of the other race," wrote Jefferson in his response to Query 14.[59] Black bodies and blackness for Jefferson and for others of his era proved an impenetrable threshold to reason. They were distasteful. Wielding the tools of enlightenment, Jefferson rationalized the Negro belonged at the back end of the social and political forces that would advance American civilization, in the same manner he designed their spaces of interminable servitude to occur below ground. While all men were born equal, as natural rights proponents advocated, to Jefferson, the Negro possessed neither the aptitude to reason nor faculties to appreciate beauty or liberty. "The people" did not include Negroes. The prospect of a free black American was both unreasonable and unimaginable to the sage of Monticello.

Mabel O. Wilson

2

American Architecture in the Black Atlantic

William Thornton's Design for the United States Capitol

Peter Minosh

In November of 1792, William Thornton (1759–1828) arrived in Philadelphia from a two-year stay on his family's slave-holding plantation on the island of Tortola in the British Virgin Islands. He carried his proposed architectural design for a new capitol of the United Sates. Thornton had lived in Philadelphia for four years prior and had found some success as a physician, inventor, and amateur architect, yet he had never planned on returning to the city. Instead, he had hoped to be sailing for western Africa with a contingent of freed slaves in order to participate in a new colony that would reconfigure the political geography of the Atlantic World.

This essay considers Thornton's design for the United States Capitol in relation to racism, slavery, and notions of American enlightenment. Against, and perhaps underlying, the multiple ideologies of freedom, liberty, and equality that have been projected onto the neoclassical architecture of the Capitol, it is well understood that this "temple of liberty" was in fact built by enslaved people. Enslaved laborers literally built the material edifice that presently stands in Washington, DC. We can equally say that slavery "built" the Capitol inasmuch as the national resources—financial and material—necessary for such an undertaking were provided by (that is, appropriated from) enslaved people. This essay proposes a third register by which slavery "built" the Capitol: that slavery *construed* it by being foundational to the political imaginary within which it was formed.

This demands another mode of "reading" neoclassical architecture. Rather than parse the various significations intended in the spatial and formal organization of the building, I will attempt to define a horizon against which such an architecture could take form at the end of the eighteenth century. This entails privileging an understanding of the racial systems within which the Capitol is entangled over an examination of its autonomous form or content. I will examine how the Capitol operates among the set of cultural, economic, and material phenomena that configured the social imaginaries that we call racial whiteness and blackness.

Following W. E. B. Du Bois, I take this architecture to present a racial "double consciousness" by exemplifying hybridity of white and black subject positions in its monumental representation; following Paul Gilroy I situate this double consciousness within the Atlantic World.[1] The neoclassical design of the Capitol has been taken to represent the classical virtues of an American enlightenment. I argue that the proper subjects represented in this monument to representational democracy are not the citizens of the Republic, but the enslaved people excluded from political and architectural representation. By examining Thornton's preliminary designs for the Capitol in consideration of the greater trajectory of his philosophical projects and political activities, we can discern in this neoclassical edifice the terms of an irresolvable crisis between the enlightened Republic and its foundation within a regime of chattel slavery. In order to offer such an interpretation of the Capitol, I will first discuss Thornton's plans for slave manumission and his formulation of a universal orthography. These will shed light on the political and philosophical systems in which Thornton formulated his design.

Throughout his early life Thornton traversed a transatlantic network that was coextensive with the Second Atlantic system: he was raised in the British West Indies, educated in England, received his professional training in Scotland, began his medical practice back in England, and established his career in the United States.[2] We might say that Thornton was a subject of the Atlantic World, and as such, we can take his neoclassical design for the Capitol as a vision for the political and economic reorganization of that world during the final decade of the eighteenth century. In this moment, just after the ratification of the US Constitution, slavery remained a "peculiar institution" that could credibly have dissipated with the Slave Trade Act of 1794 that limited American involvement in the trade. But by the end of that decade the plantation system was firmly established in the American South with inland cotton becoming the nation's main export commodity for the global market.[3] The 1807 Act Prohibiting Importation of Slaves solidified the position of slavery in American economic development, as chattel slavery

Peter Minosh

became an inelastic market and a vehicle for investment capital.[4] In this essay, I read the implicit racial politics of Thornton's design for the US Capitol Building centrifugally through a unique set of archives—personal correspondences, legal proceedings, philosophical treatises, religious pronouncements, and architectural drawings—produced while he traversed this particular route across the Atlantic system.

William Thornton and Slave Manumission

What brought Thornton back to his childhood home in Tortola was a contact, made in 1788 through his mentor and fellow abolitionist John Coakley Lettsom, with Granville Sharp.[5] Sharp, who would become one of the founders of Sierra Leone, had in 1787 purchased an area of land on a West African peninsula from the local Temne chief King Tom. With the support of the British government, Sharp moved to relocate there some seven hundred to eight hundred "Black Loyalists" living in London—these were black Africans formerly enslaved in the United States who had fought for the British during the Revolutionary War with the promise of manumission. In England, they had largely been forced into a condition of indigence, and their presence was unwelcome by the political estab-lishment. Sharp established the eponymous Granville Town as a site of black repatriation in Africa (figure 2.1).[6] Thornton sought to become involved in Sharp's settlement, and in 1789 he organized the "Union Society" in Newport, Rhode Island, to recruit two thousand free northern blacks to the cause while planning to join the settlement himself in the capacity of "superintendent."[7] His intention in travelling to Tortola was to manumit the seventy to eighty enslaved people bequeathed to him in the settling of his father's estate and to formally petition the legislature of the Virgin Islands to entrust him to lead an expedition, similar to Sharp's, to relocate them.[8]

Thornton, like Sharp, imagined that the west coast of Africa would offer an alternative to the European mercantilist mode of the colonial project. It was to be a new kind of colony above the fray of the old-world battle for empire, populated by a new kind of colonist who would refuse any implementation of slavery. Granville Town, they hoped, would not be subject to any exclusive trade arrange-ments imposed by foreign powers, and would consequently be able to sign treaties and exchange goods with multiple nations. According to Thornton: "Every European power would, no doubt, be glad to accept, upon easy terms, the trade of one of the richest colonies in the world. They would have no expense to support, might send their own vessels, could never be jealous of a power which, whilst pacifically inclined, would never increase, and indeed the basis of the government would be founded in peace."[9] Set apart from Europe, the Americas, and, especially, the West Indies, an African settlement would be precisely the type of economic

Fig. 2.1 John Matthews, *A View of Sierra-Leone River, from St. George's Hill, where the free Black settlement was made in the year 1787*, 1791. Courtesy of the Schomburg Center for Research in Black Culture, The New York Public Library.

free zone that could become the basis of a new laissez-faire political economy in the Atlantic.

In addition to the natural resources of Africa that had long been staples of the transatlantic trade—gold dust, ivory, gums, wood, drugs, and spices—Granville Town would import the trades and skills of the British West Indies, cultivating cotton and indigo for export to Europe and sugar to the United States. While former American and Caribbean slaves were to till the earth of Granville Town, freed northern American blacks would play much the same role as their northern white counterparts—taking part in trade and commerce and spreading the social and ethical values of enlightened citizens.[10] Freed northern blacks would thus serve as a proxy civilizing force for former slaves and Africans alike. Thornton explained, "The Negros of the Northern Countries, who have been amongst Christians . . . would easily be induced to live a regular life, and by example the rest, as well as the Natives, might become a sober religious people."[11] An independent colony of freed blacks would provide a model to replace the system of transatlantic slavery. According to both Sharp and Thornton, ideological claims of universal freedom and equality had been prevented from fully taking root in the Americas largely due to the presence of slavery. Their aim was to impart to Africa a version of American enlightenment that had thus far been inaccessible to the United States. Moreover, by removing and relocating American slaves, and thus

Peter Minosh

removing a foundational contradiction of American democracy, Thornton believed that the United States might also gain access to the promise of enlightenment that had eluded it.

While the commercial operations of the African colony would be overseen by free blacks from the northern United States, Thornton sought to draw its labor force from his own holding of slaves in Tortola. In his proposals to manumit these slaves we can locate a tension between enlightenment notions of individual sovereignty and a paternalistic treatment of freed slaves. Of the seventy to eighty enslaved people bequeathed to him in the settling of his father's estate, Thornton considered only a handful to be suitable for resettlement in Africa. Many, he believed, lacked the discipline or work ethic to be given immediate freedom; those whom he did not consider ready for independence in Africa were to remain in Tortola, but under modified conditions. He sought to adapt his inherited land toward "inducing the most ungovernable of [his] people to become good members of society." Thornton proposed to divide his estate into a number of lots, each to be offered, at a nominal fee, to an enslaved person for a period of six years. Those who "found the benefit of society" and "enjoyed the reward of their own labor" would be granted their freedom and have the option to remain on that plot indefinitely or to join the settlement in Africa. Those who refused to abide by the laws of the community or whose behavior remained "intemperate or improper" would be "fined in liberty or property," that is, they would lose their land and be returned to the condition of slavery.[12]

Whatever its pretense, Granville Town remained within the cold terms of exploitation founded upon multiple regimes of violence: violence upon the land that exploited mineral resources and razed native species to cultivate the products of the global marketplace; violence against individuals that displaced societies from territories staked for cultivation; and the racialized violence against subjects destined to toil for the cause of commerce.

Thornton's alternative to the large-scale plantation economy of the British West Indies consisted of a system of independent plots to be tended by freeholders who would engage in autonomous association through agricultural exchange. In effect, he would transform enslaved laborers into Jeffersonian yeomen. Yet the elimination of slavery by the removal of blacks from the United States squared neatly with the Jeffersonian mode of segregationist abolition that considered blacks to be morally and intellectually inferior and considered their presence—free or not—to be a barrier to establishing an enlightened democracy.[13] For Thornton, this effort was ultimately a disciplinary regime—an instrument of social reform devised to transform the corrupted and dependent enslaved peoples into social individuals. The violence of the plantation lurks behind this putative freedom. While the formerly enslaved peoples were to labor as "*free* tenants for life" they were not allowed to leave the plantation; this freedom existed only inasmuch as they remained subjugated to the systems of Atlantic commerce in either the British West Indies or Africa. To leave this reorganized plantation—to either refuse labor or its social obligations—would be to depart from the freedom lent to them. Were any formerly enslaved people to disobey, they would lose their rights to property and to freedom.

Black Loyalists and freed slaves were not simply to be repatriated to some ethnically natural locale to revive a premodern mode of existence. They were to remain the immanently modern subjects of the Atlantic system: bodies transported *yet again* to alien lands in order to open up new resources for ballooning global commodity markets. The ambitions of this project, modeled on an American vision of free and open trade of agricultural goods by an autonomous people, were to produce model citizens of a global economic liberalism. But they would ultimately only have remained subjects of the racial violence of global commerce.

In mid-November of 1788 Thornton was hearing reports that the African colony was diminished by disease and threatened by "enraged and jealous natives."[14] He came nowhere near his goal of recruiting two thousand northern blacks to join his emigration company, and those he did recruit never made firm commitments. There remained too much uncertainty for the would-be settlers regarding whether Granville Town was to be a free settlement or a British colony. Free northern blacks would never submit to becoming colonial subjects of the British Empire in which slavery remained legal.

By the time Thornton departed for Tortola in October of 1790, Granville Town had collapsed. Of the 700 Black Loyalists and their descendants committed to leave for the colony only 440 were to be found on the day of departure—most of whom refused to embark and were rounded up by force. Only 276 survived the journey to Sierra Leone, with many of the remaining soon dying of disease. Within three years many of the white settlers had abandoned the settlement and taken up the slave trade. The settlement was conclusively dispersed after an attack by the neighboring Temne people in misdirected retaliation for two of their own villages being torched and plundered by French slave traders.[15] In 1791 an act of Parliament established the Sierra Leone Company, which placed the area under the mercantilist control of the British Empire. Sharp wrote to Thornton strongly advising him against travel to Africa.[16]

Upon his arrival in Tortola, Thornton's reason for returning there was already lost. Having abandoned his life in the United States and with no route to Africa, Thornton was left to flounder in the West Indies. He attempted to at least free the enslaved peoples he had inherited, but a provision of British Virgin Islands law stood in the way. According to the regulations governing slavery, anyone wishing to manumit their slaves had to pay a yearly security of ten pounds per person. The

Peter Minosh

intent of the law was to prevent plantation owners from freeing enslaved peoples who had either been maimed or were too old to be productive as a way of ridding themselves of the burden of their care. Thornton thus proposed to the legislature that this fee be lifted in the cases of former slaves who were of a productive age and could reasonably support themselves. At a time when the population of blacks and whites in Tortola was proportionately ten to one, the legislature of the British Virgin Islands rejected Thornton's proposal. Any freed blacks must leave the colonies, and with the option of Africa foreclosed, there was nowhere left for them to go. Having failed to accomplish any of his plans for slave manumission in Tortola, Thornton took up writing a manual on orthography and began his designs for the Capitol. Thornton redirected his considerations on slavery to a philosophical and aesthetic plane and through these projects we can examine the irresolvability of an enlightened democracy founded upon racial violence.

Universal Orthography as Enlightenment Desire

Thornton's chief philosophical work, *Cadmus, or, A Treatise on the Elements of Written Language*, received a medal from the American Philosophical Society in 1793. It indicates the larger philosophical system within which his design for the Capitol was conceived. As its extended title claims, Cadmus sought to "[illustrate], by a philosophical division of speech, the power of each character, thereby mutually fixing the orthography and orthoepy."[17]

For Thornton, orthography—the proper spelling of words—and orthoepy—their correct pronunciation—should be self-same. It was only by received convention that they became distinct fields. He considered the conventional understanding of speech—the set of vowels and consonants by which one could determine discrete syllables making up individual words—to be an inherited burden of Europe and proposed a universal orthography to reform writing. These claims illustrate both the ambitions and limitations of his philosophical system.

Thornton's orthography aimed to simplify writing by looking to the individual sounds produced in spoken languages. This system—in essence, a basic phonetic alphabet—was composed of thirty characters divided between vowels and aspirates, wherein "a vowel is a letter that is founded by the voice, whence its name. An aspirate is a letter that cannot be found but by the breath." Over time, Thornton's orthography would incorporate all of the world's languages into a single system. New words would not require transliteration and existing words, in any language, could be universally employed.[18] As Thornton put it: "If then we fix a certain character to each sound, there will be no more difficulty in writing with a correct orthography than in speaking with one, as we speak letters, which form words, that make sentences; and I must repeat that thus ought we, in reading sentences, to read words, by reading letters; and thus will the tongue and pen express every idea with perfect uniformity."[19] Thornton sought absolute transparency between words and ideas. This writing derived from speech supersedes speech itself by serving as the common ground of a universal system.

Thornton's proposal for a new orthography, then, must be understood both as a continuation of European Enlightenment considerations of language and as a uniquely American rejection of old-world conventions. Hence his introduction declared to its intended audience of his colleagues in the American Philosophical Society: "You have corrected the dangerous doctrines of European powers, correct now the languages you have imported, for the oppressed of various nations knock at your gates, and desire to be received as your brethren. . . . The American Language will thus be as distinct as the government, free from all the follies of unphilosophical fashion, and resting upon truth as its only regulator."[20] Thornton was confident that his system would be effective in teaching the deaf to speak. The difficulty in teaching the deaf, he reasoned, lay in the impasse of the reproduction of sounds. If one could not reproduce a sound that one could not first hear, then a universal orthography preceding sound would resolve this impasse as pronunciation would become but the application of a written system. The practical claims of Thornton's system were that travelers could easily pick up languages with little instruction or assistance. As people would begin to write with a common orthography there would come to be no distinction in dialects between the different classes, and all people would easily learn to read.[21]

Thornton likely derived his ideas on orthography from the work of Thomas Spence, an English radical best known for his ideas on land reform. Like Thornton, Spence saw spelling reform as a project to release the natural capacities of the individual from inherited social constraints.[22] In his 1782 supplement to *Robinson Crusoe*, Spence imagined his orthography put into effect in the fictional worlds of Daniel Defoe: "As they could now learn as much in a Month, as formerly in a Year, the very poorest soon acquired such Notions of Justice, and Equity, and of the Rights of Mankind, as rendered unsupportable, every species of Oppression."[23] He thusly named his script Crusonean and published many of his political pamphlets (as well as the supplement to Defoe's novel) entirely in that script.

Thornton's understanding of the necessity for a rationalized orthography came about through a series of racial encounters. Two years before the publication of *Cadmus*, in a letter to the Council of the Virgin Islands in which Thornton discussed his plans to form a settlement of freed slaves in Sierra Leone, he mentioned his efforts to both learn the Temne language and devise a system of writing for it.[24] *Cadmus*, it seems, grew out of an effort to transcribe a language that he did not speak into a written language so that he could gain access to it. Yet despite this gesture toward African languages, Thornton's claims upon the universal actually normalize English as the universal standard of all human speech. He estimated

Peter Minosh

that a universal alphabet would contain fewer than fifty characters, the majority of which were already assigned as, he claimed, "the European may be considered as containing the great outline of all."[25]

While attempting to teach one of the enslaved men of his plantation to read he concluded that the only thing preventing the slave's realization of his natural capacities was an outmoded, inherited orthography. He describes this moment in a letter to Lettsom: "The cause of my considering the subject at all was the difficulty I had in teaching a negro servant to read. I was tortured by his want of intellect, and considering the subject, I found the language was faulty, for the man understood when I gave the words properly spelt."[26] In wiping away the received political and philosophical conventions that enforced such racial differentials, Thornton believed that he could unleash the natural capacities of the individual. At stake in this was the universal dissemination of knowledge within a new democracy. To offer universal access to both knowledge and public debate— regardless of race or class—would destroy systems of privilege and create an order in which all could participate on equal terms.

The system that would allow those without a voice to be heard is the same that would inculcate those without political standing into the universality of enlightenment. Yet Thornton would bring about no *ephphatha* by which the deaf were induced to speak; this universality was immanently *particular*. This universal system, ostensibly independent of class or race, fashions the racialized speech of white Europeans as normative. Thornton tried to teach an enslaved person to read in order to grant him access to enlightenment, but this enlightenment was univocal. Utterances are only possible within its particular language suppressing a bidirectional interaction, or a translational politics.[27]

Thornton's Capitol Building

When Thornton learned in early 1792 of the competition to design a new Capitol for the United States the deadline had passed and a number of designs had been submitted. None of these, however, was entirely satisfactory to Thomas Jefferson, who oversaw the project. Thornton had already proven himself as a capable architect in his design for the Library Company of Philadelphia, described by his contemporaries as the first American building in the "modern stile [*sic*],"[28] and Jefferson received Thornton's request to submit a late entry with enthusiasm. The frontrunner had been Étienne Hallet, a French-trained architect whose design combined an American Federalist architecture modeled on Pierre Charles L'Enfant's Federal Hall in New York (which served as the first US Capitol) with Louis Le Vau's baroque Collège des Quatre-Nations.[29] Hallet's layout for the Capitol arranged the American legislative system according to the organization of the French National Assembly, suggesting a precedent for American gover-

Fig. 2.2 William Thornton, United States Capitol, Washington, DC, elevation, "Tortola Scheme," 1793. LC-DIG-ppmsca-30938. Courtesy of Library of Congress.

nance in French political institutions. Jefferson, however, was never fully convinced by Hallet's design, perhaps finding the baroque monumentality ill-suited to his ambition for a "Temple of Liberty" appropriate to an agrarian democracy.

The Library of Congress identifies drawings of a sprawling Georgian complex as the scheme that Thornton brought back with him from Tortola in November of 1792 (figure 2.2).[30] On his return to the United States his work took on a decidedly neoclassical character. His approved design, formulated after 1794, organized the plan around two identical circular spaces. A central rotunda in the interior of the building was to serve as a gathering space for the separate branches of government. Directly adjacent to this, a cyrtostyle circular portico breaking the envelope of the building was to serve as a mausoleum, or "Temple of Virtue," for George Washington (figure 2.3).[31]

For Thornton the distinct branches of the federal government required neither separate sites nor distinct representation. In plan, the spaces required for each branch of government fit neatly into a unitary rectangular enclosure. A building to house the entirety of government was a unique problem in the 1790s. The Parliament at Westminster had stood in its then present form since the sixteenth century and architectural experiments for spaces of political representation were taking place in revolutionary France, yet each of these presupposed a unique representation for the people in contradistinction to a strong executive.[32] Jefferson's program, however, called for the executive to be absorbed into a building for the meeting of Congress. Rather than a house in which representatives of the people would balance out executive authority, all components were to operate in perfect accord; the two houses of Congress, the hall of the Supreme Court, and apartments for the executive are arrayed around the empty space of a central rotunda where all could gather.[33]

If the plan of the Capitol described the resolution of differences into a unity, the elevations speak to the tension at play in the slave-holding democratic repub-

Peter Minosh

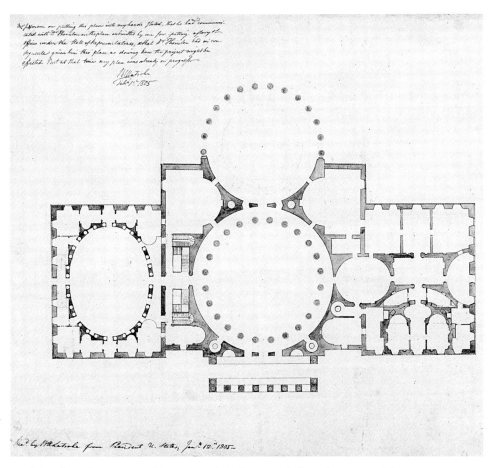

Fig. 2.3 William Thornton, United States Capitol, Washington, DC, floor plan, approved design, 1794–1797. LC-DIG-ppmsca-31440. Courtesy of Library of Congress.

lic. The new Capitol was to be sited atop a landscaped berm that would front the urban space of Washington, DC, to the east and overlook a mall to the west.[34] This placement offered a complex architectural problem necessitating dual elevations that would be both intimate to the urban condition surrounding the building while maintaining the monumentality required for it to provide a visual terminus of the extensive mall. Few of the entrants capitalized on this opportunity; most offered centralized pavilion plans that treated the east and west elevations the same or (more often) ignored the west elevation entirely.[35] Thornton's design, however, offered a distinct architectural response for each of the two main elevations. In doing so, it proposes a dual character that mediates the urban and pastoral ambitions of American enlightenment.

Thornton's east, city-facing, rotunda supports a stepped dome fronted by a classical propylaea to replicate the Roman Pantheon between two mannerist wings (figure 2.4). This low, horizontal composition gives civic representation to

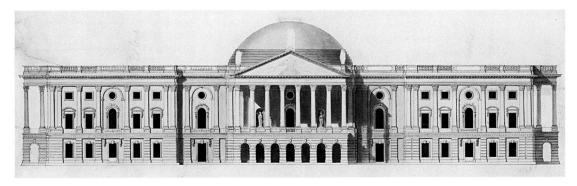

Fig. 2.4 William Thornton, United States Capitol, Washington, DC, east elevation, approved design, 1794–1797. LC-DIG-ppmsca-07219. Courtesy of Library of Congress.

the Capitol: its central portico is fashioned after L'Enfant's Federal Hall with its raised platform to serve as the public stage for presidential inaugurations.[36] It is one of the monumental edifices that would anchor a public square, per L'Enfant's vision, to establish a vast urban capital.[37] The west rotunda breaks the envelope of the building while projecting a colonnade topped with a classical tholos beyond its rectangular perimeter (figure 2.5). It forms a *tempietto* on the National Mall. This temple, like the many classical tholoi of eighteenth-century English landscape gardening, would rest atop a rolling pastoral landscape. Like those English gardens, this is not a productive landscape, but a pastoralism that could be configured precisely because the sites of agricultural production had been displaced to the slave-holding plantations of the American South.[38] In the English gardening tradition, the noble estates were transformed into picturesque landscapes as agricultural production shifted to the colonies. We might take this American counterpart to signal a similar misalignment between the sites of production and those of civic representation: while the plantation economy makes this picturesque landscape possible, all of its components have been removed from the capital.

This scheme is almost certainly modeled upon Charles de Wailly's 1764 design for the Château de Montmusard in Dijon, France. Montmusard is organized around two identical circular spaces determining the central axis of the building that each break its rectangular envelope. This design brings together two distinct chateau typologies: a cyrtostyle salon projecting east into the garden to evoke the feudal country estate and the compact single-story block of the western elevation recalling the urban typology of the Parisian *hôtel*.[39] An examination of the two faces of the Capitol presents a similar series of dialectical oppositions: L'Enfant's cosmopolitan urbanism and Jefferson's agrarian ideology, southern informal markets and northern finance capital, slavery and free labor. While these seem to be at odds, a look at the commodification of enslaved people within American chattel

Peter Minosh

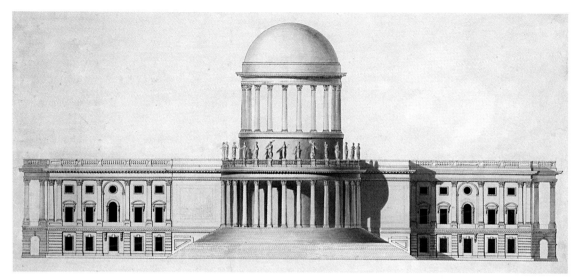

Fig. 2.5 William Thornton, United States Capitol, Washington, DC, west elevation, approved design, 1794–1797. LC-DIG-ppmsca-19858. Courtesy of Library of Congress.

slavery shows them to represent the two components of a contiguous system of wealth production.

As American financial infrastructure became increasingly dependent on the wealth contained in the personage of enslaved people, a means of securing that wealth proved necessary. Restrictions on the transatlantic slave trade beginning in 1794 created an inelastic market in chattel slavery, stabilizing the market so that the property value of the enslaved could operate as security for investment. This grew into a sophisticated financial operation. In its early phases the value of enslaved people was used to secure other investments, but it was soon realized that that value itself had to be secured. As slave capital was increasingly recognized as a mode of wealth like any other, the enslaved became fungible—transitioning from the material basis for securing wealth to a commodity itself to be securitized.[40]

Thornton, following Sharp, had understood liberal economics to be incompatible with monopolized labor.[41] In the final decade of the eighteenth century the incorporation of the violence of the plantation into systems of finance capital formulated a new type of subjecthood for enslaved peoples that was perfectly aligned with the slave regime. In a republic founded in the realization of the rights immanent to the individual, the enslaved were resolutely under the purview of their owners. Enslaved people had no explicit relationship to the republic—they were neither subject nor citizen, with no immanent rights and granting no legitimation to the state.[42] In a regime of individual sovereignty, slavery precipitated a dissolution of a sovereign individual in which enslaved peoples became biopolitical subjects regulated by free markets.

Two distinct readings of the Capitol become possible. The first presupposes a (white) sovereign citizen of a democratic republic to be its proper subject. Two façades of the Capitol describe two distinct territorial configurations—the urban and the pastoral—representing two distinct social, environmental, and economic systems. Each with matching rotundas—one, the tomb of the first president and dedicated to Virtue, the other, a space for all of government to gather. These determine the central axis of a plan that configures the disparate branches of government into a unified design within a uniform envelope. This reading, which was presumably intended by Thornton, is an enlightenment vision that resolves different political and social configurations through symbolic spaces of representation and gathering within an ideal plan. It presupposes an enlightened subject: a sovereign individual with recourse to universal reason. This subject, however, is racialized in a system that excludes enslaved peoples from individual sovereignty.

Thornton's architecture of American enlightenment thus remains haunted by a racialized other, demanding another interpretation. This one situates the Capitol back at its origin in the Atlantic World and has enslaved peoples as its proper subject. Once the ideal plan of the Capitol proves a site of privilege, we can see it as maintaining a double bind that fashions its political order in a universality that is particularized in the condition of racial whiteness. This condition extends centrifugally to the opposing façades that place the civic pantheon where the different branches of government unite in dialectical relationship to the tholos of the landscape garden. The economic order displayed in the resolution of the urban and the pastoral could only have come through an abject configuration of enslaved peoples as commoditized subjects of a biopolitical regime. An incommensurability lies at the heart of Thornton's architecture: that the American enlightenment he tried to configure is negatively determined through the absolute rejection of blackness as a site of political sovereignty. This confluence of the ideal and the abject is, perhaps, its very modernity. The absence upon which this whiteness is configured never truly disappears; it manifests aesthetically at the very sites of its erasure.

Just as in his colonization schemes and his work on orthography, the otherness that needed to be expunged from Thornton's Capitol was never actually resolved—it was merely displaced. His colonization schemes would rid the republic of its bad faith while perfectly maintaining the networks of global capital and the place of blacks within them. His orthography privileged European speech under the guise of universal participation, formulating a colonial double bind by presenting its unequal access to knowledge as a failure on the part of the excluded. The absolute transparency between citizen and state fashioned in the Capitol claims to provide universal access to government, but it ultimately renders unseen and unheard the multitude of the unrepresented enslaved—robbing them of their voice. It fashioned a regime of violence as disinterested reason of the democratic republic.

Peter Minosh

The Universalization of the American Republic

In 1800, after all of his plans for manumission and black resettlement had come to nothing and his design for the Capitol had been taken over and altered by others, Thornton extended his political ideas into a proposal to unify the entirety of the Americas into a single order. His "Outlines of a Constitution for the United North and South Columbia" described a united political body encompassing the entire Western Hemisphere.[43] The continents would be divided into thirteen states: North Columbia with five (largely adhering to the present-day latitudinal divisions between Canada, the United States, and Mexico), South Columbia with seven, and the "all of the West India and Islands" comprising the thirteenth. A capital of the unified continent, the District of America, would be centrally located at the Isthmus of Darien (presently, Isthmus of Panama). Much like its American model, the federal district would lie outside of the political determination of the states.

The boundaries of the individual sections were to be demarcated along geographic coordinates rather than natural boundaries. The division of states was explicitly imaginary, serving only to determine political representation. For Thornton ideal governance would become the new universal measure: "The cosmometry or measurement of the world, with relation to longitude, shall commence at the Supreme Seat of Government."[44] No conflict between states would arise as commerce would pass freely between them and all would offer equal protections; "whoever is a citizen of one, is a citizen of all; and . . . his rights extend through the whole!"[45] The government of the Columbias would mirror that of the United States, with a president, fifty-two representatives, twenty-six senators, and thirteen federal judges—four, two, and one from each state, respectively.

In his plan for a unified North and South Columbia, Thornton sought to universalize the political system of the United States to encompass the New World. The empire would be divided into states (thirteen no less) whose abstract political boundaries would allow for the greatest political representation while not interfering with commerce. A federal district of "Americus" would be located roughly at the center point of the empire, and government would be divided between its executive, a legislative, and judicial branches. But in this scaling of the American political system from the particular to the general, something, he hoped, would change as geographical conflicts might dissipate at greater scales. Perhaps for Thornton it is the particularity of American democracy itself that engendered a north–south divide. Perhaps remaining imbued within the European order— its networks of trade, its construction of the Middle Passage, and its ongoing battle over colonies—prevented the fulfillment of the United States' democratic self-realization.

The slave regime that was most foreign to Thornton's personal vision was sustained by the exchanges between the agricultural wealth of the New World and the economic power of the Old. Thornton's scheme necessitated the abolition of this other space of slavery while maintaining the global commercial order that it engendered. Here we must recall that Thornton's American enlightenment was, in the last instance, the purview of planter and merchant interests. Moreover, Thornton's home in Tortola—from which he penned his treatise on orthography and drafted his design of the Capitol—was a mere 250 miles from revolutionary Saint-Domingue, directly in the path of the maritime routes that transported commerce, refugees, and revolutionary ideas between Europe's West Indian colonies. In this light we might take all of Thornton's plans as attempts at a moderate revolution that might resolve burgeoning racial tensions before they brought about a generalized insurrection.

•   •   •

Thornton, in his classicism, might best be understood as a failed Ulysses of the Atlantic World. He pursued his ever-receding horizon of abolition from the sugar colonies of the British West Indies, to the English Society for the Abolition of the Slave Trade and the French Société des amis des Noirs, to the intellectual abolitionist circles of the American republic, to his unrealized journey to the fleeting free black colonies of western Africa, to the center of the American government. But Hermes, the God of commerce, always steered the winds to his disfavor and his ambitions remained just beyond his bow. The legislature of the British Virgin Islands rejected his petition to manumit the enslaved, the Girondists of the Société des amis des Noirs were killed by the Terror, the Union Society of Newport dissolved, Granville Town was overrun, and, finally, his Capitol was left unrealized. In the wake of these failures his vision only expanded, as if the scale of the Atlantic was not too vast, and the mercantile institutions of the Middle Passage not too embedded, but his ambitions simply too limited; his enlightenment vision could only operate at the scale of the universal. He ended his hapless pursuit of the receding horizon of manumission and determined that all would adhere to the absolute. His vision expanded outward from the capital of his Americus at the Isthmus of Darien, to encompass the Western Hemisphere in its entirety. All would have an equal voice in the universal tongue. The manumission societies and free settlements would be proven unnecessary. The moderate revolution would be won, and the West Indies would become a state within a hemispheric republic. We can look out at this expanse from the Capitol, with its immanent incommensurability expanding centrifugally with the enlightenment reason that it instantiates.

Peter Minosh

3

Drawing the Color Line

Silence and Civilization from Jefferson to Mumford

Reinhold Martin

If, in considering what it has meant for architecture to be modern, we trace a line from past to present, our line must at some point cross, parallel, break, or merge with that traced by what Max Horkheimer and Theodor W. Adorno referred to as an implacable "dialectic of Enlightenment," where life-as-imagined meets life-as-lived. Drawn, according to these two thinkers, by capital and its avatars but with programs of racial superiority in close attendance, this dialectic or something like it has directly or indirectly guided many attempts to understand modern architecture's aspirations to emancipation, the tacit subject of which was and remains most frequently white.[1] Predominant among these efforts are accounts that recognize cultural forms as ideological constructions—in a word, myth—the architectural history of which is one of prolonged ruination that culminates, for the European and North American neo-avant-gardes at the end of the twentieth century, in what Manfredo Tafuri memorably called the "ashes of Jefferson."[2]

For Tafuri, Thomas Jefferson was not first and foremost a slave owner, nor was he first and foremost white; rather, he was an abstraction, an allegory of the proto-bourgeois artist-intellectual and a precursor to the Euro-American avant-gardes whose thought and actions, bound to the Enlightenment ideal of reason, were betrayed from the outset by the antagonism of agrarianism and industrial capitalism into which they were born. Tafuri's racial blindness is itself ideological, and there are other, more complete and subtle accounts of Jefferson's architectural contribution and its contradictions.[3] But as historians come more clearly to understand the racial conflicts that architecture's modernity has long entailed, wherever and whenever that modernity is said to have taken hold, we must come to terms with the conflicted preconditions of our own knowledge. My aim is therefore an object lesson in anachronism, via an alliance of dialectics and discourse analysis, with the former abbreviated to mark Enlightenment's contradictions, and the latter developed in a modified Foucauldian vein with media-theoretical assistance.

Race as History as Civilization

To the extent that it appears at all in the literature on architectural modernism, of which Tafuri's work remains exemplary in its sophistication, race most frequently appears on the ideological plane. Ideologies of racial supremacy join with pseudo-Darwinian scientism, for example, in culturalist paradigms of degeneracy of which the 1937 Nazi purge of *Entartete Kunst* (degenerate art) is exemplary. But race, we must remember, did not always connote socio-biologically. Rather, as Michel Foucault emphasized in his later work, prior to the nineteenth century Europeans understood the races at least in part to refer to warring peoples with different histories, different languages, and different traditions—like the Gauls, the Franks, the Normans, and the Saxons. As subsequent studies of race and racism have shown, the eighteenth century division of the human species into subgroups ("varieties" was a common term) implied hierarchy and thus paved the way for the scientific racism that arose in the mid-nineteenth century, but the two were not identical.[4] The anthropological classification of peoples into physical "varieties" did converge with a philosophical anthropology of "character" that, in turn, flowed into both nineteenth-century nationalisms and racisms. But prior to 1800, although white supremacist ideologies had circulated for centuries, race, even when applied to nonwhite, non-European peoples colonized by European powers, was most commonly understood in civilizational terms that referred to generational lineages more than to physical classifications per se.[5]

As Ann Laura Stoler has shown, Foucault overlooked ways in which the social relations of colonialism shaped European subjectivity, not least with respect to bourgeois sexuality and the "defense" of white patriarchy against perceived internal enemies.[6] Still, Foucault's optic allows us to see how, by the end of the nineteenth century, the concept of race had been adapted in Europe to differentiate the white conquerors from their colonial or enslaved subjects, and internally, Christians from Jews. Before that, Foucault provocatively argued, race struggles of subordinate against dominant groups supplied the paradigm for revolutionary struggles more generally, including the class struggle. Only later do we see the emergence of what he calls "state" racism, in which the state is called upon to defend itself against an inner racial enemy, of which the German case is paradigmatic but to which we must also add the post-Reconstruction United States under Jim Crow.[7]

It is in this sense that we might think again about the oft-repeated assertion by W. E. B. Du Bois, made in an address to the first Pan-African Conference in 1900, that "the problem of the Twentieth Century is the problem of the color-line."[8] Knowing well that to ignore or downplay race differentials and what was called "race prejudice" would be to submit to the ruling powers, Du Bois attempted to shape the struggle against state racism as a race struggle in the sense of a struggle among peoples with distinct histories. In other words, he confronted one concept of race with another. Arguing a few years earlier that "we must acknowledge that human beings are divided into races," Du Bois exhorted his fellow African Americans to "rise above the pressing, but smaller questions of separate schools and cars, wage-discrimination and lynch law, to survey the whole question of race in human philosophy and to lay, on a basis of broad knowledge and careful insight, those large lines of policy and higher ideals which may form our guiding lines and boundaries in the practical difficulties of every day."[9] Rejecting biological distinctions as determinant, the young Du Bois nonetheless insisted instead on "deeper differences . . . spiritual, psychical differences—undoubtedly based on the physical, but infinitely transcending them."[10]

Perhaps for tactical reasons, Du Bois echoed the earlier race struggles described by Foucault when he claimed that "the forces that bind the Teuton nations are, then, first, their race identity and common blood; secondly, and more important, a common history, common laws and religion, similar habits of thought and a conscious striving together for certain ideals of life."[11] Race, in other words, was for Du Bois a matter of history much more than it was a matter of biology. It may well be that, as Kwame Anthony Appiah has shown, when Du Bois wrote in 1911 that "we ought to speak of civilizations where we now speak of races" he had not entirely freed himself from what Appiah calls the "illusion of race" from a logical point of view.[12] But neither then nor in his later "Marxist" phase did Du Bois construe race as a mere ideological phantasm; he saw it, instead, as a socially and historically produced ground that had to be remade before it was unmade. Slavery had separated generations from a history that a few decades of freedom were scarcely enough to rebuild. Hence his call, which Du Bois repeated in different forms and put into practice throughout his long life, for "race organizations: Negro colleges, Negro newspapers, Negro business organizations, a Negro school of literature and art, and an intellectual clearing house, for all these products of the Negro mind, which we may call a Negro Academy."[13]

Du Bois spoke these last words at the inauguration of the American Negro

Academy in 1897. On the same occasion, Alexander Crummell, the academy's first president, delivered an address titled "Civilization, the Primal Need of the Race." Crummell, a pan-Africanist minister whom Du Bois eulogized in *The Souls of Black Folk*, was representative of the black intelligentsia circa 1900; as such, his words stand here not so much for a particular doctrine as for the common sense of race counter-discourse as Du Bois also understood it. "Civilization" was, for Crummell, the bedrock of racial being, again in the sense of race-as-history: "To make *men* you need civilization; and what I mean by civilization is the action of exalted forces, both of God and man."[14] Crummell thus understood civilization firstly as a product of the mind that was embodied in European culture by the likes of Socrates, Aristotle, Plato, and Euclid: "For civilization is, in its origins, ideal; and hence, in the loftiest men, it bursts forth, producing letters, literature, science, philosophy, poetry, sculpture, architecture, yea, all the arts; and brings them with all their gifts, and lays them in the lap of religion, as the essential condition of their vital permanence and their continuity."[15]

It is tempting to conclude that Crummell is meeting here the myth of white civilization with a counter-myth, a new Olympus ("the lap of religion"), the groundwork for which the Negro Academy would lay. But more likely, by "civilization" he is referring to what Du Bois called in his remarks the "common history, common laws and religion" from which races are made. Where "race" and "race organizations" are the instruments of what Foucault called a "counter history," a history with which the vanquished confront their conquerors, a history not only of cruelty and injustice, but of achievement and, as Du Bois put it, a "striving together for certain ideals of life." Du Bois would write such a history many times over during the course of his career. Mabel O. Wilson has explained in detail how these and related efforts drew on and contributed to modern forms of public exhibition.[16] In order to take some measure of what this problematic could have meant for modern architecture more narrowly, I want to take up this civilizational understanding of race—of race-as-history—in two contexts that relate to Du Bois's lifelong project. That project is represented here by his support of the American Negro Academy, which was devoted to African American classical education, and thereby to building institutions and a public sphere equal but to some degree opposed to those still rooted in the European Enlightenment.

Technics and Race

A little further on in his remarks, alluding to the still simmering debate between Du Bois and Booker T. Washington regarding black vocational versus collegiate education, Crummell continues: "But civilization never seeks permanent abidance upon the heights of Olympus. She is human, and seeks all human needs. And so she descends, recreating new civilizations; uplifting the crudeness of laws, giving scientific precision to morals and religion, stimulating enterprise, extending commerce, creating manufactures, expanding mechanism and mechanical inventions; producing revolutions and reforms; manufacturing needles for the industry of seamstresses and for the commonest uses of the human fingers. All these are the fruits of civilization."[17] In the language used by Du Bois and Crummell, one measure of civilization, including that of the diasporic black civitas to which "race organizations" like the Negro Academy were dedicated, was a capacity to convert ideals into instruments. Du Bois rehearsed this principle many times when he argued for prioritizing liberal collegiate education for African American youth, especially those to whom he initially referred as the "talented tenth," over the vocational training advocated by Washington and others.[18] Technics, in this account, followed from civilization and not the other way around. Dialectically, however, the color line is a technological matter as well as an ideological one.

Along with the changing concepts of race alluded to by Foucault, from civilizational race struggle sanctified by the law to scientific racism as bureaucratic normalization, the enforced, mutual constitution of racial hierarchy and universality changed dramatically in the United States during the nineteenth century. This was due in part to the reorganization of knowledge associated with the new research universities and their disciplines. Many of these lent pseudo-scientific support to the new sociobiological racism.[19] What Du Bois called "the double life every American Negro must live, as a Negro and as an American" resulted in part from the contradiction, and mutual constitution, of race and nation as practiced in these institutions, which put universal and particular into epistemic conflict.[20] In other words, this "double life" belonged to a historically specific "discourse network" (to use Friedrich Kittler's terminology) given to constructing universals— including the category of universal civilization—in a particular way with particular means, rather than simply being an ideologically determined universal in itself.

Du Bois, who maintained a lifelong interest in the political history of the Kaiserreich, was educated in Germany into what Kittler called the "discourse network of 1900." With this terminology Kittler differentiates two post-Enlightenment literary paradigms, classicism-Romanticism and modernism, according to the media complexes that underlie them, "universal alphabetization" and "technological data storage," respectively.[21] His claim is that two starkly different "writing-down systems" (*Aufschreibesysteme*, or discourse networks) essentially wrote "reason" and by extension (and although he pointedly does not use the term) Enlightenment, differently. They thereby shaped, respectively, the European-Germanic "age of Goethe" and what we might call, allowing for modernism's displaced author-function, the later "age of Nietzsche," according to the material specificity of written discourse and its technological infrastructure. Reason, on this account, is an entailment of a specific discourse network, as is its silent partner, race.

Though the Kantian ideal of Enlightenment based on literacy and a community of readers and writers remained very much alive in Du Bois's civilizational-pedagogical program, the "double life" (or double consciousness) to which Du Bois referred was not simply a dialectical inconsistency. It was and remains epistemologically constitutive, as Du Bois recognized in advocating for "race organizations" for the reconstruction and maintenance of black history, or what we can call with Kittler, data transmission and storage, in books, classrooms, and curricula. In other words, the color line is not merely an unfortunate obstacle to the full exercise of reason and its entailments, nor does it simply obscure an underlying class conflict, though the significance of the latter would emerge more fully in Du Bois's later work. Rather, the color line was among the technical preconditions for the Enlightenment public sphere and for the republic of letters. As such, its erasure could not and cannot be based only in universal literacy, as Du Bois recognized. The color line could only be erased by being redrawn as a kind of institutionalized, automatic writing, in a paradoxical doubling and redoubling of the public sphere—white and black—as differential repetition according to the possibilities and limits of what Walter Benjamin might have called its "mechanical reproducibility."

Moreover, anything like universal knowledge or a universally knowing human subject is only thinkable in the first place through very specific intermedial relays. This means that the conception of regulating ideals is itself a technical, practical matter. Like the chain that binds master to slave in Hegel's dialectic and in the process brings both into reciprocal, asymmetrical being, those intermedial relays secure relations of domination and subordination even as they help to constitute the subject of universal knowledge and of universal education.

By the end of the nineteenth century, this was the discursive and political work done by "civilization," understood by intellectuals like Du Bois and Crummell as well as by their white contemporaries to signify a realized set of attributes possessed by all peoples but differently, in consequence of their different histories and traditions. The practical, pedagogical requirement for admission into these histories was therefore not only the alphabetization required by the republic of letters. In the cruelest of tautologies, only an a priori history—a civilizational archive or "data storage"—guaranteed admission into "civilization" circa 1900. We can follow these two steps, of admission into (and exclusion from) the republic of letters and of the technical consolidation of "civilization," through two examples from modern architecture's archive, both of which entail the technological production and reproduction of race differences. In the first, a mechanical device designed by Jefferson stages the master-slave dialectic. In the second, the paths of Du Bois and the cultural critic Lewis Mumford briefly intersect, and the sovereign master dissolves into the bureaucratic matrix of "technics and civilization."

Reinhold Martin

Fig. 3.1 Étienne-Louis Boullée, cenotaph for Isaac Newton (project), 1784. Section. Colored wash. Courtesy of Bibliothèque Nationale de France.

Silence, ca. 1800

Among the most well-known architectural examples of Enlightenment made literal is the French architect Étienne-Louis Boullée's unrealized proposal for a cenotaph for Isaac Newton from 1784, with a central armillary sphere that would periodically light up in a starburst of fireworks that made the Copernican cosmos visible, in a performance of universality compatible with Newtonian physics (figure 3.1). By 1825, Thomas Jefferson had translated this figure, via a series of mediations, into the library rotunda at the University of Virginia, for which he projected an unrealized planetarium (figures 3.2 and 3.3).[22] The University of Virginia was built in part by enslaved people and by their descendants.[23] Jefferson was a slave owner, and the republic of letters that formed there, as well as in the dining room and library of his Monticello home nearby, was built on and by slavery (figure 3.4). In his writings, Jefferson differentiated the enlightened reason allegedly cultivated in that dining room from what he regarded as the inferior faculties of enslaved Africans and, to a lesser extent, Native Americans, both of whom he regarded principally as "subjects of natural history."[24] To that extent, Jefferson's racism participated in a modified version of the civilizational paradigm, by drawing and enforcing a color line that distinguished two histories: one civilizational and one "natural." *Notes on the State of Virginia*, Jefferson's guidebook for foreign

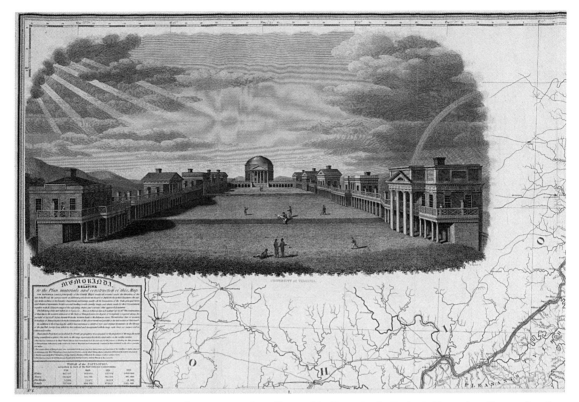

Fig. 3.2 Thomas Jefferson, University of Virginia rotunda and lawn, 1826. Engraving by Benjamin Tanner from Herman Boye's *Map of Virginia*, 1827. Albert and Shirley Small Special Collections Library, University of Virginia.

and domestic visitors, also provided an early textual basis for a biologically and anthropologically formulated state racism, written by a statesman.

Once inside at Monticello, these same visitors were enjoined to participate in reasoned discussions that were frequently lubricated by French wine made available by dumbwaiters connecting the dining room to the wine cellar below, where an enslaved person stood ready to supply the bottles (figure 3.5). As its name suggests, the purpose of the dumbwaiter was to exclude black voices and black ears from the conversation above. The dumbwaiter, then, did not merely regulate the boundaries of a sphere that was reserved, in a Kantian sense, for the public use of reason; it helped to produce that sphere by minimizing interference and distortion, and restricting transmission and communication in a manner that ontically differentiated master from slave.

Like the noise in the channel of a communications circuit, the hearing, speaking bodies of enslaved people were not external to the system of enlightened public reason as practiced at Monticello. Nor were they simply its invisible, silent operators, confined below decks, as Adorno and Horkheimer might have had it, while Jefferson-as-Odysseus strained toward the sirens' enchanting call.[25] They were the entire system's pre-dialectical, constitutive inside, which, like a body's internal

Reinhold Martin

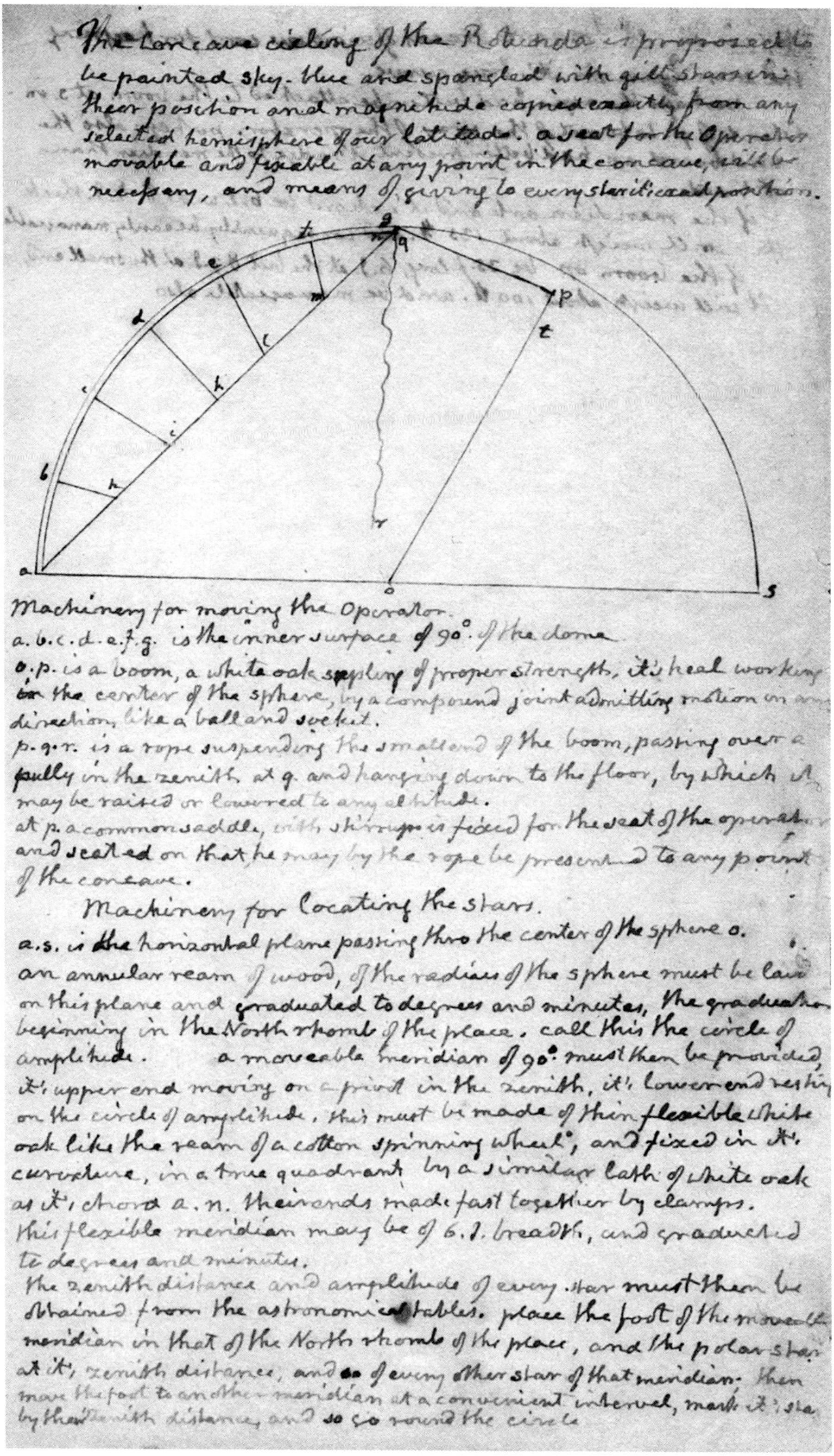

The concave cieling of the Rotunda is proposed to
be painted sky-blue and spangled with gilt stars in
their position and magnitude copied exactly from any
selected hemisphere of our latitude. a seat for the Operator
movable and fixable at any point in the concave, will be
necessary, and means of giving to every star it's exact position.

Machinery for moving the Operator.
a.b.c.d.e.f.g. is the inner surface of 90°. of the dome.
o.p. is a boom, a white oak sapling of proper strength, it's heel working
in the center of the sphere, by a compound joint admitting motion in any
direction, like a ball and socket.
p.q.r. is a rope suspending the small end of the boom, passing over a
pulley in the zenith at q. and hanging down to the floor, by which it
may be raised or lowered to any altitude.
at p. a common saddle, with stirrups is fixed for the seat of the operator
and seated on that he may by the rope be presented to any point
of the concave.
    Machinery for locating the stars.
a.s. is the horizontal plane passing thro' the center of the sphere o.
an annular ream of wood, of the radius of the sphere must be laid
on this plane and graduated to degrees and minutes, the graduation
beginning in the North rhomb of the place. call this the circle of
amplitude.   a moveable meridian of 90° must then be provided,
it's upper end moving on a pivot in the zenith, it's lower end resting
on the circle of amplitude, this must be made of thin flexible white
oak like the ream of a cotton spinning wheel, and fixed in it's
curvature, in a true quadrant by a similar lath of white oak
as it's chord a.n. their ends made fast together by clamps.
this flexible meridian may be of 6.I. breadth, and graduated
to degrees and minutes.
the zenith distance and amplitude of every star must then be
obtained from the astronomical tables. place the foot of the moveable
meridian in that of the North rhomb of the place, and the polar star
at it's zenith distance, and so of every other star of that meridian. then
move the foot to another meridian at a convenient interval, mark it's stars
by their zenith distance, and so go round the circle

Fig. 3.3 Thomas Jefferson, proposed device for mapping astronomical charts onto the rotunda ceiling,
    University of Virginia (unrealized). Pocket memorandum book, 1819. Page 2, recto. Albert and
    Shirley Small Special Collections Library, University of Virginia.

Fig. 3.4 Thomas Jefferson, Monticello, 1770–1809. West facade from the northwest. Historic American Buildings Survey, n.d. Library of Congress, Prints and Photographs Division.

background noise, had to be made silent with every pull on the dumbwaiter in order for that system to function. Their material silence, which was produced rather than merely enforced by the space and its hardware, was just as integral to the Jeffersonian republic of letters as was the wine in the glasses, the books in the library, the chatter of the dinner guests, and the oral recitations performed by students at the nearby University of Virginia aspiring to a place at the table.

The dumbwaiters that connected the Monticello dining room with the wine cellar below were probably installed sometime around 1809, during the last phase of construction on the estate prior to Jefferson's death in 1826. Their design may have been based on similar devices built into table legs in the Parisian Café Mécanique, which Jefferson most likely visited during his time as minister to France from 1784 to 1789.[26] Monticello's dining room door, which turned on a central pivot, was equipped with shelves on one side so that enslaved people could discreetly ascend the narrow staircase from the kitchen, located in the basement of the southern dependency wing, and deliver plated food without entering the room. Another enslaved person (or perhaps the dinner guests themselves) would then place the dishes on another type of dumbwaiter, which resembled a wheeled cart with a stack of four shelves (and was probably adapted from another French model known as an *étagère*). Wine could be retrieved at any time by the host, a member of his immediate family, or, if necessary, by Jefferson's enslaved personal

Reinhold Martin

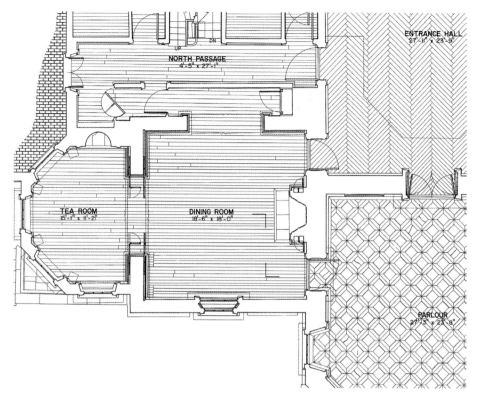

Fig. 3.5 Thomas Jefferson, Monticello, 1770-1809. First floor plan. Detail showing dining room, with dumbwaiters built into the fireplace (*center right*) and the service door (*upper left*). Drawn by Timothy A. Buehner, Isabel C. Yang, Hugh D. Hughes, Sandra M. Moore, and Jonathan C. Spodek, Historic American Buildings Survey, 1989-1992. Library of Congress, Prints and Photographs Division.

valet, Burwell Colbert (figure 3.6). All of this was designed to encourage in Jefferson's carefully chosen dinner guests something very close to what Immanuel Kant called in his remarks on Enlightenment "the inclination and the vocation for *free thinking*" intrinsic to "man, who is now *more than a machine*, in accord with his dignity."[27]

Among those guests was the literary portraitist of Washington society, Margaret Bayard Smith, who duly reported as follows: "When [Jefferson] had any persons dining with him with whom he wished to enjoy a free and unrestricted flow of conversation, the number of persons at table never exceeded four, and by each individual was placed a dumb-waiter, containing everything necessary for the progress of the dinner from beginning to end, so as to make the attendance of servants [slaves] entirely unnecessary, believing as he did, that much of the domestic and public discord was produced by the mutilated and misconstrued repetition of free conversation at dinner tables, by these mute but not inattentive listeners."[28] It is no small irony, then, that at least one of the moveable dumbwaiters was likely made by an enslaved woodworker, John Hemmings.[29] Much has been written

Fig. 3.6 Thomas Jefferson, Monticello, 1770–1809. Dumbwaiter built into dining room fireplace.
Courtesy of Thomas Jefferson Foundation.

about the lives of slaves at Monticello, including those fathered by Jefferson with Sally Hemings (unrelated to John), and several first-person testimonies have survived. In one of them, Isaac Jefferson, a tinsmith and a blacksmith, further associated this white man who was "more than a machine" with mechanically aided reading and writing: "When writing he had a copying machine: while he was a-writing he wouldn't suffer nobody to come in his room: he had a dumb-waiter: when he wanted anything he had nothing to do but turn a crank and the dumb-waiter would bring him water or fruit on a plate or anything he wanted. Old Master had an abundance of books: sometimes would have twenty of 'em down on the floor at once: read fust one, then tother."[30]

This silence of these "mute but not inattentive listeners" casts Jefferson's proposed "Bill for the More General Diffusion of Knowledge" (1779) in a peculiar light.[31] That bill, which was presented to the Virginia legislature but failed to pass, is an important document in the eventual establishment of a public school system in the United States.[32] It describes a whole administrative landscape into which the existing College of William and Mary (where Jefferson studied) and the not-yet-established University of Virginia were—in principle—to be integrated. In Jefferson's proposal, the faculty of the college presides over the public school cur-

Reinhold Martin

riculum, joined by various political bodies at different scales. The republican decentralization of governmental functions that it envisions is based on a division of the land into "hundreds," a unit of territory larger than a town but smaller than a county. In each hundred would be a primary school for both male and female students. These would aggregate into school districts comprising several counties and served by a secondary boarding school, a "grammar school," with ten or twelve (de facto white) male students, chosen by examination, in residence. From there, only the most accomplished students would be given scholarships to study at the college.

In this way, territory, population, and education were organized in an ascending scale into a pyramid of knowledge, at the actual, incomplete apex of which would eventually stand the University of Virginia, with its central organ for managing the attention of young white men, the library. Colleges and universities in Jefferson's day were noisy places, not least because knowledge was frequently reproduced out loud, in the recitation rooms that Jefferson incorporated into the professors' houses that lined the Virginia lawn. Silent reading in preparation for recitations or written exams was done mainly where the books were kept, in the central library rotunda.

This library and its books conjugate with Monticello's dining room; both belong to the material substrate out of which an intergenerational republic of letters was built. Both presupposed an agrarian order of property that included slavery among its conditions of possibility. In the dining room, silence served "enlightened" conversation; in the library, silence anchored the aesthetic education of the white southern gentry. For the library, too, was a spatio-technical device for eliminating noise and other distractions, its "book room" elevated above the lawn and washed from above with a dome of indirect sunlight. Silent reading in this library, which was bound like Boullée's domed cenotaph to the still-glowing embers of Enlightenment, was a precondition for a form of classical learning that was, in itself, a precondition for admission into the public conversation that filled the mediapolitically managed silence of Monticello's dining room.

Thus, the entire library–dining room and university-plantation apparatus belonged to the "discourse network of 1800" that produced sovereign author-reader-speakers, beginning with Jefferson himself. In this, the dumbwaiter drew one of countless color lines, or lines of racial subjugation as exclusion. During Jefferson's presidency, the United States sought to contain the slave uprising in Saint-Domingue that led to the establishment of Haiti as a sovereign nation, fearing that the uprising would spread to the American South. As state policy, this fear indicated that the chain that binds master to slave, which included instruments designed to secure the slave's silence, implicitly recognized the race struggle, which was not a struggle against racism per se (although racist discourse was abundantly present even among "enlightened" figures like Jefferson) but against forcible, racial subordination. Along this axis, from the anti-colonial revolt in Saint-Domingue to the antislavery struggles that led up to the American Civil War, to the anti-colonial struggles of the nineteenth and twentieth centuries, figures like Du Bois forged counter-institutions and a counter-history, within a discourse network in which history, or "data storage," correlated with civilization.

Civilization, ca. 1900

When Lewis Mumford published *Technics and Civilization* in 1934, by many accounts he dramatically transformed the historical study of technology, or what Mumford suggestively called "technics," in scholarly or semi-scholarly circles.[33] Less clear are the book's effects on the study of "civilization." Mumford has surprisingly little to say on this topic, despite the term's prominence in his title. What he does say is concentrated in an early chapter on mechanization, when he describes "The Profile of Technics." The "civilization" to which Mumford refers there, which arises between the tenth and the eighteenth centuries, is explicitly Western and is technologically defined: "Indeed, the age of invention is only another name for the age of man. If man is rarely found in the 'state of nature' it is only because nature is so constantly modified by technics." This Mumford summarizes with the "valley-section," an idealized landscape running from mountains to river valley, borrowed from the Scottish geographer Patrick Geddes: "In a figurative sense, civilization marches up and down the valley-section."[34] Civilization here is technological culture, from mines and quarries at the mountaintops, with the associated arts of refining, smelting, smithing, and casting, to hunting in the surrounding forests with weapons that also enable war, to forestry, milling, and woodworking, which eventually yield the mechanical lathe, to herding and agriculture below the wood line, and with these, textiles and tents, to, finally, a river-borne and seaborne fishing and boating culture bound together by nets and baskets.

From "the order and security of an agricultural and pastoral civilization" born in Neolithic times comes, says Mumford, "not merely the dwelling house and the permanent community but a cooperative economic and social life, perpetuating its institutions by means of visible buildings and memorials as well as by the imparted word."[35] This is Mumford's working definition of civilization: a material environment through which life is sustained and meaning is transmitted. Mumford occasionally attaches ethno-racial characteristics to this definition, for example when contrasting premodern stereotypes, as in "the polite and pacific cultures of India and China, and the mainly urban culture of the Jews."[36] But by and large, the idealized "valley-section" guides him "from the dawn of modern technics in Northern Europe" during the Middle Ages through the two great techno-cultural "phases" that he also borrows from Geddes, the "Eotechnic" and the "Paleotechnic." Optimistically, Mumford thinks he sees a third, "Neotechnic" phase emerging around him in the New Deal–era United States and, more ominously, in a Europe where mechanized, industrial war clouds have visibly begun to gather.

When race appears in *Technics and Civilization* it is in the sense of a universal "human race" or in the sense of rival civilizations discussed above. Only occasionally is there a hint of racial hierarchy, as when, during the nineteenth century, "coal-industrialism" drives a European nationalist bourgeoisie to pursue "imperialistic policies of aggression among the weaker races."[37] Or when the same period witnesses "the misapplication of the Malthus-Darwin theory of the struggle for existence, to justify warfare, the nordic race, and the dominant position of the bourgeoisie."[38] But this latency comes to the fore in two episodes from within Mumford's own civilizational habitus and, eventually, refracts back upon his history of technics when he comes to assess Thomas Jefferson's standing as an architect.

The first of these two episodes involves the 1922 publication of *Civilization in the United States: An Inquiry by Thirty Americans*, which was edited by the journalist Harold E. Stearns and conceived within the New York literary circles in which Mumford was a key figure.[39] The omnibus volume, a compendium of the times in the spirit of the French encyclopedists but much abbreviated, could not disguise its contributors' impassioned disappointment with their subject. "We wished to speak the truth about American civilization as we saw it," wrote Stearns in his preface, "in order to do our share in making a real civilization possible."[40] Contributions ranged from politics (H. L. Mencken) to "the intellectual life" (Stearns) and "the literary life" (Mumford's friend Van Wyck Brooks), from "radicalism" (George Soule) to "sport and play" (Ring W. Lardner). None ventured to define the term "civilization" itself, although its de facto whiteness is made plain by a careful, lengthy essay on "racial minorities" by the historian Geroid Tanquary Robinson, a Europeanist by training who later became a specialist on Russia and the Soviet Union. Stearns writes in his preface that "whatever else American civilization is, it is not Anglo-Saxon," and Robinson duly lists "the Indian, the Jew, the Oriental, and the Negro" as "the country's most important racial minorities."[41] Rejecting claims of biological hierarchy, Robinson calmly inventories the social and economic dimensions of "race-prejudice" in America, stressing the underlying role of economic competition, and concludes that as long as recognizable differences remain, so will racial prejudice exist among the majority. The horizon of his analysis is assimilation, from within which perspective "the cultural shipwreck of the Negro on the American shore has thus placed him more completely at the mercy of the majority than the other minorities have ever been."[42]

Mumford's entry on "The City," which opens the volume, makes no mention of race but aims instead at the perceived inhumanity of "metropolitanism," or a "metropolitan civilization" concentrated in cities with a population of 500,000 or more, of which by 1920, according to Mumford, there were twelve.[43] Here already is Mumford's advocacy of the regionalism he had learned from Geddes, and his chief concern lies with those forces that "drain money, energy and brains" from regional centers into those twelve engines of commercialism and of industrial capitalism.[44] What would become known as the "Great Migration" of rural African Americans to northern cities had begun, if slowly, but where Robinson saw and noted racial segregation, Mumford saw only "the long miles of slum that stretch in front and behind and on each side" of New York's theater district. For Mumford at this point, urban inequality was primarily existential rather than economic or racial: "In spite of the redoubtable efforts of settlement workers, block organizers, and neighborhood associations, there is no permanent institution, other than the public school and the sectarian church, to remind the inhabitants that they have a common life and a common destiny."[45] This sentiment rhymes with Stearns's prefatory observation that "it is curious how a book on American civilization actually leads one back to the conviction that we are, after all, Americans."[46]

Among the other contributions to *Civilization in the United States* was an entry on "scholarship and criticism" by Mumford's close friend, the former Columbia University literary scholar Joel E. Spingarn. At the time, Spingarn, who like all of the volume's other contributors was white, chaired the board of directors of the National Association for the Advancement of Colored People (NAACP), an organization to which he had belonged since its founding in 1911.[47] In 1916, following his dismissal from Columbia over a dispute concerning academic freedom, Spingarn hosted a gathering of NAACP leaders and associates at Troutbeck, his family estate in Amenia, New York.[48] Du Bois, who attended, wrote of the gathering that "we ate hilariously in the open air with such views of the good green earth and the waving waters and the pale blue sky as all men ought often to see, yet few men do. And then filled and complacent we talked awhile of the thing which all of us call 'The Problem,' and after that and just as regularly we broke up and played good and hard."[49] Spingarn had first invited Mumford to Troutbeck in 1921, after which Mumford and his wife Sophia Wittenberg would regularly spend summers there and would eventually go on to make Amenia their family home.[50] By 1933, when Spingarn (who was by then the organization's president), Du Bois, and their increasingly conflicted colleagues at the NAACP decided to convene a second "Amenia Conference" at Troutbeck, Mumford was a close neighbor.

On August 20, 1933, Mumford wrote to Catherine Bauer, with whom he was in the midst of an intimate relationship, that "yesterday, at Spingarn's invitation, I went to Troutbeck Lake, where Joel is secretly entertaining a secret conference—placarded by signs along the road: 'This way to the Amenia Conference: Amenia

Conference 1 Mile'—of young Negroes, thirty-three of them, chiefly between twenty-five and thirty-five years of age: the coming leaders of the race."[51] Though Mumford did not participate in the conference, he spent an afternoon and evening among the guests, all of whom could be counted among Du Bois's "talented tenth," including Du Bois himself. But if what Du Bois euphemistically called "The Problem"—in other words, the color line—was the first Amenia conference's principle concern, Mumford found Spingarn's African American guests "tussling with the eternal dilemma of all intellectuals today: how to be a communist without wilfully [*sic*] swallowing the fierce ignorances, the blind hatreds, the wilfull [*sic*] dogmatisms of the orthodox revolutionists who are preparing for a final pitched battle between communism and capitalism."[52] Like the NAACP itself, the second Amenia conference was riven by tensions between reformist and socialist or Marxist factions, the latter of which Du Bois had come to represent. By no means, however, did these ideological struggles overshadow a mutual concern with "The Problem." On the contrary, as in Du Bois's earlier and ongoing work on black institutions, they were driven by it, and Du Bois among others at the conference advocated black nationalism within the framework of class solidarity.[53] Mumford, though clearly taken by this debate, was unable fully to assimilate its terms, noting even decades later that his friend Spingarn did not share Du Bois's "communism."[54]

In 1932, the year before his brush with black nationalism at Amenia, Mumford had contributed a catalogue essay to an exhibition that would come for generations to define "modern architecture" in the United States and well beyond. "Modern Architecture: International Style," cocurated by Henry-Russell Hitchcock and Philip Johnson, ran from February 10 through March 23, 1932, at the Museum of Modern Art (MoMA) in New York. Two years later and immediately following a relationship with the black café singer Jimmie Daniels, Johnson would turn decisively toward racist-populist and fascist politics, a turn that culminated in his enthusiastic presence—at the invitation of the German Propaganda Ministry—at the annexation of Poland by the German Wehrmacht in September 1939.[55]

Mumford's essay addressed the 1932 exhibition's ancillary survey of mostly European experiments in mass housing, a project assembled by Bauer, Clarence Stein, and Henry Wright with limited input from Mumford, and shown separately from Johnson and Hitchcock's influential interpretation of modern architecture's formal attributes.[56] Echoing the tone of *Civilization in the United States*, Mumford began in stride: "The building of houses constitutes the major architectural work of any civilization"; and again: "The house cannot remain outside the currents of modern civilization"; and again, later: "the typical American house is a disgrace to our civilization."[57] He was writing *Technics and Civilization* at the time, and so unsurprisingly automobiles, airplanes, telephones, power lines, and large scale bureaucracies join central heating, refrigerators, radio, and "the near prospect of television" as the technological a priori of modern housing. Again race is absent from the text, although Johnson's imminent political commitments bring it implicitly closer to the exhibition's frame. Seen in this retrospective light, the absence is a presence. In this essay as in his contemporaneous writings, Mumford subsumed a racial politics represented shortly thereafter by Du Bois on his left and Johnson on his right into a techno-politics of "civilization" where technological systems, including mass housing, played an intermediate, enabling but not determining role: architecture as technology as civilization.

Color Lines

In 1941, Mumford delivered a series of four lectures at Alabama College published as *The South in Architecture*, the second of which was dedicated to "The Universalism of Thomas Jefferson." Mumford's Jefferson was an exemplary amateur, an "all-round man" or "Renaissance gentleman" who embodied the "many-sidedness of the pioneer."[58] Acknowledging those eighteenth-century institutions including despotism and slavery that possessed "an underlying harmony with Roman civilization," Mumford saw in Jefferson's neoclassical designs at Monticello and at the University of Virginia an eloquent anachronism. Wed to a civilizational past (Rome), Jefferson could not, according to Mumford, perceive "that two kinds of universal language were now being spoken: a dead language, that of the classics, and a live language, that of the machine."[59] Like the Cartesian separation of soul and body and despite his ingenious utilitarianism, Jefferson kept the two separate, encasing Monticello's "artful" mechanisms—its "cannonball calendar" and its indoor weathervane, as well as the university's rational planning—within the "dead language" of Latinate classicism. Still, says Mumford, "all these mechanical improvements were fun; make no doubt of that. Some of them were really admirable, like the two-way dumb-waiter, which brought a full bottle of wine up from the cellar to the dining room, while the empty bottle was going down."[60]

As we have seen, the Monticello dumbwaiter was more than merely artful and hardly admirable; using Mumford's language, we can say that it made slavery "modern," in two ways. First, by mechanizing the silence of those supplying the wine. Second, by deploying that silence as a precondition for the cultivation of a republican public sphere populated by reflective, speaking subjects. But we can now also see that the two universalisms, the mechanical and the classical, that Mumford found competing in Jefferson's architecture were really one, that of "technics and civilization," where the former term was a precondition for the latter. The only problem was, in Mumford's eyes, that the two were out of sync.

If, in 1900, Du Bois prophesied that "the problem of the Twentieth Century is the problem of the color-line," by 1800, when Monticello was well under construction, we can already see that line being drawn, not by what Mumford regarded as the civilizational anachronism of slavery, but by the mechanization of silence and universality that he mistook as an incomplete avatar of modernity. This was the function of "civilization" in *Technics and Civilization*: to convert the technologically and environmentally borne particular into a universal. For the relevant dialectic was not only one of master and slave but one of silence and voice. Like slavery itself, this line underwrote the contradictory alliance of reason and capital that preoccupied Horkheimer and Adorno, and Tafuri after them, if only because it so easily slipped out of sight for those moderns who, from Jefferson to Mumford, found it difficult to see the color of their own skin.

For Mumford, civilization was stored in history, which was in turn stored in an environmental technics that ranged from the "valley-section" to modern housing, with race appearing only in faint outline. Like Tafuri's, his Jefferson was obsolete, if only because Jefferson's architecture failed to reproduce artistically the mechanical universality of his household gadgets. But what therefore appeared to Mumford as a mismatch between technics and civilization, a dumbwaiter in a Roman ruin, was the technical a priori of the color line. This was Rome—or Enlightenment—not as ideology per se but as the discourse network of republicanism and literacy called civilization; not slavery as unfortunate imperial residue, but as precondition: the middle passage as a historical-technical delinking from "civilization" (Africa, the valley-section, environment) that Du Bois, Crummell, and countless others sought to rebuild, essentially, as Rome with "Negro institutions." Both Mumford's universalism and Du Bois's particularism were thereby elicited by the vast, sociotechnical apparatus to which Jefferson's dumbwaiter belonged, which deracinated, subordinated, and effectively silenced an entire population. The difference between the two turned not on whether but *how* that population, understood by the Euro-American nineteenth century as a race, could or should be considered in civilizational terms. Or, to put it differently, whether "race" and "civilization" were universals or particulars.

In 1928, as Mumford was beginning the work we have considered, there appeared in New York an English translation of *Moderne Rassentheorien* (*Modern Racial Theories*, 1904), under the title *Race and Civilization*, by the Austrian sociologist Friedrich Hertz. The treatise explicitly challenged scientific racism, or what Foucault would later call "state racism," on the basis of environmental rather than biological factors. Hertz's preface to the English translation echoed the argument of his opening pages: "Race has become a political slogan. Pan-Slavism and Pan-Germanism have played a fateful part in history, and already we are hearing of Pan-Islamism and a Pan-African race movement. It is not difficult to see the close connection between the race argument and national antagonism. . . . In nationalistic ideology almost everywhere belief in race is a dominant factor. Its emergence has caused the intensification of national antagonism which has become such a danger to our civilization."[61] This was not what Foucault described as a society defending itself against perceived racial enemies, but against the enemy of "race" as such: it was civilization against race, including the racial emancipation sought by Pan-Africanism as well as Pan-German race hatred. In this respect, the discourse of "civilization" to which Mumford's belonged drew a line different from that drawn by the sociobiological apparatus of state racism. The new line retraced the older one drawn by the civilizational understanding of race, but it did so in order to wage war against race in the name of civilization. In architecture this line, which was traced out of Enlightenment thinking, was called "modern." But if Mumford saw it tentatively sketched by Jefferson's dumbwaiters, the persistent silencing and subordination of those below by those above had already been converted into a new form of bondage, which Du Bois recognized as the twentieth century's "color-line." If, as Mumford argued, civilization was technics, the question posed by Du Bois was whether this line could be made redundant, not by erasing it but by reproducing it. Whether, that is, those below could join those above by cutting the chain of "civilization" that bound them.

4

From "Terrestrial Paradise" to "Dreary Waste"

Race and the Chinese Garden in European Eyes

Addison Godel

Between the opening of the eighteenth century and the middle of the nineteenth, the status China held in Europe underwent a dramatic shift—a change evident in shifting perceptions of the Chinese garden. In the early decades of the eighteenth century, European intellectuals, relying on the accounts of Jesuit travelers, cast aside earlier "fairy tales" of Asian cultures. Demonstrating a pre-racial, quasi-universalizing theory of artistic and cultural difference, they recognized in Chinese gardens a distinct national character, to which they granted legitimacy in the texts and drawings of architectural treatises. A few decades later, frustrated British trade ambitions informed readings of Chinese difference that emphasized exoticness, and the Chinese garden became viewed in terms of sensuality and the sublime. Finally, in the late eighteenth and early nineteenth centuries, a developing philosophical construction of race as a central feature of world history coincided with a new perception of the gardens as emblems of ostensibly ahistorical decrepitude. This last attitude served to justify European imperialism, and specifically the 1860 destruction of the Chinese emperors' world-famous, eight-hundred-acre garden complex, the Yuanmingyuan, by an Anglo-French military expedition. As a British soldier put it: "When we first entered the gardens they reminded one of those magic grounds described in fairy tales; we marched from them . . . leaving them a dreary waste of ruined nothings."[1]

That arson, European interpretations of Chinese gardens, and the larger transformation in European reckoning with the Chinese "other" have all been subjects of considerable study. In this chapter, I seek to triangulate these interrelated narratives in order to highlight the emergence of race as an organizing category.[2] While eschewing straightforward causal links between world history, philosophy, and design culture, I hope to reveal, by pinpointing important milestones in each, that architecture's chinoiserie experiments represent more than an attempt to add novelty to rococo garden pavilions through the addition of curving roofs and Qing motifs. It is not my purpose to show that architects' clients were directly inspired by close readings of continental philosophy, or that the British military took its cues directly from debates over chinoiserie. Rather, I emphasize the discursive echoes sounding between these expert fields, which indicate chinoiserie as a key site in the development of a theory of the Chinese "race"; European responses to the Chinese garden both reflect and anticipate the articulation of race as an ordering concept in philosophy, and its application (through the lens of national character) as justification for imperial policy.

Pre-Racial Commonality and China in Fischer, Leibniz, and Attiret

Scholars have long recognized that European conceptions of China in the seventeenth and early eighteenth centuries were structured by the available sources of information on the still-distant country.[3] The widely circulated reports of Jesuit missionaries, working from proto-colonial trading posts, were crucial in debunking the received medieval vision of "Cathay," a land of magic and monsters. The Jesuit sources were, however, biased by the desire to find a China ripe for Christianization; they thus emphasized, for example, the role of the Confucian ethical code, seemingly free of explicit heresy, and other moral doctrines. The Chinese, they suggested, were essentially like Europeans, missing only the Christian revelation. Beginning around the 1680s, European rationalist philosophers would fold this jesuitical view of China into Enlightenment thinking, praising Confucianism as the application of universal, natural reason to ethical and political problems.[4] This model of the world imagined Europe and China as equally removed from (Christian) divine origins, possessing equal access to universal reason.

Such a rationalist universalism informed a landmark architectural treatise, the *Entwurff einer historischen Architektur* (Outline of Historical Architecture), first presented in 1712 by the Austrian court architect Johann Bernhard Fischer von Erlach.[5] In architectural circles, the *Entwurff* has been regarded as the "the first general history of architecture," even "the first universal architectural history."[6]

Moving beyond Greco-Roman classicism, it expanded the scope of architecture to non-European and particularly Asian architecture. This inclusiveness, though pointedly not extended to the architecture of numerous other world cultures viewed by Europeans as "primitive" or "savage," predated the development of European colonialism in Asia, and the development of comprehensive theories of race or "human variety," in the words of the era's philosophers. At this stage, it was not differences in physiology but in national taste that attracted discussion, and these in turn were trumped by psychological tendencies assumed to be common to all the included cultures, as we see in the terms used to discuss seemingly disparate structures.

Fischer's East Asian plates and descriptions in the *Entwurff* rely on the accounts of missionaries, with his only named sources being the Jesuits Guy Tachard and Martino Martini. He doubtless also benefited from the intellectual pursuits of his Catholic Hapsburg patrons, who likely shared the Jesuits' enthusiasm for a Europe-like China. The buildings and pageants they commissioned from Fischer employed symbols associated with "the ideal of a world-wide Christian empire beyond Europe, by the conversion of East Asia and the Americas."[7] It is therefore unsurprising that the *Entwurff* evinces the period's conception of non-European cultures. In the book's outlined sequence, buildings from China, termed "modern" (*neuen/moderne*), appear in the third volume, after Roman architecture and alongside Arabian, Turkish, Persian, and Japanese works, while buildings from other cultures are excluded without comment, reflecting a priori assumptions that I attempt to capture with the qualified term "quasi-universal." Those included are organized chronologically (running from the ideal of Solomon's temple to Fischer's own designs) but not teleologically; Fischer does not link his own work to any particular source, and he bypasses the post-Roman European architecture typically seen as leading to his own baroque style.[8] The book nonetheless encourages the use of any of the structures it depicts as a model for contemporary architecture, commenting that these buildings serve not only to "please the eye of the Curious" but also to "embellish their Minds, and tend towards the Cultivation of Arts in general."[9]

China, specifically, is depicted as an advanced, well-administered civilization. Of the nine Chinese scenes in the *Entwurff*, four depict bridges, captioned in terms that stress technical achievements like long spans, tall arches, and negotiation of difficult terrain. This is unsurprising, as Chinese technology, especially porcelain production, was widely perceived as advanced, and had also been a subject of Jesuit investigation. In turn, scenes of spectacular pageants, akin to those Fischer designed, posit China as a site of abundance and social order. Fischer presents Chinese monumental architecture as conforming to his own highest standards of the architectural ideal, filling the evidently large gaps in his knowledge

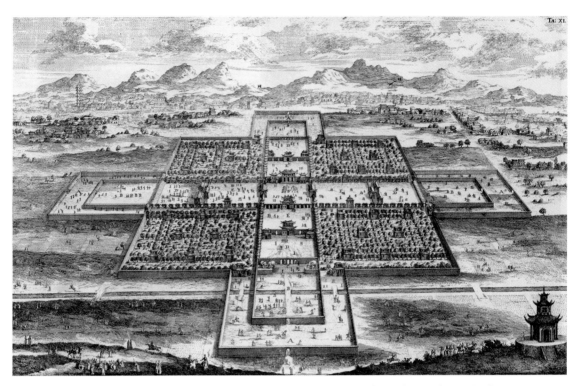

Fig. 4.1 View of the Forbidden City in Johann Bernhard Fischer von Erlach, *Entwurff einer historischen Architektur* (1712).

(and his brief texts) with description that he would surely have considered to be flattery.[10]

Fischer seems to have derived his scenes of Chinese architecture from a 1665 book by the Dutch trade attaché Johan Nieuhof, adapting the illustrations in ways that reinforce the Europeanness of forms Nieuhof had already distorted.[11] Both authors, for example, illustrate the Forbidden City as a Greek cross assembled from rectilinear courtyards, with large, vague gardens tucked into the interior corners (figure 4.1). This bizarre rendition is correct only in that the palace is indeed vast, axial, symmetrical, and several times gated. Fischer added a baroque, open-country site, like that of the Hapsburgs' Schönbrunn Palace (on which he worked), and rendered the corner gardens as approximations of internally symmetrical, four-square, Italianate models. Depicting a set of linear-edge buildings framing courtyards, the drawings are consistent with then-current European designs, such as that for the Dresden Zwinger, a palace begun around 1710 by Fischer's contemporary Matthäus Daniel Pöppelmann for the Saxon elector Augustus II. Augustus, the sponsor of a porcelain works, would later commission from Pöppelmann a country palace, Schloss Pillnitz (substantially completed by 1730), on a baroque plan with a Chinese-style roofline and decorative motifs. That design suggests a semblance between baroque and Chinese palaces; Fischer's

　　　　　　　　　　　　　　　Addison Godel

Fig. 4.2 Chinese garden scene in Johann Bernhard Fischer von Erlach, *Entwurff einer historischen Architektur* (1712).

drawings of these two types seemingly insist upon it. Moreover, his depictions of each also resemble his version of Solomon's temple, implying that both Chinese and central European architecture derive in equal measure from divine precedent.

Fischer also compounded Nieuhof's errors on Chinese garden rockeries. Both correctly comprehended these structures as multilevel organic forms in naturalistic settings, but severely overscaled them as seven-story extravaganzas set in open wilderness (figure 4.2). Fischer replaced Nieuhof's outward-thrusting stone grotesque with a more self-contained, spiraling composition. His "Chinese" rockeries suggest a cathedral-scale rendering of baroque sculptural details: the plastic, pitted forms of Solomonic columns (a baroque favorite) or the "Plague Column" Fischer executed in Vienna. Viewing humankind through assumptions of fundamental similarity, Fischer assumed that what he did not know about China would be essentially similar to what he did know about Europe.

This idea of similitude between European and Chinese architectural forms sustains the *Entwurff*'s universalist claims. All architecture, to Fischer, shares certain "general Principles" like symmetry and the visual support of weak elements by strong ones. While "Nations dissent no less in their Taste for Architecture, than in Food and Raiment," he claims such stylistic differences are merely "Whims" authorized by "Custom."[12] Thus, Fischer's apparent presumption in fabricating

Chinese design elements was not an imperial imposition before its time, but a reflection of his belief in universal access to reason. Of course, the Enlightenment universal is always already bound up in the problem of confining Europe's others to a state of affectable externality,[13] but Fischer sincerely imagines Europeans as benefitting from the study of Chinese examples, and invites artists reading the *Entwurff* to compare its examples and make a "judicious choice" as to stylistic devices.

This Jesuit-informed belief in commonality may also explain why Fischer made no use of Nieuhof's numerous drawings of Chinese *people*, images that emphasize difference from northern Europeans in costume, custom, and physiognomy. Fischer's panoramic views, populated by minuscule stick figures, may suggest a domineering European eye, but they also give only hints of foreign costume, and are absent details that would later constitute racial cues. Ultimately, the *Entwurff's* short treatment of China posits it as fundamentally similar to Europe, if perhaps more advanced. Its Chinese people possess great skill and artistry, but they are neither the magicians of Cathay nor the racialized bodies of later imperialism. Fischer's contemporary, the Saxon philosopher Gottfried Wilhelm Leibniz, offers a point of comparison. While passing references to human variety in Leibniz's writings were taken up much later by the originators of racial science, and one early text calls for the European conquest of "semibeast" peoples (not including the Chinese), ultimately, inherited races were incompatible with Leibniz's universalist, monadic theory. The mature Leibniz brought up physiognomy only to dismiss its usefulness as an area of study; varied appearance "does not prevent all the human beings who inhabit the globe from being all of the same race, which has been altered by the different climates." Linguistic study would reveal the shared Hebraic origins of all languages, emphasizing the world's unity. This theme, akin to the contemporary belief that Chinese script might be the pre-Babel "language of Noah," is reminiscent of the parallels Fischer's illustrations imply.[14]

A report specifically concerning Chinese garden practices, written by the Jesuit missionary Jean Denis Attiret in 1743, completes our picture of this early eighteenth-century quasi-universalist attitude. Attiret had been working as a painter at the Qianlong Emperor's recently completed garden palace, the eight-hundred-acre Yuanmingyuan outside of Beijing. Attiret's account of this garden was important in establishing its European reputation, and his correspondence retains Fischer's admiration while avoiding his descriptive errors. In the garden, Attiret wrote, "Every thing is grand and truly fine": the place's size, its unfamiliar design, its variety, and its objects of "exquisite taste." But while the garden is termed "a terrestrial paradise," and its pavilions said to resemble "those fabulous palaces of the fairies," Attiret's description of its details is realistic and well-observed.

Addison Godel

Attiret's report also expresses a pluralistic, if ambivalent, evaluation of Chinese and European cultural achievements. Chinese architecture is posited as inferior to its French and Italian equivalents, but Chinese technology in fireworks and lighting "infinitely surpasses" that of the same two countries.[15] Attiret's evenhanded, Fischer-esque conclusion is that "for our parts, we think differently and with reason." Differences of taste stem from experience rather than innate traits; Attiret's tenure has led his "eyes and taste [to] become in some degree Chinese," so that "without pretending to decide which ought to have the preference . . . the manner of building in his country pleases me much." A description of a Chinese garden might strike a European as "ridiculous" and of "a disagreeable appearance." But upon firsthand experience, Attiret argued, one would find the apparent irregularity artistically composed, and a beauty not perceived at first sight. Attiret's view of culture is, again like Fischer's, absent a theory of race. Attiret refers to physiognomy only once in this letter, to explain why European missionaries could never operate in secret ("our figure is too different"); such differences are secondary to a commonality that permits a French Jesuit to "become in some degree Chinese."[16] Attiret's dispatch appeared, however, as the Jesuit-derived image of China was waning. As European mercantile advances grew more persistent and aggressive, and incipient theories of race grew more developed, respect for Chinese achievements faded.

"A Distinct and Very Singular Race of Men" in Chambers and Blumenbach

The intellectual vogue for Chinese ideas in eighteenth-century Europe took different forms. In Great Britain, ideas about China were shaped less by missionary reportage than by mercantile contact—the accounts of traders, and the representative goods they brought back. Trade in porcelain, silks, wallpaper, and furniture grew considerably in the early eighteenth century, responding to the growing popularity of "fashionable novelties" and especially tea. By the 1740s, English factories made Chinese-style goods, and British merchants fruitlessly pressed Chinese officials for trade concessions. Frustrated British observers increasingly characterized the Chinese as greedy and cunning, though sometimes still praising their "arts and manner off governmentt" in the same breath. Even successful trade ventures reduced China's reputation by making the faraway country seem more responsive to British desires. By the century's last quarter, many British people had come to view China in terms of its contemptible *difference* from Europe, and even those who continued to borrow from Chinese culture emphasized its difference in terms that underscored a proximity between the Chinese mind and the natural landscape.[17]

In the aesthetic realm, British chinoiserie—a free-form adaptation of "Chinese" devices that emphasized exoticness—reached its apex just as the tide of opinion

Fig. 4.3 Chinoiserie menagerie pavilion at Kew Gardens, designed by William Chambers in the 1750s. Engraving by Charles Grignon, published in William Chambers, *Plans, Elevations, Sections, and Perspective Views of the Gardens and Buildings at Kew, in Surry* (London: J. Haberkorn, 1763).

was turning. Chinoiserie, while sometimes still alluding to China's perceived philosophical and moral wisdom, generally deployed Chinese forms as a novel means of rebelling against the neoclassical order, not unlike the Gothic Revival and picturesque landscape styles (to which chinoiserie is closely related). Most historical and contemporary discussions of British chinoiserie concern small objects, interiors, and garden pavilions, easily fitted into an aesthete's consumption and lifestyle, and offering, as the historian David Porter argues, a "tincture of sublimity" that provoked contemplation of an "unfathomable" other. It is this context that produced the work of Sir William Chambers, known as much for his neoclassical facades as for the chinoiserie pavilions he designed for London's Kew Gardens (figure 4.3). In the 1740s, he briefly visited Guangzhou (then known as Canton) as a supercargo with the Swedish East India Company. This experience supported his claim in 1757's *Designs of Chinese Buildings, Furniture, Dresses, Machines, and Utensils* to offer a corrective to the excesses of uninformed chinoiserie.[18] The book includes an essay on garden design principles, the first of two texts by Chambers that together reveal a rapidly transforming interpretive framework for cultivated Chinese landscapes.

Likely lacking the firsthand experience that supported his handling of temples and other topics, Chambers's discussion of gardens in *Designs* borrows its outline

Addison Godel

of principles from earlier English sources. However, he departs from these texts by establishing a hierarchical framework of difference, insisting that he does not wish to "promote a taste so much inferiour to the antique, and so very unfit for our climate." For Chambers, study of Chinese designs satisfies "curiosity," as in Fischer, but no longer serves to cultivate taste. Rather, the Chinese structures and details he refers to as "toys in architecture" may simply be "useful" to an architect seeking ideas for gardens or rooms; "inferiour" spaces can be rendered as chinoiserie, since "variety is always delightful; and novelty . . . sometimes takes the place of beauty."[19] This dismissive tone may indicate a bid by Chambers to shield himself from opponents of chinoiserie, or to position himself in a wider debate concerning the appropriate uses of varied styles and architectural "characters." Simultaneously, his comments reflect an ascendant theory of differential national development absent in Fischer and Attiret—one in which "nation" and "race" become interchangeable, though incompletely articulated. While Chambers refuses to place the Chinese in "competition" with Europeans, according to his text, Chinese people still comprise a "distinct and very singular race of men[,] inhabitants of a region divided by its situation from all civilized countries; who have formed their own manners, and invented their own arts, without the assistance of example." Nonetheless, he goes on to say, they are "great, or wise, only in comparison with the nations that surround them." The 1750s saw an emerging intellectual speculation among Europeans on the origins and relative "place" of Chinese civilization, but "race" was not yet a coherent or scientific concept, and Chambers does not elaborate on it. Chambers does reprint illustrations of Chinese dress (akin to in Nieuhof's treatise), possibly indicating an attention to physiognomy (figure 4.4). More significant is the link between "race," "nation," and an implied narrative of development and influence. Common historical roots and inherent human abilities fade, so that Chambers finds it remarkable that China could possess quasi-European qualities without the European "example." Chambers also affirms as widely held the idea that China's culture has "continued without change for thousands of years," an emerging trope that would become embodied in formalized Eurocentric theories of history, to be discussed shortly.[20]

In *Designs*, Chinese gardens are discussed chiefly in terms of their semblance to "nature," and the careful techniques by which "irregularity" is produced. Whether China was seen to possess a corresponding regularity is unclear, as Chambers leaves undiscussed the orthogonality, axiality, and symmetry evident in his drawings of Chinese temples. Geography becomes a determining factor, as the nature of mountainous terrain is said to inspire Chinese gardeners to "avoid all regularity." This labeling of a physio-geographical origin point for culture is consistent with the thinking of the period's materialist natural philosophy, and resembles "climatic" theories of human variety. Although this essentialism seems to diminish

Fig. 4.4 Illustrations of Chinese dress, engraved by Charles Grignon, and printed in William Chambers, *Designs of Chinese Buildings, Furniture, Dresses, Machines, and Utensils* (London: published for the author, 1757).

the individual subjectivity of Chinese garden designers, Chambers elsewhere characterizes them as possessing not merely "judgment and experience," but also "genius."[21]

Chambers's second major text on Chinese landscape, the 1772 *Dissertation on Oriental Gardening*, is quite different. At first, it appears to retain traces of universalism, and in some ways is less dismissive of Chinese art than *Designs*. Chambers suggests that Chinese gardens would be viable models for Western gardens because gardening's "effects upon the human mind [are] certain and invariable," describes "Oriental grandeur" as a goal to which Europeans should aspire, and echoes Attiret's ambivalence concerning whether Chinese gardens are "better or worse" than European ones. The role of the Chinese garden is to offer a "judicious mixture," avoiding two European tendencies: the too-formal classical garden, and the too-naturalistic picturesque garden of Lancelot "Capability" Brown.[22] This reduction of Chinese forms to a just-right porridge for an authorial Goldilocks was a popular rhetorical device at the time, but Chambers extends the approach into wild exaggerations (or "amusements," as he later claimed in defending them from critics).[23] The *Dissertation* as a result demonstrates a shift away from viewing China and its art forms as objects for serious study and reportage, as compromised as the Jesuit accounts may have been, and toward a casual and cavalier use of Chinese design (as well as goods).

Thus, the neutral tone of the book's initial sections gives way to a parade of bizarre inventions, more appropriate to the nascent genre of Gothic fiction; the text may even have inspired aspects of William Beckford's *Vathek* (1786). Chambers takes the idea of a garden that artfully stages a series of differentiated scenes as the basis for a division between three kinds of Chinese gardens—"the pleasing, the terrible, and the surprising," a widely noted variation on Edmund Burke's 1757 essay on the sublime and the beautiful. It is in the discussion of the "terrible" gardens, and their "sublimity," that Chambers is most inventive. These gardens, experienced in part as boat rides through "dark caverns," are reminiscent of twentieth-century haunted mansion rides and feature fearsome bats, vultures, wolves, jackals, implements of torture, volcanoes, earthquakes, pyrotechnics, and electric shocks.[24] This vision, obviously without Chinese precedent, extends Chambers's theme of Chinese control over nature to a broader realm of sensory stimulation. Moreover, while Chinese designers remain "men of genius, experience and judgement," the depiction of the garden's *owner* is an Orientalist fantasy. Served by eunuchs, he reclines in specially designed furniture, admiring "amorous paintings" while concubines perform songs, pantomimes, and "lascivious posture-dancing."[25] Chambers inverts the real purpose of many Chinese gardens—the secluded cultivation of scholarly, artistic subjectivity—to posit a sensual, materialist playground, a projection of his era's playboy fantasies.

Sensation and variety are prominent themes in mid-eighteenth-century aesthetics, not limited to discourse on China. The later passages in Chambers's *Dissertation* might be compared to the text of Jean-Francois de Bastide's 1758 novella *La Petite Maison* (*The Little House*), which stages a seduction through a rococo garden pavilion's variously atmospheric rooms, or the 1760s debate on "monotony" between Giovanni Battista Piranesi and Pierre-Jean Mariette.[26] In Chambers, these preoccupations dovetail with a developing Orientalism that prevents us from reading sensuality and variety as neutral aesthetic concerns. As Porter suggests, chinoiserie's decline may have stemmed from these very qualities, as much as from shifts in elite tastes, as China became associated with the sublime, and not the beautiful: it was a site of bodily thrills and earthly delights, not universal reason, even as it was placed hierarchically beneath Europe in its development.[27] Chambers still equivocates on Chinese subjectivity and intelligence, but the stage is set for China to fully occupy the materialized, racialized exteriority that scholar Denise Ferreira da Silva has recently posited as co-constitutive of European transcendental subjectivity.[28]

In this light, Chambers's evolving treatment of Chinese subjectivity may be juxtaposed with the long eighteenth-century prehistory of racial science, in which one key figure is the German naturalist Johann Friedrich Blumenbach. His *On the Natural Variety of Mankind* was published in 1775, three years after the *Dissertation*, inviting us to consider the underlying assumptions shared by European intellectuals of the late eighteenth century—notwithstanding the obvious differences in backgrounds, interests, and audiences—in comparison to those shared by the English gardener.

On the one hand, Blumenbach rejects the idea of separate human species, insisting that one variety "does so sensibly pass into the other, that you cannot mark out the limits between them," as seen specifically in the case of skin color. Nonetheless, Blumenbach identifies several "varieties of mankind," which in his final scheme numbered five, derived from climate and "mode of life." The first "variety" comprises Europeans, and an initial Asian grouping was later subdivided to distinguish northern peoples (e.g., Siberians) from those of China, Korea, and Southeast Asia. Despite his onetime claim that mental capacity and physical appearance had not "the slightest relation," this southern Asian group is "distinguished [by] depravity and perfidiousness of spirit and of manners." The Chinese in particular, he writes, are "less content than any other of the inhabitants of the world, with the natural conformation of their body," and use so many "artificial means to distort it, and squeeze it, that they differ from almost all other men in most parts of their bodies."[29] While Blumenbach introduces this claim to demonstrate that variety in human skull measurements stems from "the mode of life and art," rather than

Addison Godel

Fig. 4.5 Chinese figures by Daniel Chodowiecki, illustrating one of Johann Friedrich Blumenbach's five "human varieties" (Menschenvarietäten) for the 1806 edition of the *Beiträge zur Naturgeschichte* (Contributions to Natural History).

biology, it is interesting that he imagines the Chinese as master manipulators of nature, treating their bodies as Chambers imagines them treating their gardens.

This association is reinforced by a set of illustrations of the "five varieties of humanity," created by Daniel Chodowiecki for a later Blumenbach text and recently analyzed by the art historian David Bindman. Here, the typical male Chinese figure, removed from Fischer's urbane crowds, is set in a chinoiserie garden pavilion, in close contact with landscape and with a female figure (who may represent a concubine à la Chambers) (figure 4.5). Chodowiecki's renderings imply a close fit between culture, skin color, physiognomy, landscape, and architecture. Bindman, probing Blumenbach's universalist tendencies, asserts that despite the descriptive text's physiognomic detail, the images avoid "flat faces and slanting eyes," and emphasize "the possibilities of differentiated, but harmonious, ways of life among the world's peoples, and of improvement by the cultivation of nature."[30] Framing these images in the history of Chinese garden accounts, I suggest, paints a more troubling picture. If Chinese design was exploited for its associations with the sensual—in Ferreira da Silva's terms, the external, material, and affectable—

then the titillating or sublime experience it provoked may be a microcosm of Europe's encounters with the Chinese other. Chinoiserie offered a moment of safe, thrilling contact with the overwhelming, unfathomable "Orient," sublimating Europe's inability to impose itself on a vast portion of the planet. As a racial and imperial theory avant la lettre, it helped pave the way for the conceptualization of the Chinese as not only fundamentally different, but also as inferior and without claim to world-historical subjectivity.

Herder, Hegel, the Yuanmingyuan, and a Racialized China

By the time of the Opium Wars—imperial conquests in 1839–1842 and 1856–1860 that arose from the eagerness of British traders to gain privileged access to Chinese products and markets—this shift in European perceptions of Chinese character was complete. Experts now described a stagnant culture bereft of new inventions, while greater availability rendered Chinese products banal.[31] These changes in attitude coincided with an increasing racialization of European aesthetic discourse and accounts of Chinese physiognomy; this can be seen in changing attitudes toward gardens, and in the looting and burning of the once-fabled Yuanmingyuan by British and French troops over the course of two days in 1860. The premeditated destruction was intended not to provoke Chinese surrender, which was already at hand, but to convince the Chinese of their inferiority to British military and cultural authority.[32] With the defeat of what had once been understood as a great civilization, European hegemony apparently faced no rival claimants to mastery of the world.[33] While the arsonists' own memoirs barely mention conventional racial signifiers like physiognomy, they reflect the development of "Chinese" as a coherent racial category linked to a world-historical teleology that posited China and its people as fundamentally ahistorical.

Biological divisions among "races," attached to claims about "spirit and manners," became increasingly prevalent in late-eighteenth-century thought. Explicit racial categories are entangled with universal reason in the historical philosophy of Johann Gottfried Herder, who outlined in various essays and the *Ideas on the Philosophy of the History of Mankind* (1784–1791) the possible unification of world history as the continuous unfolding of a variegated "humanity's" God-given gifts of reason and justice. To Herder, each culture deployed these gifts by the means available to it, and in so doing made some contribution to humanity. In Herder's theory, these available means are the locus of racial difference: within the one human species, physiognomic variations emerge in response to climatic factors, and are cemented by custom. Custom and physiognomy in turn delimit the possibilities for the use of universal reason. The Chinese are defined by their racial status as an "unmixed . . . Mongol tribe," for which the evidence is physical ("their features"), cultural ("their gross or odd taste, yes even [their] clever artfulness"), and geographical (the "earliest seat of their culture"). The description incorporates stereotyped physiognomic detail ("small eyes, snub noses, flat foreheads," and so on); these features directly inform cultural accomplishments, with the "auditory organs of a Mongol" yielding a language "of three hundred and thirty syllables." A "basic Mongol makeup," possibly related to the way nature has "bountifully endowed their little eyes," gives rise to "dragons and monsters" in folklore, a "careful minuteness of irregular figures" in drawing, and "formless jumble" in gardening. Thus, race leads directly to cultural forms, but Herder also outlines an indirect path: nomadic Mongol origins give rise to deep-seated cultural traditions that promulgate "childlike obedience," preventing the development of artistic autonomy. By either path, Chinese art comes to embody a "deranged sensibility" lacking "a feeling for inner calm, beauty and dignity." Thus, universal human qualities are channeled through racially determined biology, resulting in cultural forms ranked in a Eurocentric hierarchy. According to Herder, all cultures' art displays "the plan and design of a reflecting understanding," but in different degrees—from "the shapeless artificial rocks, with which the Chinese ornaments his garden, to the Egyptian pyramid, or the ideal beauty of Greece."[34] The Chinese garden, far from proof of a gardener's "genius" as in Chambers, is, in such a formulation, the product of qualities intrinsic to a Chinese racial heritage.

In Georg W. F. Hegel's lectures of the 1820s, Asia and China were drawn into a less consistently racialized but even more explicitly teleological and Eurocentric narrative of world history. Hegel's "world-historical nations"—sites for his "world spirit" to enter consciousness—can only exist in the geographical circumstances of Europe and the Middle East, where the natural world is forgiving enough for man to "assert his spiritual freedom." The Chinese, though not subjected to the parade of physiognomic and cultural details by which Hegel dismisses Native Americans and Africans, serve his historical structure by failing to live up to it. Asian geography, he writes, directly affects "the character of [its] peoples and history"; its mountains and plains yield only nomadism and agriculture, and without a linking Mediterranean, East Asia's societies remain enclosed within themselves rather than having to grapple with other nations. Thus, the region does not enter into world history, but rather "lies suspended, as it were, outside the historical process." Its only possible relation to history is through exploration by other nations.[35] Asian societies, then, exist to provide a moment of contact with the ahistorical, furthering Europe's self-revelation of historical purpose and "world spirit."[36] As in Herder, the natural, material world has preempted individual Chinese action; the result is a nation destined for European imperial incursions.

Hegel's conceptualization of Chinese institutions as not merely long-lived, but unchanging, was increasingly common by his time. To Nicolas de Condorcet, China's state was one of "shameful stagnation"; to John Stuart Mill, "stationariness"; to Leopold von Ranke, "eternal standstill."[37] Herder saw the country as "a "dormouse in its winter sleep," an "embalmed mummy," whose arts stood "as they were centuries ago" and whose laws "continually pace round the same circle."[38] Following the first Opium War, travelers described a "stationary nation," "half-civilized," whose people were "sleepy or dreaming."[39] The preponderance of biological metaphors links these concepts to Chinese bodies and to their racialization.

Others have linked the perception of China as declining or frozen to the destruction of the Yuanmingyuan;[40] I would like to specifically emphasize the importance of the emerging racial imaginary, and treat memoirs of the 1860 assault as this period's notable garden texts. Encircling the Chinese in racial and world-historical schemas, European military officers recognized a garden—now a space of earthly indulgence and bodily torpor—as a critical site in the forcible redefinition of European-Chinese relations. Officially, the sacking of the Yuanmingyuan's hundreds of pavilions, following the conclusion of major operations in the second Opium War, was an act of retaliation for the murder of members of a European diplomatic delegation, but the gratuity of the destruction suggests other forces at work. The narrative of British army chaplain R. J. L. McGhee, who witnessed the destruction, is revealing even in its vague chronology. Attiret could date the garden's construction to two decades in the early eighteenth century, but McGhee saw its pavilions as having been built "many, many hundred years ago"—"the admiration of ages, records of by-gone skill and taste." Despite the nineteenth century's pretensions to historical insight, the suspension of China outside of history leaves McGhee to shroud the palace in timelessness. Conveniently, this confirms the "stern but just necessity" of British domination and the destruction of the garden's "most enchanting beauty."[41]

To others, the Chinese existed in coherent, linear time, but in a narrative of decline. They spoke of cities in ruin and crumbling pagodas, evidence that following some earlier, distant period of perfection, the empire had "been retrograding rather than advancing."[42] Another Yuanmingyuan arsonist, Garnet Wolseley, found advanced decay in the garden he was sacking, notwithstanding its "magic grounds described in fairy tales," mentioned earlier. To him, the Yuanmingyuan's ponds, once evidently fed by "very pretty little cascades," were now full of "stagnant water." Such signs of physical ruin demonstrated not the destructive effects of European interference on China's economy and society, but rather the internal decline of Chinese administration—a decline that, he commented, "has allowed [the gardens] to become what they are." The garden's remaining beauties were even cast as the source of racialized decadence; its "very gorgeousness . . . has been one great promoting cause of the luxury and effeminacy which have served to debase the late rulers of China, causing the descendants of fierce warriors to degenerate

Addison Godel

into mere enervated debauchees." Growing up in the gardens, and apparently more susceptible to material influence than Hegel's Europeans, the emperors came to "an indolent, dreamy, and unpractical manhood," cut off from historical progress as "the greatest of all copyists under heaven." Here Wolseley echoes not only Chambers's reclining potentates, but Herder, who claims that "a nation bedded on warm stove tiles, drinking warm water from morning till night" inevitably lacks "the martial as well as the reflective spirit."[43] Thus, the conversation around the Yuanmingyuan discursively knits together Chinese bodies, products of Chinese design, and Eurocentric theories of history in a way that must be understood as racial. Just as Hegel viewed Asian geography and Herder viewed "Mongol" lineage, the British viewed the Yuanmingyuan as a generator of inferior bodies and an inferior worldview. In turn, they thought, these produced military defeat and the destruction of the garden. Burning the garden was a material means of forcing the timeless "copyists" into their appointed role in a racialized, European history of the world.

Although McGhee and others expressed some regrets concerning the Yuanmingyuan's destruction, such sentiments were fading legacies of an earlier period.[44] The arson, like the war to which it served as postscript, made clear that the new order of European-Chinese relations presumed the annihilation of Chinese independence. Without the development of race as a category defining and delimiting Chinese art and society, could educated Europeans have destroyed a garden celebrated as a masterpiece a century before? Would a Europe that still revered the Chinese garden have constructed an image of a Chinese race whose inferiority and ahistorical condition demanded conquest? In this light, Chambers's garden fantasies mark a step away from the quasi-universalist gestures of Fischer, and toward the radical inscription of difference increasingly articulated by Blumenbach, Herder, and Hegel, and insisted upon by the Yuanmingyuan arsonists of 1860. More than a quirky subspecies of rococo, or a piece of the picturesque garden mode, chinoiserie in architecture and landscape design served as a site for the theorization of Chinese difference, and part of the grand rethinking of European-Chinese relations over the course of the long eighteenth century.

PART II

RACE AND ORGANICISM

5

Henry Van Brunt and White Settler Colonialism in the Midwest

Charles L. Davis II

The various stages in the slow developments of civilization from barbarism are marked by a corresponding series of visible monuments, in which may plainly be read the character and quality of the social conditions out of which they grew. The true value and significance of these almost ineffaceable records have never been duly recognized.

Henry Van Brunt, "Architecture in the West" (1889)

The best critical surveys of modern architecture tend to credit the birth of American modernism to a series of transatlantic disciplinary exchanges between professional architects in the United States and western Europe.[1] This literature celebrates the writings and buildings of figures such as Henry Hobson Richardson, Frank Furness, John Wellborn Root, William Le Baron Jenney, Louis Sullivan, and Frank Lloyd Wright for producing an indigenous style of modern architecture—an American architecture—that equaled the rigor and sophistication of Continental architectural styles while representing the social and political realities of life in the States. The international frameworks of these studies successfully recover the European pedigree of this national building style by characterizing its development as a synthesis of the socially progressive ideas of European theory and the pragmatic realities of domestic building culture. Yet an outward focus on European trends unduly masks some of the key domestic influences that determined the practical reality of architectural practices in the United States. This is especially the case when one considers the ways in which architectural styles were used as political tools to legitimize particular strands of cultural nationalism in the nineteenth century. Even the best historical surveys have failed to expose the white nativist associations that bound period definitions of American character that underwrote the meaning of American architecture. When leading architects used the label "American architecture" to identify an indigenous style of building, who did they believe this style was indigenous to in the States? What definitions of racial and ethnic identity most informed their conceptions of American character? And were these definitions broad enough to encompass the racial diversity present at that time? It is only by situating a disciplinary history of American architecture within the political contexts of the nineteenth century that we can fully interpret the tacit associations this movement accrued in the past.

The dialectics of race and nationalism within American architectural theory were an inherent aspect of political control as exercised through the competition for land ownership and the control of local resources. A popular narrative to emerge in defense of an exclusively white Christian nation was the credo of Manifest Destiny, which pitted white colonial settlers against indigenous peoples, formerly enslaved Africans, and other migrant laborers of color. The dispossession and redistributions of Native lands was a routine aspect of wealth building in North America, but a physical record of this exchange was not always preserved within the land itself. Architecture was often tasked with providing a symbol of the desired course of civilizational change for successive generations. This chapter analyzes the ideological function of American architecture in promoting an exclusively white definition of American character. It uses the writings and buildings of Henry Van Brunt, the Beaux-Arts-trained American architect who moved his Boston architectural practice to the Midwest to complete a series of signature commissions for the Union Pacific Railroad in the 1880s and '90s, as a period case study of the political functions of architectural style. Van Brunt is an ideal choice here because his career is representative of the types of cultural distinctions and the avant-garde positions on architectural style taken by elite designers then practicing on the East Coast: his exposure to and emulation of the principles of architectural organicism from Continental Europe and the US reflect his critical engagement with the notion of a living architecture shaped to reflect present conditions. A close reading of the developmental models that emerge from his theory of organic architecture will uncover the racialist discourses that subtended the politicization of architectural style theory as it migrated from the East Coast to the developing Midwest.

Van Brunt's relocation to the center of the country was characteristic of a broader professional migration of elite architects westward, either in person or through the opening of satellite offices. The local conditions of the Midwest prompted many of these professionals to struggle with their aesthetic dependence on European revivalist styles to visualize the essence of American character. A lack of urban density in comparison to what they were used to back east was accom-

Charles L. Davis II

panied by a rougher physical terrain that required extensive leveling, dredging, and irrigation. For some, these conditions suggested a different formal approach to city building. The subsequent search for an autochthonous national building style that replaced the former use of revivalist styles raised certain contentious questions about the ideal racial constitution of the nation, something that has yet to be widely recognized in contemporary architectural historiography. As Martin Berger notes in his book *Sight Unseen: Whiteness and American Visual Culture*, the aesthetic practices of white cultural elites were an important indicator of what made them different and therefore worthy of leading the country. These aesthetic distinctions naturalized their grasp on power by codifying and disseminating elite ideas about space, dress, and politics among people of a different social class and race.[2] If these views were adopted as social norms, then it became that much easier to see elite notions as normal for all people. During the seventeenth, eighteenth, and nineteenth centuries, different racial and ethnic groups migrated to North America to settle in the territory that was later identified alternately as the American West, the Middle West, or the Midwest. In the inevitable competition for political influence that ensued between white settlers, indigenous peoples, and other nonwhite groups, romantic portraits of whiteness from paintings of settler culture to distinctive portraits of Gilded Age elites served an instrumental political function. One example is the Hudson River school painters who led the way in creating a visual and material matrix for representing the norms of whiteness in aesthetic fields such as landscape painting and architecture.[3] Wealth and privilege had a face, and the racial identity of this face was very important. Architectural style and material culture became emblematic of specific racial and ethnic groups, either as a natural product of their experimentation or as an aspirational statement on how things should be. Van Brunt's writings and buildings served a similar function in early America as his work emerged alongside the divisive rhetoric of Manifest Destiny and the rejuvenating cultural potential of frontier life.

During the three decades that Henry Van Brunt lived in Kansas City, Kansas, he completed a series of speeches, papers, and essays in trade journals and popular magazines that outlined the generative principles of an autochthonous American architecture. He intended these writings to serve as a practical guide for both architects and business elites in channeling the future trajectory of building culture in the Midwest. The historical timeline he created to explain the evolution of architectural style advances along a progressive and teleological model of vernacular development that begins with the material culture of white settlers and ends with the birth of a unique American architecture. Van Brunt considered himself to be situated somewhere in the middle of this trajectory, but moving toward the completion of a new stylistic expression. He praised the structural clarity of the "temporary makeshifts" of "border life" that followed the universal laws of nature, which he believed provided the true basis of all beauty in art.[4] Yet he did not consider the rudimentary architectures of frontier settlements to be sufficient to reflect the full range of needs and values that were emerging from the increasing modernization of the country. Instead, he hoped that avant-garde constructions in the American frontier would precipitate a new wave of design standards for contemporary users that would elevate the fine arts in America. This theory of architectural style is notably influenced by the racialist thinking of the French architect Eugène-Emmanuel Viollet-le-Duc who wrote ethnographic histories of architectural style in the 1860s and 1870s.[5] Van Brunt not only read the French architect's theories in their original language, but he later produced an authoritative English translation and critical introduction to Viollet-le-Duc's collection of essays, *Discourses on Architecture*, for American audiences.[6] The racial conflicts between white and nonwhite groups that fueled the progression of building culture in Viollet-le-Duc's historiography provided a structural parallel for Van Brunt's consideration of life on the frontier.

Van Brunt's designs for a regional station on the Union Pacific Railroad took shape in a social and political context mired by the nativist ideologies associated with nineteenth-century railroad culture. Local boosters such as William Gilpin encouraged the construction of a transcontinental railroad in a grand effort to promote the geographical expansion of "Aryan" culture in the United States. Since this expansion was reliant on the dispossession of Native lands and the relocation of nonwhite groups, Gilpin's theory made the transcontinental railroad a physical emblem of white cultural nationalism in Kansas City and of white colonialism abroad. The clearest illustration of this potential global infrastructure is Gilpin's drawing of the "Cosmopolitan Railway," which shows a winding ribbon of railroad tracks moving through the most developed predominantly white nations of the earth. According to Gilpin, this rail line would take occasional forays north and south of the central meridian through these countries, guaranteeing an efficient route for the future colonization of less developed peoples (figure 5.1). The cultural pedigree and evolutionary rhetoric of Van Brunt's architectural theory likewise elevated the symbolic status of railroad culture as a visual sign of American progress. For example, Van Brunt's teleology of form naturalized the proprietary standards established within the Union Pacific Railroad, which gradually increased the durability of local railroad stations as they became important nodes in its infrastructure. This cost-saving measure essentially began each node on the rail line with the construction of a makeshift station that emulated the simplicity of construction used by white settlers in surrounding territories (figure 5.2). In many cases, these structures were carried directly on railroad cars to their local destinations. As time progressed, the more important nodes were expanded as the local population grew, and in the cases of the most important sites, new and opulent

Charles L. Davis II

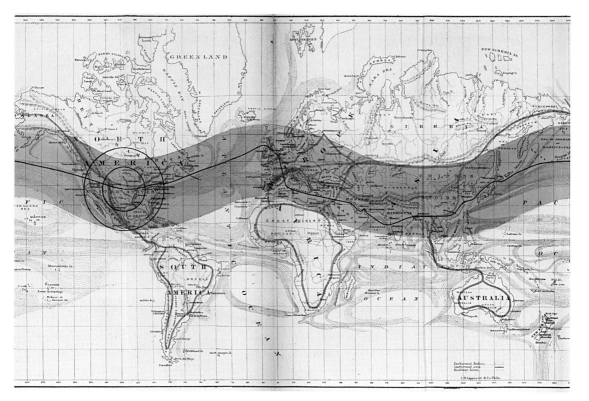

Fig. 5.1 "The Isothermal Zodiac and Axis of Intensity Round the World; and the Line of Cosmopolitan Railway and Its Longitudinal Feeders," in William Gilpin, *The Cosmopolitan Railway* (1890). Courtesy of David Rumsey Map Collection, Stanford University.

buildings in a modern or urban style were erected in their place. Van Brunt's modernist style for depots that reached the most advanced stage of circulation dramatized in his evolutionary narrative for American architecture—a trajectory that was didactically illustrated by the naturalisms of his masonry materials, which communicated the rising city's deep and abiding relationship with nature. He completed designs for the most important regional depots of the Union Pacific line, such as those located in Cheyenne, Wyoming; Ogden, Utah; and Portland, Oregon (figure 5.3).

Racial Interpretations of Place in the Midwest, ca. 1860–1900

A brief survey of nineteenth-century literary and artistic conceptions of white settler culture demonstrates the importance of architectural imagery for romanticizing the white domestication of the midwestern landscape. From Laura Ingalls Wilder's *Little House on the Prairie* to D. W. Griffith's *Birth of a Nation*, romantic portraits of America's racial origins popularized the notion that white immigrants provided the best racial stock for breeding a democratic culture that would flower around the country. In and around Kansas City, local writers and artists used at

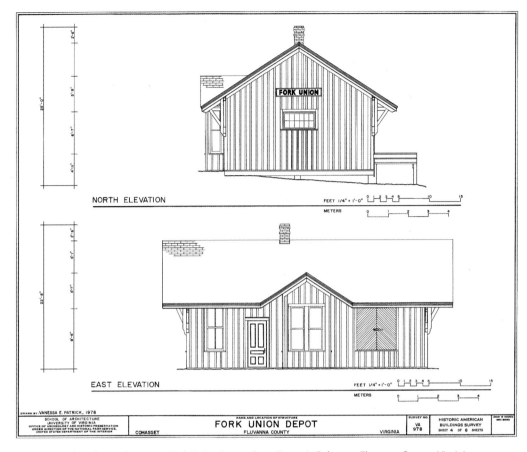

NORTH ELEVATION

EAST ELEVATION

DRAWN BY: VANESSA E. PATRICK, 1978

SCHOOL OF ARCHITECTURE
UNIVERSITY OF VIRGINIA
OFFICE OF ARCHEOLOGY AND HISTORIC PRESERVATION
UNDER DIRECTION OF THE NATIONAL PARK SERVICE,
UNITED STATES DEPARTMENT OF THE INTERIOR

COHASSET

FORK UNION DEPOT
FLUVANNA COUNTY

VIRGINIA

SURVEY NO.
VA
978

HISTORIC AMERICAN
BUILDINGS SURVEY
SHEET 4 OF 6 SHEETS

Fig. 5.2 North and east elevations–Fork Union Depot, State Route 6, Cohasset, Fluvanna County, Virginia (1908 construction). Drawings from survey HABS VA-978 (1933). Courtesy of Library of Congress.

least two rhetorical strategies to legitimize white settlers' claims to indigenous lands. The first consisted of the mechanization of Native American material culture in novels and films that demonstrated the settlers' ability to advance beyond the current state of indigenous vernacular culture toward a more modern ideal. One common trope of this mechanization took the form of the "iron horse," or the steam-powered railcar that replaced the horse-led hunting and gathering culture of the Plains Indians. A second strategy employed a climactic argument that extended the latitudinal area bounding the so-called temperate zones of western Europe across the globe to suggest that white migrants would also establish a civilized culture in the New World. In both of these strategies, the intercontinental railroad proved to be an important infrastructural component for spreading white civilization.

Novels such as Robert Michael Ballantyne's *The Iron Horse; or, Life on the Line* (1871) first popularized new labels for steam-powered trains nearly a decade before railroads finally came to Kansas City.[7] In the chapter entitled "History of the Iron

Charles L. Davis II

Fig. 5.3 Union Pacific Railroad Depot building, Cheyenne, Wyoming (1876). Courtesy of *Wyoming Tribune Eagle*.

Horse," Ballantyne establishes the European origins of rail technology by describing the transatlantic path of innovations that contributed to the growth of rail travel. He uses two principal phrases—the "steam wagon" and the "iron horse"—to suggest the mechanization of the dominant forms of manual travel, that of horseback and stage coach travel. This tradition of mechanization continues in American films such as John Ford's *The Iron Horse* (1924), which became an archetypal visual representation of the racial dynamics of western expansion. The bicoastal geography indicated by the subtitle of Ford's film, *A Romance between East and West*, summarizes the racial tensions operating within the wake of railroad expansion: in order to connect the physical extents of the continental railroad, the Native American culture of the Plains had to be replaced. In filmic representation, this nonwhite indigenous culture was attacked on two fronts—through the local threat of white settler culture and the national threat of railroad expansion. In one famous poster for *The Iron Horse*, we see a Native American perched on a rock looking out over the plains below. In the distance is the iron horse, intruding upon his territory. The clouds overhead form the shape of dancing bison—a fundamental component of Plains Indian life as a source of food, shelter, material for religious culture, and so on. This imagery stages a standoff between the natural life of the plains and the territory's eventual mechanization. In a second poster, we see the same scene from the perspective of the Euro-American settler. Standing aloft on the right side of the frame is the central character of the film, Davy Brandon, a Pony Express rider who dresses like a lost member of the Lewis and Clark expedition. All of the comforts of settler life are poised behind him, ready to move westward. The iron horse in this image magically skips over the divide of the broken hillside on the back of a colorful rainbow.

The colorful rainbow of Ford's film recalls another image that employs a climactic argument to legitimize the settler control of indigenous lands. This image, which emerged in Kansas City, originated from local booster William Gilpin, the former territorial governor of Colorado and a self-proclaimed "mountain man" of the Midwest.[8] The central image of Gilpin's 1890 treatise *The Cosmopolitan Railway* is an "international" rainbow whose trail expands the latitudinal bands of European nation-states to new territories in the Midwest—suggesting that whites would prosper in the New World as they had in the Old World. Gilpin's theory of white urbanization (the eventuality of frontier settlement) was predicated on the vast global dissemination of railroad infrastructure.[9] Despite the seemingly inclusive sound of the subtitle of his book, *Compacting and Fusing Together All the World's Continents*, Gilpin identified this international travel route as an efficient means of extending the colonial efforts of so-called Aryan nations. He outlines this exclusive racial ideology in chapter 7, entitled "Race Problems and Proclivities," in which he associates Aryan man with the doctrine of scientific progress: "During the last five hundred years, the races that have acquired new territory and have planted new colonies, that have made grand discoveries in the scientific world and have invented machines, that have written books which the world will not willingly let die and have collected the wisdom of the ages in vast libraries, are all members of the great Aryan family of nations."[10] In addition, Gilpin plainly states the important role of European immigration in this march toward progress, which the railroad can only accelerate at the global scale: "The migratory propensity of this race is one of its dominant characteristics. It has, of course, its periods of repose as well as its periods of progress. Doubtless the discovery of America, which afforded the Aryans such vast fields for colonization, retarded the reclamation of Africa and Asia. But a new migratory wave within the last decade has swept over Arya. . . . What the old Roman roads and aqueducts were to the greatest of ancient empires, the railroads and the systems of irrigation are to the Aryans of the nineteenth century."[11] These arguments are imbued with the exclusive racial rhetoric and divine ordinations of Manifest Destiny that propelled white Christian migrations into the Midwest. However, in Gilpin's mind this was only the first step. Outlining what he called the "Indo-European Monroe Doctrine," he proposed the forceful dispossession of nonwhite indigenous territories and the re-enslavement of Africans in the New World, which was to be followed by the complete colonization of Africa and Asia; the railroads were to serve as a vital infrastructure for this new regime. His plan was to connect all of the lands held by Aryans on each continent in a region that he called the "Isothermic band" of the globe. This area was demarcated by the geographical origins of the most prosperous white peoples who ever lived in one comprehensive graphic. The racial outliers were clear insofar as the natives of Africa, Australia, and South America were outside of this barrier, and the European territories to the north were characterized as less vigorous than those lying within the band. Gilpin added a circle, or target, over the midwestern territories of the United States since he believed that the most advanced developments of Western civilization were going to take place in that region (see fig. 5.1).

While Gilpin's racial ideology made up one of the most extreme and explicit theories of white cultural nationalism created in the States at the time, its general principles echoed the racialist models of history outlined in European and American histories of architectural style. During his move to the Midwest, Van Brunt took the opportunity to document the local vernacular culture then emerging in the Midwest in speeches to the American Institute of Architects as well as in published essays. His articles and speeches are some of the most representative interpretations of American architects looking to build up the West at this time. Architectural historians have tended to credit Van Brunt with being a successful popularizer of avant-garde theories of architectural style while chiding him for merely imitating the most popular design approaches of his day. It is these very qualities, however, that make him an ideal case study for examining the dominant strains of American architectural discourse.

Van Brunt's Evolutionary Model of Vernacular Development in the Midwest

The clearest summary of Henry Van Brunt's thinking on American architecture appears in a series of essays published by *Atlantic Monthly* in the years leading up to his move to Kansas City to manage the construction of the Union Pacific's midwestern depots. Two essays from this period—"On the Present Condition and Prospects of Architecture" (1886) and "Architecture in the West" (1889)— demonstrate the increasing prominence that Van Brunt placed upon the vernacular architectures of white settlers.[12] Before his move to the Midwest, Van Brunt is clear that the precedents for American architecture are not likely to be found in the historical styles of western Europe. Yet it is not until after he arrives in the Midwest and has more intimate experiences with its local culture that he specifically cites the material culture of white settlers as a new origin point for domestic developments.

Van Brunt begins his outline of an evolutionary model of vernacular development in "On the Present Condition and Prospects of Architecture," which was published three years before his move to the Midwest. He opens this essay by describing the polarities recorded in a literary review of translated Arabian poetry that he found fitting to describe the gap that separates the architectural designs of "primitive races" from those of "modern architects" of the nineteenth century.[13] While the modern architect is relatively advantaged by a "far more learned and versatile" historical record of the past, the growing complexity of Western civilization places him in "an atmosphere infinitely less favorable to purely artistic achievement."[14] This creative poverty forces designers to develop the rigorous science of history to recover the epistemological basis for architectural design that primitive race groups instinctively used to solve their problems: "Those were days when styles were visibly unfolding toward perfection; when the practice of architecture broadened from precedent to precedent without distraction or bias; when temple followed temple, church followed church, chateau followed chateau, in a reasonable development and natural growth of architectural forms, confined within practicable limits. The study of the architect was limited to a type which all understood, and there was an orderly, intelligible, and harmonious evolution of styles."[15] According to Van Brunt, it was an intuitive conception of architectural typology that provided the epistemic basis for primitive man to produce new building precedents in history. This language was not accidental as researchers in the natural sciences used type theory to demonstrate the underlying unity within variety that connected all organic life. This theory of nature posited that the physical variations of all organic species—from microscopic life to animals and human beings—were predicated on the gradual transformation of a fixed set of archetypal forms that adjusted themselves to fit their surrounding contexts. Thus, at a structural level, Van Brunt's evolutionary model of vernacular development extends the universal basis of form generation in nature to a modern process of architectural design.

The scientific framing of "On the Present Condition and Prospects of Architecture" establishes an inherent relationship between the essential qualities of race and style, which become clearer when we examine Van Brunt's strategic use of the term "character." Van Brunt undertakes a comparative analysis of "French character," "English character," "Italian character," and "American character" to describe the essential qualities of the national architectural styles produced by the most prominent Christian and liberal nations of his day.[16] His timeline places all four national building styles at the apex of Western civilization, which he sites as beginning with the pagan architectures of Egypt, Greece, and Rome before transitioning to basilican churches and cathedrals. The individual character of each style was achieved by making a series of gradual changes to domestic architectural forms that better aligned them with the social aims of each group. This process made each national style "an exponent of [local] manners and customs."[17] The specific motivation driving the formation of national character was, respectively, political conquest in England, a "brilliant court culture" in Italy, religious revolution in France, and political liberty and commercial experimentation in the United States. According to Van Brunt, architectural character was organically connected to the social conditions of each group. For example, French architectural style, with its formal principles, when used outside of France became "an unfruitful exotic" that "degenerates into cold conventionalism. Its blossoms invariably die in crossing the English Channel, and when imported to this side of the Atlantic there is nothing left of it but branches and withered leaves."[18] This was an important principle for Van Brunt because he believed that when it came to the birth of an American architecture, stylistic revivalisms were a dead end.[19] The unique national culture of the United States nearly mandated that the architect should abandon his reliance on European historical precedents for a renewed emphasis on local and domestic productions.

After Van Brunt arrived in the Midwest in 1889, he turned his eye more pointedly toward the vernacular structures of white settlements. Written the same year, his essay "Architecture of the West" extends the general characterizations of his earlier timeline of domestic vernacular developments, citing "the emergencies of border life" as a starting point in midwestern developments that would crest with the innovative and pragmatic commercial structures being completed by avant-garde architects in Chicago and Minneapolis.[20] Van Brunt's conception of American architectural development had become more Darwinian as is evident by his explicit references to the relative "fitness" of architectural forms: "Like all other experiments in the evolution of forms, only the fittest remain."[21] He also cites the racial composition of the nation-state as one of the most prominent social factors influencing architecture: "The common and distinctive architectural forms in these older communities of the world are the results of established customs and ancient traditions, which have their roots not only in characteristics of politics, race, and religion, but in the soil itself, which has furnished the materials of building, and, through these, has dictated the forms by which they are most readily adapted to meet the wants of mankind."[22] Van Brunt's essays from the mid- to late-1880s suggest that he wished to measure American progress alongside that of other white Christian nations, presumably because the political structures of these cultures paralleled the grand ideals of American democracy. He also believed that the most transparent expression of American culture—its architecture—would likely emerge from the local conditions of white ethnic migrants settling in the United States. According to Van Brunt, American building style would constitute a "complicated organism," capable of adjusting its form to fit its regional environment.[23]

During the late 1880s and '90s, Van Brunt wrote an essay crediting American architect Henry Hobson Richardson with developing a completely unique aesthetic interpretation of the Romanesque that renovated the latent potential of this lost historical style in novel ways.[24] While Richardson's eclectic approach did not constitute the independent growth of a national style that Van Brunt desired, its singularity made it an appealing first step. Van Brunt's architecture builds upon the "Richardsonian Romanesque," experimenting with its tectonic and spatial features—with its rustication, modern yet Gothic-influenced articulation, and use of local materials—to produce a mature style of building that could be used in growing cities of the Midwest. What is most interesting about his approach, however, is not what he copied from Richardson but how he modified the style for the Midwest. James F. O'Gorman has summarized the visual typologies that Richardson originally established in order to visually and materially adapt his designs to the urban, suburban, and rural contexts of the nineteenth century.[25] In the dense urban fabric of Boston and Chicago, Richardson created taut rectilinear masses for buildings that reflected the capitalist division of land into regular, individual parcels. By contrast, he replaced the smoothed lines of his urban masonry detailing with the aggregation of rugged stones in an irregular geometry in order to respond to the wide-open spaces found in suburban and rural contexts.

Richardson's approach to urban form is perhaps most clearly visible in his design for the Marshall Field's Wholesale Store (1885–1887) in Chicago, Illinois. Although located in the Midwest, Chicago had become a center of a new national architectural style by the late 1880s. Richardson's choice to create minimal rectangular forms of monumental scale and symmetry reflects the formalism of the urban grid that gave the city its rhythm. Van Brunt and his business partner Frank Howe followed Richardson's monumental style in several of their designs for Kansas City, such as the Emery Dry Goods Store (1899). Yet many of their works also deviated from Richardson's by employing more picturesque massing to acknowledge the relative lack of density that was still a fundamental part of Kansas City's urban landscape. Examples of this include works such as the Gibraltar Building (1888) and the Kansas City Club (1888). The sculptural character of these freer-formed buildings, with their rounded projections and rusticated crowns, reveals a material and aesthetic playfulness that Richardson usually reserved for his suburban projects, such as the Oakes Ames Memorial Hall (1881) in North Easton, Massachusetts.[26] This sculptural character was also present in early examples of white settler culture. Because Van Brunt drew on the norms of Richardson's architectural practice, many architectural historians have labeled him, perhaps unfairly, as a timid purveyor of the Richardsonian Romanesque style. This judgment is usually justified by Van Brunt's inability to properly imitate his peer's style directly or to emulate his rigorously structured plastic sensibility for aligning architectural forms with their immediate surrounding contexts. However, a more

Charles L. Davis II

positive view of Van Brunt's work emerges if one analyzes his designs for the ways in which their picturesque formal qualities reflect the current state of urban culture in the Midwest and transform their central motifs to channel the potential of their future developments. He was not looking at what was, but at what things might become.

One of the building typologies that Van Brunt brought from the Northeast to the Midwest was that of the railroad depot, and he borrowed much from Richardson in many of his most spectacular designs. However, he also attempted to innovate the contextual use of this kind of building in a way that transcended that of his peer. For Richardson, who designed railroad depots for freight and commuter trains outside of the city limits, this typology was primarily a suburban building form. He drew sketches of depots with domineering rooflines that emulated the character of surrounding forests while matching the datum line of the ground that elevated passing trains. In these compositions, the roofline provided a steady linear reference against which people would move back and forth as they exited and entered the train. As Janet Greenstein Potter notes in her study of midwestern train stations, this spatial organization was common to the modest train stations that made use of rustic materials such as unfinished lumber to create one-story "shacks" that contained a ticket office and freight storage.[27] Van Brunt inverted the urban-suburban typologies of Richardson's practice when designing plans for major depots in the Midwest, even when the cities associated with these stations were not yet very dense. The most spectacular of these projects is his design of a Union Pacific depot in Cheyenne, Wyoming—which was still a small town in the 1880s. For this project, Van Brunt transformed Richardson's prominently used hip roof to bring a more civic type of architecture to suburban depots.[28] This approach freed him to create a more picturesque profile along the roofline to articulate the functional spaces lying behind each volumetric projection in the facade. His aesthetic formula was usually accompanied by a highly projecting bell tower that served as a beacon within the urban landscape.[29] Van Brunt's formal treatment of this typology departs drastically from the vernacular detailing and modest scale of outlying junction stations for freight trains by anticipating the larger scale and complex interior organization that would come to mark future commuter stations. His didactic visualization of the future of American architecture was not limited to the building's exterior scale but extended to his treatment of the interior, as well. The first depot that had been built in Cheyenne, which was completed in 1865, consisted of a series of supporting wood-framed structures with board and batten siding (see figure 5.3). The utilitarian character of buildings of this type was so prominent that an 1865 editorial in the *Cheyenne Daily Sun* compared it to a modest cattle shed.[30] Yet Van Brunt maintained a physical memory of this structure in his final design—suggested by the way that the exterior facing

Fig. 5.4 View of east wing, south-southeast side (track side), Union Pacific Depot, Cheyenne, Wyoming (1887 construction). Drawings from survey HABS WYO,11-CHEY,5–16 (1974). Courtesy of Library of Congress.

of the building seems to engulf the window mullions, which are scaled to the iron and wood frame within (figure 5.4). In a tectonic sense, Van Brunt's design for the Cheyenne depot literally demonstrates how one transforms the structural logic of a post-and-lintel-framed building into one that is more appropriate for a rising metropolis. The interior lodging spaces of the original 1865 building gave way to dedicated office spaces in the 1887 design, around the time when dense urban centers began to accommodate visitors in stand-alone hotels of their own.[31]

When it suited him, Van Brunt could apply Richardson's organic design principles to allow for a more picturesque assemblage of programmatic elements to hang over the street, rise above the roofline, or cut into the mass of a building to emulate the sparse and rambling condition of a growing urban context. By contrast, when Van Brunt wished to express the monumentality of a civic program he could resort to Richardson's urban language, even when such a structure was surrounded by nothing but open landscape. The clearest example of this can be found in his design for the Spooner Library (1894), which was constructed on the periphery of land set aside for the completion of the University of Kansas (figure

Charles L. Davis II

Fig. 5.5 Spooner Library, University of Kansas, Lawrence, Kansas (between 1894 and 1910). Courtesy of Library of Congress.

5.5). Although the institution's surroundings were rural, Van Brunt imagined a time when the university would become as complex as a city in its own right. In light of this, he used Richardson's language innovatively to create architectural forms that established a projective dialogue with their contexts. Never completely suited to merely respond to existing or normative patterns of density, Van Brunt was decisive in setting a standard for leading his peers in future aesthetic and formal development.

Despite the fact that the racial discourses of Manifest Destiny radically conditioned the production of nineteenth-century American art and architecture, architectural historians have only recently begun to account for these influences in their critical histories of modern architecture. There exists a need to examine the political function of national architectural styles in territories where competition between white settlers and nonwhite peoples inherently colored the ideological function of architectural form.[32] This chapter uses Henry Van Brunt's writings on architecture in the Midwest to analyze the ways his evolutionary theory of vernacular development legitimized the white hegemony of the Midwest. A close reading of Van Brunt's writings reveals the increasing importance of white material culture in his conception of American architecture during the 1880s. This shift occurred as he relocated his architectural firm to Kansas City to complete a series of depot commissions for the Union Pacific Railroad. The literal function and institutional history of the railroad likely contributed to Van Brunt's ideals. He inherited a racialized conception of midwestern culture in the form of popular writings and illustrations of American railroad culture, which associated the "iron horse" with a mechanization of white vernacular cultures around the world. This ethnographic theme was evident in local booster theories such as William Gilpin's *The Cosmopolitan Railway* as well as European theories of architectural organicism that Van Brunt translated from French to English. The proprietary standards for gradually improving rail depots within the Union Pacific Railroad also seemed to naturalize Van Brunt's evolutionary thesis of vernacular development by expressing a stylistic teleology that moved from simple and modest forms to monumental structures. By the 1890s, Van Brunt's Richardsonian designs for train depots at Cheyenne, Wyoming, and Ogden, Utah, represent a didactic mode of design that was intended to elevate public taste in the Midwest. These structures created a synthetic architectural form that combined the simple tectonic detailing of utilitarian structures of white settler colonies with a monumentalizing masonry shell that pointed toward a new and modern architectural style.

As train travel caused Kansas City to grow between 1890 and 1910, new architectural programs emerged to commemorate the wide range of vernacular cultures that were lost to new patterns of industrialization. These institutions consisted of formal and informal cultural clubs that produced a comparative analysis of the spiritual and aesthetic ideals of world cultures, annual festivals that memorialized the importance of natural resources for the growth of the city, and an explicit ethnographical display of the Native and white settler cultures that had been displaced by recent rail travel and economic development. All of these elements maintained the public perception that the vernacular roots of American democracy were still present despite the increased mechanization of frontier life. Shortly after Van Brunt arrived in Kansas City, he was asked to lend his support to the creation of a historical society that would establish a collection of primary artifacts dedicated to local culture.[33] An 1896 article in the *Kansas City Daily Journal* notes the general theme of the collection—"the History of this Vicinity and the West"—which was meant to house all forms of vernacular culture in the region, past and present. The collection was to contain "the scattered relics of Spanish, Mexican, and Indian domination" that had been displaced by the territorial annexations resulting from Manifest Destiny, as well as the "relics of jayhawkers and bushwhackers" and other elements of "border ruffianism" that had been displaced by the industrial trajectory of the state. This narrative parallels the evolutionary model Van Brunt describes in his architecture theory, although it is more expansive by including both white and nonwhite vernacular cultures. It is interesting to note that the curators of this potential collection chose not to celebrate the white frontier culture with phrases such as "mountain men," as had been popular during the 1860s and '70s. This marks a distinct shift in attitude toward the immediate past as local leaders hoped to shed certain attitudes toward settler culture during these booster years. Such an attitude would continue throughout Van Brunt's time in the city and would not change until nearly two decades after his passing. In this sense, the architect's progressive narrative for the cultural evolution of the region was matched by a social, economic, and political aspiration to continue modernization in every respect.

Van Brunt's architectural designs helped to secure the longevity of white settler culture in the region, even as he hoped to elevate it to a new cultural plateau. As we witness contemporary revivals of white cultural nationalism in the United States, it is important to remember that the defense of and legitimation of whiteness is a consistent theme of American culture. While progressives tend to focus on the most negative forms of racial pride in the figural representations of Civil War heroes and the preservation of Confederate street names, it might be more beneficial to remember that the built environment contains a wide range of material evidence of our nation's experimentation with Anglo-American racial identity. Reconsidering the history of modern architecture through the lens of its racial ideologies will enable us to speak more intelligently about the long-term material legacies of such thinking in the present.

6

The "New Birth of Freedom"

The Gothic Revival and the Aesthetics of Abolitionism

Joanna Merwood-Salisbury

On the evening of April 27, 1865, the National Academy of Design opened its fortieth annual exhibition, the first held in a magnificent new Gothic Revival building on the corner of Fourth Avenue and Twenty-Third Street in New York City. The occasion was somber: the Civil War had just ended, and the building was draped in black mourning bunting for President Abraham Lincoln who had been assassinated less than two weeks earlier. Inside, visitors to the exhibition ascended a grand staircase to the second floor gallery where they were confronted with one of the largest and most controversial pieces in the show, a colossal plaster sculpture depicting the figure of a black woman reclining on one elbow, the other hand raised to her brow in gesture of despair. This was Anne Whitney's *Ethiopia Shall Soon Stretch Out Her Hands to God* (also known as *Africa*) (figure 6.1). An allegorical representation of the plight of the African peoples under slavery, *Africa* was one of many forms of artistic production created in direct response to the national crisis of the Civil War. Describing the cultural framework of this period, the art historian Kirk Savage wrote, "The shift from slavery to freedom precipitated by the Civil War was the cataclysmic event and the central dilemma of the century. . . . [It] reverberated throughout public space in countless ways, some obvious

Fig. 6.1 Anne Whitney, *Ethiopia Shall Soon Stretch Out Her Hands to God* (or, *Africa*), ca. 1864. Courtesy of Wellesley College Archives

and others subtle."[1] Concentrating primarily on sculpture, Savage has written about the importance of aesthetic representations of race during the war and subsequent Reconstruction period, and of the propagandistic and memorializing functions of art as a vehicle through which concepts of race were reinforced.

Beginning with the critical reception of Anne Whitney's *Africa*, this essay examines the racial dimension of the movement toward "naturalism" that swept through the fine arts in America beginning in the 1840s. Focusing primarily on Peter B. Wight's monumental National Academy of Design building, it suggests the presence of racial thinking in the transition from neoclassicism to Gothic Revival–style architecture in the United States, a transition previously seen as a matter of aesthetics or fashion, removed from and undisturbed by its political context. Known chiefly as an homage to the English art critic John Ruskin's beloved Venetian Gothic, Wight's Academy building is one of most prominent examples of Gothic Revival architecture built in the United States during the mid-nineteenth century (figure 6.2). The style was becoming popular throughout Europe and its current and former colonies during this period, though its forms and meanings were adapted and interpreted differently in different geographic locations. While the context of the Academy building's construction against the

Fig. 6.2 P. B. Wight, National Academy of Design, New York, 1865. General view of the building from the opposite corner. *National Academy of Design: Photographs of the New Building*, with an introductory essay and description by P. B. Wight (New York: S. P. Avery, 1886). Courtesy of Metropolitan Museum of Art.

backdrop of the social and political upheaval of the Civil War has been acknowledged in architectural history, the centrality of that national crisis to its design has not. This essay discusses the relationship between the adoption of the Gothic Revival style for the Academy building and the broader aims of its patrons and its architect as members of the northern antislavery coalition. Like Whitney's *Africa*, the building was intended as an aesthetic expression of abolitionist ideals. Whitney's approach was figurative: she sought to elicit abhorrence for the practice of slavery by representing its human consequences. Without explicit reference to race, Wight, a disciple of Ruskin, relied on the symbolism of the Gothic Revival (both its aesthetic form and its explicit reference to craft production) to convey

Joanna Merwood-Salisbury

complementary ideals of creative and social freedom. As this essay will explore, the building embodied a concept of "free labor" that had particular connotations in the context of mid-nineteenth-century America, one that helped shape ideas about the racial landscape of the nation after the war.

Anne Whitney's *Africa* and the Aesthetic of Abolitionism

It is illuminating to compare the reception of Wight's Academy building to that of Anne Whitney's *Africa*, which was featured in the inaugural exhibition held there in the spring of 1865. In both cases critics juggled claims to naturalism with fealty to historic models in order to judge the aesthetic success of the work. And in both cases the meaning of the work was tied to the antislavery cause. Produced in response to the Emancipation Proclamation of 1863, *Africa* was a deeply felt contribution to the debate over slavery.[2] Inspired by Enlightenment thinking, the international movement to end the global slave trade began in the eighteenth century. In the United States calls for the abolition of slavery gained momentum in the 1840s, ignited by the question of whether the practice would be permitted in the new western territories.[3] Supported by a broad and multiracial coalition of activists, the movement was especially strong in Quaker and evangelical Protestant churches in New England. A member of a well-off white family, Whitney was affiliated with the Boston-based abolitionist movement. While others wrote editorials and gave speeches in favor of the cause, she used her skill as an artist to depict the humanity, intelligence, and self-awareness of the black race (as it was imagined at that time), and black women in particular. As is evident in its longer title, *Africa* was inspired by Psalm 68:31: "Princes shall come out of Egypt and Ethiopia shall soon stretch forth her hands unto God." Referencing this biblical verse, the statue celebrated the African continent as a center of ancient civilization. Opposing theories of black racial inferiority, it dignified contemporary African peoples as equals in the eyes of God. Rendering *Africa* both legible and sympathetic to her intended audience, Whitney gave her a neoclassical form, half clad in a toga and with noticeably Greek features. As art historian Melissa Dabakis has noted, Whitney took a constructivist approach to her subject, assuming that one could simply visually recode racial representation.[4] However this attempt at aesthetic translation was not uniformly well received. While her intent was to lend *Africa* the dignity of Western artistic tradition, Whitney struggled to reconcile classical iconography with the stereotypical representations of black female bodies familiar to her audience. This struggle became a central theme in the critical reception of her statue.

Africa became an object of fascination, attracting more attention than any other artwork on display at the Academy's 1865 exhibition. In the art press, Whitney's attempt to render a black woman in neoclassical form attracted ambivalent, if not openly hostile, responses. While some critics praised her ambition, others criticized the statue for its lack of "realism." *Africa*, they said, did not represent a "real negress" because the features and hair were too Anglicized.[5] The language used to denounce the piece suggests that while Whitney's visual vocabulary deliberately resisted popular stereotypes, some critics were disappointed not to see those stereotypes reflected:

> The face is not the negro face nor any variety of it, nor is the head the negro head. Miss Whitney has only half dared, and between realism and idealism has made a woeful fall. She has shrunk from the thick lips, the flattened nose, the woolly hair; and in striving to suggest forms which a great artist would have accepted with a brave unconsciousness, she has succeeded in making only a debased type of the Caucasian breed. . . . Call a statue "Africa" and it is the first essential that the forms should suggest, at least, the African race.[6]

The same suggestion was made more kindly by Whitney's friend, Thomas Wentworth Higginson, a Unitarian minister and prominent abolitionist, who suggested that "Africanized features" would be an "added triumph" to the message that the statue conveyed. Of *Africa*, he wrote, "She must rise as God made her or not at all."[7] In other words, racial body markers represented an essential and innate truth that could not and should not be eliminated. Because *Africa* was seen as an inauthentic figural representation of the black race, she was deemed unworthy as an aesthetic representation of the abolitionist cause.[8]

One of the most critical reviews of *Africa* appeared in a local art journal, the *New Path*. Published by the "Association for the Advancement of Truth in Art," the *New Path* was founded in 1863 by the architects Peter B. Wight, Russell Sturgis, and several like-minded friends. Heavily influenced by John Ruskin and the English Pre-Raphaelite movement, they were passionately opposed to conventional forms of artistic representation, believing that only strict adherence to nature could produce original and vital art forms.[9] The magazine's criticism of *Africa* echoed that given to a contemporary statue, the American sculptor Harriet Hosmer's *Zenobia in Chains* (1859). Exhibited at the Great Exhibition of the Industry of All Nations in London in 1862, this statue depicted the Queen of Palmyra (Syria) walking in the procession of her conqueror, the Roman emperor Aurelian. While *Africa* was deemed too idealized to depict a black woman, the *New Path* rejected Hosmer's decision to stain the skin of her marble figure a pinkish brown, and criticized the sculptor for giving the queen the "face of a common, housekeeping type."[10] Whether augmented by accepted visual markers of racial difference or not, the use of historical models was deemed insufficient and unhelpful when it came to the artistic representation of enslaved black women. Hosmer and her fellow sculptors were advised to abandon allegory altogether and to put their skills to better use portraying contemporary heroes of the abolitionist movement. Significantly, the magazine suggested a white woman, Harriet Beecher Stowe, as a real life abolitionist heroine worthy of artistic representation.

In contrast to the unsatisfactory *Africa*, the *New Path* critic pointed to other works in the exhibition he believed more truthful and aesthetically pleasing. It so happened that the fortieth exhibition of the National Academy contained a portrait of a contemporary African American woman: Elihu Vedder's *Jane Jackson, Formerly a Slave* (1864). This modest tondo depicted the bowed head of an older woman, her face partially obscured by a headscarf. Vedder had drawn the portrait from life, using a local street vendor as a model. The *New Path* praised it as "wonderfully fine, full of expression and full of truth."[11] From the perspective of the critic, Vedder's painting was notable for its naturalism: his depiction of Jane Jackson was that of an authentic African American woman. In its review of the Academy's fortieth exhibition, the *New Path* put things in proper order. According to the magazine's worldview, abstracted, allegorical representations of black women as queens or other symbols of nationhood were rejected, while "realistic" depictions of black Americans were praised when shown in their expected contexts. Most significantly the *New Path* review concluded by suggesting that both Whitney and Hosmer would be better tasked with another form of sculpture: carving naturalistic ornaments for the as-yet-unfinished National Academy of Design building.[12] In one sense this comment was demeaning; the two women were recognized artists fully capable of creating aesthetic products in their own right. To suggest they take on the role of architectural carvers was to belittle them. However, in drawing attention to these ornaments the critic for the *New Path* had another intention. Carved by stonemasons working under the conditions of "free labor," they are key to understanding the larger political meaning of the Academy building.

The National Academy, the Gothic Revival, and the Emerging American Race

Designed when he was only twenty-three-years old, Wight's National Academy building was a major public commission heavily freighted with meaning because of its program and because of the time and place in which it was built. Beyond its pragmatic function, public architecture assumes a semiotic role as an emblem or sign of cultural identity, and in this period cultural identity was defined in terms of race. In the evolutionary thinking of the nineteenth century, a race was considered mature only when it fully embraced the arts, when it discovered its own forms of aesthetic expression. In these terms the United States barely registered because its peoples were not considered established as a coherent racial group with an intelligible formal aesthetic. In his *History of Architecture in All Countries* (1862–1867), the Scottish architectural historian James Fergusson claimed that the puritanical beliefs of the English colonial settlers had hampered the evolution of a national style.[13] In this sense North America was on a par with the African continent, he claimed; the poverty of vernacular architecture in both places reflected a lack of cultural development. For Fergusson, Americans were simply too pragmatic to bother with art. The result, he argued, could be seen in their "ugly" cities and architecture, in the haphazard and indiscriminate use of ornament on their buildings. The typical American, he wrote, would be perfectly satisfied by the "invention of a self-acting machine" that would produce plans of cities and buildings in classical and Gothic styles, "at so much per foot square, and save all further trouble or thought."[14] The same criticism was frequently voiced in the *Crayon*, a New York–based art journal published from 1855 to 1861.[15] While the country had a wealth of raw material at its disposal, the *Crayon* claimed, this material was seldom put to use in the manufacture of "articles of taste and refinement—matter made beautiful."[16] Instead designers relied on feeble imitation of foreign models, frequently mingling different architectural styles together indiscriminately. The result, in the buildings of contemporary New York, especially the commercial palaces lining Broadway, was vulgarity. The solution, the magazine editorialized, was to promote national schools of art in order to educate Americans in good design and to elevate their taste as consumers.

In this critical context, the new National Academy of Design building was to be both agent and symbol of change, proof that Americans had developed an aesthetic sense reflecting a mature culture. Founded in 1825, the Academy was a private organization modeled after the Royal Academy in London and supported by well-off patrons from the emerging mercantile class.[17] Under the influence of Hudson River school painters Thomas Cole, Asher B. Durand, and George Caleb Bingham, it focused on promoting naturalistic art, rejecting aesthetic convention in order to more truthfully represent the American landscape and its people. Prior to 1865 the Academy had no building of its own, offering classes and exhibitions in a series of rented rooms including the gallery of the Society Library on Leonard Street, and the Tenth Street Artists' Studios. Following an aborted attempt to construct its own premises at Broadway and Bleecker Street during the 1850s, in 1860 the organization explored the purchase of a new site with the aim of erecting a permanent building. In November of that year the trustees, with Durand as chairman, purchased a rectangular lot on the northwest corner of Fourth Avenue and Twenty-Third Street.[18] Only a few blocks north of Union Square, then the city's most stylish shopping and entertainment district, this was at the time a fashionable area. With regard to the proposed building, the trustees set out a basic brief: it was to be three stories tall, with rooms for a School of Design on the ground floor, a suite of reception rooms and a lecture hall on the first floor, and exhibition galleries above. They invited three local architects to compete for the commission: Richard Morris Hunt, Leopold Eidlitz, and Jacob Wrey Mould.

There was little doubt that the entries would be in the Gothic Revival style. Popularized in Germany, France, and England, the style was already well established in New York City, especially for churches. Existing examples included Richard Upjohn's Trinity Church (1841–1846) on lower Broadway and James Renwick's Grace Church (1843–1846) and Church of the Puritans (1846), both in Union Square.[19] These churches followed an English pattern, with a greater emphasis on ornamental features such as pointed arches than on fealty to Gothic construction methods. In reaction to the work of Upjohn and Renwick, Eidlitz and Mould promoted a different kind of Gothic, massive and robust rather than spindly and ethereal, suitable for secular buildings as well as religious ones. While Eidlitz's St. George's Church on Stuyvesant Square (1846–1856) was relatively restrained, Mould's All Souls Unitarian Church (1855) at Fourth Avenue and Twentieth Street had caused a sensation. Built for the liberal Rev. Dr. Henry Whitney Bellows, All Souls introduced New Yorkers to so-called structural polychromy, in which the natural color of building materials was displayed to decorative effect.[20] With alternating courses of starkly contrasting dark-red brick and pale-yellow stone, All Souls attracted unflattering comparisons to both a zebra and an uncooked beefsteak. By the 1860s tastes had changed and this vigorous and colorful form of Gothic Revival architecture was increasingly accepted as the most appropriate style for public buildings, overturning the neoclassical model that had dominated American architecture since the late eighteenth century.

The National Academy of Design building was to be the most fully realized expression of the mid-nineteenth-century Gothic Revival built in New York City. After petitioning to be included in the competition, the young Wight presented drawings for a building no less audacious than Mould's All Souls. Described in the press as "Italian Romanesque" in style, his design clearly referenced Ruskin's beloved fifteenth-century Doge's Palace in Venice. Taking the form of a cubic palazzo, it was notable for its Gothic arches and for the colorful effect of its stone and marble facades, with horizontal bands of alternating colors on the lower floors and a diagonal checkered pattern above.[21] This effect was magnified by a blind facade on the upper floor, concealing the top-lit exhibition galleries. The absence of windows allowed for an uninterrupted surface of decorative stone and marble topped with an elaborate marble cornice and pierced only by six circular ventilation openings filled with delicate medieval tracery. Besides the use of fashionable polychromy, the principle feature of the facade was a grand entryway featuring a double flight of steps leading up to a highly ornamented entrance door topped by a steep gable (figure 6.3). Every column supporting the stairway was surmounted by a unique capital decorated with carvings depicting plants and foliage (figure

Fig. 6.3 P. B. Wight, National Academy of Design, New York, 1865. Entry staircase from the southwest corner of the building showing the newels of the stairway. *National Academy of Design: Photographs of the New Building*, with an introductory essay and description by P. B. Wight (New York: S. P. Avery, 1886). Courtesy of Metropolitan Museum of Art.

6.4). The boldness of this design clearly appealed to the trustees: although Wight was by far the least experienced of the competitors, and his design was considerably more expensive than what they had allowed for, in March of 1861 they announced him the winner of the competition. The *New York Times* called it "one of the handsomest buildings in the United States, and different from any other edifice in the City. It will combine many novel and beautiful characteristics in the highest style of art and taste. . . . The Gothic renaissance will be the chief style of architecture, with some florid adaptations of the still more modern day."[22] During the following year Wight was asked to make some changes in order to keep costs down. In the process the rounded arches became pointed Gothic ones and the polychromic effect was reduced to only two colors, blue-gray and white. However the realized design, completed in 1865, was not significantly different from his original competition entry. In 1866 the *North American Review* said of it: "It is the first attempt in our country, so far as we are aware, to revive a system of constructive building and natural decoration which has been for a long time neglected in

Joanna Merwood-Salisbury

XI. VIII.

VII.

IX. X.

Fig. 6.4 P. B. Wight, National Academy of Design, New York, 1865. Detail of column capitals. *National Academy of Design: Photographs of the New Building*, with an introductory essay and description by P. B. Wight (New York: S. P. Avery, 1886). Courtesy of Metropolitan Museum of Art.

Europe as well as in America. . . . The only architecture which deserves the name of fine art is based upon laws of constructive beauty and harmony, derived from the study of nature, and adapted to the changing natural wants of man."[23] As this quotation suggests, the Gothic Revival, which seems so heavily mannered to us today, was valued chiefly for its naturalism.

American critics were particularly attracted to the adaptability of the Gothic. Although it was borrowed from a much earlier age, they believed it was ripe for further development. In the biological terms in which architecture was understood, the style had the potential to evolve. While it retained the authority of history, at the same time it had an innate and essential natural logic that would lend its newest expressions the aura of complete originality.[24] As with the fine arts, naturalism was the highest ideal for mid-nineteenth-century American architects. In an essay entitled "American Architecture" (1843, reprinted in the *Crayon* in 1855) the sculptor Horatio Greenough criticized many of his peers for their use of thoughtless mimicry and encouraged them to look instead to the natural world for inspiration: "As the first step in our search after the great principles of construction, we but observe the skeletons and skins of animals. The law of adaptation is the fundamental law of nature in all structures."[25] Crucially, Greenough did not reject the concept of style altogether, and by the 1850s the Gothic style was widely seen as the most beautiful and useful because of its naturalism, or innate organicism. Though clearly based on historical models, its use implied strict adherence to nature and natural principles as the primary model for the arts.

Beyond the purported naturalism of the Gothic Revival, the style's association with the medieval social world and with social reform in the contemporary age also held appeal, even for pragmatic Americans. Eloquently expressed by Ruskin and by Augustus W. Pugin in relation to English society, this association held particular meaning in the context of the upheaval of the Civil War. When the American republic was established in the late eighteenth century, the Greek Revival style was widely adopted for its public architecture. Americans built in this style to reinforce their claim as worthy inheritors of the democratic tradition begun in ancient Greece. The rejection of that style in the 1840s, it has been suggested, was partly because the symbolism of the porticoed Greek temple had become tainted by an outdated idea of nationalism, in particular as a state founded on and supported by the practice of slavery.[26] However it is likely that this negative connotation took hold only later, particularly with reference to the image of the plantation house with its classical pediment and colonnade. Those searching for an overt link between the vogue for the Gothic Revival and an emerging American understanding of race and racial difference may find it in the nineteenth century "Anglo-Saxon" movement described by historian Reginald Horsman.[27] As Horsman explains, beginning in the early part of the nineteenth century many

Joanna Merwood-Salisbury

Americans of northern European origin sought a common national identity in the mythical "Aryan" tribe of northern Europe. According to popular lore the Aryans were a strong, independent, and practical people who had for centuries been steadily conquering westward territories, from their origins in Asia, across the European continent, and eventually the Atlantic. For adherents to this particular narrative of American origins, the Gothic style symbolized the racial connection between the new American race and medieval Germanic tribes with Aryan roots (an idea that was enshrined in the writing of the young Theodore Roosevelt).[28] While there is no evidence of that association in contemporary descriptions of the Academy building, this idea was to become expressed overtly in architectural discourse just a few years later, for example, in the writing of Chicago architect William Le Baron Jenney.[29]

In seeking to understand the meaning of nineteenth century historicism and eclecticism (in which elements of different historical styles are mixed together) for American architects, some scholars have argued that the orientalized Gothic Revival style popularized by Ruskin was attractive because it suggested a privileged cultural and racial lineage of which they might claim to be descendants. In his multilayered analysis of Frank Furness's Pennsylvania Academy of the Fine Arts in Philadelphia (1872–1876), the art historian Martin Berger discusses Furness's eclectic incorporation of Near Eastern, Moorish, and Saracenic architectural motifs.[30] Earlier in the nineteenth century, he notes, such motifs had typically denoted Jewishness and were used in the design of synagogues. The adaptation of these orientalized elements for a fine arts museum, he proposes, signified the passing of culture from Jerusalem (the biblical Holy Land) to the United States: "Unconcerned with stylistic accuracy or geographic precision, a wide cross section of Americans liberally interpreted a host of Near Eastern references as signs of the link between their cultural and religious heritage and an ancient Jewish past."[31] This interpretation is suggestive, and might also be applied to Wight's National Academy of Design building, which shared a similar program, patron, and clientele. However, in the concluding section of this essay I would like to explore another argument, one that might be read in parallel with Berger's. This argument is concerned less with the question of architectural product (the form taken by the building), and more with that of architectural production (the way in which it was built). As we know, for Ruskin and for Pugin the Gothic Revival indicated a rejection of modern architecture with its exploitative division of labor, and an embrace of medieval craft methods of production in which architectural creation was believed to have been a collaborative and cooperative activity. Famously, Ruskin saw this style as a metaphor for a more perfect social harmony. In particular he was obsessed with craft as an antidote to what he saw as the inhumanity of modern industrial production processes. For Ruskin, the medieval stonemason was the ideal model of a free man: drawing on his own skill and imagination to produce his work according to his own methods and pace, he was his own master. By contrast the industrial worker, engaged in back-breaking repetitive tasks and discouraged from thinking for himself was nothing more than a slave to the machine. In the following section I would like to suggest that the Ruskinian celebration of "free labor" associated with the Gothic Revival style had a particular resonance with the "free labor, free soil" ideology of the newly formed Republican Party in the United States, the ideology that was to provide the foundation for ideas of American racial identity in the postbellum years.

The National Academy of Design and the Ideology of Free Labor

When the National Academy of Design building opened in 1865, the construction of a prominent public building in the Gothic Revival style communicated a strong political message in the face of the contemporary crisis. One of the few public buildings realized in New York City during wartime, it was a form of aesthetic propaganda for a particular view of the future of America and the American race, at a time when the city was socially and politically polarized. Besides presenting an innovative and attractive version of the Gothic Revival style, the building was also highly ideological. The moral associations of the style, born out of religious sectarianism in the United Kingdom, were here employed to bolster the cause of the antislavery coalition. Borrowing heavily from Ruskin's favored Venetian Gothic, valued for its admixture of various racial-national styles, both Eastern and Western, the architecture of the National Academy building represented the evolution of different European colonial races into a new American one, relieved of their dependence on the southern slave economy, and coded as white.

The Civil War represented a huge threat to the continued prosperity of New York City. The growth of the American economy in the first half of the nineteenth century was due in large part to the expansion of the plantation system in the south.[32] By the 1840s, the city occupied an important position as a national center for manufacturing and trade. The expansion of its economy was accompanied by rapid population growth as new sources of labor were imported to service industry, and also by ethnic, religious, and racial conflict. While migrants were vital to the success of the manufacturing economy, at the same time they were resented and shunned. So-called "nativists" (predominantly Protestant, American-born workers) clashed with Irish Catholics and free blacks who were willing to work in dangerous conditions for lower wages. The entire city was segregated by class and race: as the wealthy moved farther north up the island of Manhattan, following the path of real estate development, recent immigrants from Europe were consigned to the crowded blocks below Houston Street. Meanwhile the free black community was relegated to far-flung areas such as "Seneca Village," a settlement in the northwestern area of what is now Central Park. City politics were also divided along ethnic lines. After the vote was extended to non-property-holding white males in 1825 the Democratic Party took control of city hall. The party of the working class, the Democrats supported white workers in their claims for improved labor conditions (higher pay and shorter working hours) while at the same time supporting the practice of southern slavery.

From the early nineteenth century racial, class, and religious conflict was enflamed by the debate over abolition, with the various arms of the Protestant church the most adamant proselytizers for the cause. In 1835 the Congregationalist General Assembly passed a resolve stating that "the system of slavery, as it exists in our land, is a sin against God and a violation of the inalienable rights of man."[33] At the Congregationalist Church of the Puritans on Union Square and at nearby Unitarian All Souls the Reverends George B. Cheever and Henry Bellows preached highly contentious weekly sermons condemning the practice. In the 1850s Cheever's sermons drew large crowds, especially during his monthly "prayer for the enslaved" services. Like his Brooklyn-based rival Henry Ward Beecher, Cheever played a powerful role in bolstering support for the abolition of slavery amongst his well-to-do congregation and also in influencing business leaders to support his cause, flattening the complex political and economic positions surrounding the debate into a simple and unassailable moral choice.

But while religious ministers preached the sinfulness of slave ownership, local merchants and their employees had a vested interest in the continuation of the practice. Abolitionism was particularly condemned in the working class press. In 1860 the Democratic Party–supporting *New York Herald* described the Reverends Cheever and Beecher as being locked in a struggle "to see which shall pay the most profound homage to the Almighty n*****. It is to him, rather than to Almighty God, that the incense of prayer and praise is offered."[34] For more than half a century the city had benefitted enormously from the expansion of the cotton economy. In this context, workingmen, merchants, and industrialists alike had strong motivation to support the southern states in the lead up to the Civil War.[35] The outbreak of war in April 1861 caused the majority of New York Democrats to join, reluctantly, with President Lincoln in support of the defense of the Union. However, while the city united in support of Congress and the Union army, it remained deeply divided over the issue of race. This division flared up in July of 1863 during the so-called draft riots, in which working-class white opponents of the draft burnt down a draft office, igniting a riot that quickly spread all over town.[36] The riot was suppressed by the military after three days, but not before the homes, businesses, and bodies of people suspected of supporting abolitionism, both rich and poor, black and white, were violently attacked. Appalled by these events, members of a self-described "intellectual aristocracy" united by wealth and social standing and with a strong sense of civic responsibility dedicated themselves to supporting the local black community and redoubled their efforts to free those enslaved in the Confederate states.[37]

This is the backdrop against which the design and construction of the new National Academy of Design took place. For the members of the Academy, support for abolition was a signifier of class, religious, and political affiliation. Commissioned and designed by members of a powerful minority elite, largely supporters of the newly formed Republican Party, the Academy building was the aesthetic expression of self-declared moral authority over their political opponents. Their new premises was an expression of faith in the future of the nation established on new basis, one in which the old economic alliance between New York City and the southern states was destroyed. The Reverend Bellows summed this up in a speech on the occasion of the laying of the building's cornerstone: "You cannot have true Freedom without true Religion and true Art; nor true Religion without true Art and true Liberty."[38] In this way Bellows tied religious, social, and artistic freedom together, as the joint cornerstones of the American nation.

As a dedicated Gothic Revivalist, Peter B. Wight shared this belief in the essential link between artistic and social freedom. Discussing the Academy building, he emphasized his belief that it was the product of creative freedom rather than lifeless copyism. Several months before the building was completed he signaled his intentions in an article published in the *New Path* entitled "An Important Gothic Building" (his friend Russell Sturgis was the likely author). Published between May 1863 and December 1865, almost exactly coincident with the Academy building's construction, the *New Path* was ideally suited as a publicity vehicle to promote its merits as an exemplary public monument. Sturgis wrote, "The building is designed entirely in accordance with the views on architecture previously expressed in this journal. Indeed it is the first building in America that has been so designed. Two main principles are key: first, that all buildings should be designed in the medieval spirit, in other words should be 'Gothic' and not revived classic of any school; second that all carved ornament should be designed by the workmen who cut it, under such superintendence and instruction as the artist in charge may find necessary."[39] Of all the elements of the Academy building, Wight was proudest of the ornamental carvings based on real plants and flowers. Influenced by Ruskin's passionate advocacy for the dignity of labor in the production of art and craft, he was eager to explain how they had been made. Far more than merely supplementary, these carvings epitomized the spirit of the entire venture. The decorative capitals atop the columns, he explained, were "representative of the facts of nature, generally of leaves."[40] Working under his direction, stonemasons had used real models and photographs to create their own sculptural versions of ivy, oak, chestnut, and maple leaves, along with roses, lilies, and azaleas.

Joanna Merwood-Salisbury

The capitals of the four shafts supporting the arch over the drinking fountain were each carved with a different plant: wild blood root, fern leaves, *Nabalus*, and Indian turnip or jack-in-the-pulpit.

Here Wight was drawing on a well-known model: the Ruskin-inspired Oxford Museum of Natural History (1855–1860) by architects Thomas Deane and Benjamin Woodward. The *Crayon* had earlier cited the Oxford Museum as an important precedent for American museums, suggesting it as a model for the proposed new Museum of Natural History in Cambridge, Massachusetts.[41] Representing natural forms (geological, animal, and vegetal), the choice of materials, decorative schema of the capitals, and wrought iron ornaments of this museum were designed to supplement the museum's mission to educate the public in the natural sciences. According to Ruskin's edict, the stonemasons were encouraged to create freehand ornaments using their own skill and observational power in the Gothic manner. Inspired by the English example, Wight was convinced that the close involvement of craftsmen in the design of carved ornaments for the Academy building "has promised so much for the future both of the workmen and of the arts in America. The workmen were the designers here."[42] As Wight recognized, this process involved valuing the stone carvers' time, not just the objects they produced: it was only possible because the trustees of the Academy allowed him to employ them under a separate contract, by the day, rather than a under contract for services delivered. In this way the artisans were free to take the time necessary to produce truthful and beautiful ornaments.

The carvings created by these men and the sculptures created by Anne Whitney and Harriet Hosmer represented the ideal of American freedom in different ways. While Whitney and Hosmer depicted the degradation of slavery figuratively, the naturalistic ornaments embodied a more abstract ideal of free labor borrowed from Ruskin. Although the sentiment had English origins, the concept of "free labor" employed in the Academy building had a particular meaning in the context of the Civil War. In particular, it had parallels in contemporary political speech. In the rhetoric of the Republican Party, the doctrine of free labor was the principle on which the antebellum nation would be established: all workers would be free to choose the conditions under which they worked. While Republicans did not make abolitionism a part of their original political platform, as the war progressed it became a useful rhetorical tool in the attempt to break up the huge economic and political power of the southern slaveholding states. As historian Anthony E. Kaye explains, Republicans overturned southern rhetoric about the importance of slavery to national prosperity, an idea enshrined in the three-fifths clause of the original Constitution, by reformulating the stakes of western expansion: "They redefined the exclusion of slavery in the western territories as the fulfillment of northerners' aspirations as independent producers. This antislavery vision of expansion was articulated in an ideology of free labor that . . . defined the lot of small commercial farmers as the antithesis of slavery and the foundation of the north as a good society."[43] In the Gettysburg Address of November 1863, President Lincoln was explicit in linking the future of the nation with the abolition of slavery. The practice was not only un-Christian, he claimed, it was also contrary to the founding principles of the republic. Freeing the slaves would mean freedom for all. Even the international workers movement took up this idea. Karl Marx wrote in first volume of *Capital* (1867): "In the United States of America, every independent workers' movement was paralyzed as long as slavery disfigured a part of the republic. Labor in white skin cannot emancipate itself where it is branded in black skin."[44] Believing the war would inspire a great movement for workers' emancipation worldwide, Marx's conclusion was premature. He did not foresee that the free labor ideology would lead to the amassing of great capitalist fortunes generated by factories rather than by plantations, that the freeing of enslaved peoples in the southern states would promote rather than retard the expansion of exploitative systems of production, now industrialized rather than depending on raw human labor.

The rhetoric of free labor had ominous implications for the question of race in America. At the core of the argument was the goal of the industrial North seizing control of the western territories from the slaveholding South. In theory the natural resources of these new territories would be exploited by free whites, leading to a decline in dependence on enslaved black workers and a lessened demand for black labor. Some abolitionists even advocated the expatriation of former slaves to Africa to avoid the founding of a free black class. In this way of thinking, a new American race would emerge on the western frontier, made up of immigrants from the United Kingdom and northern Europe. While still seen as members of different races, the Irish, Germans, Scandinavians, Bohemians, and Slavs were believed more easily assimilated into "American" behaviors, values, and customs—a process celebrated in the writing of Theodore Roosevelt and Frederick Jackson Turner around the turn of the twentieth century. Turner and Roosevelt wrote of the American occupation of the western territories "as the new center of gravity of the nation," a place where a new American race was being formed out of migrants from the Old World.[45] Freed from reliance on black labor and the accompanying threat of miscegenation, this new American race would be "colored white" in the words of historian David Roediger.[46]

In the nineteenth century, the progress of the architectural arts was seen as a reflection of national, and therefore racial, evolution. This theme was central to the discourse on public architecture in New York City during the 1850s and '60s, as evidenced by articles published in the *Crayon* and the *New Path*, in which the central question for the emerging profession was: What kind of architecture would

Joanna Merwood-Salisbury

the American race produce? The aftermath of the Civil War seemed to offer an answer to that question for supporters of the Union cause. In the rhetoric of the time, the nation had emerged out of the conflict stronger than ever, and the crisis was credited with germinating new social and aesthetic forms. President Lincoln and the members of the National Academy of Design both used biological language to describe these outcomes. For Lincoln, the end of the war had resulted in a "new birth of freedom." Emancipation had become an essential component of American national identity (though the meaning of freedom remained ambiguous in a society still firmly attached to the idea of a racial hierarchy). For the Academicians, the war was a "regenerative force" that would produce new and better forms of art and design, and Peter B. Wight's National Academy of Design building was one of its very first expressions. Although based on a historic model, the Gothic Revival–style building was an architecture modeled on organic principles. In its use of natural materials and ornament based on native plants, built by craftsmen in charge of their own labor, it reified the belief in the evolution of a free "native" American race. Not to be confused with Native Americans, this race would be bred in the new western territories from the strong biological rootstock of European settlers, and would be identified as white.

After moving to Chicago following the great fire of 1871, Wight was one of a generation of architects who sought the aesthetic expression of the concept of the American race on the western frontier.[47] While he soon abandoned the Ruskinian Gothic as a visual style, he never gave up his belief in the essential truthfulness of the Gothic Revival and the appropriateness of its principles for modern American building. Through his work as a designer, a critic, and a mentor to the young architects of the Chicago School, he went on to play an essential part in the transformation of the Gothic Revival from a morally correct style to a rational constructive principle, a transformation that enabled the next generation of American architects to untether the concepts of "truth to materials" and "constructive expression" from their original historicist framing into a new and particularly American form of modernism, one that continued to communicate a racialized concept of American identity. Celebrated as a naturalistic product of free labor, Wight's Gothic Revival National Academy of Design helped shape an aesthetic projection of American whiteness.

7

Structural Racialism in Modern Architectural Theory

Irene Cheng

Recent scholarship has revised traditional narratives of architectural modernism (emphasizing industrialization, capitalism, and avant-garde aesthetics) to instead stress the historical contexts of imperialism, colonialism, and migration.[1] We can now recognize that modern architecture was shaped as much by "internal" historical forces as by the kinds of transnational encounters enabled by empire and globalization—epitomized by epiphanies before "primitive huts" at world expositions, experiments in construction techniques first undertaken in the colonies, and countless episodes of travel and emigration. Yet the specific role of racialism—the idea that humankind can be divided into indelible and unequally endowed biological groupings—in the entanglements of modernity, history, empire, and architecture has not been sufficiently recognized.[2] What I want to develop here is the hypothesis that ideas about race were constitutive to the development of modern architectural theory. Specifically, concepts regarding different population groups' distinct mental-cultural aptitudes and pasts helped construct concepts of historicity and architectural progress that were critical to the very idea of what it means to be "modern" and therefore to architectural modernism. If it has become a commonplace that twentieth-century architectural modernism was unthinkable without nineteenth-century historicism—without Europeans becoming aware of their own distinct and relative place within world history—then we must also recognize that this historical self-knowledge required the comparative study of other peoples and cultures, both civilizations from the distant past as well as the racial others that Europeans encountered through imperial expansion, cultures of collection, print publications, and world expositions.[3] In the nineteenth century, many prominent architects searching for an architecture of the future believed that the answer lay in finding the laws or genetic principles governing historical cultural development. Racial theorists—who posited that history was synonymous with racial history—provided several leading architectural thinkers with a useful explanatory framework. Race science became one of several emerging "human sciences" that architects drew on for epistemic legitimacy and to derive a rational, historically conscious theory of design.[4]

While this essay will focus primarily on the most egregious instances, it's fair to say that most nineteenth-century European architects and theorists consciously or unconsciously shared several racial beliefs: First, that mankind could be divided into distinct biological groups marked by inherited physical and intellectual traits; second, that different races and cultures produced characteristic forms of building—identifiable as "styles"; third, that processes of racial evolution, diffusion, and hybridization could help explain transformations in architectural style and, correspondingly, that architecture could be read as evidence of racial history. Lastly, most believed that the variety of architectural forms, and the peoples that produced them, could be hierarchically arrayed along a temporalized scale of progress from the primitive to the modern; the latter was often associated with Germanic (Aryan) peoples who were seen as pioneering the ushering of industrial materials and methods into architecture. Below, I elaborate on how each of these racial ideas manifested itself in late nineteenth-century architectural theory, and how they eventually became subtexts of an emerging modernist architectural consciousness.

The Rise of Race Thinking in the Nineteenth Century

The first half of the nineteenth century witnessed an acute intensification of racialism in Europe.[5] To be sure, eighteenth-century white Europeans held ethnocentric and aesthetic prejudices about the new peoples encountered through colonial conquest and exploration. And it's often said that the modern concept of race was invented during the Enlightenment by natural philosophers such as Carl Linnaeus, Johann Friedrich Blumenbach, and Georges-Louis Leclerc, comte de Buffon, who drew on the period's obsession with classification to produce some of the earliest racial taxonomies. Nevertheless, most thinkers before the nineteenth century hewed to the Christian belief in the essential unity of humankind. Blumenbach, who wrote one of the first modern treatises on race, articulated a relativist view that the "innumerable varieties of mankind run into one other by insensible degrees."[6] The dominant eighteenth-century explanations for racial difference pointed to climate and environment, leaving room for the possibility of adaptation and progress. (Buffon famously thought that Africans who moved to cold climates would whiten in complexion over several generations.[7]) Civilizational hubris was thus tempered by a fundamental belief in human equality and biological uniformity, as well as a tentativeness about the causes of human diversity.

By the early nineteenth century, such attitudes increasingly gave way to a pervasive belief in starkly distinct and deeply engrained racial natures that either caused or retarded cultural development, accompanied by a marked increase in Europeans' sense of their own civilizational superiority.[8] Historians have cited numerous reasons for the rise of virulent race thinking during this period. Chief among these were slavery and imperialism: it is no accident that the slaveholding United States and the leading imperial powers France and England harbored the strongest proponents of racial theory and "science."[9] Beliefs about the inherent superiority of European civilization helped justify imperial subjugation and racial slavery—economic systems that surged to meet large-scale industrialization's need for raw materials and expanded markets. As Hannah Arendt observed, political and economic imperatives drove race science and belief rather than the other way around.[10]

Nineteenth-century racial thinkers aspired to "scientificity." This meant they continued the eighteenth-century obsession with classification, but now focused increasingly on precise measurement, especially of crania, to prove the permanence of racial attributes. Older ideas of cultural and population groups being distributed across geographic space gave way to chronological schema that arrayed different races along a hierarchical and developmental timescale, from the primitive to the most advanced. As the classificatory table was replaced by the historical timeline, European race theorists initiated what the anthropologist Johannes Fabian has called the "denial of coevalness" of the other, consigning nonwhites to a time and a stage of development before and below contemporary Europeans. The period also saw a growing fascination with narratives of racial evolution, decline, diffusion, and hybridization as underlying causes of historical change.

All of these tropes of racial theory were mirrored in architectural thought. In the middle decades of the nineteenth century, architects hotly debated whether they should continue imitating the immutable model of divine nature (the classical position) or, following the model of the biological and geological sciences, try to uncover the objective laws of historical change governing how societies and their cultural products evolve over time. Proponents of the latter position saw their viewpoint as not only more modern and up to date, but also as potentially authorizing the use of various nonclassical styles, from the Gothic to the eclectic to a

Irene Cheng

yet-to-be-discovered modern idiom that would take advantage of new materials like iron and glass. For supporters of classicism, any architecture outside the antique tradition was basically irrelevant. Thus, ironically it was often the more "progressive" advocates of architectural change fighting entrenched academic classicists who turned to anthropology and race science to bolster their ideas about modernity, history, and cultural production. Within this cultural and intellectual context, racial thinking manifested itself in architectural thought in at least three main ways: in the growth of typological theories tying each nation to a race with its own distinct architecture—now with an emphasis on the mental attributes of a population in contrast to the earlier attributions to climate or environment; in narratives of architectural history premised on evolution, diffusion, and hybridization of populations; and in the arrangement of architectural forms into linear and developmental scales, from primitive to modern. Over time, racial themes evolved from a nationalist emphasis on finding the appropriate architecture for a particular country to finding the best expression for the present—that is, for the modern period.

Racial Typologies of Architecture

Paradoxically, it was the arch-classicist and French academician Antoine-Chrysostome Quatremère de Quincy who opened the door to an expanded typology of architecture informed by ethnography. Sylvia Lavin has called him "the first architectural theorist to make a radical break with the tradition of monogenesis"— that is, to suggest multiple origins for architecture besides the classical temple-cum-hut famously idealized by Marc-Antoine Laugier.[11] Influenced by the ethnographic theories of Cornelius de Pauw and Lord Kames, Quatremère de Quincy in 1788 wrote an essay positing not one but three original types of architecture: the cave, created by a hunting people, which would give rise to the monolithic stone architecture of Egypt; the tent, the abode of shepherds and the ur-form of Chinese wooden construction; and the hut, invented by a farming people, which would form the basis of Greek architecture.[12] Whereas the cave led to a monotonous architecture with no outlet for further improvement, the tent was too impermanent and light for meaningful evolution. Only the happy medium of the hut, with its combination of lightness and strength, was susceptible to progressive development. Quatremère de Quincy's theory was still more mythological than empirical, but nevertheless offered a harbinger of subsequent more anthropologically derived, materialist approaches to explaining global architectural diversity. It also foreshadowed a trope of Europeans being considered the people capable of progress and historical advancement, while other groups were condemned to historical stagnation.

We can witness how architectural history became more explicitly racialized over the course of the nineteenth century by comparing Quatremère de Quincy's typology to that proposed by Edward Freeman in *A History of Architecture* (1849).[13] Freeman repeated the schema of the Chinese tent, Egyptian cave, and Greek hut as original types, but added a fourth—the Gothic cathedral whose structure mimicked the "deep forests of the North."[14] Whereas Quatremère de Quincy had cited geography and habit as the conditioning forces for these primitive typologies, Freeman posited a deeper force: "An unfathomable Law of Divine Providence has divided the offspring of our common parents into widely distinguished races: there are certain definite marks stamped deep upon the physical and moral constitution of each, upon their habits, their tone of thought, and above all, their language."[15] This deeper force was race—which Freeman understood in idealist terms as a kind of national genius, traceable to an ancient bloodline. For Freeman, the Gothic, with its soaring vaults and "barbaric grandeur," embodied the purest expression of the "stern and hardy virtues" of the Northman.[16]

In Freeman, we can see one of the guiding axioms for nineteenth-century architects seeking to make sense of the diversity of global architectural forms: the principle that architectural monuments reflected the culture and people who created them at a specific time period—that buildings were the "veritable writing of peoples," as the French critic Hippolyte Fortoul put it in 1841.[17] This idea was already incipient in Johann Winckelmann's attribution of the greatness of Greek art to the felicities of Greek climate and culture.[18] And it was given additional support by the ethos of national romanticism, inspired by Johann Gottfried Herder's notion that each ethnic group possesses a unique *Volksgeist*. Yet the idea of different population groups producing distinct characteristic architecture acquired a more explicitly racialized valence in the nineteenth century, as architects absorbed the tenets of racial science to promote the idea that intrinsic mental characteristics of various peoples could be manifested in constructional systems and ornamental forms. Eric Michaud has given the name "racial attributionism" to the idea, which became dominant in art history, that "individual objects were determined by 'styles,' styles were determined by peoples or nations, and nations by their racial components."[19] Examples of casual racial attributionism were common in mid-century architectural writing. We see it in Owen Jones's *Grammar of Ornament*, a tremendously influential compendium of global ornament generally regarded as promoting a liberal cosmopolitan appreciation of non-Western design.[20] In the book, Jones repeatedly associated formal properties of ornamentation such as proportion and geometry to racial-national mental attributes. For instance, Jones was particularly dismissive of Turkish ornament, which he described as having coarser curves than Persian or Moorish, because it was carved rather than incised. Although he acknowledged the differences were "almost impossible . . . to explain by words," he nevertheless held that the eye could easily distinguish

Irene Cheng

Arabian.   Moresque.   Moresque.

Fig. 7.1 Comparison of "Arabian" and "Moresque" ornament from Owen Jones, *The Grammar of Ornament* (1856). Courtesy of the Getty Library.

between the "works of the refined and spiritual Persian, the not less refined but reflective Arabian, or the unimaginative Turk"[21] (figure 7.1). Stereotypical mental attributes were thus imagined to be legible in aesthetic forms—in proportion, the curvature of a line, the choice of color.

Perhaps the most systematic racial typology of architecture of the period can be found in the writing of Eugène-Emmanuel Viollet-le-Duc, who was deeply influenced by race theorists of the day, especially Joseph-Arthur, comte de Gobineau, author of *Essai sur l'inégalité des races humaines* (1853–1855)—a text promoting the superiority of the white race that would have a notorious afterlife in twentieth-century Germany.[22] Racial ideas pervaded Viollet-le-Duc's writing after 1860, appearing in the *Dictionnaire raisonné de l'architecture française* (1854–1868) and *Entretiens sur l'architecture* (1863–1872), and constituting the central organizing trope of *Histoire de l'habitation humaine* (original French 1875, English translation 1876). The latter, a quasi-allegorical history of dwellings from primordial times to the present, was intended for a juvenile audience—a fact that is more damning than exculpatory; it also did not prevent the work from being read seriously, especially by architects in the United States. Viollet-le-Duc organized the book into chapters, each linking a racial group to a distinct typology of dwelling. He began several chapters with descriptions of the physical and mental attributes of the race, focusing on the traits codified by nineteenth-century race theorists—hair and skin color, the shape of the eyes, the slope and height of the forehead—supplemented with caricatured physiognomic illustrations (figure 7.2). A Central Asian nomad was described as having "copper-coloured oily skin," "a projecting and wide forehead," "loop-like eyes with black pupils," and a "thick short nose," all of which give

Fig. 7.2 Composite of illustrations of racial types from Eugène-Emmanuel Viollet-le-Duc, *Histoire de l'habitation humaine* (1875). Courtesy of University of California at Berkeley Libraries.

Fig. 7.3 Himalayan dwelling, home to the ancient Arya, from Eugène-Emmanuel Viollet-le-Duc, *Histoire de l'habitation humaine* (1875). Courtesy of University of California at Berkeley Libraries.

him a "repulsive aspect."[23] Viollet-le-Duc's characterizations followed the racial stereotypes of the day: Blacks were an "abject race," the Semites were simple, contemplative, and calculating; and the "Arya" were "of great stature and brave . . . like superior beings, born to command."[24] Following the scheme laid out by Quatremère de Quincy, Viollet-le-Duc associated each racial group with a distinct dwelling type, material, and constructional method—the Chinese with trellis-like houses relying on a principle of "agglutination" of wood members, the Turanian race with small stones and mortar, and the Arya with wooden frame construction. The timber house was described as a kind of racial signature, visible even when the Aryans mixed with other races.[25] Or as he put it in another text: "Frame construction characterizes the Aryas, and everywhere one finds it, we are sure to see an immigration, or at least an Aryan influence"[26] (figure 7.3).

What implications did such racial typology carry for architects of the mid-nineteenth century? In the conclusion to *Histoire de l'habitation*, Viollet-le-Duc argued that a knowledge of racial history could be a key to the finding a progressive and national architectural style, implicitly challenging the classical position that there was one transcendent, universal style. Evoking the gnostic dictum "Know thyself," he wrote that by becoming "acquainted with the elementary characteristics of his race or of the races from which he descended," modern man could "improve his dwelling in accordance with his natural proclivities and aptitudes" and, more grandly, "pursue that path of true Progress to which thy destiny calls thee."[27] Racial typological knowledge was essential to discovering a contemporary romantic nationalist architecture, a point he gestured to in *Histoire*: "Every civilized nation has begun to inquire . . . whence it comes, and what are its elements; and it is consequently endeavouring to adopt those original forms in art which are adapted to the genius and requirements of the race to which it belongs. This movement is already very apparent in England, in Germany, in Sweden, and in Russia and it is becoming daily more marked."[28] Viollet-le-Duc extended this argument in *L'art russe* (1877), where he proposed that modern Russian architects look to their Slavic roots for inspiration.[29] But the architecture that he championed most fervently throughout his career was the French Gothic of the twelfth and thirteenth centuries, which he adored for its supposed structural rationalism and its manifestation of a spirit of progress. He called the Gothic the "style arising out of our own genius," as opposed to the borrowed idiom of classicism or the incongruous mixtures of eclecticism.[30] We have already seen with Freeman how racial theory could underpin romantic Gothic revivalism, a view shared by others, including Daniel Ramée in France and George Gilbert Scott in England. Scott called the Gothic the "native architecture of our own race and country," one found in nations "wholly or partially of Germanic origin, in whose hands the civilisation of the modern world has been vested."[31]

What is important to note about Viollet-le-Duc, however, is the particular way he makes this connection between the Gothic and race, via the notion of a special aptitude for rationality. Viollet-le-Duc theorized that the Gothic had emerged from a free class of lay artisans and builders working in newly free French communes in the twelfth and thirteenth centuries. The racial origins of this class lay in the Gallo-Roman peoples who possessed a "natural genius" defined by "supple and innovative natures," and who were "quick to seize upon the practical side of things. They were active and energetic, given to reasoning things out; and they were driven by good sense as much as they were by imagination." These people "never stopped trying to improve."[32] This idea that a white race—whether it was Viollet-le-Duc's "Gallo-Roman" or "Aryan" or the "Anglo-Saxon" in England and America—had a special proclivity for independence, rationality, practicality, and

Irene Cheng

innovation, which was reflected in its architecture, would be critical in modernism's ability to adopt racialized ideas while shedding explicit racism in the early twentieth century.[33]

Racial Diffusion and Hybridization

A corollary to the idea of racial attributionism was the theory that stylistic changes reflected the main motive force of historical change itself, which was understood to be the movements and interactions of different racial groups. The prevailing view among racial theorists of both the monogenist and polygenist schools—opposing groups of thought that cited the origins of humankind from either one or multiple origins—was that the major racial stocks had been established long ago. Since then, the races had spread across the globe, either conquering or crossing with other races.[34] In the nineteenth century, a number of romantic historians, beginning in France but rapidly spreading throughout Europe, popularized the idea of history as a chronicle of racial struggles.[35] The French historians François Guizot and Augustin Thierry (1795–1856), for example, interpreted contemporary French social and political structures as resulting from ancient interactions between races of Gauls, Romans, and Franks. Such narratives were mapped onto the class conflicts of contemporary France: it was often claimed that the French nobility were derived from the Frankish invaders, whereas the commoners and bourgeoisie had descended from a Gallic population. Romantic historians pointed to the fifth century "barbarian invasions" to construct a narrative of a northern people who regenerated a feminine, decadent Roman Europe, propelling it into modernity.[36] Gobineau would extend this racial view of history, famously arguing that race mixing, while widespread and occasionally beneficial—including for the development of the arts—generally led to degeneracy, loss of vigor, and decline of civilizations over the long term.[37]

The idea that history was shaped by racial conflicts, migrations, and admixtures influenced art and architectural historians in the nineteenth century. Michaud has argued that in the early decades of the century, the racial opposition between Germanic and Latinate cultures became one of the principle interpretive tropes structuring historical and art historical writing in Europe.[38] As we have already glimpsed with Freeman and Viollet-le-Duc, racial history was sometimes cited to support romantic nationalist critiques of classicism and eclecticism. But the thesis of racial migration as cause of stylistic development was not limited to proponents of the Gothic. The Englishman James Fergusson, an advocate of the neo-Renaissance, relied on it in penning numerous histories that were some of the first "global" histories of architecture. Fergusson explicitly aimed to write architectural history as ethnography, and deployed race as a central structuring principle. As he explained in the first volume of his *History of Architecture in All Countries* (1865), the characters of the races were constant and unchanging, and the migrations, conquests, and mixture among these racial groups gave rise to different architectural styles. "Progress among men, as among the animals, seems to be achieved not so much by advances made within the limits of the group, as by the supercession of the less finely organized beings by those of a higher class," he wrote.[39] Thus, Fergusson explained that it was the migration of one branch of Aryans southward and their intermixture with a Turanian (yellow) race that had produced the "brilliant" but "evanescent" civilization of classical Greece. The combination of the artistic feeling of the Turanian with the common sense of the Aryan is what enabled creations such as the Parthenon. Yet he also linked miscegenation to inevitable aesthetic degeneration, claiming that when two dissimilar races mixed, they tended to produce a more brilliant but short-lived "stock."[40] Fergusson interpreted Indian architecture through this lens, describing it as having declined from a purer, earlier Aryan-Buddhist phase to a later period characterized by a mixture of Hindu and "Muhamaddan" styles.[41]

For Viollet-le-Duc also, architecture history was the product of racial migrations and interracial struggles. Here again we see the influence of Gobineau, although the architect had a much more positive outlook than the degeneration-obsessed racial theorist.[42] Viollet-le-Duc echoed Gobineau's and Fergusson's understanding that under the right circumstances, racial mixture could be the source of artistic achievement, writing in the *Dictionnaire*: "Any artistic explosion . . . in history is produced through the contact of two different races, . . . [the] intellectual fermentation of natures endowed with different aptitudes."[43] He repeated the idea that Athenian architecture was attributable to a racial mixture of Aryans and Semites.[44] Elsewhere, he posited that the monuments of Uxmal, Tulum, and Chichén Itzá were created by a white race—or possibly a mixture of white and yellow—migrating across the Bering Strait; he was convinced that the present inhabitants of South America could not be responsible for such monumental constructions.[45] Even more insistently than in Fergusson, the protagonists of Viollet-le-Duc's racialized architectural history were the Arya, whom he described in *Histoire de l'habitation* as a self-sufficient nomadic tribe pushed out of their homeland in the Himalayas. As they migrate west, the Arya subjugate, enslave, and intermix with local populations, spawning new racial subgroups—including the Dorians (Aryan-Hellenes), the Franks (Aryan-Germans), and the Gauls (Aryan-Celts).[46] As one character in the book voices: "The man of noble race [the Aryas] is born to fight to establish his power over the accursed races, and to be the master of the earth."[47]

Viollet-le-Duc's racialized approach to architectural history met with contemporary objections, but nevertheless influenced and resonated with other architects

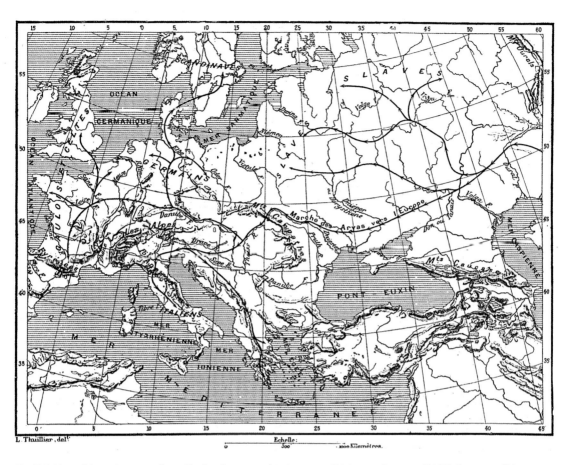

Fig. 7.4 Map of Aryan Invasions, from Charles Garnier and A. Ammann, *L'Habitation humaine* (1892). Courtesy of University of California at Berkeley Libraries.

of his time.[48] In their *L'Habitation humaine* exhibit at the 1889 Paris World Exposition, Charles Garnier and Auguste Ammann would pick up on the idea of Aryan migration as the motive force in the diffusion and development of modern European culture, even including a map depicting Aryan movements in the exhibition catalog (figure 7.4). Joanna Merwood-Salisbury has demonstrated that nineteenth-century American architects like William Le Baron Jenney, Henry Van Brunt, and John Root read the racial architectural histories of Viollet-le-Duc, Garnier, and Fergusson, and absorbed their ethnographically framed accounts of architectural history to formulate the notion that a new American race (composed of mixed Europeans, inheritors of Aryan-Saxon blood) would bring about a strong, virile architecture in the American West.[49] Variations of an Aryan myth thus permeated European and American architectural histories, contributing to French, American, and English architects' self-understanding of their own special roles and capacity for creating a new modern architecture.

Racial Timelines

A great many of these racialized architectural histories depicted white Aryans as agents of historical change whose architecture was uniquely capable of progress and development. Other, weaker groups were implicitly or explicitly portrayed as prone to stagnation or conquest. This differential racial capacity for progress reflected the theories of anthropologists, who in the nineteenth century began transposing the spatial dispersal of human groups into a temporal schema.[50] Races were no longer understood simply as diverse populations inhabiting various areas of the globe, but as occupying different positions in the timeline of history, in a kind of temporalized reprisal of the Great Chain of Being. Such theories offered various schema for dividing history into stages. Europeans labeled certain groups as "passive," "savage," "primitive," and "childlike"—generally Native Americans, sub-Saharan Africans, and inhabitants of the recently discovered South Sea Islands—placing these at one end of the timescale; Europeans invariably positioned themselves at the opposite end. The consensus among many anthropologists, race scientists, and historians was that European societies had evolved through historical time, whereas non-Western cultures remained "arrested" at their moment of inception, suspended in a nonhistorical mode. The introduction of evolutionary theory added another valence to this hierarchical timescale: now the "lower races" were ones that had evolved least, represented atavisms, or were biologically weaker and thus disposed to being dominated. Technology and empire enabled Europeans to imagine themselves as predestined by biological aptitude to advance, conveniently ignoring that their economic and technological development was enabled by raw materials, labor, and markets appropriated through imperial conquest, while disrupting colonized countries' own trajectories.[51]

This hierarchical, racialized temporal scale was reflected in numerous architectural histories of the period. While chronological arrangements were not new, almost all narratives before the nineteenth century were limited to European and Near Eastern examples and reprised the supposed lineage of Egypt to Greece to Rome to western Europe. Growing awareness of the wide range of cultural production from around the world presented European architects with a conundrum over how to transpose geographical space into the linear, chronological arrangements. The arbitrariness behind white Europeans' placement of other cultures in a linear timescale can be seen, for instance, in Fergusson's changing position on where to place the architecture of Asia and America within his chronology. In his 1855 *Illustrated Handbook of Architecture* (1855), they were cordoned off in a separate section in the beginning of the book. A decade later, in *History of Architecture in All Countries from the Earliest Times to the Present Day* (1865), he inserted these

Fig. 7.5 Charles Garnier and A. Ammann, *L'Habitation humaine* exhibition at the 1889 Universal Exposition in Paris. Courtesy of Gramstorff Collection, Department of Image Collections, National Gallery of Art Library, Washington, DC.

continents' production between the volumes on the Medieval/Byzantine and Modern periods (i.e., European architecture from the Renaissance forward).[52] The author brushed aside objections to his imprecise chronology, reasoning that these traditions were of "far less consequence" than the European, and anyway, being based on instinct rather than intellect, they were incapable of progress.[53]

Another prime example of the civilizational developmental timeline manifested in architecture can be found in Garnier and Ammann's aforementioned exhibit of human habitation at the 1889 Paris Exposition. At the exhibit, reconstructed examples of houses from around the world were arrayed in a linear arrangement, from "primitive" to advanced, all under the shadow of the Eiffel Tower (figure 7.5). The message was clear: some cultures were assigned to prehistory, or no history at all, whereas others were hurtling into an engineered future of iron and glass. This microcosmic timeline was mirrored in the exhibition as a whole, where a hierarchy was established between the Western countries on the Champ de Mars and non-Western architectures on the Esplanade des Invalides (itself bifurcated into a few societies represented in monumental architectures and others relegated to ethnographic villages). In the accompanying book *L'Habitation Humaine* (1892), Garnier and Ammann placed Chinese, Japanese, Eskimo, Aztec, Incan, African, and Australian dwellings in a section entitled "Peoples Isolated from the General Movement of Humanity"—this followed a section devoted to civilizations shaped by "Invasions of the Aryans" encompassing Europe, Iran, and India.

One ostensible complication in these linear timescales that must be mentioned is the phenomena of modernist primitivism, which impacted architecture as well as the visual arts. Owen Jones is exemplary of primitivist ideology, which sees African or Oceanic cultural products as key to the "regeneration of a tired, degenerate, vulgarized, mechanical European civilization," as Robert J. C. Young puts it.[54] In *Grammar of Ornament* Jones critiqued what he saw as the degraded industrially produced ornament of the day, counseling his fellow Europeans to learn from the aesthetic output of more "primitive" cultures: "If we would return to a more healthy condition, we must even be as little children or as savages: we must get rid of the acquired and artificial, and return to and develope [*sic*] natural instincts." Jones thus distinguished between the artificial culture of the modern West and the "savage," "natural," "childlike," "instinctual" culture of the non-West. It is important to recognize how primitivism, although ostensibly valuing non-Western cultures, relies precisely on the idea of the linear developmental scale—that some cultures are closer to nature while others are more historically developed. Although Jones argued for the universality of the instinct to ornament, his words repeatedly affirmed the idea of a scale of progress: "As we advance higher, [we go] from the decoration of the rude tent or wigwam to the sublime works of a Phidias and Praxiteles."[55] Jones's book followed an ostensibly crystal-clear chronological schema—beginning with examples of the "Ornament of Savage Tribes" (which he connected to tattooing practices) and ending with examples of European (Elizabethan and Italian) ornament, before finally closing with several plates of leaves illustrated "from nature" intended to serve as models for contemporary English design (figure 7.6). This kind of racial timeline of architecture would be given iconic form in Banister Fletcher's Tree of Architecture diagram, which depicted the development of architecture as stemming from multiple ancient origins: While the branches depicting non-Western architecture are short and end close to the trunk, constituting so many "dead ends," a stout central trunk rises in the center tracing the progress from Greek to Roman to various early modern European national architectures, up to the modern revival styles at the peak (figure I.1).

Irene Cheng

Female Head from New Zealand, in the Museum, Chester.

Fig. 7.6 Tattooed Maori face, from Owen Jones, *The Grammar of Ornament* (1856). Courtesy of University of California at Berkeley Libraries.

Toward a Deracinated Modern Architecture

Racial theories of architecture did not simply disappear in the twentieth century, but underwent a process of sublation. David Theo Goldberg has described a shift between two kinds of racialism occurring in the mid-to-late nineteenth century, from an older ideology of racial naturalism which positioned non-Europeans as inherently inferior, to a racial historicism that deemed these same groups as immature and less developed. Racial historicism, Goldberg writes, underpinned movements like abolition, assimilationist colonial regimes, as well as more recently the ideal of color blind "racelessness" as the political teleology of modernization.[56] This shift from racial naturalism to racial historicism is reflected in the way that the narrative of a racial developmental timeline began to predominate over the older ideas of racial typology and diffusionism in architectural discourse. As nationalism gave way to a cosmopolitanism among elite European cultural practitioners, the question "In what style shall we Germans / French / English / Americans (or Anglo-Saxons / Aryans / Gallo-Romans) build?" increasingly gave way to the problem: "What is modern architecture?" The notion of a temporal progression from primitive to modern was retained, but the attendant concept of inherent racial fixity was sublimated. In the process, race became first subtext and then a specter of modernism.

This process of the sublation of race can be witnessed in the writing of Adolf Loos, an architect who bridged the nineteenth and twentieth centuries in more ways than one. Often lost in the contemporary understanding of Loos as prophet of unornamented modernism is the way his definition of the modern is deeply steeped in the racial logics of the previous century. Indeed, in his famous essay "Ornament and Crime" (1913), Loos borrowed Owen Jones's association of ornament with "primitive" peoples but went even further in arguing that the use of ornament should not just be reformed but abolished. In labeling ornament a "crime," Loos declared it an aesthetic practice suited only for "Papuans," criminals, and other inhabitants of the lower rungs of the evolutionary ladder and not for modern Europeans. In his intentionally provocative treatment, ornamentation—or its lack—became an index of cultural development, a process that he described colorfully in terms of a racial timescale with a recapitulationist spin: "The human embryo in the womb passes through all the evolutionary stages of the animal kingdom. When man is born, his sensory impressions are like those of a newborn puppy. His childhood takes him through all the metamorphoses of human history. At two he sees with the eyes of a Papuan, at four with those of an ancient Teuton, at six with those of Socrates, at 8 with those of Voltaire."[57]

The racial subtext of Loos's modernist credo was not limited to the association of ornament with the lower racial and social orders, but also incorporated the affiliation of Aryanism with progress. Across the corpus of his writing, the inhabitants of New Guinea (at the time split under French, German, and British colonial authorities) and "Red Indians" occupied one end of Loos's scale of progress, while white men—particularly the English and Americans—occupied the other. He idealized these two nations because to him they best embodied "Germanic culture" (*germanische Kultur*)—even more than his native Austria or Germany, which he believed had become too "Latinized" and where a lingering attachment to ornament was a sign of degeneration. As the above analysis suggests, Loos was drawing on well-established racialist tropes. In the same way that Fergusson and Viollet-le-Duc had seen the Aryans as the active agents of history, Loos equated future progress with the extension of a specific racial genius: "It is Germanic culture which, like a mammoth under the ice of the tundra, had been preserved intact in the British Isles, and now, alive and kicking, is trampling down all other cultures. In the twentieth century there will only be one culture dominating the globe."[58] This conquering Germanic culture would be unornamented, utilitarian, and modern. It would differ from the ethnically heterogeneous Austro-Hungarian Empire, where an hour's train journey from Vienna, Loos observed, "We meet people who appear to us more foreign than people who live thousands of miles above sea level. We have nothing in common with them."[59] Written in the context of Vienna, a city seen as straddling the eastern and western halves of the empire, Loos's perspective was that of the German-speaking metropolitan condescending toward those in the provinces, including Slavs, Czechs, and other "atavistic" ethnic minorities.[60] In contrast, Loos imagined that in America there were no such laggards, no chasm between city and country dwellers, no racial inequality: the people walked faster, they bathed more frequently, the workers labored more efficiently. As Janet Stewart has observed, Loos's American utopia was an "Anglo-Saxon" America, the America celebrated in the Chicago World's Fair.[61]

Loos equated the universalization of Germanic culture with the modern society of the future. His views departed from the nineteenth-century race-and-architecture theorists in one regard, however: for Loos, Germanic culture was not the privileged domain of Germanic people. At the end of the essay "Plumbers," Loos raised the "shameful" possibility that the "Japanese could attain Germanic culture before the Austrians."[62] Although this ironic statement was an obvious instance of nationalist baiting, it also evidenced a shift from the naturalist racialism characteristic of the previous century, toward a historicist racialism in which modernity was still implicitly associated with northern and/or western Europeans, but not intrinsically or exclusively. It was only a step further to erase the term "Germanic" while retaining a definition of modernity premised on what had been established as Germanic racial attributes—inventiveness, rationality, practicality, and a will to improve and progress. The imperative to be up to date, or modern, began to trump adherence to a specific racial-national tradition.

In the 1920s, spurred variously by an anti-nationalist ethos following World War I, socialist internationalism, and a belief in technology and global trade's connective, leveling capacities, most avant-garde architects began to speak a language of internationalism—proclaiming their desire to supersede national differences and to construct a common, universal modernism.[63] In 1932 Henry-Russell Hitchcock and Philip Johnson formalized, coopted, and some would say perverted these internationalist impulses within European avant-garde architecture when they organized the International Style show at the Museum of Modern Art. In the process, they not only divested modernism of its political charge (an oft-cited critique), but also stripped away the vestiges of racial-national particularity in favor of a putatively universal aesthetic suited to the present and future. Modernism was to be raceless. The new architectural style, they wrote, "exists throughout the world, is unified and inclusive, not fragmentary and contradictory."[64] The pretense of universalism was belied by the fact that of sixty-two projects in the published catalog, only one was by a non-European or non-American architect (Mamoru Yamada of Japan). Thus, a style whose characteristic features of lack of ornamentation and utilitarianism had been associated only half a century earlier with the superiority of a particular race was now tied to the transcendence of national and racial divisions.[65] Yet like the ideology of color blindness that it mirrored, modernism continues to be haunted by its racialist genealogy, which has yet to be fully exhumed.

Irene Cheng

PART III

RACE AND NATIONALISM

8

Race and Miscegenation in Early Twentieth-Century Mexican Architecture

Luis E. Carranza

The deepest and most disturbing lesson taught by the Ciudad Universitaria [University City] is the questionable role that contemporary architecture has played, in some instances, away from its birthplace. . . . The powerful stirring of native impulses should force upon our architects a re-evaluation of building concepts, in relation to ethnic traditions and needs. Has our generation, in an exuberant realization of technical forms for a technical civilization, stepped carelessly over the subtle and irrepressible demands of populations outside the orbit of technology? It is perhaps time for us to learn from the mistakes of too-ardent camp followers that even economic leadership can be much more effective when it respects and encourages the cultural inheritance of peoples.

Sybil Moholy-Nagy, "Mexican Critique" (November 1953)

Sybil Moholy-Nagy's "Mexican Critique," one of the earliest international evaluations of the new campus for the Universidad Nacional Autónoma de México (UNAM), is paradoxical in its observations (figure 8.1). One is not sure whether she is ruthlessly criticizing the architectural direction that Mexico took and that reached a particular culmination in the early 1950s or if she is subtly suggesting that architects throughout the world need to learn from the Mexican example. Her position here is doubly paradoxical as her piece harshly criticized most of the architectural decisions that tied the university to other (international) modern experiments and that gave it its modernist character. Nevertheless, at the crux of her observations is the role that ethnicity—whether for good or bad—has played in the development of this modern style of architecture in Mexico. What is clear is that she didn't see the university's design as one example in a long process that, on the one hand, was centered on investigations about which Mexican historical roots or traditions could be applied to modern architecture and that, on the other

Fig. 8.1 Gustavo Saavedra, Juan Martinez, and Juan O'Gorman (Juan O'Gorman murals), Main Library, Universidad Nacional Autónoma de México (UNAM), Mexico City, 1946-1952.

hand, was partially based on a discourse of miscegenation. That discourse would ultimately find itself articulated in art, architecture, and in the desires for plastic integration that found an idealized expression in the construction of the University City.

At the beginning of the twentieth century, cultural debates in Mexico revolved around the revival of pre-Hispanic traditions because these represented the Mexican "race," pure and uncorrupted by the colony, in contrast to a nationalist architecture derived from a contemporary understanding of the people, their character, and culture that would have been forged from the colonial period through modern times. Both positions were central to the project of creating a sense of Mexican nationalism centered on notions of common heritage, language, and traditions that would reduce conflicts between different social groups. As this nationalism was also rooted in contemporary ideas of race and racial mixture as means to characterize a "people," the influence of late nineteenth-century European racial discourses and their contestation in the early twentieth century

Luis E. Carranza

played a central role in its definition. Similarly, notions of the effects of racial mixing and eugenics that tinged some of the arguments for nationalism were translated as broader concepts to characterize forms of social or cultural change rather than racial ones. Definitions regarding the purity of the Mexican race and of a Mexican hybrid race—or mestizo, as it would be called—were central to the development of theories and projects for a nationalist architecture as well as contested terrains in regard to what defined the modern Mexican people in the first half of the twentieth century.[1] In this way, the very definitions of race could be seen, in and of themselves, as expressions of "fictive ethnicities," to use Étienne Balibar's term. These "constructed" forms of ethnicities were intended to interpellate subjects into a collectivity as a way to propose (or impose) a sense of unity and historical mission congruent with the ideals of the state and in opposition to a universalistic representation of the people.[2] The very idea of race was extremely labile and open-ended within the Mexican context; it was used as more of a descriptor of a historical lineage or social construction of identity than as a notion of biological difference.

During the Mexican Revolution (1910–1920), a keen interest in and awareness of the importance of the pure, "uncorrupted" past began to develop as a reaction to the Europeanizing tendencies of the Porfirio Díaz regime, which the revolution removed from power. As a result, in the aftermath of the conflict, the pre-Hispanic past was not only championed and idealized, but it also came to stand as an example of the true spirit of the Mexican race. As such, it could still have a strong impact in the present. The social agenda inherent within the Mexican Revolution seems to have enabled many cultural producers and intellectuals to rethink the pre-Hispanic past. This type of thinking was exemplified in Manuel Gamio's *Forjando Patria* (Forging Nationhood, 1916), published during the revolution (figure 8.2).

Gamio, a Columbia University–educated anthropologist who studied under Franz Boas,[3] argued that social equality could be achieved through education and changes in social relations between the indigenous population and other social classes. This view reflected Boas's own ideas of the processes of cultural development, which upended the belief that certain races were culturally "inferior." Instead, in *The Mind of Primitive Man* (1911), Boas argued that knowledge was an expression of the environment, social conditions, and the role of traditions of different groups.[4] As a student of Boas, Gamio saw the modern understanding of "primitive" cultures ultimately as a reflection of the contrast between the observer's and "primitive" person's particular environment, social configuration, and relationship to tradition. Such outlooks, he believed, could be overcome with a different perspective on how culture was produced.

For Gamio, art was one field in which cultural barriers could be removed. He

M. GAMIO.

ORJANDO
PATRIA

PRO=NACIONALISMO

MEXICO·   MCMXVI·

Fig. 8.2 Manuel Gamio, *Forjando Patria*, cover, 1916.

sought to foster an appreciation for pre-Hispanic art despite dominant modern and Western aesthetic sensibilities. Gamio believed that in order to appreciate pre-Hispanic art, one needed to be familiar with the culture that had produced it. He understood that in order to redeem and create a shared national culture—one of the bases for a strong nationalism—a transformation and melding of aesthetic taste needed to take place. This meant uniting the preferences of the indigenous class, which he saw as based on pre-Hispanic traditions, with those of the middle class, which were based on European traditions. Furthermore, he argued, it was unfair to judge pre-Hispanic cultural artifacts through a European lens and, at the same time, attempt to emulate the pre-Hispanic by simply copying its forms and styles; this, he said, would only create a confused and desolate hybrid.[5]

Mexico had the three elements that made a country strongly nationalistic according to Gamio: it was composed of a people who were members of the same race, spoke the same language, and shared the same culture or cultural manifestations. Most importantly for him, its people also had a shared past. This determined what they valued in the present as well as what they understood about their country in political, social, and ethical terms. Because of these shared elements, Gamio postulated that the unification of the different races and classes would lead to the disappearance of linguistic and cultural barriers and a modern, coherent, and homogeneous culture would arise—a position in line with contemporary theories regarding the construction of Mexican identity through the cultural mixing of races. For Mexican art to be truly Mexican, Gamio wrote, it had to be "its own; it had to be national; it had to reflect in an intensified and embellished way the joys, the sorrows, life, the soul of the people."[6] And for him, the means to achieve the full understanding of present Mexican culture was being materialized by the revolution itself, in the way that it was hybridizing the different races and classes. Gamio concluded *Forjando Patria* by noting that the Mexican Revolution allowed for "the fusion of races, the convergence and fusion of cultural manifestations, linguistic unification, and economic equilibrium between the social groups."[7]

While some artists and architects were developing a syncretic art—backed by José Vasconcelos under the Ministry of Education and discussed later in this chapter—others followed a strand of Gamio's beliefs and explored the possibilities of cultural production based solely on pre-Hispanic ideals. This difference became central in debates regarding nationalism in modern art and architecture in Mexico. One of the advocates for pre-Hispanic architecture was Manuel Amábilis. Born in Mérida, Yucatán, Amábilis studied at the École Spéciale d'Architecture in Paris.[8] Throughout his life, much of his architectural works and writings responded to the pre-Hispanic and, more specifically, Mayan legacy of Mexico. Amábilis's writings—such as *La Arquitectura Precolombina de México* (1929, reprinted 1956),[9] *Donde* (1933), *Mística de la Revolución Mexicana* (1937), and *Los Atlantes de Yucatán*

(1963)—addressed the importance of drawing on pre-Hispanic historical sources for the development of a modern Mexican culture. He also served as professor of architectural theory in the School of Architecture at the National University in Mexico City.

Amábilis's general idea of architectural production for Mexico was centered on the importance that he placed on "abstract aesthetic systems" (*modalidades abstractas de estética*) that could be found throughout pre-Hispanic art and architecture. While considering himself a traditionalist, he contended that the imitation and reproduction of arts, decorative details, and styles of the past was inappropriate for the present since contemporary needs were different. Rather than simple imitation, Amábilis called for a different form of traditionalism: "My belief is precisely based on the fact that I consider, probably to the surprise of our young architects, that architecture must be *functional*, as it has never ceased to be. In fact, if we define our architectural traditionalism as the archive—enriched through time—of the technical and aesthetic systems of our race, it is evident that this archive is one of the functions that our architecture needs to express."[10] The contemporary Mexicans, in turn, were capable of understanding, interpreting, and translating pre-Hispanic works into the present precisely because these existed in and resulted from the same, specific geographical location. The Spanish colonizers, and the recent dictatorship of Porfirio Díaz, he believed, were not able to erase the "racial sediment" of Mexicans, as it was part of the "ethnic roots of the people."[11] Here, as in other of Amábilis's writings, "race" stood as a metonym for the distinctive cultural, aesthetic, and other traits of pre-Hispanic peoples who occupied what is now contemporary Mexico.[12]

The task of the postrevolutionary government was to make race operative as a construction that would question class structures and introduce the Mexican people to traditional heritage. In this way, according to Amábilis, the state would "raise class consciousness" and "place in front of the people all of the social values, so that by knowing what they are capable of doing they can rekindle within their soul, at the conjure of its past greatness, the creative impulse characteristic of the Mexican race. . . . [By awakening the race from] its long sleep, a resurgence of Mexican art, well adapted to our actual conditions, will take place."[13]

Amábilis sought to bring the collective unconscious of traditions and sensibilities that had lain dormant since pre-Hispanic times into the present environment and social configurations where they would adapt to become more universal, cosmopolitan, and hybridized. This meant, for example, that modern architecture would be functional in its response to "the functions characteristic of the Mexican people and not the French, German, or North American."[14] Again and again, Amábilis's call was for contemporary architects to understand the customs of the Mexican people as well as their "idiosyncrasy and racial characteristics."[15] Modern architecture in Mexico would have to be rooted both in the past and in the present climate, topography, and character of the people, and respond to modern scientific advances, construction, materials, and sensibilities. Through this, Mexico would be part of and contribute to the universal culture.

Paradoxically, Amábilis's architectural works—such as the Templo Masónico (Mérida, 1915), the Mexican pavilion for the Ibero-American Exhibition (Seville, 1929), the Parque de las Américas (Mérida, 1945), and the Monumento a la Patria (Mérida, 1951)—are highly ornamented and stylized through the use of pre-Hispanic decorative motifs, ornaments, and references, even though their general organization and plans are based on the abstract principles that he advocated theoretically. Although he believed that the characteristic elements of and foundations for his work would be innately understood by viewers, he relied on a formal architectural and ornamental language based on pre-Hispanic forms that would not only be intelligible and accessible to the people but that would also speak directly to them.[16]

Another line of development for modern architecture in Mexico following the revolution was centered on the idea of miscegenation. During the revolutionary struggles in Mexico, a group of architects and intellectuals met to define the character of what architecture in Mexico should be. At the core of their discussions was the role and importance of race and racial mixture characterized by Spanish colonial architecture. For them, this architecture was representative of the "true character" of Mexican identity: it was based on the imported styles from Spain, but manufactured by the indigenous population who interpreted many of the forms idiosyncratically and altered and localized them. Architects Federico Mariscal and Jesús Acevedo noted the importance of the mixture of races both in the past and for the future as a means to not only empower the (primarily indigenous) population but also to legitimize its cultural production.

These discussions were part of broader philosophical and political considerations that would ideologically frame the notion of *mestizaje* (racial mixture) as foundational to incorporating the "Indian" population into the modern state. It should be noted, however, that the use of the term or idea of "race" within the concept of mestizaje was more of a social construct (rather than based on biological traits) that referred, broadly speaking, to the cultural and social characteristics of individual groups. As Allan Knight notes, "A range of characteristics determined 'racial'—or, we should properly say, *ethnic*—identification: language, dress, religion, social organization, culture and consciousness. Since these were social rather than innate biological attributes, they were capable of change; the ethnic status of both individuals and communities was not immutable. By dint of education, migration, and occupational shifts . . . Indians could become mestizos. . . . Clearly, therefore, the process of *mestizaje*, sometimes seen as basically racial, is in fact social: 'mestizo' is an achieved as well as an ascribed status."[17] In mestizaje, therefore, race becomes a discursive category that is part of the state's ideological project for the integration or acculturation of the indigenous into the broader population. Historian Kelley Swarthout has described this as the consolidation of a racially and culturally heterogeneous population into a unified culture that would lessen the impact of racial, cultural, and class differences on the state's desire of unity and progress after the revolution.[18] Through mestizaje, a new modern Mexican identity was forged based on the assimilation of the indigenous population or popular masses and their culture into the new regime through education, by rejecting the parochialism of indigenous groups, and through the exaltation of a unified patriotic collectivity.

What characterized this new identity was its uniqueness: mestizaje, it was argued, defined the distinctive condition of the Mexican people, their culture, and their future. It highlighted the importance of the European or Hispanic tradition at the same time it emphasized the value of indigenous cultures. In short, it incorporated the Indian and its culture into "universal" Western civilization. Mestizaje ideology gained importance as it appeared to stand in contrast to President Porfirio Díaz's general promotion of positivism, a philosophical doctrine based on scientific method and social evolution—advanced by his advisors, known as the *cientificos* (scientists)—and his belief that European culture represented the highest point of human achievement.

The paradox of Díaz's government was the fact that Díaz himself was mestizo. And while he promoted foreign immigration and investment, which were associated with the development of infrastructure and business and modernization of the country, this immigration was later cited as one of the causes of xenophobia and brutality against the indigenous population. Díaz was also lauded as an example of mixed racial heritage and as the leader of what could be described as the mestizo bourgeoisie. So while his government embraced positivism to develop its sociopolitical and economic policies, positivist theories of race never found a steady ground in Díaz's government.[19] Instead Díaz and the cientificos adopted social Darwinist theories that pointed to the deficiencies of the population that was unfit, poorly educated, and born into poverty. Positivism, as the historian Leopoldo Zea has argued, became a tool to direct the transformation and modernization of Mexico through government's technocratic and scientifically guided rule.[20] This was expressed not only in the educational, governmental, and economic projects under Díaz's government but also in its promotion and emulation of European (in particular Parisian) neoclassical and Beaux-Arts architecture. Díaz's overthrow, then, marked a shift away from positivism and the embrace of Spanish colonial architecture over a Beaux-Arts style.

Thinking about what architecture could be produced outside of the parameters

Luis E. Carranza

established by the Díaz regime, architects Jesús Acevedo and Federico Mariscal argued that colonial architecture was a paradigmatic example of built mestizaje and, as such, was an apt style for modern postrevolution Mexico. In this case, the aim was to suggest that architecture could express not only the hybrid character of the Mexican people but also that it was possible to instrumentalize the idea of racial mixture in order to develop new aesthetic principles.

Between 1914 and 1918, during the revolutionary period, Acevedo delivered a series of lectures defining the character of a truly Mexican architecture. For him, architecture always represented the race that constructed it. As such, colonial architecture in Mexico was truly Mexican: "The fact was that the indigenous people learned the different professions that make up the arts . . . at the moment of translating, with admirable dedication, the foreign designs that served as models for them, something of the native and inaccessible hid within their work. . . . Nothing more natural . . . that when the colonizers implanted any style and architectural tendency, these would be modified by that dark current; always latent in the native."[21] Acevedo defined race as something not based on biological traits but rather understood as an expression of pre-Hispanic sensibilities and traditions. An ungenerous reading of Acevedo would note that his notion of race simply suggested a condition of inherent otherness—what was not European or European in character. He defined the native, for instance, as docile in contrast to the European, or as a mere tool to be used by the colonizers. This otherness was characterized by stereotypes; he noted, for instance, that the Mexican architectural laborer had "Asian" faculties, meaning an ability and interest in precision and fine detail work.[22]

It is also clear that for Acevedo architecture was the expression of human life. As such, it had "the imprint of the race [upon it]," as he would note elsewhere.[23] Clearly influenced by William Morris, whom he cites in other moments of his talks, Acevedo understood architectural production in a materialist sense: as an expression (or effect) of human life and the social system within which it was produced. He believed that people give architecture its character and that the only way for architecture to advance and become more modern is through the use of new materials.[24] Since it did not adapt to "the needs of constant progress," colonial architecture stopped evolving in the nineteenth century, according to Acevedo. It did not conform, for instance, to the imported architectural styles, and, as a result, the relationship between the people and their architecture was lost.

The education that Acevedo received in the Beaux-Arts curriculum of the Academia de San Carlos and his work under the French architect Émile Bénard—who had been hired by Díaz to design the Legislative Palace—most likely put him in contact with the theories of Eugène-Emmanuel Viollet-le-Duc, which became important for the postrevolution functionalist movement. Viollet-le-Duc proposed that new architecture be based on functional, national, and social premises. Design, he argued, was based on the program and the habits of the culture for which it was built.[25] These are similar to the requirements for modern architecture noted by Acevedo. However, Viollet-le-Duc—under the influence of Arthur de Gobineau—added that the evolution of architecture was also based on the natural or biological "imperturbable" laws of science, and, as such, race was a factor that defined it.[26] Acevedo defined architecture's relationship to race, instead, as based on cultural developments over the long duration of the colony.

It was necessary, then, to return to the colonial style as it contained the "roots of the Mexican tree whose harvest we must work hard at."[27] Although devoted to the overhaul of colonial architecture, Acevedo did laud the style for not only re-creating a monumental architecture, but also for instituting different means of production. Indigenous labor was essential to the construction of colonial-style buildings, and, according to the architect, "The worker, invariably destined to machine labor as a consequence of our sad social regime, must occupy its new position as teacher, as creator, as artist!" In this way, Acevedo channeled Morris and John Ruskin's theory of the workers as agents free to express themselves through their work and Ruskin and Morris's understanding of work as more than just disinterested production and the working environment as a place worthy of attention and reform.

Federico Mariscal similarly advocated for the resurrection of colonial architecture in 1914. By pointing to how society, life customs, geography, and climate informed different architectural works, Mariscal showed that a national architecture represented both the natural and the social. Such an architecture represented "the life and more general customs characteristic of the whole life of Mexico as a nation. The current Mexican citizen, who forms the majority of the population, is a result of the material, moral, and intellectual mixture of the Spanish and aboriginal races that populated the Mexican land."[28] In other words, what was "Mexican" was the expression of the syncretism of a people and its culture that resulted from colonization. Like Acevedo, Mariscal saw colonial architecture as an evolution of imported foreign architectures. However, as importations continued after the wars of independence (1810–1822), they stopped expressing "Mexican" life and became alien to the people and the place of their construction, and, as such, they stopped evolving into what could be a modern, nationalist architecture.[29] This national architecture would emerge, according to Mariscal, from the study and understanding of the colonial period. By correcting the problems caused by the eclectic importation of foreign styles in the nineteenth century, the monumental legacy of the past could be re-created and bring about a rebirth of Mexican architecture and art.

These ideas would become foundational for the development of the artistic and architectural program proposed for the Department of Public Education by José Vasconcelos. As early as 1916, Vasconcelos, echoing Acevedo and Mariscal in a lecture to the Sociedad de Bellas Artes in Lima, Peru, proposed that architects should search for "threads through which they could structure their development; these arc, for example, certain successes of our national inheritance—such as the architecture of the time of the Colony. . . . The three centuries of Mexican architecture are still the best aesthetic realization of the Latin American race."[30] Vasconcelos's vision for a neo-colonial architecture—like Acevedo and Mariscal's—called for a mixture of the Spanish and indigenous races, ideas, and artistic traditions: a new aesthetic syncretism.

For Vasconcelos, colonial architecture not only created a spiritually elevating and inspiring environment, but it also represented Mexican character. He prized the grandiose and monumental in colonial architecture, full of light and vast spaces—as evident in his well-known statement: "Only the races that don't think put the ceiling at the height of their heads!" The designs of the schools for the Department of Public Education under his direction were thoroughly colonial in style and, as a consequence, to be read as Mexican. They were to reflect an authentic culture based on traditions and to meet modern educational needs. In addition, they served as the vehicle for and representation of Vasconcelos's transcendental beliefs: "We must continue building in [an architectural style that responds to the old colonial tradition], because we have the obligation to continue to create an autochthonous culture. . . . We reject the wooden house because it does not adapt to the ideal expression of our race coupled, as the ancients had, with the eternal. In this way, we will reject everything that is inferior to the ethnic and aesthetic potential of the Mexican."[31] Like Mariscal before him, for Vasconcelos an autochthonous Mexican architecture was always a result of the mixture of Spanish and native cultures—a complex cultural development that resulted from the specific natural environment and social configurations.

It was in his book *La Raza Cósmica* (The Cosmic Race, 1925) that he proposed a more far-reaching theory about the importance of miscegenation for Latin America. Here, he argued for the coming of a fifth race resulting from the mixing of all other races. In this vision, aesthetics were seen as the highest point of human achievement and the mixture of races (with their attendant cultures) would lead to the greatness of the fifth race. In this way, Vasconcelos reacted to contemporary theories that linked social progress to racial purity, such as those of Gobineau, whom he mentioned in his prologue to the 1948 edition of *La Raza Cósmica*.[32] This syncretic character became the guide that Vasconcelos employed as the basis for the architecture and decorative program of the headquarters of the Secretaría de Educación Publica. Vasconcelos made this clear in the last sentence of the theoretical section of *La Raza Cósmica*:

To express [the ideas of the cosmic race] that today I am trying to explain . . .
I tried to give them shape in the new Palace of Public Education in Mexico.
Without enough elements to make precisely what I wanted, I had to conform to
a Renaissance Spanish construction, with two courtyards, with arcades and
walkways that give the impression of a wing. In the panels of the four angles in
the first courtyard I had someone make allegories of Spain, Mexico, Greece, and
India, the four particular civilizations that have the most to contribute to the
formation of Latin America. Afterwards, under these four allegories, four large
stone sculptures should have been placed representing the four great contemporary races: the White, the Red, the Black, and the Yellow in order to show that
America is the home of all and that it needs them all. . . . All this to indicate that
we will arrive in America, before any other part of the globe, to the formation of
a race created with the treasures of all of the previous ones, the final race, the
cosmic race.[33]

The building relied on a modernized version of the colonial style that reflected the
synthetic culture of the cosmic race. This architectural syncretism was based on
the stylistic mixture of colonial architecture with modern materials, such as reinforced concrete, and the introduction of modern programmatic elements. It was
clear in Vasconcelos's inauguration speech for the building that his intentions were
to make the structure a part, symbol, and activator in the process of postrevolution
reconstruction. Within the context of the utopian aesthetic and philosophical
theories that Vasconcelos developed, this synthesis and transformation would be
incomplete without the mediatory capacity of painting and sculpture, used in a
referential and didactic manner, to transform the somewhat self-referential and
autonomous qualities of the emerging architecture. These representational, legible,
and collective systems were to educate the diverse elements of the population
about the sociopolitical transformations taking place in postrevolutionary Mexico.

Second, Vasconcelos's requirements included the sculptural expression of racial
miscegenation in the Hispano-American culture through Manuel Centurión's
allegorical reliefs of the four races: Quetzalcoatl, representing the Mexican race;
Plato, representing the race of Greece; Buddha, representing the Indian race; and,
an image of the ship, Las Casas, representing Spain at the height of its colonial
power (figure 8.3). Additionally, Ignacio Asúnsolo was to carve four statues to
represent the "white, black, red, and yellow" races, also to be placed in the first
courtyard, which was to be called the "Court of the Races." Only one of the statues
(that for the white race) was ever modeled in plaster (figure 8.4). For Vasconcelos,
these statues indicated the racial evolution of humanity. As he put it, "Latin
America boasts in possessing the contribution of the four human types and is
preparing to build, with all of these and by demolishing all prejudices, the truly

Luis E. Carranza

Fig. 8.3 Manuel Centurión, *Quetzalcoatl: The Mexican Race, Court of the Races*, Secretaría de Educación Pública, Mexico City, 1922. Image from Secretaría de Educación Pública, *Edificios Construidos por la Secretaría de Educación Pública en los Años 1922-1924* (Mexico, 1924).

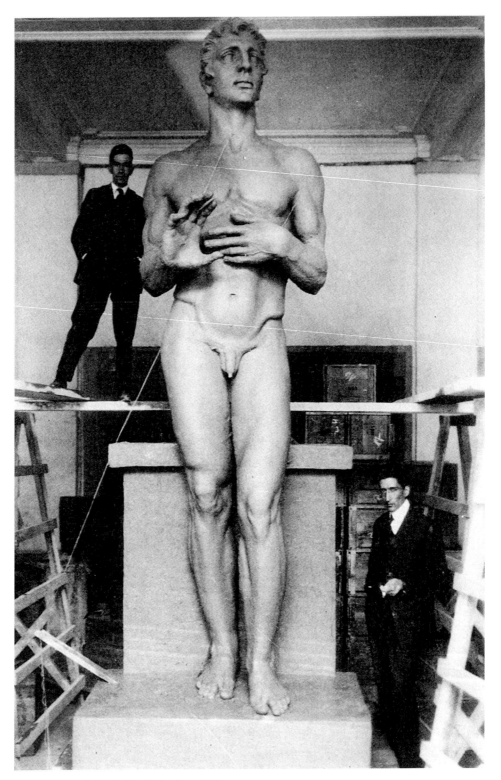

Fig. 8.4 Ignacio Asúnsolo, *The White Race*, 1922.

universal type." In the second court, Centurión carved reliefs on the corners representing branches of the plastic arts: sculpture, painting, music, and architecture. While the reliefs in the first patio represented the primary, racial, and cultural components of the cosmic race, the second patio contained its aesthetic components. The exaltation of these ideas through their architectural placement also suggests the importance that they held, symbolically, in the formation of a new racial and aesthetic culture.

For the mural program at the site, Vasconcelos encouraged the artists to focus on autochthonous cultural production, the syncretic condition of the people and their traditions, as well as the influences of time and past cultures. In addition to Vasconcelos's interests and requirements, the murals were guided by the *Manifesto of the Syndicate of Technical Workers, Painters and Sculptors* (December 1923): "The noble work of our race, down to its most insignificant spiritual and physical expressions, is native (and essentially Indian) in origin. With their admirable and extraordinary talent to create beauty, peculiar to themselves, the art of the Mexican people is the most wholesome spiritual expression in the world and this tradition is our greatest treasure. Great because it belongs collectively to the people."[34] This call for a nationalist art echoed the debates on architectural syncretism that sought work that represented the collective spirit. In addition, distinctions between "high and low" art would be eliminated through the incorporation of popular traditions into the new creative developments; in this way and through its placement in public spaces, art would become a part of life.

Ultimately, it was syncretic synthesis that Vasconcelos advocated as appropriate for Mexico and, broadly speaking, Latin America. This is clear, first, in his conception of Universópolis, the city destined to be the center of the cosmic race. Located in the Amazon, the metropolis would dispatch armies and planes to educate people instead of conquering them. For Vasconcelos, the opposite of Universópolis was Anglotown, the place from which colonizing troops were sent to dominate the world and eliminate rival races. This was, undoubtedly, part of Vasconcelos's critical campaign against the United States and its meddling in Latin American affairs. In Universópolis, everyone would be equal, nationhood would be transcended, and a more universal sense of community achieved. Its culture would be founded on free will and the metaphysical and mystical qualities of the arts. In addition, modern means of communication and education would dissolve geographical boundaries that, in turn, would lead to an "accelerated fusion of the races."[35] Reproduction of the species would become guided by aesthetics and education and, in Vasconcelos's schema, a form of eugenics guided by beauty would "prevent the mixture of the most divergent types." Instead of a Darwinist form of selection that mechanistically controlled the mixture of races and eradicated those

Fig. 8.5 José Chavez Morado, *Return of Quetzalcoatl*, School of Science, Universidad Nacional Autónoma de México (UNAM), Mexico City, 1952.

that didn't fit, for the cosmic race "selection will be spontaneous, like the artist who, from all the colors available, chooses only the ones that best fit his intentions."[36] For Vasconcelos, Universópolis and the ideas behind it served as an alternative to creating nations that, according to Marissa K. López, would "replicate an evolutionary logic of race and perpetuate the colonizing forces of Anglo capital."[37]

The synthesis that Vasconcelos was after and the importance that he placed on the arts can be seen expressed most clearly in his promotion of plastic integration that would become a hallmark of modern architecture in Mexico. The 1952 campus for the UNAM is emblematic of this influence. Not only is it clear by the integration of art into its buildings, but also through its seal (which includes a map of Latin America) and its motto—*por mi raza, hablará el espiritu* (through my race, the spirit shall speak)—coined by Vasconcelos. Even in the 1950s, artists such as Francisco Eppens and José Chávez Morado included in their murals for the various university buildings references to mestizaje and, paradigmatically, the "races" or cultures of Vasconcelos's cosmic race (figure 8.5). In turn, references to pre-Hispanic architecture continued but in a more abstract spirit and with less direct decorative references. At the UNAM, for instance, Alberto Arai's Fronton Courts were lauded for their simple, abstract forms that evoked pyramids. Even when more specific elements were introduced into the designs, such as the use of the Atlanean statues of Tula or the colossal Olmec heads in public museums or pavilions designed by Pedro Ramírez Vázquez in the late 1950s and 1960s, these were

Luis E. Carranza

used to highlight the contrast between modern forms and materials and those of the past.

By the 1950s the utilization of race as a discourse as it had developed from the revolutionary moment became linked more to a broader, more ideological desire to express a Mexican national identity than to a transformation of what Vasconcelos called the "technical forms for a technical civilization." In other words, race was used to express visually Mexico's simultaneous historical legacy and its emerging modernity. The constructed notion of race and ethnicity proved to be a malleable tool for the expression of the desire of architects and, ultimately, the state, to define its uniqueness in order to achieve social cohesion by incorporating, in a utopic way, the majority of the population. By developing an ideology based on the fusion or hybridization of antagonistic or different social groups or forms, the state could ultimately remove antagonisms that held back the modernization of the nation. In this way, the search for built mestizaje and the glorification of pre-Hispanic works were guided by an ideological desire to unify the population through the mythifying of its "racial" history as a uniquely Mexican response to the placeless modernity of the West.

9

Modern Architecture and Racial Eugenics at the Esposizione Universale di Roma

Brian L. McLaren

Two days before "Fascism and the Problems of Race," better known as the "Manifesto of the Racial Scientists," appeared in *Il Giornale d'Italia* on July 15, 1938, the powerfully placed state architect Marcello Piacentini published an essay in the same newspaper titled "Balance Sheet of Rationalism."[1] The publication of this essay at the same moment, and in the same venue, as the first public pronouncement of the Fascist racial campaign is a clear indication of the close connection between the emerging racial discourse in Italian politics and the discourse on architecture in the late Fascist period. With regard to this political debate, the "Provisions for the Defense of the Italian Race" was officially passed into law by the Fascist government, with the intention to defend Italy against racial impurities of all kinds.[2] This was the most comprehensive of a series of measures that were put in place between September 1938 and July 1939 that led to limitations on marriage as well as constraints in the fields of education, the national economy, the Italian military, and all sectors of the government. As a result, not only were so-called Aryan Italians prohibited from marrying other races, it was forbidden for Jews in particular to be in a position of authority over them or to teach them. The consequence of these and many other highly contentious political measures was that Italian politics moved away from "Mediterraneanism" and in favor of asserting the Nordic and Aryan origins of the Italian people—thus conjoining Italian racial policies and those of German National Socialism.[3]

This racial discourse was closely tied to equally heated debates in the fields of art and architecture. In art, these disputes centered around what the most retrogressive critics of the time considered the impure and subjective qualities of modern art—and especially the danger of foreign influences. In light of the broader political discourse, which argued that Italian identity could be linked to biology, this general appeal to control the aesthetic principles of contemporary art can be understood as a call to purify its genetic code. In architecture, in addition to the state control of cultural matters, these disputes were tied to the issue of autarchy. This economic policy called on Italian industry to utilize materials from within the Kingdom of Italy following the invasion of Ethiopia in 1935 and related sanctions by the League of Nations. As a result, there were limitations on the use of steel and reinforced concrete that moved architecture away from modern systems and toward more traditional building methods—in what can be considered a direct attempt to define its genetic material.

This paper will trace the impact of this broader debate through the transformation of the Piazza e gli edifici delle Forze Armate (Piazza and buildings of the Armed Forces), designed by the architects Mario De Renzi and Gino Pollini. This project began in 1937 as two separate competition entries for one of the permanent buildings at the Esposizione Universale di Roma or E42—a world exhibition planned for 1942 but that did not take place due to Italy's entry into World War II. The evolution of the project, which included merging the two schemes and several changes to its program, ended somewhat silently during wartime as the abandoned construction site of the Edifici del Corporativismo, dell'Autarchia e dell'Assistenza e Previdenza Sociale (Buildings of Corporatism, Autarchy and Social Security). This essay frames the E42 project within the racialized architectural, and political, discourse of late 1930s and early '40s Italy, traced through prominent art and architectural publications of the era. Through exploring the historical trajectory of the E42, this essay argues that the aesthetic control exercised during the competition process met with the material limitations imposed by the wartime conditions to instantiate contemporary theories of racial eugenics within architecture.

Parallel research in other geographies and time periods includes architectural historian Charles L. Davis II's examination of the fusion of theories of race and style in the writings of Eugène-Emmanuel Viollet-le-Duc.[4] In particular, Davis's discussion of the metaphorical assimilation of race in Viollet-le-Duc's theory, found in the internal functioning of architecture rather than an external anthropomorphism, supports a conception of style as a form of eugenics that would regulate architecture's internal principles—an argument similar to that found in this essay. Also relevant to this study of the architectural impact of Fascist racial policies is an understanding of what architectural historian Mabel O. Wilson contends took place in the United States during the period of immigrant assimilation immediately following World War I, which she describes as "paranoid efforts at 'racial containment,'" supported by a racist discourse of eugenics.[5] In the Italian context, these concerns were generated by the immediate circumstances following the Italian conquest in Ethiopia, where the threat of miscegenation intermingled with the militaristic logic of empire. Notably, Mussolini had already expressed his views ten years earlier in his speech to the people of Reggio Emilia, when he called for establishing policies and programs that would remake Italians along Fascist lines.[6] This mild form of eugenics, which encouraged a high birth rate, was paired with policies and programs aimed at shaping the Italian character externally to form Mussolini's racial strategy through the early part of the 1930s.[7] After the Ethiopian conquest, and with some frustration with the lack of progress of his campaign to remake Italians, Mussolini pursued a more aggressive approach that included his so-called "Reform of Customs" that attacked the Italian bourgeoisie.[8] As historian Aaron Gillette argues, by the late 1930s Mussolini increasingly believed that races could be "physically and psychologically" transformed through a combination of internal and external pressure.[9]

In response to this body of research, this essay contends that the most powerful political and cultural assertions—and particularly those in the realm of art and architecture—arose from a fearful and reactive need to assert a "pure" Italian identity against the threat of international, foreign, or Jewish influences. It further maintains that Fascism's racial ideologies were a product of fear and weakness rather than strength, and that the architecture of the period bears the mark of this combative stance. In so doing, this essay addresses a body of built work that has been either entirely ignored or inadequately theorized in the existing scholarship. Exceptions to this tendency include historian Emilio Gentile's *Fascismo di pietra*, which argues that Mussolini's efforts to create "modern Romans" through the regime's racial and anti-Semitic campaign was physically manifested in state-sponsored projects such as the Foro Mussolini and Esposizione Universale di Roma.[10] This essay aims to provide more substance to Gentile's arguments through a close look at precisely how these racial theories were operationalized in the review, decision making, and design refinement of a single project. Also relevant to this discussion is the theorization of race as a form of, after Michel Foucault, biopolitics. According to Foucault, biopolitics emerged at the moment when "the biological came under state control" in response, in part, to concerns about health, hygiene, and racial purity.[11] The concept of the biopolitical, in Foucault's theorization, reached its apotheosis in state racism and genocide during the twentieth

Brian L. McLaren

century. In reference to Nazi Germany, Foucault argues "once the State functions in the biopower mode, racism alone can justify the murderous function of the State."[12]

Art, Architecture, and Racial Eugenics

In the discourse on modern architecture during the Italian racial campaign, there was a grave suspicion about purportedly international or foreign sources of modern Italian architecture—with allusions to northern European, Bolshevik, and Jewish influences. The direct connection between the political discourse on race and the parallel debate within the arts is apparent in the racialization of art discourse. This is reflected clearly in the rhetoric of Sicilian architect Giuseppe Pensabene for example, who, through the course of the 1930s, began to espouse the racist ideology of the Fascist state.[13] Of particular note are a series of essays by Pensabene that appeared in the weekly *Quadrivio* in early 1938 that called for the creation of a national culture free of impure "modern" (that is, Jewish) influences.[14] He conveyed a similar message in *Difesa della Razza* through a pair of essays, "Our Art and Jewish Deformation," in October and November 1938—which was at the height of the Italian racial campaign. In this context, Pensabene made a distinction between the authentic traditions of Italian art, which were tied to realism, and "subjective painting," which he described as "a form [of art] that came from a psyche alien to us."[15] He goes on to argue that Italian artists who followed modern artistic movements, such as expressionism, cubism, and Dadaism, created a situation where "now arbitrary and entirely subjective, art is no longer resolved in works, but only in trends."[16]

The views of Pensabene were echoed by journalist Telesio Interlandi, who published "The Question of Art and Race" in the newspaper *Il Tevere* on November 14, 1938—just three days prior to the approval of the Italian racial laws.[17] His central argument was that the importation of foreign influences in the arts over the past decades had created a climate in which Italian artists were compelled to work in a way that was against their instincts. In reference to modern art, Interlandi bluntly states: "We believe that 'modern' is a trap set by Judaism and Jewish sympathizing intellectuals to continue to interfere with our artistic life."[18] Just ten days later, founder of the futurist movement Filippo Tommaso Marinetti responded to Interlandi in the pages of *Il Giornale d'Italia*, in an essay entitled "Italian-ness of Modern Art," where he argues that modern Italian art was initiated by artists who were neither Jewish nor Bolshevik.[19] After providing a detailed summary of the wide range of tendencies within modern Italian art, Marinetti concludes his essay by sarcastically stating: "The attempt of *Il Tevere* to attribute merits and defects to Jews is for them an undeserved praise, while it offends the Ministry of Popular Culture and the Confederation of Professional Artists who safeguard modern

Italian artists, and is especially insulting and destructive to the prestige of the Mussolinian Empire."[20]

The debate over race and modern Italian art culminated in the pages of the journal *Le Arti*, which began publication in October 1938 under the direction of the minister of National Education, Giuseppe Bottai, a powerful and complex figure within the Fascist regime.[21] In a note from February 1939, "Discussions on Modern Art," the editors assembled the various opinions on this issue including the essay by Interlandi and responses by Marinetti and others.[22] While the editorial position of *Le Arti* was said to follow a "rigorously objective attitude," this objectivity was premised on a search for artistic movements that, according to the editors, genuinely reflected contemporary Italian politics and culture. The assumption was that "only through judgment, which is knowledge, will it be possible to distinguish real originality, a new and historically justified reality, from fictitious reality."[23] This approach is clearly reflected in an essay by Bottai in the same issue of the journal entitled "Modernity and Tradition in Today's Italian Art." In directly referencing modern art and the contemporary political issue of race, he warns that "this relationship does not act so much between art and race, in its most current and accepted biological significance, as between the *concept* of art and the *concept* of race, which . . . enunciates the new consciousness that Italy has of itself, of its own traditions, its own civilian mission."[24] According to this view, modern art would express the concept of race to the extent that it was an integral part of Fascist culture. Thus, rather than residing in the nationality or racial origin of the artist, it was subsumed into the broader expression of the Italian (and modern) tradition of the artwork.

In reflecting on the problem of modern art as it was discussed during the Italian racial campaign, there emerged two distinct lines of critique in the writings of Pensabene, Interlandi, and others—one that focused on the artist, as bourgeois, Jewish, and decadent, and a second that concentrated on the artwork itself, on its *ebraizzazione*, that is, its racial impurity. It is in this second category, which deals with the internal rules of the artwork—in short, its style—that the relationship between art and race can be best understood. The goal of commentators like Pensabene was to invoke a eugenic process within the discipline of art—thereby eliminating the external influences whether they be Jewish, African, or otherwise foreign to the Italian peninsula. This critical debate was actualized through the state bureaucracies whose responsibility it was to control or otherwise judge artistic production through direct intervention in the educational system or through competitions. As historian Marla Susan Stone argues, there was a battle for culture in Italy that shaped the processes and outcomes of state patronage during what she identifies as the most restrictive phase of Fascist official culture, between 1937 and 1943.[25] Indeed, it was especially by means of institutional mechanisms, such as the National Fascist Syndicate of Fine Arts (1927–1943), and art competitions, such as the Premio Cremona (1939–1941), that artistic taste in late 1930s Italy was shaped eugenically.

In architecture, there was a similar racialization of critical discourse, tied to the long history of condemnation of international influences by conservative critics like Marcello Piacentini, which dated back to the founding manifestoes of Italian rationalism of 1926–1927.[26] In his review of the First Italian Exhibition of Rationalist Architecture, which was held in Rome from March 29 to April 30, 1928, Piacentini made a not-so-subtle connection between the exhibition and the first Communist International.[27] He then rebuked the participating architects for their relation of the beautiful with the structural, as well as their use of foreign elements such as flat roofs and horizontal windows, which he called "the new international drugs of architecture." In commenting on the rationalist approach to architecture, he further scolded these architects, stating: "Let us leave these dry and metaphysical speculations to the men of the North."[28] The racial connotations of this line of criticism were explicitly stated in a separate essay by Piacentini from 1931, which argues that the search for a properly national expression for modern architecture was dependent upon "the questions of climate, of the temperament of the various races, and of the traditions of the civilizations."[29]

This racialized critique escalated through the course of the 1930s through a series of public competitions, such as the two-stage design competition for the Palace of the Fascist Party in Rome (1934–1937). In a morning session of the Chamber of Deputies on May 26, 1934, Alberto Calza Bini, secretary of the National Syndicate of Fascist Architects, took the floor in support of a bill to fund public improvements to the site of the competition. During the course of this rather animated session the work of the younger generation of Italian architects was openly disparaged by prominent members of the chamber, such as former party secretary Roberto Farinacci, who bellowed with unwavering conviction that "modernism is finished!"[30] Reporting on these events in the pages of *Casabella* in June 1934, editor Giuseppe Pagano admonished the members of the Chamber of Deputies for "the same old ridiculous and demagogic stone throwing against 'exoticism,' against 'architectural leveling,' against 'modernist abortions,'" while sarcastically thanking them for providing a "cold shower" to modern architects.[31] This wake-up call included numerous references to the danger of external influences that need to be considered for their racial overtones, such as a final speech by Francesco Giunta, who protested against "Teutonic architectural trends" while pleading, "We must not end by importing from other people too distant from us in spirit, in origins, in traditions."[32]

This line of critique was extended in the "Balance Sheet of Rationalism" of Piacentini, as the criticism of foreign influence in that essay was set against the backdrop of the Italian racial campaign. In this context, he argues that the positive qualities of Italian rationalism—what he calls "the pursuit of simplicity, of clarity, and the predominance of the essentials of construction"—were offset by its errors and misjudgments, such as its employment of "large windows better suited to Nordic countries."[33] Beyond his continuing disparagement of international, and in particular northern, influences, it is important to note that Piacentini offers an operative reading of Italian rationalism through a racial lens. Indeed, there are unquestionably some broader motivations in his praise of rationalism's "return to rhythm" and "value of proportions"—something he believed would lead it to "the fundamentals of great ancient architecture."[34] These arguments were followed in a second essay in *Il Giornale d'Italia*, which describes an architectural renewal found in "the fundamental forms of our spirit and our race."[35] In this context, turning to the "divine harmony, the clarity, the nobility" associated with the best aspects of Italian rationalism ultimately meant a "return to the great Roman conceptions." Piacentini also advocated the use of material and products that, in his words, "our soil produces" instead of things from abroad, which was an argument that directly reflected the Mediterranean racial theories of the time.[36]

It is important to note, though, that accusations against Jews, northern Europeans, and the Bolsheviks were not limited to politically reactionary critics. As architectural historian Richard Etlin has noted, there was an "internecine warfare" among the ranks of rationalist architects during the racial campaign. For instance, the architect Giuseppe Terragni charged that *Casabella* editor Pagano was either Jewish or a Jewish sympathizer.[37] However, the opposition between realism and subjectivity found in the criticism of modern art was rather more nuanced in the case of rationalist architecture, which from the beginning proclaimed that "the new architecture" was based on logic and rationality.[38] Nevertheless, just as in the arts, the reactionary decisions that defined the identity of a modern architecture for the Fascist state—which inevitably led to a racial idea of ancient renewal—were strictly applied by members of the various state bureaucracies that presided over public projects as well as the juries that were part of the public competition processes. As a result, architectural taste during the late-Fascist era was similarly shaped along eugenic lines.

An Architecture of Racial Purification

Just over one year prior to the passing into law of the "Provisions for the Defense of the Italian Race" by the Fascist government, a public competition was held for the design of the Piazza e gli edifici delle Forze Armate, the initial stage being held between October 25, 1937, and February 21, 1938.[39] This was the last of four major public competitions held for the most important permanent buildings and public spaces for the Esposizione Universale di Roma. As an "Olympics of

Brian L. McLaren

Civilization," the E42 was intended to assert the historical and contemporary importance of Italian culture on a world stage, and thus legitimize Mussolini's geopolitical ambitions. Like the world's fairs of the late nineteenth and early twentieth centuries—which historian Charles Rydell argues were hegemonic efforts to convey social and technological progress "laced with scientific racism"—the E42 offered a "symbolic universe" that would affirm Italian cultural, technological, and racial superiority to its domestic and foreign visitors.[40] This broad purpose was described in the initial proposal by Giuseppe Bottai as intended "to highlight all of the progress and all of the discoveries of over twenty-seven centuries of human activity."[41] However, in contrast with the metropolitan and colonial displays at the 1931 Paris Exposition coloniale internationale, which Patricia Morton argues attempted to maintain racial hierarchies in the face of the threat of hybridity, this imperial exhibition was almost exclusively preoccupied with the problem of a "pure" Italian identity. In this regard, a more pertinent comparative is the German Pavilion at the 1937 Paris Exposition internationale, whose recourse to the antique in its architecture and statuary, art historian Karen Fiss argues, reflected "the National Socialist ideal of beauty and racial purity."[42]

In the case of the Piazza e gli edifici delle Forze Armate, racial purity was thematized in the descriptive language of the call for entries, formalized in the design constraints of the competition, and strictly enforced by the jury and through subsequent oversight by the Architecture, Parks, and Gardens Service of the E42. The broad expectations for the competition were conveyed in the call for entries, which stated that "even in the most modern functional forms, the basis of architectural inspiration must be the classical and monumental sentiment in the pure sense of orientation of the spirit."[43] This idealist vision subsumed functionalism to the apparent inner spirit of the design. The competition called upon its entrants to "express the essential characteristics of Roman and Italian architectural art in the masses and in the bold and imposing lines" of their designs.[44]

This eugenic approach was given more concrete expression in the urban design guidelines and programmatic requirements in the call for entries. The project was to be located on a piece of high ground at the eastern terminus of an east-west axis that crossed the central artery of the E42, the Via Imperiale. The three buildings were to be arranged to create a "constructed environment" for the Italian armed forces, responding to "the need to create an organic and unified composition."[45] The detailed program of the buildings was intended to glorify the past and present accomplishments of the Italian military. Each branch was to be represented through a narrative of its development as well as an impassioned display of sacrifice: the Edificio del R. Esercito featured a "solemn temple of the glories of Italian warriors," the Edificio della R. Marina incorporated the memorabilia of the navy, and the Edificio della R. Aeronautica included a shrine to heroes of the

Fig. 9.1 Mario De Renzi, Piazza e gli edifici delle Forze Armate, Stage I, 1938. View. *Architettura* 17, Special edition (December 1938): 889. Author's collection.

air force.[46] Notably, all of the Italian armed forces were compelled to trace their origins back to the Roman period.

This strong direction was supported by the input of the jury, which presided over this process. It was chaired by Cipriano Efisio Oppo, a painter and art critic with strong nationalist sentiments who was vice president of the E42. The attitude and aesthetic values of the jury are evident in their decision making, as well as in the input they provided to the competitors, which tended to favor proposals that created a sequential, axial experience. This compositional preference is evident in the positive jury comments for the first stage proposal by De Renzi, which was praised for its "exceptional sculptural strength and nobility of design," and the criticism of the entry by Pollini for the fact that it lacked "the requested emotions of grandeur and strength that only a powerful organization of architectural masses can produce"[47] (figure 9.1).

The continuing refinement of the projects by the competitors demonstrates how administrative structures were able to significantly reshape public projects in the late Fascist era. In his second stage proposal, De Renzi made a significant shift in the approach to his design, ultimately configuring three main buildings to frame an urban space, and placing the Edificio del R. Esercito as the central element. According to the jury, the resulting grouping created a "strict, steady rhythm

Brian L. McLaren

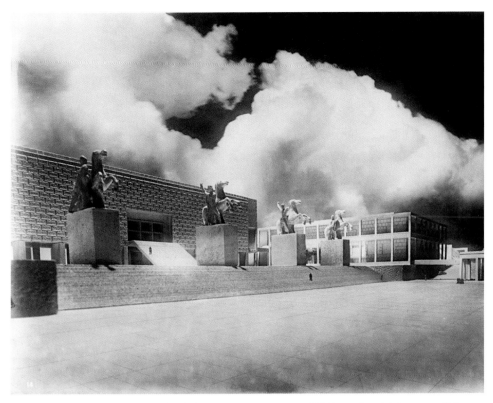

Fig. 9.2 Gino Pollini, Piazza e gli edifici delle Forze Armate, Stage II, 1938. View of model. Courtesy of Museo di Arte Moderna e Contemporanea di Trento e Rovereto, Fondo Gino Pollini.

that, rather than generate monotony, made a powerfully expressive composition."[48] The jury was equally positive about the stage two submission of Pollini, which offered a large square divided into two distinct spaces—one for larger assemblies and rallies and a second that was more intimately framed by the three buildings. Following the review of the stage two proposals, the jury decided to award the first prize and commission to De Renzi and Pollini. The directions given to the two architects was quite clear: the form of the buildings and their positioning would be De Renzi's, and the internal arrangement would come from Pollini (figure 9.2).[49]

As these results demonstrate, the desire expressed in the call for entries for the architects to express "the essential characteristics of a Roman and Italian architectonic art" became more than just a subtle directive—it was an operative demand that the jury enacted through the competition process.[50] This approach also characterized the continuing refinement of the project under the management of the E42. Under the supervision of Marcello Piacentini, director of the Architecture, Parks, and Gardens Service, not only were these architects to merge their two projects into a single scheme, they were called upon to respond to the economic demands of its construction and a change in program. The revised project reacted to the budget constraints by shortening the two wings that frame the central urban space by thirty meters—resulting in a more focused and centralized design.[51] In the case of the program, which saw the Edifici delle Forze Armate become the Edifici delle Comunicazioni e Trasporti (Communications and Transport Buildings) as part of a redefinition of the E42 master plan, the highly charged narrative and symbolic program of the former design gave way to the creation of a more ordinary and conventional exhibition building.[52] When looking at the full evolution of the project up to December 1938 it seems clear that there was a process of refinement that resulted in the emulation of Italy's ancient sources, and that gave rise to stifling circumstances of an artistic climate that Stone describes as a "historicist, coercive, and censored patronage style."[53] No less so than with the artwork of the times, the building project of De Renzi and Pollini was a reification of Italy's racial laws, which—anxious to extinguish the perceived danger of miscegenation—sought refuge in a pure Italian race (figure 9.3).

Autarchy in Architecture

Not only did the Italian racial campaign provoke an intense debate concerning the identity of modern Italian architecture, one that intimately connected it to the idea of racial purity, it foregrounded the architectural, and in particular material, implications of the already well-established campaign for autarchy. Although latent within many of Fascism's early economic, political, and cultural views, this policy was first presented by Mussolini in a speech to the National Assembly of Corporations on March 23, 1936—less than two months before the end of the Ethiopian conflict and his declaration of an Italian empire.[54] Looking back at this speech, there seems an exact parallel between his argument that the defense of the nation required an autonomous Italian economy free from foreign authority, and the contentious rhetoric proclaiming the importance of protecting the Italian race from foreign influences. In fact, as Gillette has noted, the idea of genetic purity in Italy was tied to racial autarchy—a specious notion proffered by Mussolini that although Italians were deemed to be members of the Aryan race, they constituted an autonomous racial subgroup that had not changed since Roman times.[55] As Stone argues, this political policy had an exact parallel in the regime's support of cultural autarchy, where all forms of expression were "based only on elements authentically Italian and Fascist."[56]

While there was no immediate discussion of the implications of this policy on architecture, in December 1937, an article entitled "Aspects of the Problem of Autarchy in the Construction Field" appeared in the Milanese professional journal *Rassegna di Architettura*.[57] This essay is somewhat typical of the economic and technical interpretation of autarchy in architecture, which was largely concerned with the supply and cost of modern materials like steel and reinforced concrete. This situation changed with the beginning of the Italian racial campaign in the

Fig. 9.3 Mario De Renzi and Gino Pollini, Edifici delle comunicazioni e trasporti, 1938. View of model. Courtesy of Archivio Centrale dello Stato, Carte Gaetano Minnucci, Buste 142, Fascicolo 258, Sottofascicolo 2, photo 1724.

fall of 1938. In an essay "Architecture of the Italian Race," rationalist architect Carlo Enrico Rava argues that the "principle of race" was "a natural corollary to the great autarchic battle to which every aspect of the life of the Nation is committed."[58] He further contends that being called to use "construction materials that are all and only Italian" would allow architects to attain a character that is "spiritually, politically and racially" Italian.[59] It is important to note, however, that not all architects viewed this issue in the same light. In the September and October 1938 issues of *Casabella*, Pagano offers a blistering critique of the policy and its negative influence on modern Italian architecture.[60] In this discussion, Pagano maintains that there was an unresolvable conflict between "our premises of pride in modesty, of honesty and of clarity" and what he called "the pomp of the rationalized monumental"—a direct slight against Piacentini for his influence on the site and buildings of the Esposizione Universale di Roma.[61]

It was in this highly contentious context that De Renzi and Pollini began the last phase of design of the newly renamed Edifici delle comunicazioni e trasporti. In this effort, these architects were attempting to reconcile their initial design with the demands that were coming from the E42.[62] This already difficult process was further impacted on September 3, 1939, when Germany entered World War II.[63] As the architects would later write in a letter to the Architecture, Parks, and Gardens Service, in September 1939 they began what was essentially a new project. This revised design was, they wrote, "based on constructive characteristics completely different from those of the first project (structure in masonry rather than reinforced concrete), and for which a completely different architectural expression was required."[64] In addition, the E42 was in the midst of a major revision to the master plan. As a result, the Edifici delle Comunicazioni e Trasporti became part of the Italian City of the Corporate Economy, which with no small amount of irony included the Exhibition of Autarchy. However, in examining the evolution of the design by De Renzi and Pollini, the transformation of the building had less to do with the change in program than with the political pressures of autarchy under the wartime conditions—which resulted in a building that was described as a "renewal of the classical tradition in modern Italian architecture."[65]

In the project's final iteration as the Edifici del Corporativismo, dell'Autarchia e dell'Assistenza e Previdenza Sociale, the frame became the dominant element, with travertine used in the wall cladding as well as in the freestanding columns. This material selection supported the formal approach of the project, that is, the material addressed a specifically Italian (and Roman) identity while also reflecting its autarchic character. As noted in an essay on the use of marble and travertine at the E42, not only did these materials represent a literal connection to Italy's past, but also they were the most Italian of materials, as travertine was quite literally drawn from quarries throughout the country.[66]

Under the pressure of the policy of autarchy, the reinforced concrete frame that in Italian rationalism referenced both modern and classical traditions had surrendered to a trabeated structure comprised of fully embodied travertine columns. Despite the fact that this compromise was simply a product of a change in the construction system of the building, its result was quite profound. The expression of the central pavilion of the grouping, which was originally a powerfully blank facade with blind relieving arches, had given way to a classical frame that rendered that central pavilion as a statically composed temple structure. For all three buildings, the dramatic and expressive play between solid and void that existed in the original proposals by De Renzi and Pollini had ceded to a more neutral expression arising from the rhythm of the repetitive structure. Not only did the implementation of protectionist economic policies lead to the sublimation, in a material sense, of architectural expression as marble replaced concrete, but also it caused the racialization of architectural principles that led, in the case of the Edifici del Corporativismo, dell'Autarchia e dell'Assistenza e Previdenza Sociale, to a silent and lifeless version of the classical. Reflecting on this change, it would seem that the creative void that opened up within Italian society as a product of the Fascist

Brian L. McLaren

Fig. 9.4 Mario De Renzi and Gino Pollini, Edifici del Corporativismo, dell'Autarchia e dell'Assistenza e Previdenza Sociale, 1943. General view under construction. Courtesy of Archivio Centrale dello Stato, Carte Gaetano Minnucci, Buste 142, Fascicolo 258, Sottofascicolo 2, photo 4880.

pursuit of cultural autarchy had resulted in the complete loss of the expressive qualities of architecture (figure 9.4).

•　　•　　•

The last phase of evolution of the Edifici del Corporativismo, dell'Autarchia e dell'Assistenza e Previdenza Sociale during the wartime is perhaps most illustrative of the impact of racial eugenics on the architecture of the late Fascist era. Although the progress of construction at the E42 had gradually slowed, in the early months of 1942, almost two years into the wartime effort, the quota of steel to these projects was cut off and the supply of concrete was almost nonexistent.[67] By the end of the year it was reported that the progress of De Renzi and Pollini's project had halted, while for all buildings the construction was "practically paralyzed."[68] The issue of the labor force was especially problematic, as the workers, who were largely from the Roman *campagna* and beyond, had to return to their homes because of Allied air raids. During the course of Italy's participation in World War II, the worksite of the Esposizione Universale di Roma was gradually abandoned, facilitating its transformation in unforeseen ways. The photographs of the project from this time show its desolation, poised somewhere between a construction site and a ruin. In Foucault's discussion of biopower he describes the function of racism as being "to fragment, to create caesuras within the biological continuum" and ultimately to establish "the break between what must live and what must die."[69] In considering these thoughts relative to the impact of Fascism's state-sponsored program of racism on architecture, what Foucault describes as "the elimination of the biological threat" was perhaps tied, in the Edifici del Corporativismo, dell'Autarchia e dell'Assistenza e Previdenza Sociale, to the death of modern Italian architecture.

Brian L. McLaren

10

The Invention of Indigenous Architecture

Kenny Cupers

What is indigenous architecture? An example that might come to mind is the traditional German farmstead, nestled in the agrarian landscape or perhaps part of an old village, as is suggested in an early twentieth-century photograph of Golenhofen (figure 10.1). The farmhouses of this picturesque village feature half-timbered facades, clipped gable roofs, dormers, and a variety of pitched roof shapes. Yet despite exhibiting such age-old German building styles, the entire village was meticulously planned and built from scratch just a few years before it was photographed for publication in the magazine *Deutsche Kunst und Dekoration* (German Art and Decoration) in 1906.[1] The ensemble encompassed not only farmsteads but also a church, a school, workers' houses, an inn, a bakery, a poor-house, and even a small public laundry and a fire station, built with material and technologies imported from Berlin. Golenhofen was located in Prussia's eastern, Polish-dominated province of Posen; the village is now in Poland, and bears the name Golęczewo. But at the close of the nineteenth century, this seemingly time-less German hamlet was part of a rural modernization and territorial control project.

Even though indigenous architecture—architecture of, for, and by people native

Fig. 10.1 The village of Golenhofen in the province of Posen, designed by Paul Fischer. Source: "Eine deutsche Dorf-Anlage in den Ostmarken," *Deutsche Kunst und Dekoration* 18, April–September 1906, 536.

to an area—conjures up a sense of timelessness, it is itself not a timeless concept. It was invented in the nineteenth century, and would have important repercussions in the one to follow. By the time Golenhofen was built, there was a well-established discourse in Germany about what architecture was considered native. Even though intellectual elites tended to reserve the term "native" for non-Europeans they considered inferior, they approached rural communities in European provinces with similar assumptions about the innate connection between architecture, land, and racialized notions of human difference. While anthropologists looked for indigeneity in the colonized other, folklorists, as they would come to call themselves, tended to approach the material culture of rural Europe in a like-minded manner in which anything from dress to building came to index ethnic identity. As the notion of the nation gained increasing importance in the nineteenth century, locating the indigenous within one's own society was not only important in order to define that society as modern, but to be grounded and communal in that modernity.

In the course of the nineteenth century, architecture became ever more intensely charged with the task of representing human difference in terms of race. Architecture became part of a powerful set of "invented traditions" used by elites to bolster national pride and the supremacy of whiteness.[2] Imperial Germany is a particularly instructive context to examine how these anxieties about race shaped the discourse of indigenous architecture. Germany lagged behind in the formation

Kenny Cupers

of a national consciousness when compared to England, France, or the United States. The region's multiethnic population and its extreme fragmentation in territorial sovereignty challenged a sense of nationhood both before and after German unification in 1871. Beyond these challenges in the construction of nationhood, Germany also experienced rapid urbanization and mass migration in the late nineteenth and early twentieth centuries, which propelled desires for belonging and rootedness. The concept of *Heimat* (homeland) and its architectural productions such as at Golenhofen were crucial to German nation-building as much as they were strategies to cope with modernization and globalization.[3]

Despite much scholarship that unpacks this cultural and political role of architecture, scholarship on the twentieth century has often continued to accept architecture's claims to represent ethnic identity at face value. This tends to mask the history of modernism as the self-evident spread of "international" architectural principles, forms, and styles. Even the proposition of what has been termed "critical regionalism"—a combination of International Style aesthetics with "local" or "regional" elements—rests on an assumed direct relationship between architecture, ethnic identity, and geographic environment. This assumption becomes particularly problematic for the history of architecture in formerly colonized parts of the world. Up until today, indigenous claims remain central to anti-colonial struggle, and architecture can play a significant role in such struggles. The concept of indigeneity has indeed been mobilized by colonized peoples in the effort to attain self-rule and continues to shape post-independence nationalism, particularly in Africa. But history shows that the kind of work that the idea of indigenousness performs when applied to architecture has not always been emancipatory. Indigenous architecture was promoted and produced by metropolitan elites before it was mobilized by colonized peoples for their own purposes.[4] At the time of Golenhofen's construction, Germany was, after all, both a nation-state under construction, and an empire with colonial ambition both overseas and in Europe. Its architecture was not only an invented tradition for domestic purposes; it was also an instrument of colonial oppression.

Heimat and Lebensraum

In his bestselling *Kulturarbeiten* volumes, published between 1901 and 1917, architect Paul Schultze-Naumburg argued that to protect Germany from the unsettling consequences of industrialization and urbanization, architecture needed to be what was called *bodenständig*—literally rooted in the soil. Styles needed to be native, just like plants, to their environment rather than imported from abroad; he was especially critical about the use of Italian renaissance and French styles in Germany's burgeoning industrial cities. "Rooted" architecture, by contrast, would safeguard the Heimat—an idea that was central to the *Heimatschutz* movement, the environmental and architectural preservation movement that Schultze-Naumburg helped found in 1904. Germans, like other Europeans, made categorical distinctions between their own native populations and the natives elsewhere. The term *eingeboren* (native) was used for Africans, while Heimat and *Bodenständigkeit* were reserved for those individuals indigenous to Germany. Architectural historians have tended to translate bodenständig as contextual or regional, but "indigenous" is in fact a more illuminating translation in this context, since its usage allows one to critically approach the imperial distinction between colonizer and colonized. Despite its romantic provenance and anti-modern overtones, Bodenständigkeit—and the aesthetics associated with it—were fundamental to the development of modern architecture.[5]

Schultze-Naumburg was not the first and certainly not the only one at the time to focus on architecture indigenous to Germany. In 1894, the Berlin Architects' Association (Vereinigung Berliner Architekten) had already begun commissioning a systematic study of the German farmhouse, leading to the publication in 1906 of the encyclopedic book *Das Bauernhaus im Deutschen Reiche und in seinen Grenzgebieten* (figure 10.2).[6] Such studies of German building traditions were part and parcel of the rise of folklore studies, which developed first in the Austro-Hungarian Empire. Since its founding in 1863, the Österreichische Museum für Kunst und Industrie had been exhibiting regional arts and crafts objects to represent the multinational identity of the empire, and during the 1870s, this focus was expanded to include farm buildings.[7] In contrast to the acknowledgment of its multiethnic regional character in Austria-Hungary, however, folk art in Germany was more often cast as naturally unified.[8] Just as the notion of a local Heimat contributed directly to German nationalism, as scholars like Celia Applegate have demonstrated, so was local folk art—whether from the Schwarzwald or Thuringia—understood as a direct expression of the German people, or *Volk*.[9]

Folklorists such as Robert Mielke, cofounder of the Heimatschutz movement, and Oscar Schwindrazheim, who founded the association Volkskunst in Hamburg in 1889, considered folklore to spring from the countryside and thus not from the city. Their unspoken assumption was that rural buildings were more indigenous than urban ones. This rural ideal relied on the romantic intellectual tradition of Johann Gottfried Herder and the work of Wilhelm Heinrich Riehl, one of the founders of German *Volkskunde* (ethnology). In his four-volume *Die Naturgeschichte des Volkes als Grundlage einer deutschen Social-Politik*, written between 1851 and 1869—the most famous volume of which is entitled *Land und Leute* (Land and People)—Riehl emphasized the essential German-ness of the landscape. The book contrasted the agrarian landscapes of France with the forest landscapes of Germany, and found in the latter the uniqueness of its national character. Riehl

Kenny Cupers

Fig. 10.2 Cover of *Das Bauernhaus im Deutschen Reiche und in seinen Grenzgebieten* (Dresden: Verlag von Gerhard Kühtmann, 1906).

understood German culture, more than any, as anchored in the land, and thus organically grown through nature and history. His anti-urban and anti-modern ideology had a long-lasting influence on German intellectual culture in the second half of the nineteenth century.[10]

By the turn of the twentieth century, through the work of Schultze-Naumburg, Mielke, and others, these romantic ideas had developed into a more deterministic mapping of German architecture onto the national territory. Architectural forms, styles, and details were systematically projected onto territory in order to suggest that racial identity was rooted in the land, and that local homelands could be subsumed under the umbrella of the German "race." At the same time, the folk-loric celebration of Germany's man-made landscapes, by Heimatschutz advocates and reform movements such as the *Wandervogel*, was not foreign to imperialist ambitions, and in many ways correlated with emerging geopolitical theories. The concept of Lebensraum (literally, living space), developed by the geographer Friedrich Ratzel, best encapsulates these imperialist ambitions. Lebensraum was defined as "the geographical surface area required to support a living species at its current population size and mode of existence."[11] As an evolutionary rationality of environment, Lebensraum impacted older concepts such as Heimat, which were based on more static connections between people and the land, as formulated by Riehl earlier in the century. Ratzel's concept thus signaled a revolution in how space was understood: social and political space was no longer essentially fixed but could now be conceived of as a vital category.[12]

Lebensraum is one of the most well-known German political concepts of the twentieth century. After the treaty of Versailles, radical conservatives harnessed it to argue for the establishment of a new German empire, and the Nazis subse-quently employed it to legitimize the invasion of Poland. But its political impact was felt even before that; the concept was formulated in 1901 to legitimize German settler colonialism. Ratzel's concept was a way of extending biological principles to geography, casting the Darwinian struggle for life as, essentially, a struggle for space.[13] By conceptualizing the state as an organism rooted in the soil, he suggested that just like plants spreading their roots, a people needed to expand its territory or die. This idea, of environment as a category of life itself, resonated with a range of turn-of-the-century reformers, including Heimatschutz advocates. Opposed to turning to the widespread urbanization, industrialization, and internationalization of the time, and a corresponding instrumentalist view of nature and human society, these advocates held up biology as the guiding principle for social and political affairs. And it was this kind of naturalist nativism that undergirded the deploy-ment of indigenous architecture in the German Empire—from the Prussian coun-tryside to sub-Saharan Africa.

Kenny Cupers

Systematic Settlement

Golenhofen was a rural modernization project of the Prussian Settlement Commission. Between its establishment in 1886 and 1918, this state organization settled close to 150,000 Germans in farming villages in Prussia's eastern provinces of Posen and West Prussia. Around the time of Polish independence in 1918, the Settlement Commission proclaimed to have built 57 churches, 479 schools, and more than 700 other public buildings, in addition to thousands of farmsteads.[14] Central to such "internal colonization" efforts, as Germans called them, was the aim of strengthening German national identity in the eastern provinces. Resettling German farmers and workers was a way to oppress Polish people, and this goal was explicitly formulated by the Settlement Commission at its outset.[15] Polish resistance only grew in the following decades, in part as a response to the work of the Prussian Settlement Commission. Land prices skyrocketed because Polish farmers were eager to buy back land from German settlers, which led to new legislation in 1908 to allow the direct expropriation of Polish farmers.[16] But the oppression ultimately failed; it only further heightened Polish nationalism. In the period 1896–1914, the Polish anti-colonial movement gained 181,437 hectares of land.[17]

German officials cast Polish farmers as backwards, their agricultural techniques as inefficient, and their architecture as primitive. Tropes of colonial ideology thus seem readily applicable to the resettlement project. Yet despite some parallels with overseas colonialism and the increasingly racialized understanding of German-Polish differences, the category of race worked quite differently in Prussia than it did, for instance, in the empire's African colonies. Although Germans saw the Poles as inferior, they were still incontestably European. Polish people had official citizenship in the Prussian state and there were no interdictions on Polish-German marriages or explicit segregation policies.[18] In fact, the determination of German and Polish nationality was often an ambiguous and contradictory exercise. Since the beginning of the nineteenth century, Prussian statisticians had used linguistic status as the determinant of nationality.[19] Yet, in practice, categorical distinctions between Germans and Poles were often extremely difficult to make—in some regions language was to determine nationhood, while in others "behavior showing adherence to the German state [Staatsgedanken]" was proposed as a supposed determinant.[20] The region's Jews, living mostly in cities, were sadly caught in between German nationalism and its Polish response.

The Prussian Settlement Commission was not solely motivated by an anti-Polish agenda. It was in fact part of a larger set of programs focused on rural modernization. In other parts of Germany, including those without a marked non-German presence, a range of organizations pursued internal colonization as a way to rationalize rural land use and increase agricultural productivity.[21] The German countryside had been emptying throughout much of the nineteenth century as peasants moved to cities or abroad. German governments responded by launching programs that would repopulate the countryside and expand agricultural productivity. Like other programs, the Prussian Settlement Commission aimed to transform large land holdings into smaller farmsteads. Social as much as it was economic in its aims, this measure would counter rural proletarianization by strengthening the German rural middle class.

Architecture and planning played a key role in this project. Village layouts such as Golenhofen's aimed to create a community of German settlers while providing each farmer with enough land for sustenance and independence. During the first years of the commission's activities, settlers were responsible for building their own farmsteads, using their own skills and building traditions. However, the commission soon took charge of the massive building operations, from the provision of materials to design and construction. The project's chief architect, Paul Fischer, was responsible for the designs. Although he remains virtually unknown in architectural history today—he is not to be confused with the more well-known architect Theodor Fischer—Fischer was well-versed in architectural debates of his time and was particularly drawn to Heimatschutz ideas.[22] In the first half of the 1890s, Fischer pursued an extensive survey of the farmsteads constructed by the first settlers to Prussia, who came from as far as Hungary and the Baltic. A decade into the commission's building experience, Fischer concluded that neither self-building by the farmers nor custom design by his office was ideal. The first method was economically inefficient, and the second led to buildings that were often unsuited to farmers' needs. Consequently, Fischer implemented a new system of building that was both centrally administered and adjustable to local needs and circumstances. The commission's central administration would pay for wages and materials, so building production could be significantly streamlined.[23] At the same time, designs were to be customized by individual estate managers.[24] Such a system required pre-approved, standardized designs, which Fischer compiled in a series of catalogues (figure 10.3).[25] The designs were inspired by his survey of the kinds of structures settling farmers had built for themselves. Fischer understood his work as a process of collecting of Germanic building traditions, inspired by the self-building practices of migrating farmers from lower Saxony and Westfalen to Hungary, mobilized for a rationalized design and construction system.

Reflecting the contemporaneous debates within the Deutscher Werkbund, a German association of architects, designers, industrialists, and artists, Fischer's work was shaped both by a romantic, anti-urban nationalism and the imperative of standardization. In fact, despite the ethos of standardization that underlay the commission's building production, Fischer was adamant about stylistic diversity.

Kenny Cupers

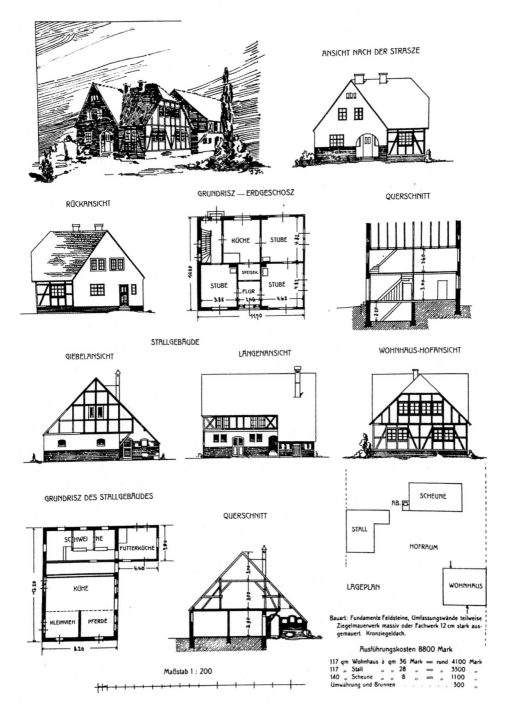

Fig. 10.3 Farmstead design by Paul Fischer. Source: Paul Fischer, *Ansiedlungsbauten in den Provinzen Posen und Westpreußen* (Halle a.S.: Ludwig Hofstetter, 1904), 3.

None of the commission's dozens of churches was the same. The goal of creating a feeling of place by promoting architectural difference reflected the ambitions of Heimatschutz designers. Architectural forms inspired by native traditions—even if these regions were located a thousand kilometers away—would help settlers feel at home. Whether the farmers trying to establish livelihoods in new surroundings cared much for the intricate half-timbering is unclear. Many may in fact have preferred more rudimentary, economical buildings. The ultimate goal of the Prussian Resettlement Program, however, was not simply to build homes, but to reinforce the homeland. This is what informed the creation of a rational system of so-called indigenous architecture that was meant to make centuries of Polish presence in eastern Prussia irrelevant.

Building a New Homeland

Compared with other major European powers, Germany came late not only to the business of nation-building, but also to the colonial project. Only with the Berlin Conference of 1884–1885 did Germany become an imperial power and begin to officially acquire colonial possessions in Africa (now Namibia, Tanzania, Cameroon, and Togo), the Pacific (New Guinea and Samoa), and China (port concessions). In these overseas colonies, architecture was similarly used to construct a homeland, and building was accompanied by violent practices of dispossession and annihilation. This was particularly true in Namibia. Soon after its formal colonization in 1884, armchair colonists began to portray German Southwest Africa as an ideal territory on which to expand German Lebensraum. While the region's existing polities had participated in capitalist exchange for centuries, and local societies had been reshaped by long-distance trade and migration from the Cape Colony, the relatively short period of German colonization (until 1915) constituted a radical moment of rupture—not so much for bringing the region into the dynamics of global capitalism than for ruthless annihilation and the systematic dispossession of African land and wealth.[26] After the genocidal war with Namibia from 1904 to 1908, the German colonial state aimed to transform those who had survived into a landless proletariat, to destroy their culture and political organization, and to force them into serving as a disciplined labor force for white employers.

While white settlement remained nevertheless sparse, and fewer than 15,000 Germans moved to Namibia during the German colonial period (compare this with the 150,000 settlements in eastern Prussia alone), settler colonialism in Namibia constituted a radical restructuring in the ownership, use, meaning, and construction of the landscape. As they moved to this region's dry highlands and deserts, German settlers relied not only on African forced and wage labor, but at least initially, on local building techniques. The architecture of the region's existing peoples included domed huts, first represented in early nineteenth-century drawings. Germans called these *pontoks*, to mean any dwelling type built by and for natives. In addition, the settlers adopted the Afrikaans word *hartbeeshuis* to typify the dwellings built by groups of mixed African and European descent. Just like their builders, German colonists understood such dwellings as a hybrid type, built using "native" techniques but essentially "European" in form.[27] By reducing architectural form to racial type, colonists denied both the variety and historical change of dwelling cultures in precolonial Namibia.

In a pamphlet distributed to the first settlers, the German Colonial Society explained how to use such native building techniques. For the roofs, the pamphlet suggested weaving together small trunks and twigs, rather than using corrugated metal.[28] Not only was corrugated metal expensive to import from Europe, it also collected the intensive desert heat. Over the following decades, however, corrugated metal—together with all sorts of building elements such as windows and doors—was increasingly imported for roof construction and became the colony's standard roof material. Similarly, for masonry walls, builders gradually replaced local stone with factory-produced cement blocks as they became locally available. Despite the growing influence of such modern building materials, or perhaps because of it, Germans increasingly insisted on the Bodenständigkeit of their new architecture.

In the colonial imagination, farmsteads were often thought of as naturally rooted in their new homeland—just as they would have been in Germany. This idea of natural rooting was suggested in drawings and paintings, such as those by Erich Mayer.[29] But it was more than just imagined or represented. Architecture effectively served to transform the colony into a new, German homeland. Half-timbering and clipped gable roofs constituted often self-conscious strategies to emphasize German-ness in a geographical and climatic environment that continued to estrange and threaten colonial settlers. Industrial corrugated metal roofing was made to emulate complicated roof forms and details, including turrets, clipped gables, and dormers. Despite the fact that these could be historically found across much of northern and central Europe, and had more to do with the European popularity of the neo-Tudor style than with historical German farmhouses, colonists understood these elements to be essentially German. Moreover, these elements were often given a new function. Dormers rarely functioned as dormers, for example; they were instead used to allow natural roof ventilation and to mitigate the considerable heat built up under the metal roofs. The veranda became a dominant feature of rural architecture, and could be seen in rudimentary farm buildings as well as in more extravagant, architect-designed farmsteads.[30] Built across colonial Africa and South Asia, the veranda was inserted in a growing stylistic vocabulary of German Southwest African architecture. Despite its quasi-global spread, the veranda came to be portrayed as a new element of specifically German architecture for the new Heimat.[31]

Of course, the creation of a new homeland was hardly a matter of architectural form or style alone. It required systematic efforts to physically dispossess Africans and segregate their bodies in time and space. Control of the colonized population entailed creating enclaves, building fences, and enforcing curfews.[32] The building of white settlements such as Windhoek also entailed the creation of native settlements, locations, or *werften*—a form of segregation that was later formalized in the South African apartheid system.[33] In this process, the pontok was no longer understood as indigenous architecture, but rather came to shelter a landless class of refugees in marginalized enclaves or, during the Namibian war, in concentration camps.[34]

Since the beginning of German colonial rule, African resistance had prompted intensive militarization, which continued to shape the production and meaning of the Namibian built landscape at large. German colonization had left a sprawl of military infrastructure, in particular forts, across the country, especially along the line that would become to delineate the "Police Zone," as the Germans called it, demarcating the southern two-thirds of the country where colonial control could be maintained.[35] But militarization shaped civilian architecture as well. This was perhaps most striking in the crenellations that appeared on many private residential buildings. Housing projects for officers adopted the layouts and sometimes even the massing of forts.[36] Even though such military architectural elements might just as well be found in the residential architecture of Berlin's leafy suburbs at this time, they attained a meaning particular to the colonial context of German Southwest Africa.

The prison of the coastal town of Swakopmund, designed by Otto Ertl and finished in 1909, suggests how militarization and Bodenständigkeit collided in this context.[37] Like other prisons, the building was organized by strict segregation, with separate entries and cells for white and nonwhite prisoners. With a mastery unusual for the colonial builders in the empire's overseas colonies, this building displayed many of the stylistic tropes of the Heimatschutz movement, replete with medieval-looking cornerstones, half-timbering, turrets, and protruding gables (figure 10.4). The architect's idea for the prison was that all its building materials should be "appropriate to the local climatic conditions," and therefore he chose ashlar stone masonry.[38] This aim seemed to be lifted from Schultze-Naumburg's ideas about Bodenständigkeit as outlined in the *Kulturarbeiten* volumes. Yet in a colonial context where architectural design served to legitimize the dispossession of exactly those who had indigenous rights to the soil, the cruel irony of these ambitions seems to have gone entirely unnoticed.

The modern invention of indigenous architecture, foundational to the

Kenny Cupers

Fig. 10.4 Prison of Swakopmund, designed by Otto Ertl, 1909. Source: Cupers, 2014.

Heimatschutz movement, was not only an instrument of cultural reform or environmental preservation in historically German cities and countrysides, but also an instrument of the European colonial project. From Namibia to eastern Prussia, architecture was mobilized to colonize land and to reinforce German imperial reign. Paradoxically, the accompanying architectural styles used the idea of indigenousness against those who had indigenous rights to the land. In the German empire, indigenous architecture was not something that was simply found, or even discovered; it was something that needed to be built and imposed. Indigenous architecture was not just about employing the local to build the nation, but about reshaping the local in order to expand empire. As it required a new, unprecedented harnessing of people and materials, empire building entailed an architectural project of indigenizing—of assigning people to specific places, making those people belong to that place, and dispossessing others. For cultural reformers in Germany, architectural indigeneity served as the medium for a new way of life, in touch with nature and tradition. For officials of the Settlement Commission and colonial governments, it allowed for the implantation of a rational system of settlement. For German settlers, it offered the opportunity to feel at home while they were far away. And for Polish landholders and African pastoralists, it was a weapon that enforced their dispossession.

PART IV

RACE AND REPRESENTATION

11

Erecting the Skyscraper, Erasing Race

Adrienne Brown

The skyscraper may seem like a strange place to tell a story about race at the turn of the century. All the architects who designed the first generation of skyscrapers that we know of were white. Iconic images of heroic-looking men working high above the city to construct these structures widely circulated through American mainstream periodicals in this period, but the presence of the many Mohawk Indians who appear in these photographs went generally unacknowledged for decades.[1] We know relatively little, moreover, about the black and eastern European laborers who dug their foundations and cast their steel supports. Even the place of the black elevator operator in skyscrapers was uncertain in this early era, as union records mark the hesitations of these organizations to allow black men to work in such close proximity to white women, who were increasingly occupying skyscrapers as workers and customers.[2] While several other architectural forms more readily suggest a connection to race either through their association with racial minorities—think plantation structures, tenement buildings, or vernacular architecture such as shotgun houses—or through direct lines of influence between architects and minority subjects—Josephine Baker's encounters with architects Le

Corbusier and Adolf Loos for instance—the skyscraper seems to be the least "raced" of all.

In my book, *The Black Skyscraper: Architecture and the Perception of Race*, I examine responses to the early skyscraper across a number of genres in order to show how the early skyscraper was both shaped by debates about racial formation emerging in the United States at the turn of the century while also shaping how race was perceived, imagined, and experienced in urban centers. While seconding the growing chorus of architects and architectural historians, many of whom are featured in this volume, pushing their disciplines to better address the historical neglect of race as a category of analysis, I came away from my interdisciplinary work on the skyscraper believing that the responsibility for thinking about race's relationship to the built environment belongs just as much to scholars of race as it is does to those of architecture. In other words, not only must architecture take up matters of race with more urgency, but critical race studies must also more fully attend to the range of ways the built environment plays a role in shaping what literary critic Anne Cheng has called the material life of race.[3]

Much of the scholarship on architecture and race has so far focused on recovering race's influence on architecture's design, attending to how architects and planners both explicitly and implicitly imagined architectures to be in service of specific raced populations or racialized ideologies while at the same time contributing to the direct marginalization or indirect neglect of others. And the early skyscraper's archive certainly lends itself to such a reading. When looking at writing emerging from the industries and professions most responsible for the skyscraper's early materialization, race's role in shaping its material and aesthetic development is a fact hidden in plain sight. It pervades period accounts of steel manufacturing and skyscraper construction in which managers used preexisting racial antagonisms between workers to better exploit their labor and in debates amongst architects about preventing a "miscegenated" facade scheme for the skyscraper from surfacing. These instances affirm William Gleason's central claim in *Sites Unseen: Architecture, Race, and American Literature* that "the built environment is always shaped in some way by race whether such shaping is explicitly acknowledged or understood."[4]

I very much subscribe to Gleason's claim and underscore the need for scholars to continue investigating the ways race shapes the built environment across different contexts, geographies, and historical eras. At the same time, I more strongly wish to pursue the inverse of this claim—that race is always shaped in some way by the built environment. While the humanities have gone through a "spatial turn," embracing an analysis of space as a way of understanding the production of the social, scholars have been slower to explore the ways that, as Dianne Harris writes, "space is equally significant in the construction of ideas about race and identity."[5]

Adrienne Brown

While Gleason's argument about the built environment's racial foundations can be corroborated using the methods and archives that have typically fallen under the domain of architectural history (if not its ideological orientations), the claim that race is always shaped by the built environment is most productively pursued and unpacked not only by architects and architectural historians but by scholars of race working from within a variety of disciplines to chart race's ontology and epistemology, its comparative formation across regions, and, even more basically, how race is perceived and felt in distinct built spaces across time. To tell the story of racial perception in any time or place necessitates considering how the built environment helps determine its operations. As architecture changes, so do the measures of race, a condition that should encourage scholars in a multitude of disciplines to think about race in more site-specific terms—decentering national and regional contexts in order to attend to the more immediate types of material landscapes that condition racial experience.

The skyscraper, originally envisioned as an economically efficient way of managing the large populations that were overwhelming downtown corridors, appears in a range of materials between the 1880s and 1930 as an obstacle to racial perception and differentiation. From its distancing apex—reducing bodies to specks—to its interior spaces housing large numbers of people who may never meaningfully encounter one another, to the shadowy mega-blocks it formed at street-level, the skyscraper called attention to the malleable nature of perception. Prompting writer Henry James to put the verb *seeing* itself in quotation marks when faced with its overwhelming size, the skyscraper suggested the ineffectiveness of emerging Jim Crow practices and the de facto segregation more common in the North to regulate racial contact in spaces in which bodies appeared indeterminate.[6] Writers representing the skyscraper during its first forty years accused this architecture of making it harder to anchor racial knowledge in either invisible blood or visible skin, unsettling what it meant to both perceive race and feel raced.[7]

But in what follows I focus on a different aspect of the skyscraper's history—considering the skyscraper not as a site where bodies more generally are perceived as raced but as a stage framing the bodies of construction workers whose labor was often viewed as spectacular, theatrical, and available for public consumption. I focus here on builder William Starrett's 1928 monograph on skyscraper construction in which race proves to be an inconvenient detail when rendering the exceedingly large onsite workforces it was his job to organize and manage. Representing his employees' bodies more like instruments belonging to the larger operational network he steered, Starrett's monograph demonstrates the role the perceivable racial detail played in determining how these men would be consumed and, not uncommonly, made disposable.

• • •

Skyscraper construction workers were nearly as iconic in the skyscraper's earliest era as these buildings themselves. Moving across high beams with seeming fearlessness, workers commonly known as "beamwalkers" attracted large crowds of people upwardly craning their necks to watch their spectacular feats of labor.[8] Beamwalkers were, as novelist Faith Baldwin described in a 1931 novel, the "star performances of this theatrical spectacle played out against the backdrop of an indifferent and challenged sky."[9] But whereas the beamwalker attracted attention because of the heights at which he worked, the many other types of laborers who worked on skyscraper construction sites alongside and below them fascinated the public due to their sheer numbers, with thousands of men working on site at any given moment. The busyness and nimbleness on display at construction sites compelled the public to stop and stare. As one *New York Times* article from 1929 notes, "While the spectacle which the building of a skyscraper presents has become a familiar one in New York, the people of the metropolis still find in it their favorite drama of the streets," going on to describe the "fascinated groups of people on the street," "endlessly engross[ed]," who "stare" with "lively interest" at the "infinite activity involving the men of a hundred trades."[10] Skyscraper construction sites were dynamic places around which urban residents congregated en masse to watch these various types of laboring bodies in motion. Within the modern city in which most large-scale industrial operations were housed behind closed doors, as tragically demonstrated by the Triangle Shirtwaist Factory fire, or situated outside the city, as was true of logging, migrant farming, and coal mining, skyscraper construction was distinct for being the largest industrial operation regularly visible to the general public within city limits.[11] But skyscraper construction sites enticed readers and viewers far beyond city limits. Images, cartoons, and articles featuring skyscraper laborers circulated frequently within American newspapers and magazines around the turn of the century, consumed by audiences who might never see a skyscraper in person but could still be awed by the death-defying feats its construction entailed.

The erection of the Empire State Building gives us a window into the magnitude of this work. Completed in one year and forty-five days, several months ahead of schedule, the 102-floor skyscraper required 7,000,000 man-hours to be built, with as many as 3,400 laborers working on site at one time during peak construction.[12] But even as the feat of building something as large as the Empire State building could be said to exemplify the power of man, affirming a teleological narrative of civilization's progression, skyscrapers seemed to simultaneously throw human agency into question, with writers wondering how it was possible to ascribe these superhuman structures to the efforts of mere men. As Mary Borden describes

Adrienne Brown

in her 1927 novel, *Flamingo*, while the city's skyscraper-filled landscape suggested "some super human agency had been at work here," upon closer inspection, "the strange thing is that men should believe they build this city."[13] Relying on "machines a thousandfold more powerful than men" for the city's erection, it seems incredible to her narrator that "the men of the city, the citizens of New York, they called themselves, thought they were doing it."[14] Given the widespread concern about the completed skyscraper as an agent of dehumanization, answers to who (or what) was capable of producing such a structure proved expansive and expansively erratic.

The spectacular nature of the skyscraper construction worker's labor, the job's inherent danger, and the incredulousness expressed by members of the public that men alone could be responsible for these seemingly extra-human structures resulted in this figure taking on an ambivalent iconicity. Referred to as a degenerate "man-monkey" and the more noble "cowboy of the sky," the beamwalker in particular was simultaneously a hero and a freak, a daredevil and an object of pity, a "nigger-head man" and a "man who knows his business," an evolved "specialist" and mechanistic cog.[15] He, like most of the other workers on the skyscraper, appeared to the public as, to use Anne Cheng's terms, an undecidable amalgamation of modernism's "three foundational, distinctive categories"—the animal, the human, and the mechanical—which, despite their "ideological separation," were often rendered as "stylistically identical" in modernist aesthetics.[16] Modernism's interest in this trio, I would add, originates in the much longer historical preoccupation with solving the representational riddle of the worker, conceived of simultaneously as an abstract surplus, a less-evolved species, a machine to be industrially optimized, and a catalyst for a future proletarian consciousness. The modernist tendency to represent the animal, the human, and the mechanical as stylistically similar must also be understood in relation to the specifically raced history of indeterminable personhood foundational to the emergence of chattel slavery.

One of the key decisions writers and artists had to make when representing skyscraper laborers was whether to focus on the living or dead. The alleged number of laborers' lives lost during the construction of Empire State in particular wildly fluctuated in the period following its completion. As historian John Tauranac explains in his history of the Empire State's erection, it was rumored that as many as one hundred men died between the demolition of the old Waldorf-Astoria and the construction of the Empire State Building in its place. Writer Edmund Wilson pegged the number at forty-eight, while a gruesome illustration in the socialist literary magazine, the *New Masses*, featuring jumbled white corpses stacked against a dark city backdrop, put the total at forty-two (figure 11.1).[17] To end such speculation, Empire State's general contracting company, Starrett Brothers & Eken, released the real figures. Out of an average of six hundred men employed in

Walter Steinhilber

42 men killed constructing the new Empire State Building . . . "the building was completed on time."

Fig. 11.1 Walter Steinhilber, "42 men killed constructing the Empire State Building . . . 'the building was completed on time.'" From the *New Masses*, June 1931.

the demolition of the Waldorf-Astoria and five thousand men employed on the construction of the Empire State building, five workers had been killed on-site: one worker was hit by a truck as he was sawing a plank; the second ran into a blast area; the third stepped off a scaffold; the fourth fell down an elevator shaft; and the fifth was struck by a hoist.[18]

The Starretts had much to gain by reigning in the erroneous accounts of construction fatalities. Picking up where the architect's role as designer left off, the builder, also known as the general contractor, was responsible for turning the idea for a building into a cost-efficient reality, supplying and coordinating the materials, laborers, equipment, and services needed for it to be finished on time and on budget. A building may have been designed by the architect, but it was produced by the contractor in concert with the laborers he gathered and coordinated to make its erection a profitable reality. The Starrett brothers actively worked to displace the perception of the architect as sole designer of a building, arguing through books and biographies that the erection of a building was an aesthetic work in and of itself, separate from, if not greater than, the formal properties of the completed product.[19] Not only were the exorbitantly inaccurate death tolls for Empire State bad for profits and for their reputation as businessmen—they were bad for their budding aesthetic reputation, threatening to sour the greatest testament to their organizational artistry.

Their most extensive argument for the beauty of the work of building appears in the 1928 monograph *Skyscrapers and the Men Who Build Them*, written by Col. William A. Starrett, the younger of the two Starrett brothers.[20] The first book dedicated entirely to the structure, *Skyscrapers* opens by recuperating the completed building type as an aesthetic object, lamenting that "the skyscraper has had to submit for forty years to the abuse and patronage of aesthetic critics, many of them architects of note." But Starrett was much more interested in connecting the skyscraper's importance to its "beauty of power," a beauty he ultimately deemed inseparable from the powerful hands of its builders.[21] In line with this thinking, most of Starrett's three-hundred-page book treats the completed skyscraper as a matter of secondary importance to the extraordinary organization of the labor force behind its construction. As Starrett writes, "When one views it as a great and complicated operation involving skill and daring, with a wealth of adventure and the joy of fulfillment of a hard task well done, the scale of bigness may again grip the imagination, and in the story of how it is all done may yet be held the romance of a triumph no less stirring than the victory of battle, or the leading of a nation into the paths of peace and prosperity."[22] It is this "scale of bigness" that Starrett attempts to capture for much of his book.

Starrett remains largely committed to rendering building in the terms of romantic masculine adventure, displacing the *New Masses*' portrait of construction as a cold factory of killing with a narrative of stirring unity. Yet his first chapter renders the scene of building on a very different scale—that of the intimate and familial—assimilating the skyscraper into progressively smaller units of belonging. *Skyscrapers* opens with the unit of the nation, declaring the structure to be "the most distinctively American thing in the world."[23] Framing the skyscraper as "all American and all ours in its conception, all important in our metropolitan life," Starrett quickly paints a picture of the nation defined by its citizens' shared appreciation for it.[24] Transitioning from a vision of the skyscraper as completed icon to its status as a large-scale construction site, he narrows the unit of belonging down to the metropolis, turning the city imagined by many as untenably heterogeneous into one "whole citizenry" united around the spectacular feat of skyscraper construction fueling "our pride of civic acquisition."[25] Construction for him is a "drama" choreographed by builders and enjoyed by "the enthusiastic spectator who gazes with admiration at some feat of skill and daring performed before his very eyes."[26] Starrett frames the scene of building as an act of communal gazing—and thusly civic polity—as city residents together "recognize it as another of our distinctive triumphs, another token of our solid and material growth."[27]

From national iconography to the more specific drama of metropolitan belonging, Starrett goes on to scale skyscraper construction down even further to the unit of family. He acknowledges four Chicagoan "chiefs" who served as the original pioneers of the skyscraper—architects William Le Baron Jenney, Daniel Burnham, John Root, and William Holabird—rendering them as folk heroes of sorts, cataloging their rough-and-tumble pasts. He then weaves his own family history into this tale of the skyscraper's invention. Not only was he "a boy in Chicago when the first skyscraper arose," but he "knew most of the architects and engineers who devised and erected them, and served as a cub under some of them."[28] Belonging to "a family of builders, one of five brothers who have designed and built a vast number of skyscrapers," Starrett ends this first chapter by turning this national epic of the skyscraper into a family yarn, referring to Daniel Burnham as "Uncle Dan" and relaying the "Scotch origin" of his own family as they proved to be integral to the expanded history of construction the book sets out to provide.[29]

Through these narrowing constructs of the nation, metropolis, and the family, Starrett stresses skyscraper construction as not just homogeneous but homogenizing, inaugurating a process of belonging that works first as a symbol, then as a stage, and finally as a domestic drama. As the national body is ultimately displaced by the familial one, the text distinctly marks the skyscraper's bloodline as Anglo-American, emerging from the Scotch origins of the Starretts in addition to the pedigrees of its four "chiefs." Erased from this intimate family tree, perhaps unsurprisingly, is an acknowledgement of the actual American Indians who worked on this structure as well as the myriad of immigrant and ethnic laborers who joined

Adrienne Brown

them.[30] In his casual use of the word *chief*, Starrett invokes the figure of the Indian while vanishing the place of his actual body—active in skyscraper construction longer than Starrett's family—from the scene of building entirely.[31]

While race becomes a way to genealogically and metaphorically mark the elite world of architects and builders as a close-knit tribe, when Starrett moves into the body of the book where he details the various stages and categories of labor required to erect a skyscraper, the language of race suddenly disappears. Not only does Starrett decline to invoke race in his descriptions of the various laboring bodies at work on the skyscraper's "scale of bigness," but he foregoes marking their bodies in any particularizing fashion. Men are tersely described solely by what they do—"work-gangs sweat and toil behind chugging, hissing air-drills," "the man tightens his pull on the now idle rope"—rather than in terms of their physical characteristics.[32] Starrett attends more to the equipment the men work with than to the men themselves. In fact, the one time a racial descriptor enters his descriptive lexicon, it is used to describe a machine—"a small winch or 'niggerhead' that looks like a steel spool" attended to by "a watchful man."[33]

A similar investment in deemphasizing the sovereign worker emerges across the seventy-two images Starrett chose to include in *Skyscrapers*. Periodical profiles of skyscraper laborers preceding his monograph tended to feature tight shots of workers' bodies juxtaposed with the abstract city above which they perch, as in the iconic *Lunch atop a Skyscraper*, or kinetically engaging the machinery they operated, as did many of the celebrated images taken by photographers Lewis Hines and Margaret Bourke-White. By contrast, the majority of the images Starrett includes in *Skyscrapers* do not feature individual laborers but instead focus on either the machinery they operated, often dwarfing them, the completed buildings they helped to construct, or capture empty or sparsely populated construction sites, giving a sense of the vastness of the enterprise in the absence of any visible workers (figures 11.2–11.4). When workers do appear relatively close in the frame, they are often looking away from the camera, their faces obscure and their bodies blurred in motion.

Starrett's decision to render individual laborers as generally nondescript in both the prose and images within his book sits in stark contrast to how skyscraper labor was being portrayed not only in photographs but a range of other forms of print media during the late nineteenth and early twentieth centuries, dutifully marking the race of laboring bodies in an almost ethnographic fashion. Juxtapose Starrett's unraced workers, for instance, with the emphasis on racial difference demarcating skyscraper laborers featured in the 1911 *Everybody Magazine* profile, "Just Wops," cataloging the "Dagos, niggers, and Hungarians" who were treated as "unintelligent, sweating workers who could be killed without counting."[34] Or see the 1905 film *The Skyscrapers of New York*, featuring a character named Dago Pete getting in

Foundation of the New York Life Insurance Building, New York. The excavation was blasted out of solid rock and is one of the largest rock excavations ever attempted in Manhattan. In the deep basement the rock had to be excavated for over 72 feet below the street level. The rise and fall of the line of solid granite of the Island of Manhattan is clearly shown along the walls.

Fig. 11.2 From William Starrett's *Skyscrapers and the Men Who Build Them* (New York: Scribner's, 1928).

a fight atop his skyscraper jobsite, or Willa Cather's short story from 1912, "Behind the Singer Tower," featuring a gang of "twenty dagos" ultimately treated as disposable by their rapacious foreman.[35] Langston Hughes wrote two poems featured in 1926's *The Weary Blues* highlighting the contribution of black labor to the skyscraper's construction.[36]

Adrienne Brown

Courtesy of Underpinning & Foundation Co., Inc.

After a tube has been driven a certain depth, a blast of air under pressure of 100 pounds per square inch is suddenly released. The explosion forces the material within the tube out of it.

Courtesy of George A. Fuller Co.

An open caisson with interlocking edges of steel sheet piling. They are made in various lengths, and when driven, present a continuous barrier against quicksand and water. Such a cofferdam is cross-braced at intervals as it is driven, and the material excavated from the inside.

Courtesy of the Foundation Co.

The enormous supply of compressed air necessary for a large caisson job is indicated by the machinery shown above. This plant was temporarily on the job for the American Telephone Company Building, New York.

Fig. 11.3 From William Starrett's *Skyscrapers and the Men Who Build Them* (New York: Scribner's, 1928).

An addition to this building in Detroit made it necessary to replace the columns below the second floor and add piers forty feet deep for the new columns. Temporary trusses were installed and the load of about 500 tons to the column was transferred to temporary piers and columns which were pretested to overload. The new columns were then installed.

Hudson Department Store, Detroit. Making the general cellar excavation after the caissons, columns, and cellar walls had been installed in pits and the steel work erected.

Courtesy of Spencer, White & Prentis, Inc.

Fig. 11.4 From William Starrett's *Skyscrapers and the Men Who Build Them* (New York: Scribner's, 1928).

Contrastingly, journalists interested in glorifying construction for mainstream and middlebrow papers as a testament to capitalism's awesome power tended to emphasize skyscraper construction sites as the domain of a heroic white workforce. A 1908 piece from the Munsey periodical the *Scrap Book* titled "Men-Monkeys Who Build Our Babels" reported ironworkers as being "principally Irish, English and American, with a sprinkling of Italian."[37] A similar article about skyscraper construction from 1908 by Ernest Poole notes the presence of an incompetent "Mac" and "a slow-minded Swede" amidst the "American English, Irish, French Canadians, Swedes, now and then an Italian" on-site before acknowledging the "two full-blooded Indians" also present. Cromwell Childe's 1901 profile of sky-scraper workers warns that "a nigger-head man"—a term describing a worker manning a specific kind of tool known as a "nigger-head," but which also poten-tially alludes to this figure's lower status on the worksite—who fails to "know his business" can put his coworkers at great risk. The article goes on to note with relief, however, that most skyscraper laborers were not in fact of such stock. First describ-ing the "absence of dialect" he heard on-site, Childe goes on to testify to the Anglo roots of most of the workers he observed: "Nearly all are workmen that are widely traveled, nearly all are American-born with any provincialisms they may have had knocked off by contact with men from other sections. Americans, Scotchmen, Irishmen, Englishmen, make up the roll of these iron-workers, with a few Canadian Indian half-breeds, who are highly esteemed for their endurance, strength, and skill." In articles like this one, the skyscraper construction sites appear the ideal melting pot, forging assimilative intimacies for the "nearly all"— deracinating those whom the author wants to claim as part of one happy Anglo family while marking out those with Indian blood as literal "breeds" unto them-selves despite their mixed ancestry. When the specters of Mohawk labor do appear, it seems to be largely in the service of securing white laboring solidarity in terms of kinship from which these men were exiled.[38]

Starrett, by contrast, does not paint an image of skyscraper construction as a model of melting-pot democracy—depicting how the act of construction folds together variously raced bodies to create a collective unit, as was a common trope for writing about labor in the period—nor does he double-down and stereotype certain jobs as held by specific ethnic groups as was the norm in the popular press. Rather, he refuses racial markers all together. For a text dedicated to bringing the machinations of skyscraper labor to the public's attention, race is a detail that goes dutifully unseen in his rendering of the "drama" of building beyond the first chap-ter. Starrett's decision to deracinate the scene of skyscraper construction fits his agenda for *Skyscrapers and the Men Who Build Them*—to redistribute the layman's attention away from the individual laborer and toward the less visible and more artful mechanisms of capitalist organization making the visage of the heroic laborer possible. In making generic the bodies of skyscraper laborers and describing them more as instruments animated by capitalist organization rather than as animating agents themselves, Starrett combats the visual power of the sovereign worker on high, an image available every day to passersby and further reinforced by the numerous images that accompanied popular stories of skyscraper construction in the press. For the inquisitive spectator whom Starrett depicts as wondering "where does it all come from? Whence these planks these rivets and forges, these hoists for material, all arrived as if by magic?" his answer ensures that the harder-to-see labor of the builder's organizational technique gets its due credit. Starrett writes of the scene of construction that "it is all a part of the builder's plan." "Yes the *things one sees* and *a thousand things unseen* come not by magic, but as the result of vigilant and organized forethought." By refusing to mark race in his descriptions, Starrett draws the reader's attention to the "thousand things unseen" by those eyes locked in on these death-defying bodies at the expense of the less visible artistry of managerial organization.

Race's strategic presences and absences in *Skyscrapers* prove integral to Starrett's efforts to portray his role as builder as something more than practical, rendering it as a practice with an aesthetic pedigree all its own. Race, a crucial detail of ethnographic curiosity in other accounts of building, becomes in Starrett's hands an inefficient remainder to be smoothed out as he would any other inefficiencies within the act of building. In a manner reminiscent of modernist architect Adolf Loos, who famously found the use of ornament in contemporary design to be "a symptom of degeneracy in the modern adult" that was a holdover from "alien" and "primitive" cultures that the white Western world had evolved beyond, we find Starrett similarly framing his organizational aesthetics in terms of sleek utility.[39] He creates a world in which particularizing details become unnecessary ornament encumbering the scene of building made light and fluid by the artistry of coordinators. Whereas Loos advocated solving the problem of ornamentation through substitution, replacing it with a more minimalist design aesthetic, Starrett solves his resistance to the "ornamental" detail of race with "the scale of bigness," a scale incommensurate with the more detailed one needed in order for perceivable bodily details believed to denote racial difference to come into focus. The typical narrative about this period situates modernist design as drawing inspiration from industrialism. Starrett suggests, however, that industrialism had its own discreet interests in depicting large industrial scenes as strategically unadorned, at least in relation to the racial detail.

There is, however, one final glimpse of race in *Skyscrapers*, exiled from the city's vertical center for much of the text only to reemerge at its horizontal periphery at the conclusion. Remaindered by much of Starrett's text, it seems appropriate that race should reappear in Starrett's description of what happens to the remaindered materials of demolished buildings upon their removal: "Go to remote parts of the city, in the tenement districts, where racial colonies huddle together in out-of-the-way sections, where thrifty foreigners are making their first struggles with property ownership, and there you will find these second-hand materials being put to good use. Sometimes these structures are grotesque and laughable; sometimes they are put together with considerable effort at design and good arrangement; but they are to building what the wearers of second-hand clothing are to the patrons of the new and fashionable shops."[40] Race, along with the outdated materials of capitalist production, are depicted by Starrett as ending up at the city's periphery, rendered here as not just spatially outside the city, but temporally beyond it as well, as "thrifty foreigners" make late attempts at urban ownership by recycling the accouterments of disassembled buildings. Garbed in the trappings of urbanity's past, these "racial colonies" are described as masquerading in the dress of a city that no longer exists. Discourse about the relative evolution of civilizations popularized by race science as well as the "race aesthetics" of someone like Loos surely shadows this vignette of peripheral "colonies" out of time.

While race strategically falls out of focus when Starrett renders urban modernity on "the scale of bigness," he conveniently scales down in this scene to bring both race and racial ornament into view, if only to more soundly dismiss their importance. But Starrett's appeal to the racial "grotesque" in this passage, framing architecture's racial afterlife in terms of reductive mimicry, ultimately depends upon the racial erasures he performs elsewhere in *Skyscrapers*. It is those earlier racial erasures that allow him in this moment to forget that members of these racial colonies, too, were present at the scene of building as both participants and spectators. With this passage, Starrett reproduces the general history of architectural modernity that has cast marginalized bodies as outside, beyond, or in non-relation to building, overlooking how race gets constructed in these very performances of non-relation. Starrett's raceless "scale of bigness" requires these smaller scale "peripheral" colonies for its own stability, demonstrating his continued need for racial perception in civic and social spheres even as he depicts his workforce as operating more efficiently without it.

12

Modeling Race and Class

Architectural Photography and the U.S. Gypsum Research Village, 1952-1955

Dianne Harris

In April of 1955, nearly every popular design magazine in the United States devoted one of its sections to six newly constructed houses—a development known as the U.S. Gypsum Research Village, located in Barrington, Illinois (now Palatine). This publicity was, in the words of the development company, one of the most carefully composed and orchestrated media campaigns about housing in recent history. From the village's inception in 1952, U.S. Gypsum (USG) executives worked closely with their corporate advertising consultants, with the National Association of Home Builders (NAHB), and with architectural photographers to develop a campaign strategy that would broadcast the suburban domesticity the village modeled into millions of American homes. They targeted twelve of the most important consumer and design magazines in which to promote the Research Village during the single month that just preceded its public opening in 1955. Each house appeared separately in periodicals including *House & Garden*, *McCall's*, *American Home*, *House Beautiful*, *Better Homes & Gardens*, and *Living for Young Homemakers*. In addition to USG's own publications, the *Business of Building*, the *Business of Farming*, and *Popular Home*, the corporation reached the building trades by publishing articles in *Progressive Architecture*, *Practical Builder*, *House + Home*,

Six architect-builder teams create
a Research Village that foretells

what's ahead *for your next house*

Fig. 12.1 Architect's rendering of the U.S. Gypsum Research Village. *Popular Home Magazine*, Spring 1955, p. 3.

and the *NAHB Correlator*. The publicity campaign held particular visual appeal and appeared remarkably consistent because it was illustrated in every instance with high-quality photographs produced by the renowned Chicago architectural photography firm Hedrich Blessing. Optimistically anticipating 40 million readers during that month alone, USG also included press releases to all of its large-scale customers. Some of the houses, such as the one designed by A. Quincy Jones, even appeared on televised broadcasts.[1] Given all this, the corporation's claim that its advertising strategy represented "the greatest concentrated editorial selling drive in home building history!" seems to have had some merit.[2] If USG managed to reach even a fraction of the 40 million Americans it had targeted, the representations of the Research Village must have made a significant impact on readers in 1955 (figure 12.1).

The houses in the Research Village, designed by architects with national reputations for their innovations in small-house design during the postwar era—Harris Armstrong, Gilbert Coddington, O'Neil Ford, A. Quincy Jones, Hugh Stubbins, and Francis Lethbridge—were not themselves remarkable enough to warrant such a publicity blitz. Each house did include innovative uses of materials or construction techniques, since the application of U.S. Gypsum materials was part of the project's brief, but formally and programmatically the houses followed most of the prescriptions that could be found in the postwar house design literature of the moment.[3] Instead, the project and the publicity program merits examination because of the ways we can now see both as belonging to a complex history of race and housing in the postwar United States, one that utilized a specific set of representational strategies to participate in and to reinforce widely held notions about belonging and exclusion in the U.S. housing market.

Projects like the U.S. Gypsum Research Village are significant not because the houses were actually available to everyone—they were not—but because they represented a modeled ideal, something to which thousands of visitors and viewers could aspire. Model homes are explicitly educational in nature, intended to instruct the viewer about specific cultural norms that are likewise informed by political, social, and economic realities.[4] They were simultaneously houses for everyone (who was identified as white) and no one, and therefore always slightly and tantalizingly beyond the immediate grasp of those who viewed them on a tour or in a magazine. Each functioned as a kind of laboratory, not because the house designs were themselves particularly experimental or revolutionary (though some used novel construction techniques and new materials) but more—especially in this case—because they were an experiment in how domestic life could be represented to a large segment of the public through either the immediate experience of touring or through the photographic images created for national dissemination in the media. In some respects, and through a representational reciprocity, the Village brought magazine images to life just as the photographs that appeared in the magazines amplified the impact of the home tour experience; the houses were stage sets for living that Hedrich Blessing photographers likewise staged, photographed, and then publicized. Because the photography firm was involved from the inception of the research village, the project seems to have been conceived with an especially photogenic aspect in mind.

Given the photographic project that accompanied the U.S. Gypsum Research Village from its very start, we must imagine the village itself and the photographs as exercises in a particular kind of sanctioned domestic voyeurism.[5] The staged family life presented in the images is literally on display, the photographs transgressing apparently private boundaries to allow the public a peek into the contrived domestic lives of imaginary homeowners and their families. This, surely, was part of their appeal.

The Research Village houses also carefully brought together corporate ideals and family values through domestic architecture. As such, they are very like the so-called postwar miracle houses, in which technological innovation was coupled with romantic notions of transformation that, ultimately, distracted from salient cultural problems such as racism or economic strife that were not being transformed or changed.[6] Such houses also served to promote the national economic

Dianne Harris

agenda, dependent then as it is now on the housing market, because they encouraged people to "upgrade" from their existing house or dwelling—an especially important notion by 1954, when the most severe postwar housing crisis had passed and housing sales had slowed for the first time since 1945.[7] As the model houses urged participation in the US housing market, they also persuaded viewers to assimilate to or to adopt a particular lifestyle that was literally "modeled" for them.

Rather than the houses themselves, the truly noteworthy aspect of the development is the suite of 147 Hedrich Blessing photographs and their deployment in the national media campaign (figures 12.2 and 12.3). Their status as images that straddled the genres of real estate photography, family snapshot, architectural photography, and corporate advertisement made them especially powerful rhetorical tools that conveyed equally compelling messages about the intersections between housing, race, class, gender, corporate capitalism, and a neoliberal spatial imaginary.[8] They are particularly persuasive because of the ways the images portray the performance and intersections of race, class, and gender, leveraging the material world of houses and domestic objects as signifiers of middle- and upper-middle-class values, race (particularly whiteness), and the (at the time) almost singularly white world of corporate capitalism and new suburban housing. In this essay, I examine these images as complex rhetorical artifacts that contributed to the enormous corpus of postwar visual culture connecting white identities with the many privileges of new suburban homeownership. As such, they powerfully (if perhaps subtly) contributed to the structures that permitted and enforced housing segregation, from the FHA's redlining practices, to the many political forces that existed in the Jim Crow era of the United States and that permitted the then-prevalent existence of "sundown towns"—communities that explicitly excluded nonwhite residents.[9]

The photographs also, as I hope to demonstrate, easily reinforced what Elspeth Brown has established in her work as a "corporate eye" that used photography in corporate advertising to create a standardization and conformity of American subjectivity through the repeated publication of specific kinds of photographic images.[10] As Brown rightly notes, corporate executives and advertisers after the turn of the century increasingly put their "faith in photographic realism to promote consumer products." The supposed "truth claims" of photography and its illusion of the real helped solidify notions that linked race, class, and gender to specific corporate capitalist ideals.[11] Importantly, Hedrich Blessing's photographers included human subjects in many of the Research Village photos—something the vast majority of architectural photographers did not do. The inclusion of figures within the houses indicates a conscious decision to use people as part of a rhetorical strategy within the corporation's carefully designed advertising campaign (figure 12.4).

Spring, 1955

Popular Home

Your How-to-do-it Magazine

Quaker City Lumber and Supply Company

presents

RESEARCH VILLAGE

a glimpse of the future in family living

Fig. 12.2 This cover of *Popular Home* was just one of many such shelter magazines that featured the U.S. Gypsum Research Village on its cover in April 1955. *Popular Home Magazine*, Spring 1955. Courtesy of Chicago History Museum.

Fig. 12.3 One of the 147 photographs made by the Chicago firm of Hedrich Blessing Photographers of the U.S. Gypsum Research Village in 1955. House designed by Hugh Stubbins. Note the white "father and son" in the left of the photograph. Hedrich-Blessing Collection, Chicago History Museum.

The cultural and political work of these images can seem more obvious now following at least two decades of scholarship that has begun to unpack photography's relationship to the production of ideological meaning. But to viewers in the 1950s, the Hedrich Blessing photographs were very likely received with little critical scrutiny, seen as truthful (if staged) depictions of desirable residences and their rightfully modeled inhabitants. As Brown again notes, photography at that time "was understood by most Americans as a transparent, objective technology," and it thus became a primary tool for use by corporate managers and executives, its "truth claims" vital to the stabilization and ideological naturalization of "racial and class hierarchies in a period of tremendous social and political change."[12] The USG Research Village photographs worked to validate the architecture they depicted, making it seem more authentic through the legitimation and reinforcement of expectations about race, class, family life and composition, and heteronormativity.

Fig. 12.4 White models demonstrated the pleasures of outdoor living on the patio of the home designed by Harris Armstrong in the U.S. Gypsum Research Village. Photo by Hedrich Blessing, featured in *Popular Home Magazine*, Spring 1955, p. 7.

They were part of a utilitarian photographic practice that pretended at documentary innocence while performing important ideological work in a US economy both built by and predicated upon a housing market intended for the social, economic, and political mobility of whites.

Despite their visual tranquility, the Hedrich Blessing images of a white domestic utopia were made during a period of tremendous and rapid societal change. Consider this: September of 1955—just five months after the April 1955 publication of the Research Village in the national media—saw the publication of one of the most important photographs of that decade, and arguably the most important photograph of a dawning civil rights era: Emmett Till's brutally mutilated corpse lying in his coffin; the photograph of Till was made in Chicago, within commuting distance from the racially restricted north suburb where the U.S. Gypsum Research Village was located (figure 12.5). The image of Till's body first appeared in *Jet* magazine and in the *Chicago Defender*; news of the photograph's publication and the reaction it generated in the black community and beyond circulated widely to a national audience in the months and years that followed. Emmett Till's murder remains a profound tragedy and a national disgrace, an unhealed wound. It now also serves as a milestone in a long, continuing, and horrific American history in

Dianne Harris

Fig. 12.5 This photo of Emmett Till's brutally mutilated body in his coffin appeared in September of 1955. Mamie Till's decision to display her son's body forced observers to publicly acknowledge the brutality of Till's murder (which had been performed in private). *Chicago Tribune*. Courtesy of Chicago History Museum.

which black men are murdered by whites without judicial consequences. Moreover, the Till image must now be read alongside a longer history of the depiction of the tortured black body in the United States, one that includes abolitionist depictions of tortured slaves, postcards of public lynchings, and more recently the video captures of police murders of unarmed black men and women.[13] Emmett Till's murder, and the published photograph of his corpse, has become part of "a crucial visual vocabulary that articulated the ineffable qualities of American racism in ways words simply could not do." As such, both his murder and the photographs of Till in his coffin "served as a political catalyst for black Americans in the then-fledgling civil rights movement," a movement that remains incomplete.[14] The image of Till's body also marks a crucial milestone in the history of documentary photography, so it seems impossible to ignore the temporal and geographical proximity of the production of these two very different (yet I believe closely linked) forms of representation and their connections to racial formation and social justice (and injustice). If the photographs of white people and houses in the Research Village portrayed an American dream, the photograph of Emmett Till's brutally mutilated body starkly revealed that America was also a place of lived nightmares for many blacks and people of color, for those who had no access to newly constructed suburban houses in places like Barrington, Illinois.

I am here purposefully juxtaposing an image of one of the most tragic events in US history, an image known to sicken viewers, with the banal photos of newly constructed residences, in an effort to understand how and why architects and members of the building trades consistently—then as now—turned away from the problems of segregation, housing discrimination, and racism and the violence they wreaked, structurally and personally, for people of color in the United States. By looking at the Till photograph alongside those of the Research Village I hope to make visible anew the structural and institutional relationships that connected the violence that was (and is) imposed on black bodies in urban settings with the apparently tranquil lives of whites living in segregated suburbs. If Jim Crow segregation was the overriding structure at play in postwar American society, then the institutions that enforced that segregation and permitted the various forms of violence I am evoking included (among others) the Federal Housing Administration's redlining practices, banks with their unfair lending practices, and the real estate industry that steered whites away from black neighborhoods.

These are not images normally considered in tandem, but doing so can help us once again reflect on the institutional networks that initially separated the audiences for these photographs, restricting the Till photograph at first to the black press intended for black audiences, and the Hedrich Blessing photos to magazines that targeted a white readership.[15] What I hope to demonstrate here is that *both* the Till photograph and those depicting the Research Village perform specific types of political work, but they do so in amplified ways when viewed together. A white viewer's initial disinclination to view the Hedrich Blessing photographs as political is precisely what makes them so ideologically powerful. Their bland and seemingly documentary nature renders opaque for white viewers the institutional structures that provided the very basis for the violence rendered so hideously and tragically visible in the Till photograph. As such, we might consider the existence of a latent racial violence that haunts the Hedrich Blessing photographs of the Research Village.[16]

Of course, the Hedrich Blessing photographers made and published their images before the photograph of Emmett Till's body appeared in *Jet* and in the *Chicago Defender*. And it is equally important to note that images of prosperous black families also appeared in the national media, though primarily in the black press, and less frequently in conjunction with stories about housing unless those narratives focused on housing discrimination, segregation, and housing inequality.[17] But the Hedrich Blessing photographers produced and published their images during precisely the same era that permitted Emmett Till's brutal murder to take place, and for his murderers to be acquitted at trial and to go unpunished. They decided to build their corporate research village in a sundown town, making it closed to blacks and others identified as nonwhite. The community of Barrington was also completely closed to Jews as reported in 1959 by the Anti-Defamation League.[18] This fact remains absent from the corporation's accounts of the Research Village, so it is impossible to know how heavily it figured in their choice of location. Because many such towns in Illinois and elsewhere in the United States were restricted, or observed "sundown" laws at the time, Barrington may not have seemed exceptional to U.S. Gypsum's executives, nor to the architects involved, and the restrictions likely made it seem, if anything, more appealing to them and to many potential white buyers as a model home site.[19] The whiteness of Barrington, though perhaps taken for granted at the time, is important when we consider that the Research Village modeled the expected identities of its inhabitants just as it modeled new ways to use U.S. Gypsum products.

To execute their project, USG executives Graham Morgan, B. George Pomfret, H. F. Sandler, and J. G. Maynard partnered with the American Institute of Architects and the National Association of Home Builders (NAHB) as sponsors. They assembled an architectural advisory panel, and the NAHB contributed three of their members for the project as well. These committees invited forty architects to submit designs; thirty-six responded, and from these they selected the final six designers including Gilbert H. Coddington, Francis Lethbridge, Hugh Stubbins, A. Quincy Jones, Harris Armstrong, and O'Neil Ford.[20] Chicago practitioner Franz Lipp served as the sole landscape architect for the project. Each architect worked with an associated builder. A Chicago contracting firm, Maxon

Construction, did all the construction so these associated builders had a relatively small role, but they were meant to represent various regions of the country, and by including them, USG involved a group of merchant builders whom they hoped could take the ideas from the Research Village and apply them in their larger projects elsewhere throughout the United States.[21] Thus, the project's exclusive locale was imagined from the start as being replicable nationally, but also as emblematic of a national suburban ideal.

Teaming the architects with merchant builders, it was thought, would help ideas from the Research Village trickle down, or as the U.S. Gypsum executives put it: "The class market today—the mass market tomorrow."[22] But the materials corporation also recognized that the vast majority of middle class homes were built by developers or builders. The American Institute of Architects (AIA) therefore hoped that including architects in this project would bring a greater share of the mass-housing market to the profession of architecture. As a USG program stated, "Through its program United States Gypsum would prove that the talented architect, teamed up with the practical home builder, can produce a better house that is more salable and still can be built on a practical basis. The good thus stimulated among the architectural profession would reflect favorably on USG."[23]

The architects were asked to design a small, low-cost house using as many new ideas and as many USG products as possible. Although the architects were strongly encouraged to use and test USG products, they were not required to do so.[24] After all, it didn't really matter how many USG products they used since the project as a whole served as an associative advertising tool. But the participating architects in the project had to strike a balance with their designs: the houses were intended to appeal to the mass market and were to be "low cost," while simultaneously appealing to the "class market." The cost for the house designed by participating architect Hugh Stubbins, for example, was estimated at between $18,000 and $22,000—twice as much as the lowest-priced house in Levittown, Pennsylvania, which could be purchased for around $11,000 in 1955, but about the same cost as the most expensive house in that same development during that period.[25]

In the 1955 issue of the *Business of Building*—U.S. Gypsum's corporate publication—Research Village was compared to the World's Columbian Exposition of 1893, the anonymous author calling it "another great exposition." Proclaiming the village "A Parade of New Ideas," the Hedrich Blessing cover photo featured the interior of the house designed by A. Quincy Jones, its vibrantly colorful living room photographed to feature a coffee table covered with magazines in the foreground. Several of the magazines on display—including *McCalls* and *Popular Home*—had published articles on the Research Village upon its completion in the spring of 1955. The *Business of Building* promoted the house designs as being intended for exceptional people, comparing the participating architects

Fig. 12.6 The everyday life of white domesticity is on display in this photograph inside the house designed by Hugh Stubbins. Hedrich-Blessing Collection, Chicago History Museum.

and USG to Ford Motor Company, who had designed the Lincoln Continental "with simple beauty that met the taste of a small but zealous market." In the minds of *Business of Building*'s editors, "there was no reason why the housing market can't have its counterpart." The houses, claimed the author, rise "above the rough-and-tumble competition of selling houses like those available in other subdivisions," noting that they were specifically designed for a "small but unsatisfied market," and for "people of advanced taste," while simultaneously predicting a mass desire for contemporary simplicity on the horizon.[26]

The USG corporate executives therefore predicted and assumed that their target audience would be white, and would consider themselves, or would aspire to be, part of an elite and segregated population, one associated with the white families portrayed in the crisp Hedrich Blessing photographs. The white models that appear in the photographs perform tasks associated with the everyday life of white domesticity, their solipsistic affect reinforcing the middle-class decorum that reflexively affirmed their white identities and thus their rightful place as home-owners in the Research Village (figure 12.6). If white suburban residents of 1955 feared a "Negro Invasion" or the violence that resulted in Till's tragically broken body, the photographs of white families blissfully ensconced in their scientifically planned research houses erased any trace of possible connections back to those fears.[27] That the photographed "families" were models rather than actual occupants mattered little—perhaps not at all—because they were understood by the corporation, photographers, and viewers to be lexical figures that were part of the known visual language of home marketing.[28] The USG executives and their advertising partners understood that an appeal to race, class, and status was a tried and true way to make their products, and the houses from which they were made, as appealing as possible. The exclusivity implied by the possession of taste sufficient to appreciate the Research Village houses was matched by the exclusivity of Barrington as their setting.

The U.S. Gypsum photographs and others like them celebrated all that was seemingly antithetical to the experience relayed just a few months afterward in the accounts of Till's murder and in the photograph of his mutilated body, yet we might see them as being closely tied to it, and to the prevailing notions that linked postwar affluence to white identity, privilege, homeownership, and spatial freedom. The suite of images, like so many other advertisements that included white families in domestic settings, assuaged possible anxieties during a time when whiteness was firmly associated with the rights to accumulate property, but when the surrounding political landscape was beginning to shift in ways that could be seen and felt. As Susan Sontag noted, photography is "mainly a social rite, a defense against anxiety, and a tool of power."[29] Photographs made to promote postwar houses in a restricted suburban setting might then also be seen as a visual defense against the challenges to power, hierarchy, and the status quo that an incipient civil rights movement may have signaled.[30]

The banality of the USG Research Village photographs—and the many others like them produced at the time—belies their rhetorical and political power and significant public impact (figure 12.7). Unlike the iconoclastic images of national catastrophe studied by Ned O'Gorman, or the overt images of power studied by Nicholas Mirzoeff, I contend that the "authority of visuality" resides equally in the repetitive suasion of banal images of ordinary subjects in common settings that nevertheless serve to classify, separate, and reinforce social and political ideals. In fact, the visually banal can be a more persuasive ideological tool because it so easily escapes our immediate attention, becoming a subconsciously absorbed background that we fail to question because we, in essence, fail to "see" it even as our minds process its unquestioned existence. That the Hedrich Blessing photos were also pleasingly high-quality images of soothingly known subjects meant that they also leveraged aesthetic properties to bind the image to the authority of the real.[31]

The photographs of houses at the USG Research Village and the many thou-

Dianne Harris

Fig. 12.7 The ordinariness of the photo and the heteronormative, white family depicted is part of the rhetorical power of this photograph depicting the patio of the home designed by Francis Lethbridge. Hedrich-Blessing Collection, Chicago History Museum.

sands of other ordinary photographs of houses that appeared in the popular and shelter magazines of the period contributed to the production of a neoliberal economic, social, and political framework—indeed, they were perhaps the ideal subject for doing so. After all, the image of a postwar house could stand symbolically for so much: democracy, free-market economics, neoliberal politics, cold war triumphs, racial orders, and more. Housing was and is a material reality, but it is also a highly representable social order through which ideas about American social life could—then as now—be transmitted extremely convincingly. Images of houses were, in many respects, a key component in a commonly understood postwar communications strategy about what it meant to be American. Instead of photographic images portraying the racial discord or unrest that characterized significant portions of the United States in the 1950s, the USG photos offered security through the affirmation of what was by 1955 an increasingly destabilized social order.

While race may or may not have been explicitly considered in the selection of Barrington as the Research Village site, class considerations were frankly expressed, and most real estate agents, developers, and architects likely understood—at least on an intuitive basis—what we would now refer to as the intersectional aspects of race, class, and gender/sexuality.[32] The corporation's stated desire to target a "small but zealous market" of homebuyers who could appreciate designs that might be a cut above average or ordinary indicated their belief appealing to race, class, and social status was sure to make their products, and the houses that contained them, as desirable as possible. The exclusivity implied by the possession of taste sufficient to appreciate the Research Village houses was matched by the exclusivity of Barrington as their setting.

Despite the fact that race is never mentioned in any of the promotional or archival materials associated with the project, questions about the impacts of race and class on housing appears to have been a U.S. Gypsum concern during the 1950s, particularly as those issues impacted the construction industry. The corporation published two books during this decade, *Building a Better Tomorrow* (1952) and *Operative Remodeling: The New Profit Frontier for Builders* (1956). *Operative Remodeling* was copublished by the NAHB and U.S. Gypsum "as a service to the 'New Face of America' program." The "New Face of America" program was in turn both sponsored by and a program of the NAHB and the "American Council to Improve Our Neighborhoods" (ACTION). In a chapter on "Merchandising and Selling," the authors recommend conducting market research to establish the audience to whom builders planned to sell: "It might show that with a big project a builder could change the entire complexion of an area, while single remodeling jobs would have to find their market among the neighbors seeking improved quarters."[33] The book's purpose was to promote the idea that builders were saving the country from the pall of urban blight through renewal projects. The meaning of phrasing like changing a neighborhood's "complexion" becomes clear when one considers that urban blight and renewal were largely terms used to describe work performed in black, inner-city neighborhoods. The book promoted the idea that builders could start by remodeling in "safe" (read white) neighborhoods where they were sure to get their money back, then move on to slums after gaining sufficient

Dianne Harris

experience. In so doing, they hoped to keep middle-aged houses from becoming slums through rehabilitation projects. The book's frontispiece states: "Better Housing, besides being an end in itself, is also the most basic instrument in stepping up the effectiveness of all public and private action. A family in a decent home is freer of disease; less prone to antisocial behavior; less likely to have delinquent children."[34] But the book was actually aimed at stimulating gentrification of older neighborhoods rather than rehabilitation of true slums, and the authors emphasized that builders should select houses that would protect "areas worth saving."[35]

Above all, the U.S. Gypsum executives were, of course, considering the maximization of profit in the building industry. Following the logic of FHA redlining practices, white neighborhoods were considered "safe" neighborhoods where real estate could most securely be turned for a profit; these books' rhetoric of families in "decent" homes that were healthy, clean, and filled with well-adjusted children tapped into at least a century of environmental determinist philosophies that asserted the importance of a well-designed home in the making of well-designed citizens, who were, by extension, envisioned as white. It is not surprising, therefore, that the Research Village project was similarly imagined and similarly represented.

By 1954, the Research Village project was fully developed, the houses designed, and construction had commenced. The publicity machine that advertised the Research Village nationwide was also in full gear. As a USG executive wrote, "Never in home-building history has such broad recognition been given to a single manufacturer's promotion."[36] Corporate hyperbole aside, USG did organize and execute a remarkable publicity blitz to accompany the opening of the village, and the Hedrich Blessing photographs played an essential role in that campaign.

A striking aspect of many of the Hedrich Blessing photographs is their relationship to family snapshots. Whether capturing an interior or exterior view, the family's activities appear only slightly more contrived than in many family photos made during the same period. A reciprocal relationship existed between the representation of white family life as seen in advertisements and the ways families then represented themselves in an effort to match that fictive imagery. With their rigidly portrayed gender roles, child-centric activities, and insistence on a portrayal of whiteness that depended on material goods—including architecture—the photographs are both specific in their depiction of a particular architectural context, and interchangeable in their conventional homogeneity. Part of their rhetorical efficacy stems from their use of standardized commercial tropes that linked white families to commodities and consumerism, and linked the quotidian family photograph to these professionally produced and commercially distributed images. The family snapshot commercialized family life, and in turn, the family in its domestic setting became the ideal subject for promoting a commercial enterprise.[37]

As Diane Hope has written, the Kodak corporation cemented the notion that American families were "white and young, headed by men, depicted as groups of attractive heterosexual couples, babies, children, teenagers, and grandparents, and staged in scenes where 'nothing but blue skies' provided locations for 'dreaming in color.'"[38] It is worth noting that Kodak and other analog films were specifically calibrated to an industry standard that maximized the representation of white skin tones, based on a set of standard reference photographs of white women known as "Shirley cards." These reference cards were calibrated to the emulsification of the film itself, which was designed to represent white skin as accurately as possible, making it difficult for photographers to accurately capture and represent darker skin tones. This, as Lorna Roth has demonstrated, was a choice made by the major film-producing corporations, based in their assumptions about the aesthetic supremacy of white skin, and their presumption that the primary consumers of their products were white. As such, film itself contributed to a cognition of white supremacy, enhancing the pervasive whiteness of the subjects themselves.[39] As a defense against change in the social order then, the Hedrich Blessing photographs were very effective visual tools that helped assuage the anxiety that other, emerging journalistic images—like the Emmett Till photograph—could generate.

For an example of the family snapshot composition, we can look at three of the Hedrich Blessing photographs that portrayed views of the multilevel interior of the Stubbins-designed house: two are taken from inside the living room, and one from outside looking in at night (figures 12.8, 12.9, and 12.10). The latter is particularly dramatic because of the effects of interior lighting, but also because of the amplifying voyeuristic effect derived from the view of interior family life taken through the large glass panes of the house from the back terrace. In this image, the father in this presumed family stands on the upper level and looks down on the mother and daughter who are playing in the ground-level living room; the lower-level dining area is also visible at the far left. Moving the photographer inside provided a view of the ground-floor living room but also allowed a daytime view of the patio with a bike and outdoor furniture on the terrace, seen through the glass. In this view, the father sits reading a newspaper, while the mother perches next to the television watching her daughter, who plays with a doll on the floor. All are engaged in leisure activities that appear satisfying and that reinforce expected gender roles for a family intended to be seen as solidly white, middle class, and following expected patterns of heteronormativity. The bike and outdoor furniture suggest a life lived beyond the confines of the interior space, yet sheltered by the terrace enclosure. A third view portrays the living room and upper level seen with the bedroom wall panels slid open, revealing a mother smiling down on her daughter in the living room below. The image is bright and sunny, pervaded by a sense of transparency to the outdoors made possible through the appearance

Fig. 12.8 White heteronormative family life captured to mimic a family snapshot. House by Hugh Stubbins. Hedrich-Blessing Collection, Chicago History Museum.

of abundant glazing. On the lowest or basement level, the photographs again emphasize the recreational aspect of the space: The mother sits on a chair next to a bench with a teddy bear and knitting yarn in a basket as she works on a sewing project. Father and son work nearby at a built-in hobby bench with a Masonite pegboard above it, making a small bracketed shelf (figure 12.6). The pegboard holds tools and displays children's art. All the images convey a world of incredibly tidy and industrious people engaged in orderly, quiet leisure in a home designed

Fig. 12.9 White models performing domesticity in the house designed by Hugh Stubbins. Hedrich-Blessing Collection, Chicago History Museum.

to ideally suit their needs—one where they can watch each other as we watch them, in photographic compositions that emphasize a visual recursiveness—all eyes in and cast upon the image see the same thing.

The Hedrich Blessing photographs were made specifically to appeal to consumers, and they displayed the Research Village houses as commodities of a specific order. They were advertising images that made an obvious appeal to class, race, and various forms of status. The new technologies and materials used in the houses

Dianne Harris

Fig. 12.10 The man looking at his family from above suggests a father looking over his white family at home, in a house designed by Hugh Stubbins. Hedrich-Blessing Collection, Chicago History Museum.

were largely camouflaged in order to make them traditionally appealing—indeed the USG materials are difficult to discern for the average viewer—so it is hard to see the photographs as useful for anything other than bolstering mainstream notions of a highly gendered domestic realm that was on the one hand safe, but on the other would also seem adventurously modern, a "research" village after all. The developers and architects, working in tandem with USG and the Hedrich

Blessing photographers, sold ideas about family happiness and well-being in a package that equally emphasized race, class, and status. The photographs provided a visual narrative: the Research Village homes could provide occupants with happy, well-behaved children, husbands content to spend time with their families, housewives with leisure time to pursue hobbies, and all the technologies necessary to maintain a clean, orderly home. They are certainly images of family togetherness. The photographic narrative, then, posits the houses as active agents, machines that make everything work, including the heteronormative, white nuclear family. In this respect, they are like the "togetherness ads" described by Marsha Ackerman that "showed nuclear families at very close quarters, each engaged in gender and age-appropriate leisure pursuits, including decorous play, games, reading and needlework, but almost never television viewing."[40] As such, they also demonstrated "how capital projects images of family life as it 'ought to be lived.'"[41]

Taken together, the photographs depict domestic worlds that are at once anonymous and known. The photographed spaces are curated to achieve an aesthetic balance that appears lived-in while being furnished with the minimum number of objects. Despite the technical prowess with which they were clearly made—the images are sharp, artfully composed, perfectly lit—they are not intended as art objects themselves. Instead, they are intended as documentary images, read as objective renderings of a particular reality that might belong to viewers who cast themselves into the domestic spaces depicted. The fact that the images disguise their rhetoric through the appearance of documentary objectivity makes them much more powerful as ideological devices.[42]

For a twenty-first-century viewer, the suite of images haunts in their own way, even if that haunting is of a decidedly and vastly different variety from that which we experience when looking at the photo of Emmett Till in his coffin. The contrivance, staging, and depiction of what we might now see as "suburban ironic" seems to prefigure work that wouldn't appear for another twenty years with the opening of the *New Topographics* exhibition in 1975. The supposedly neutral, documentary, and mundane scenes of suburban life made by photographers such as Robert Adams with their exaggerated normality also registers now a certain note of anxiety. The New Topographics photographers aimed to produce images that were quietly infused with social commentary; architectural photographers, on the other hand, have been presumed innocent in their creation of images that perpetuate exclusively white spatial realms. Somewhere between a register of the social conditions they were embedded in and a vision of the aspirational future the building industry hoped to sell, architectural photographs, which have so far largely been imagined as being vacant of such commentary, are rich artifacts for considering the construction of how Americans understood spatial boundaries, and their links to notions of racial identity, privilege, and exclusion.

Dianne Harris

PART V

RACE AND COLONIALISM

13

Race and Tropical Architecture

The Climate of Decolonization and "Malayanization"

Jiat-Hwee Chang

In the 1980s Singapore and Malaysia saw a renewed interest in tropical architecture after almost two decades of neglect and disregard for it. One of the key protagonists behind the resurgence was the Singapore architect Tay Kheng Soon. Tay's advocacy of tropical architecture was partly a response to the ethnocentric "visible politics" that the Malaysian government was promoting at the time.[1] This brand of politics was exemplified in the policies of Mahathir Mohamad, then prime minister of Malaysia, who encouraged the use of Malay symbols in architecture to enunciate national pride and identity. He was, for example, quoted as saying, "There should be no reason why a skyscraper should not have a [Malay] roof which reflects our national identity."[2]

Tay, in contrast, felt that the explicit use of symbols clearly associated with a particular ethnic group in multiethnic societies like Malaysia and Singapore was both "historically absurd" and "dangerous" as it implied "ethnic sectarianism" and "inadvertently exacerbated ethnic cleavages that lay just below the surface of new-state cultures."[3] Instead of referencing ethnic symbols in the built environment to evoke national identity, Tay believed the region's architectural identity could respond to a "more intrinsic design agenda . . . the *environment* itself," specifically the hot and humid climate of the Asian tropical countries.[4] By employing new technologies, Tay believed architects could draw on the environment to generate form and aesthetic expression that could communicate a kind of identity that transcended ethnicity and culture.

Urban historian and theorist Abidin Kusno was critical of Tay's construction of tropicality as a cultural identity discourse, which he interpreted as an abstraction of categories like "Asian," "people," and "independent identity" that invoked a trans-local pan-Asian environment absent the particularities of localized culture.[5] In this chapter, I argue otherwise by historicizing and tracing Tay's discourse to the decolonizing moment of the 1950s and 1960s. I show that instead of being based on an abstraction, Tay's tropical imagining was born out of the sociopolitical and racial tensions of decolonization in Singapore and Malaysia during the transition from colonial "plural societies" to postcolonial multiethnic societies. Tay's tropical imagining was an integral part of a modern and cosmopolitan Malayan architecture that he and his local colleagues conceived in their quest for an emancipatory architectural aesthetics capable of redressing some of the problems of colonial racialization.

Malayan Architecture as Tropical Architecture

Tay was among a pioneering group of five architecture students who graduated in 1963 from the Department of Architecture at Singapore Polytechnic (SP).[6] These students, who were the first generation of locally trained architects, were educated during the socially and politically turbulent period of the 1950s and '60s, in which cultural belongings and political allegiances were both varied and changing amid decolonization and the various competing constructions of new postcolonial nations. Influenced by the nationalist fervor of the milieu, Tay and his classmates sought to design a Malayan architecture that would contribute to the Malayan identity of the emerging nation.

At Singapore Polytechnic, Tay and his classmates were taught to design in the language of tropical modernism, deploying an approach that sought to understand and address the social, cultural, and technical problems of living in a tropical climate. For Kee Yeap, the department's first local head, the emphasis on tropical architecture meant a change of sociocultural reference, away from European colonial forms toward a pantropical orientation.[7] The sense that tropical architecture represented cultural reorientation away from colonial metropolitan references was reiterated in Tay's recollection many decades later. He argued that tropical architecture was a "quest" for an "architectural aesthetic . . . in our terms and none other" and it was "part of the context freeing oneself from the political and taste-dictates of our masters."[8]

However, if we examine Tay and Yeap's positions in relation to the larger historical context of tropical architecture in the mid-twentieth century, their belief that tropical architecture represented a reorientation of cultural reference away from the metropole appears, at first sight, to be rather perplexing if not untenable. Modern tropical architecture was, after all, invented in the metropole at around the same time. One of the key conferences on tropical architecture was held at University College London in 1953 and one of the main institutions involved in the pedagogy of tropical architecture was the Department of Tropical Architecture at the Architectural Association, London, established one year after the conference.[9] Furthermore, some of the best-known practitioners of tropical architecture in Africa and Asia were British expatriate architects like Maxwell Fry, Jane Drew, and James Cubitt and firms such as the Architects Co-Partnership,[10] Furthermore, tropical architecture has its origin as a nineteenth-century colonial discourse to help Europeans cope with the tropics, which was previously constructed as the unhealthy, uncomfortable, and backward other to the European temperate zone.[11] Although rearticulated in different forms, many of these colonial ideas and their underlying assumptions continued to shape the mid-twentieth century discourse on tropical architecture. Given this pervasive undertone, how could tropical architecture be seen as constituting a reorientation—let alone an emancipation—from European/colonial references? Rather than dismissing as misguided Tay and company's positioning of tropical architecture as Malayan architecture, we need to probe deeper and understand it in relation to the mid-twentieth century architectural debates surrounding Malayan architecture and the underlying racial tensions behind the contested constructions of Malayan identity in architecture.

Malayan Identity Formation

Between 1945 and 1963, the word "Malaya" evoked in many of its inhabitants sentiments and visions for an independent, multiracial, postcolonial nation, just when it was being reconfigured geopolitically. From the nineteenth century to World War II, Malaya referred to the three British colonies in the Malay Peninsula: the Straits Settlements, Federated Malay States, and Unfederated Malay States. After World War II, the British split Singapore from Malaya to form a separate Crown colony while the rest of Malaya became first the Malayan Union in 1945 and then the Federation of Malaya in 1948. Malaya as a formal political entity, however, ended in 1963 when the Federation of Malaya merged with Singapore, Sarawak, and North Borneo to form Malaysia. Singapore was subsequently separated from Malaysia in 1965 and attained independence involuntarily. While Singapore was also governed as a separate political entity in the 1940s and 1950s, its long historical ties with the rest of Malaya meant that it was frequently imagined by people in both Singapore and Malaya as an integral part of Malaya.

The formation of the Federation of Malaya in 1948 also marked the beginning of a twelve-year period of "emergency," or the war against communist guerrillas in Malaya. The emergency was the British colonial state's response to one of the major challenges to its power and legitimacy. These challenges arose following Britain's profound loss of prestige and legitimacy as rulers due to their inability to defend Malaya from the Japanese invasion in the early 1940s. When the British returned after the end of the Japanese occupation in 1945, Malayan independence was an inevitability. In response, the British sought to control the nature and pace of political development in Malaya. They also went about molding a Malayan citizenry that would be friendly to British interests in the region after the end of British colonial rule. It was in this context, as the British government sought to win the "hearts and minds" of the Malayans during the period of emergency, that Sir Gerald Templer, the British high commissioner in Malaya between 1952 and 1954, called for architects to design a "Malayan architecture."[12]

Any discussion of the construction of a Malayan identity in the postwar period must grapple with the legacies of colonial racialization and what British sociologist J. S. Furnivall has described as the colonial "plural society." In his study of colonial Burma and the Dutch East Indies, Furnivall argued that colonial policies had produced a society characterized by both hierarchical economic specialization and social segregation along racial and ethnic lines. It was a society in which different ethnic groups mixed but did not combine, "living side by side, but separately, within the same political unit."[13] In such societies, economic forces tended to create social tensions between competing groups and their interests, further accentuating cleavages along ethnic lines.[14] The concept of plural society is also applicable to many colonial societies beyond Burma and the Dutch East Indies, and numerous scholars have employed it to understand the socioeconomic order in colonial Malaya. In the case of Malaya, the socioeconomic segregation of the different ethnic groups was overlaid and reinforced with colonial cultural constructions and racial stereotypes.

As with some other parts of the British Empire, the British rule in Federated and Unfederated Malay States was based on trusteeship or indirect rule. In the words of historian Anthony Stockwell, the imperial rhetoric was that Malaya "was not a white man's country; it was *tanah Melayu* (Malay land) and the British had a duty to keep it so."[15] Formulated and deployed in Malaya in the late-nineteenth century to legitimize British colonial rule, this rhetoric and its underlying political ideology also meant that colonial officers in Malaya needed to study and know the "character" and way of life of the Malays in order to protect them. By the end of the nineteenth century, prominent colonial officers had already established influential portrayals of the Malays in books such as Frank Swettenham's *The Real Malay* (1900) and Hugh Clifford's *In Court and Kampong* (1897). These accounts included sweeping generalizations about the Malays that drew upon environmental and genetic explanations. They were affectionately stereotyped as easygoing but lazy, which precluded them from participating in the colonial economy. In contrast, the Chinese were considered hardworking and enterprising but untrustworthy, and the Indians were regarded as docile. Although both of the latter groups were deemed as vital to their colonial economies, they were seen as transients by the colonial state, and, unlike the Malays, the colonial administrators did not feel obliged to protect their culture and welfare. It is clear that these generalizations and racial stereotypes provided the underlying rationales and served as the justifications of the socioeconomic segregation in plural societies. Moreover, these stereotypes also informed and were further entrenched by colonial policies and administrative practices in census taking, landownership, regulation of labor, education policy, and political representation.[16] On the whole, the colonial state demonstrated a pro-Malay bias in its policies and practices because "the 'protection' of Malays [in the rapidly transforming Malaya] was the justification of the British presence while the preservation of Malay society was the guarantee of indefinite British control."[17]

The socioeconomic segregation and racial stereotyping of the ethnic groups were obviously not conducive for the emergence of a unified national consciousness required for the formation of a postcolonial nation. If anything, communalism and ethnocentrism on the one hand, and interracial tensions and conflicts on the other, were the likely outcomes. Indeed, the 1950s and 1960s in Malaya were marked by three major racial riots: the 1950 Maria Hertogh riots, and the 1964 and 1969 racial riots.[18] At the heart of the construction of a Malayan identity was therefore the challenge of addressing a colonial plural society fraught with racial tensions and conflicts. Politically, the initial response of the British was to form the Malayan Union in 1945, which gave equal rights to all ethnic groups. The Malayan Union plan provoked two main forms of opposition. The first came from Malay traditionalists led by the United Malays National Organisation (UMNO) and the local aristocracy. This group opposed the loss of the sovereign rights of the Malay sultans and the absence of special rights granted to the Malays as the original inhabitants of Malaya. The second form of opposition was a broad-based, multiethnic and secular alliance known as the All-Malaya Council of Joint Action-PUTERA (AMCJA-PUTERA). Led by the Malayan Democratic Union and Malay Nationalist Party, AMCJA-PUTERA opposed the Malayan Union proposal because it meant continued British rule and the separation of Singapore from the rest of Malaya.[19] The British proved more responsive to the former opposition. They came up with the Federation of Malaya agreement that restored the sovereign rights of the Malay sultans and guaranteed the special position of the Malays, abandoning the idea of equal rights for all citizens, regardless of ethnicity and religion.

Although AMCJA-PUTERA failed to influence the British decision, its vision of a multiethnic and multicultural Malaya that included Singapore endured in other ways, especially in the cultural realm. In the 1950s and 1960s, during a period of what Mark Ravinder Frost and Yu-Mei Balasingamchow called "creative *Merdeka*" (creative independence), writers, artists, and intellectuals of different socioethnic groups within Malaya attempted to cross racial boundaries and articulate their visions of a multiethnic cosmopolitan Malayan culture through their arts.[20] The cultural outpouring encompassed various art forms—especially the literary and visual arts—produced by different socioeconomic and ethnic groups. For example, undergraduates of different ethnicities at the University of Malaya attempted to capture the hybrid culture in their English writings by incorporating Malay and Chinese cultural and linguistic elements. Besides the multiethnic representatives of the English-educated social elite, the comparatively marginalized Chinese-educated writers, artists, and intellectuals—including the Nanyang style painter and educator Chen Chong Swee—also put forward their own visions of Malayan literature, art, and culture. Shifting away from their previous cultural orientations toward China and Chinese culture, these writers, artists, and intellectuals began to identify with Malaya as their adopted homeland and sought to further root themselves in Malaya by learning and embracing indigenous Malay language and cultural forms.[21] Often also drawing on Malayan landscape and subjects, they sought to represent and create a "creolized" culture through the arts.[22]

The cultural outpouring of the creative merdeka also spread to architecture. Before discussing a design strategy deployed in an attempt to create a multiethnic architectural culture, I want to turn to two different ethnocentric approaches to architectural representations of Malayan identity in the mid-twentieth century. In analyzing and comparing these two approaches, it is perhaps useful to return to the pro-Malay bias of the colonial state discussed earlier. In its attempt to preserve the Malay society, Stockwell argued that the British colonial state instead created "a doctored version of traditional Malay society—one in which a careful delineation of genealogy, Western concepts of justice and humanitarianism, and European models of kingship, feudalism, clan organization and land-ownership intermingled with Malay *adat* (custom), Islam and the Hindu remnants of pre-Islamic days."[23] A key component of this "doctored version" of Malay society was the British colonial state's "invention" of Malay traditions and crafts. One of the most influential British colonial administrator-scholars involved was Mubin Sheppard (born Mervyn Cecil Sheppard, 1905–1994). Assigned as one of the four British advisors to work closely with Gerald Templer to formulate cultural policies, Sheppard helped to stage cultural shows and establish institutions that promoted Malayan arts and history during the emergency. A renowned scholar in Malay culture who has written extensively on Malay history, arts, crafts, and architecture, Sheppard was one of the few British civil servants who stayed behind to work for the postindependence Malayan government after the formal end of British colonial rule. He was tasked to help to establish Muzium Negara (the National Museum)—which exemplifies the first ethnocentric approach to architectural representation—and to take charge of other cultural affairs.[24]

As the first director-general of Muzium Negara, Sheppard was the central figure behind not only the contents and curatorial direction of the museum but also its architecture, so much so that some claimed he was the "real designer" behind the building.[25] This is evident in how Sheppard went to great lengths to create a museum in what Mark Crinson has described as "Malay-house-style," a form of colonial regionalism in which highly recognizable elements and motifs of Malay vernacular architecture were exaggerated, often with minimal abstraction, and directly applied to a modern structure.[26] Sheppard's predilection for "Malay-house-style" should not be surprising. During the 1950s, when the traditional timber house was generally viewed as backward, uncomfortable, and thus undesirable, Sheppard was the first to see its potential and converted an old Malay *istana* (palace)—essentially a grander and more elaborate timber house—into a museum in the early 1950s.[27] He also specially commissioned a timber house built by traditional craftsmen for himself at Petaling Jaya in the late 1950s. Sheppard wanted the national museum to be based on the design of a traditional Malay istana—specifically the legendary Sultan Mansur Shah's istana that was built during the peak of the Malacca sultanate's power—and did a sketch to that effect. He rejected a modernist design for the museum by Ivor Shipley, an architect with the Public Works Department, and instead appointed Ho Kok Hoe, a Singapore-based Chinese architect, as the official architect.[28] With Sheppard, Ho toured different parts of the Malay heartland and they finally decided to incorporate a few architectural features from Balai Besar (literally, big hall) in Kedah in their design of the museum. Sheppard also assembled a team of Malay artisans from different parts of Malaya to incorporate "local" elements into the museum's design, such as screens with floral patterns, carved timber panels, and ornaments.[29]

Sheppard's preference for the "Malay-house-style" should also be understood in relation to the "romantic tradition in imperialism."[30] Hugh Clifford (1866–1941), the administrator-scholar who exemplified that tradition in Malaya, was Sheppard's role model.[31] Clifford saw the Malays as having "a Rousseauesque innocence, a virtue and nobility, expressed in their sensitivity and perfect manners, which was endangered by the spread of Western civilization" and Malaya as possessing the "makings of a very Garden of Eden" had outsiders been excluded.[32] Clifford felt that British administrators should encourage the Malays to preserve their traditions. During the colonial era, such a romanticization of the Malay character and the fossilization of their culture served to legitimize the British indirect rule in Malaya. When a similar attitude was adopted in postindependence Malaya by the state—particularly in the ethnocentric manner it was manifested in an important national institution like Muzium Negara—it could be read as an attempt to justify the political primacy of the Malays in the Federation of Malaya.

The second approach is often referred to as Chinese traditional revival architecture (*huazu chuantong fuxingshi jianzhu* or 华族传统复兴式建筑) and is exemplified in a number of 1950s and 1960s buildings associated with the Chinese community.[33] Chinese traditional revival architecture has its origins in the quest of early twentieth-century Chinese architects to define a monumental architectural form appropriate to China as the modern nation.[34] The Chinese traditional revival architecture was intended to be a modern Chinese style that, according to Delin Lai, "embodied the Chinese nationalist elite's expectations of a 'renaissance' of Chinese culture that would originate in a vigorous Chinese tradition but be modified according to Western classical and modern standards."[35] An architectural style conceived to reinvigorate a fallen nation in the early twentieth century took on different significance in the context of ethnic politics in colonial and postcolonial Malaya in the mid-twentieth century.

Looking at three built examples of Chinese traditional revival architecture— the Nanyang University Library and Administration Building (1954) designed by Ng Keng Siang, the Singapore Chinese Chamber of Commerce Building (1964) designed by Ho Beng Hong, and the Chung Cheng High School Administration Building (1968) also designed by Ho Beng Hong—they appear, at first glance, somewhat similar to the aforementioned example of "Malay-house-style" colonial regionalism (figure 13.1).[36] Instead of a Malay roof atop a reinforced concrete structure with motifs of Malay vernacular architecture applied to surfaces of the structure, we have a Chinese roof and Chinese motifs. Yet there is a critical difference: the Chinese traditional revival buildings were not of the political and cultural elite or the state—as was in the case of Muzium Negara discussed earlier—but of the marginalized Chinese-speaking community. Both Nanyang University and Chung Cheng High were key institutions of Chinese language education in a context where Chinese language education was unrecognized and marginalized by the colonial state.[37] While the Singapore Chinese Chamber of Commerce could be seen as representing the wealthy and influential Chinese business elite, its traditional role as the intermediary between the colonial state and Chinese community was threatened—and the prestige it acquired through performing that role was eroded—in the transition from laissez-faire colonial rule to state-dominated interventionist postcolonial rule.[38] As such, the ethnocentric approach to architectural representation in these buildings could be understood less as the

Jiat-Hwee Chang

Fig. 13.1 Exterior view of Nanyang University Library and Administration Building, from *Journal of Society of Malayan Architects*, 1959.

aestheticizing of the political primacy of a certain ethnic group than as a form of resistance against such cultural dominance.

Tropical Architecture in between the Universal and the Local

If an ethnocentric approach to architectural design in Malaya meant the exclusive use of architectural symbols and motifs associated with one particular ethnic group, what would constitute a multiethnic and multicultural approach to architectural design in Malaya? The two main professional groups that dominated the architectural scene in Malaya in the 1950s—expatriate colonial architects, mostly British, and local architects—appear to share a common position. The former group responded to the official call from the British colonial government for Malayan architecture through a series of discussions and debates in *PETA, the Journal of the Federation of Malaya Society of Architects.*[39] The journal featured numerous articles on the various types of historical architecture in Malaya. Despite giving serious attention to historical architecture, the journal's editors arrived at a consensus against the addition of elements or motifs taken directly from historical architecture—"local touches" as they called them—to mid-twentieth-century buildings.[40] This position reflected the biases of mid-twentieth-century European modernism. Modernist architects advocated a universal abstract language; they tended to be against the use of ornament and deemed the application of recognizable, unabstracted elements from vernacular architecture to be aesthetically unacceptable. As a result, these colonial architects fell back on the modernist faith in fundamental principles and agreed that Malayan architecture should, first and foremost, deal with something more fundamental: the climatic conditions of Malaya.[41]

Besides *PETA*, the other architectural journal in Malaya was *Rumah*, the journal of the rival professional organization, the Society of Malayan Architects, later renamed the Singapore Institute of Architects. Unlike the Federation of Malaya Society of Architects, which consisted primarily of British expatriates, the Society of Malayan Architects was comprised of only local architects, almost all of them of Chinese ethnicity.[42] Unsurprisingly, *Rumah* also featured articles that discussed Malayan architecture. These were sometimes explicit, as in the case of Eu Jin Seow's article on "Malayan Touch," which was an attempt to find inspiration in the traditional kampong house.[43] By seeing and evaluating the vernacular through the modernist lens of economy, functionality, tectonics, and climate-responsiveness, Seow argued that the vernacular offered lessons in "efficient planning and sound construction," revealed "so much talent in local handicraft and so many opportunities for uses and experimentation with [local] materials," and demonstrated varied solutions to "man's continual struggle . . . against the elements."[44] At other times, the discussion of Malayan architecture was implicit, embodied in allusions to the "local." For instance, in an article on the architectural education at Singapore Polytechnic, Lim Chong Keat, Tay's teacher, emphasized the "local conditions of climate, sociology, material resources and attainable techniques" in the school's pedagogy. Lim also noted that Singapore Polytechnic's architectural pedagogy should "learn from local traditions and usages" while striving for "a vital and progressive attitude in the practice and instruction of architecture."[45]

It is difficult to generalize about the local designers' position on Malayan architecture, however, given their diverse output, which included Muzium Negara and the Nanyang University Library and Administration Building, mentioned earlier as examples of an ethnocentric approach to architecture. For the more progressive among the local architects, such as Lim Chong Keat, Eu Jin Seow, Alfred Wong, and William Lim, climate was certainly one of the many local conditions to which Malayan architecture should respond. These architects' embrace of tropical architecture could be attributed to a number of factors. They were English-educated Chinese elite from wealthy and well-established families in colonial society.[46] Unlike members of the marginalized Chinese-speaking community, or

Jiat-Hwee Chang

the Malay nationalist elite who spearheaded the aforementioned ethnocentric architectural representations, there was no reason for these members of the cosmopolitan "Anglophone domiciled community" to assert any ethnocentric identification.[47] Many of these architects received their architectural education overseas in Manchester, London, and Melbourne, before formal architectural education was offered in Singapore, and they were all trained in the modernist paradigm, in which climate was regarded as an important determinant of architectural form. A central part of this modernist paradigm in the mid-twentieth century would include celebrating exemplars of tropical architecture by modernist masters such as Le Corbusier and Oscar Niemeyer in India, Brazil, and other places. For these local architects, not only did tropical architecture appear to be race-neutral, having no historical baggage, it was also associated with the modern and the progressive.

The Chinese Malayan architects did not just unquestioningly accept or internalize metropolitan discourse on tropical architecture, however. Tropical architecture discourse, they believed, had a tendency to reduce and simplify the complexity of living in a particular environment into a set of technical parameters.[48] This was especially evident in Lim's review of David Oakley's *Tropical Houses: A Guide to Their Design* (1961) in *Rumah*. Lim commented that the book appeared to be written for "naïve or underdeveloped readers" and the examples shown appeared "distilled as it were for Batsford and for Bedford Square!"[49] Batsford was the book's publisher and Bedford Square was the address of the Department of Tropical Architecture at the Architectural Association, where Oakley taught. Through this critique, Lim implied that the information in the book was so condensed that it was only suitable as a textbook for British architecture students. The book had little relevance to the readers of *Rumah*—that is, local architects who had to deal with a much more challenging set of socioclimatic conditions on the ground.

If the local architects did not indiscriminately adopt tropical architecture as prescribed by the metropole, how was the tropical architecture they produce different? First, like the artists involved in the creative merdeka, they closely studied indigenous Malay culture, specifically vernacular houses. As we saw earlier, Seow sought to draw inspiration from the vernacular in his quest for a "Malayan touch." Furthermore, the Society of Malayan Architects named its journal *Rumah*, the Malay word for house. The cover of *Rumah* featured an elevation drawing of the Rumah Melaka, or the Malaccan vernacular house. This was a measured drawing done by Wee Chwee Heng, another one of Lim's students at Singapore Polytechnic. Wee, together with Tay, were part of a group of first-year students that Lim brought on a field trip to various sites along the west coast of Malaya to familiarize them with regional variations of the traditional Malay house. To be sure, many modernist architects were fascinated by vernacular architecture, so what these local architects were doing was not particularly unusual. What is exceptional was the

Fig. 13.2 Exterior view of the Singapore Conference Hall and Trade Union House. Private collection of Lim Chong Keat.

manner in which the vernacular was incorporated into the tropical architecture they designed, especially in the case of the Singapore Conference Hall and Trade Union House (SCHTUH).

Designed by Lim together with his partners at Malayan Architects Co-Partnership, William Lim Siew Wai and Chen Voon Fee, the SCHTUH is one of the key buildings of postindependence Singapore.[50] As its name suggests, it was built to serve two main functions. First, it was designed to host major international conferences and cultural events of the newly independent nation—gatherings such as the Afro-Asian Trade Union Conference held just after the building's official opening on October 15, 1965.[51] Second, it was to be the headquarters of the unified labor movement in Singapore. Although the building is now no longer called the Trade Union House, the building was originally conceived primarily, in the words of Devan Nair, secretary-general of the unified trade union movement, "to honour a tryst" between the government and the labor movement. As the minister of Culture and Social Affairs, Othman Wok, put it, the aim was to build a headquarters that was "commensurate with the dignity of labour."[52] The multiethnic People's Action Party (PAP) government came into power during the late 1950s by allying itself with the labor movement. The control of the various trade unions by the PAP government and the subsequent establishment of tripartitism between workers, employers, and the PAP government were central to attracting foreign direct

Jiat-Hwee Chang

Fig. 13.3 Interior view of the naturally ventilated concourse of the Singapore Conference Hall and Trade Union House, with the auditorium and related conference hall facilities to the right and the facilities of the trade union house to the left. Private collection of Lim Chong Keat.

investment to Singapore, resulting in its rapid economic growth from the 1960s onward.

Lim and his partners won the commission in one of the major open architectural competitions in postwar Singapore in 1962. Architecturally, their design was conceived as a highly integrated solution to the complex site, programmatic, and environmental requirements. The original building was dominated by a large butterfly roof that unified the two main elements of the building underneath it: the auditorium and related conference hall facilities on one side and the facilities of the trade union house on the other side. Located between the two was a naturally ventilated concourse (figures 13.2 and 13.3). From the concourse, stairs led to the other levels of the buildings, including the foyer of the conference hall at the second level. All these were visible from the outside as only glass curtain walls separated the interior from the exterior. The foyer also opened out to large cantilevered terraces, which were expressed as floating concrete trays. The glass curtain walls were protected by the overhanging cantilevered roof and two long strips of louvered screens hanging from the roof. These features allowed the curtain wall to stop short of the roof, leaving gaps for hot air to escape, thus creating air movement to naturally ventilate the concourse. These horizontal elements of the building were anchored by five vertical service cores.

A cursory evaluation suggests that the design of the SCHTUH adhered to the design language and spatial strategies of tropical modern architecture, particularly in its clarity of structure, fluidity of composition, and spatial ambiguity between inside and outside. But its design also created a new and unusual effect, as Tan Kok Meng noted:

> Aesthetically, the varying portions of the facades that come under shade at changing times of the day seem to add another dimension to the elevational composition. The aesthetic is thus one of layering, of degrees of transparencies and reflectivity. This poetically brings out the qualities of tropical shade, with its rich tones, shielded from harsh tropical light. The Corbusian use, typified at Chandigarh, of chiaroscuro, of modulation of shadow versus light and mass versus voids, especially the aesthetic function in the use of the *bris-soliel* [*sic*], is most sensitively transformed here into a modulation of layers of transparencies and tactilities that almost acquires a textile quality.[53]

No wonder the SCHTUH was regarded by Tay as "an innovative attempt at evolving a modern tropical design language [in Singapore and Malaysia] that has not been matched since."[54]

The building, however, was not just designed to be in dialogue with the international discourse of tropical architecture. It was designed to emphasize and incorporate the local—the Malayan—both literally and symbolically. Lim and his partners specified local materials, particularly hardwoods like *merbau*, *mersawa*, and *keranji* for wall and floor finishes; they also employed local craftsman to fabricate the furniture and commissioned local artist Khoo Sui Hoe to paint a huge mural within the building. Just as the young architects, who were in their early thirties when they won the competition, were given the opportunity by the state to build their capacity and demonstrate their capability with the important commission, the architects themselves wanted to provide similar opportunities for these local suppliers, builders, and artists. Within the building itself, surrounded by layers of glazing, screens, and cantilevered roofs and balconies, were highly abstracted representations of traditional woven mats made of *mengkuang* (screw pine leaves or local species of *Pandanus atrocarpus*) found in Malay houses (figure 13.4).[55] Instead of screw pine leaves, the patterns were created using colorful glass mosaics.

Where did the mengkuang mat patterns come from and how could we understand their incorporation in a modernist building like the SCHTUH? As we noted earlier, Lim was interested in vernacular Malay architecture and he took his

Jiat-Hwee Chang

Fig. 13.4 View of the external wall of the auditorium covered with glass mosaics based on patterns derived from weaved mengkuang mats. Photograph taken when the building was still under construction. Private collection of Lim Chong Keat.

students on outings to study and carry out measured drawings of Malay houses.[56] Thus, the patterns could have been inspired by his knowledge of the mengkuang mats he saw in Malay houses. Such knowledge of traditional Malay arts and crafts was also common among British administrators-scholars—such as the aforementioned Mubin Sheppard—who romanticized the Malays and their cultures. Hence, Lim's use of the mengkuang pattern could also be seen as being influenced by this form of colonial knowledge. Indeed, Lim has a collection of drawings by Carl Alexander Gibson-Hill (1911–1963), a medical doctor and a prominent British administrator-scholar, who also happened to precede Sheppard as the editor of the *Journal of the Malayan Branch of Royal Asiatic Society* (*JMBRAS*). Some of the materials in Gibson-Hill's collection went to Lim sometime after he passed away in 1963, when the construction of the SCHTUH was about to commence. They included a series of large, beautiful measured drawings of mengkuang mats of vernacular Malay houses probably prepared as illustrations for articles in *JMBRAS* that Gibson-Hill was editing (figure 13.5). Seen as such, could the abstracted mengkaung mat patterns found in the SCHTUH be read as an unconscious postcolonial extension of colonial romanticism?

Fig. 13.5 One of the measured drawings of mengkuang mats originally from Carl Alexander Gibson-Hill's collection that is now kept by Lim Chong Cleat. Private collection of Lim Chong Keat.

There were, however, distinct differences between the SCHTUH and Muzium Negara in the ways "Malayness" was represented. Unlike with the Muzium Negara, where the symbols and motifs associated with Malay arts and culture were literal and highly visible on the exterior, the mengkuang patterns in the SCHTUH were highly abstracted and only appeared on interior surfaces within a modernist shell. If we go beyond formal analysis to examine the production of these architectural components to ascertain their plausible meanings, we would notice that while the Malay symbols and motifs at the Muzium were fabricated by traditional Malay craftsmen, the mosaic walls of mengkuang patterns were built by modern Chinese construction workers. Both form and process suggest that the mengkuang patterns at the SCHTUH were removed from the racial knowledge associated with colonial romanticization of the Malays.

Despite his interest in the vernacular architecture of the region, Lim has always insisted that, like other prominent southeast Asian modern architects such as Leandro Locsin and Sumet Jumsai, his own works "illustrated an unself-conscious international design criteria."[57] He argued that these southeast Asian architects were international architects through and through, and they were only coincidentally national architects. In his words: "Their national importance lies in the fact that their architects are nationals in residence, serious about their urban responsi-

Jiat-Hwee Chang

Fig. 13.6 Buckminster Fuller sketching his ideas about three-way woven basketry, triangular structures used for rafts in Bali, at the first Campuan meeting, 1976, convened by Lim Chong Keat, who is sitting next to Fuller. Private collection of Lim Chong Keat.

bilities and are not transient foreigners. Generally, the major regional practitioners have come to terms with world building techniques, and by training and experience, have been ready to design more significant projects not only in their own cities but also in other parts of the world." Lim's statement suggests a form of cosmopolitanism, one that does not distinguish, in the hierarchical sense, between the national and the international, the local and the global, subordinating one to the other. This cosmopolitanism is perhaps best captured in Lim's friendship with the visionary architect and engineer Buckminster Fuller, and particularly in Lim's enthusiasm for Fuller's rather unorthodox understanding of Southeast Asia. For Lim, Fuller "had a world-view of South East Asia" that was based on Fuller's "speculative prehistory" of the region.[58] Instead of holding the conventional view of the southeast Asian region as "a cultural Johnnie-come-lately," Fuller argued that the region was the cradle for early human civilization.[59] Fuller noted that the warm water of the South Pacific (broadly corresponding to island Southeast Asia) was the "most logically propitious place for humans to survive and prosper within our planetary biosphere."[60] Inhabitants of this region became "natural hydraulic inventors," building rafts and boats to sail and connect between landmasses. In the process, they "learned that triangles are the only structurally stable patterns for the interbracings, outriggings, and sparring of their sailing canoes and catamarans."[61] One of the main pieces of evidence that Fuller mobilized to support his argument was the three-way woven baskets found solely in the region (figure 13.6). Unlike the square, two-way woven basketry found in the rest of the world, the three-way weaves are much more structurally robust.

Through his structural reasoning, Fuller's prehistory of the South Pacific reconstructs and even helps to redeem the region. Instead of being consigned by the colonial discourse on the tropics to a geography of insalubrity and backwardness, Southeast Asia was recuperated as a zone of fundamental innovation and early civilization. Likewise, weaving was no longer just a particular form of traditional craft practiced by backward people, it had a universal structural logic that could be seen as a precursor to the three-way gridding of a sphere in Fuller's sophisticated geodesic geometry. Fuller wrote part of this speculative prehistory during his tours of the region with Lim, and at the Campuan meetings that Lim convened in the 1970s and early 1980s. It is perhaps fitting that we end this chapter on what could be described as the cosmopolitan tropical architecture of Lim and his partners with a broadened, albeit unconventional, understanding of the tropics and its traditions.

"Compartmentalized World"

Race, Architecture, and Colonial Crisis in Kenya and London

Mark Crinson

Early in Frantz Fanon's *The Wretched of the Earth* comes his famous description of the colonial world as a compartmentalized world:

> The colonist's sector is a sector built to last, all stone and steel. It's a sector of lights and paved roads, where the trash cans constantly overflow with strange and wonderful garbage, undreamed-of leftovers. The colonist's feet can never be glimpsed, except perhaps in the sea, but then you can never get close enough. They are protected by solid shoes in a sector where the streets are clean and smooth, without a pothole, without a stone. The colonist's sector is a sated, sluggish sector, its belly is permanently full of good things. The colonist's sector is a white folks' sector, a sector of foreigners. The colonized's sector, or at least the native quarters, the shanty town, the Medina, the reservation, is a disreputable place inhabited by a disreputable people. . . . It's a world with no space, people are piled one on top of the other, squeezed tightly together. . . . The colonized's sector is a famished sector, hungry for bread, meat, shoes, coal, and light. The colonized's sector is a sector that crouches and cowers, a sector on its knees, a sector that is prostrate. . . . This compartmentalized world, this world divided in two, is

inhabited by different species . . . what divides this world is first and foremost what species, what race one belongs to.[1]

The passage has all of Fanon's characteristic physical immediacy and urgency, conveyed by the prose's clogged and released cadences, the way it makes objects creaturely, and its insistent triangulation of bodies, mentalities and violence. We might quibble with the description—where are the laborers, servants, shopkeepers, the traffic in goods, including building materials, that traverse these compartments?—but its psycho-existential truth is powerfully produced by its formal system of differences. It is a Manichean society, a world divided by the interiorized impositions of "epidermalization," its differences born out of dispossession and coercion.[2] But it is also an interdependent and self-mirroring society, as shown by its recto-verso sensualities of abundance and lack, and the near repetitions of colonist's sector / colonized's sector ("*la ville du colon . . . la ville du colonisé*").

In terms of the interactions between architecture and racial discourse, however, Fanon's description only offers a promise, a glimpse. While the white feet in the sea, the solid shoes, the strange garbage, the cowering knees, all carry through into the main arguments of Fanon's writing, nothing is made of the stone and steel, the shacks squeezed tightly together. In short, it seems that Fanon's interest in the body's perspective on the world and the world's impress on the body—race as discourse and race as phenotype—are not accompanied by any extended sense of the spatio-physical specificity of that world. Nor do we find this elsewhere in Fanon's work, despite his many analogies between race and building.[3] While Fanon's thought insists on physical embodiment, equally physical matters like buildings, walls, and roads become etherealized, dissolve into background or, at best, act metaphorically. Perhaps the physical environment is a less urgent consideration than the immediate demands of psychic survival under the isolating terms wrought by colonial racism. Or perhaps Fanon in constructing an anti-colonial psychology based on anti-carceral social therapy, was avoiding the deterministic links between race and environment that played an operative role in colonial psychology. Perhaps the "sociogenic principle" would break through the compartmentalization.[4]

In what follows, Fanon's idea of a "compartmentalized world" is used to help understand the divided yet interdependent terrain of architecture as it was structured by racial discourse at this historical moment of late colonialism. The chapter starts with a colonial practice of psychology that caused actual spaces to be reshaped under its authority. It looks at resistant conceptions of space that directly challenged the logic of colonial racism. It suggests how colonial violence was enabled by the interdependent compartments of vernacular and high architecture.

Mark Crinson

And finally, it tracks how the racially compartmentalized world of the colony resonated with the metropolis at just that moment when empire was in crisis. Overall, the argument is that any fuller account of the imbrications of race and architecture must both recognize and at the same time, as a matter of historical and political necessity, break out of those compartments—colony/metropole; *la ville du colon / la ville du colonisé*; vernacular/modern—into which the built world is divided.

Villagization

Well-known to Fanon, and directly attacked by him, was the work of the leading exponent of colonial "ethnopsychiatry," J. C. Carothers, director of the Mathari Mental Hospital in Nairobi between 1938 and 1950.[5] Both Carothers and his predecessor, H. L. Gordon, were obsessed with brain capacities. Notoriously, in one study Carothers described "the African" as "remarkably like the lobotomized Western European and in some ways like the traditional psychopath."[6] Biological determinism was used to understand cultural matters such as the effects of European education and the modern city on the supposedly undersized brains of Kenyans; it was this conjuncture of biology and modernity that formed the "African mind."[7] However crude its findings, however belated its version of phylogenetic race theory, Carothers's work could not so easily be dismissed as it gave scientific justification to colonial policy.

By contrast Fanon's psychiatry was radical, in the sense that it was dedicated to improving the lot of the people studied rather than supporting the prevailing colonial regime. Fanon argued against any idea his colonized patients were innately deranged, but instead for derangement as a product of historic and sociological conditions: to use his famous phrase, "beside phylogeny and ontogeny stands sociogeny."[8] The sense of self was produced by lived experience, which included derangements such as racism and the internalized effects of racism. In this sociogenic principle the reality to be grasped was not the structure of the brain, but the structure of social relations and their construal of the individual in racial terms. In Fanon's words, "it was necessary to go from the biological to the institutional, from natural existence to cultural existence."[9] Symptoms resulted from "a distorted dialectic between the ego and the world and from the internalization of social conflicts."[10] If Carothers's ethnopsychiatry attributed everything to the ethnos, the idea of unchanging racial difference, and understood human geography as an expression of this, then Fanon took the structure of society as a given (its "historico-racial schema") and worked towards the psyche.

In 1953 British colonial authorities deployed Carothers's ethnopsychiatry to maintain colonial rule, using its findings to justify reshaping the built environment. This was a year after the start of the so-called Mau Mau Uprising, a revolt over land rights by sections of the Gīkūyū, the main ethnic group in central Kenya. The Mau Mau quickly achieved an extraordinary place in colonial mythology, seen to represent an atavistic return to violent barbarity and precolonial witchcraft.[11] Commissioned to look into the reasons for anti-colonial revolt in Kenya, Carothers produced *The Psychology of Mau Mau* in a short two months.[12] The region's Gīkūyū people—from which the majority of the Mau Mau rebels came—were deemed to suffer from mass psychosis due to their liminal condition, neither urbanized nor forest-dwelling. Displacement and alienation of living conditions were already understood as central to the problems studied by colonial ethnopsychiatry.[13] In Carothers's terms, the Gīkūyū's essential "forest psychology" had been jolted and disturbed by their new situation "in transition" between two worlds, traditional and modern.[14] The Mau Mau rebels had lost the constraining influences of their own culture, so letting loose their old "'magic' modes of thinking."[15] The problem was exacerbated, Carothers claimed, because of current land settlement patterns: disloyal Gīkūyū "have no chance to alter their allegiance in isolated country houses." As the primitive had reemerged in the Mau Mau, he argued, becoming violent anti-colonialism, so these isolated huts had to become communalized if they weren't also to foster the primitive. These huts' very existence, unscientifically scattered across an otherwise uncannily "English" landscape, was an affront to any sense that human community was reflected in architectural community.[16] Forced villagization was the answer, and not just for "emergency" conditions but for the foreseeable future. It would "rehabilitate," engendering a sense of security and communal-mindedness among the Gīkūyū as a whole.[17] And this concentration on enforced patterns of communal life would be extended with a home hygiene program teaching domesticity to Gīkūyū women so their children would be better socialized.[18] In Carothers's cosmos the new village would create and occupy a zone, both psychic and spatial, between the swirl of urban modernity and the call of jungle atavism, a new/old space invested—as will be seen later—with ideas of the vernacular.

The policy of villagization was already being used in British Malaya to combat Communist insurrection there.[19] But in Kenya, where the problem was perceived less as political than as racial and psychological, the policy needed the authority of ethnopsychiatry for its application. It was carried through on a vast scale: over eight hundred new villages were built—laid out by the police and military—with many hundreds of thousands of people forcibly removed from their homes and resettled (figure 14.1). Villagization was only one way in which space and containment were used against anti-colonial revolt, and by no means the worst. Historians have belatedly exposed the brutal "bare life" of the detention camps for Mau Mau suspects.[20] No association with villages and vernaculars was felt or intended in these camps, where barracks and tents were the usual form of accommodation.

Mark Crinson

Fig. 14.1 Nijku village, Kiambu, from Elspeth Huxley, *A New Earth–An Experiment in Colonialism* (1960).

Across the spaces of the colonized a compartmentalized world was thus reinforced, reshaped, and made police-able: the forest world of the atavistic Mau Mau, with their scrambled brains and unconstrained nature; the country world of the wavering Gĩkũyũ, isolated, with their brains vulnerable to reversion; and finally, the world of the secured, made-loyal Gĩkũyũ, given their demarcated villages, their petri dish for proper community.

Land and Home

Even before the Mau Mau revolt the Gĩkũyũ had articulated their own understanding of land and home in forms that were resistant to colonial culture. *Facing Mount Kenya*, for instance, the anthropological study written by the Gĩkũyũ (and future Kenyan president) Jomo Kenyatta provides a legalistic defense of Gĩkũyũ conceptions of proprietorship and elaborates on Gĩkũyũ domestic space, and would become particularly resonant in the 1950s. Kenyatta presented dual forms of authority to his metropolitan British readership: as a Gĩkũyũ elder, and as an

African using the discipline of anthropology learnt from his teacher Bronislaw Malinowski. Kenyatta teased his readers by using another clearly stereotyped authority, portraying himself masquerading as a warrior in the frontispiece photograph (figure 14.2). Here Kenyatta was shown wearing an animal skin and fingering the sharp point of a spear, both hastily acquired for the shoot (he had been living in London for several years and studying at the London School of Economics).[21] Native informant, subaltern native subject, and ethnographer were made one and the same.

Central to Kenyatta's book was the ascription of rationale, history, and intricate anthropological meaning to Gīkūyū modes of land tenure and patterns of inhabitation. This was a Malinowskian functionalist account of precisely those things that Carothers would ignore. Gīkūyū were presented as agriculturalists who depended entirely on the land. But the connection was deeper than this, for the earth was considered the "mother" of the tribe and, as "it is the soil that nurses the spirits of the dead for eternity," so communion with ancestral spirits was perpetuated by contact with the land.[22] Land was owned individually and collectively (by family, not tribe) through a complex system of tenure through which a right to own land arose from labor spent developing it.[23] This system, including common land for grazing and woodlands held in common, was underpinned and explained by rich tribal legends, some of which had predicted the coming of Europeans. But although understood as temporary settlers initially, Europeans soon claimed the land as Crown Lands, with the Gīkūyū designated "tenants at will of the crown."[24]

Also significant for Kenyatta were the meanings invested in Gīkūyū huts. He spent what might otherwise seem an excessive amount of time describing hut building: the transfer of fire, the different functions of the woman's hut as opposed to the man's, the speed of building and the collective effort that went into it, the selection of a plot (emphasized as "one that has been lawfully acquired"), the relation to various taboos, the foundation ceremony, and the marking of foundations and digging of postholes.[25] Thus far all was done by men, but then women took over the thatching while singing songs. Feasting followed and an address by the ceremonial elder, who chanted a prayer blessing. Then the homestead was declared open and a fire was lit. A book that had announced itself in the familiar titillating terms of the frontispiece, had become an elaborate anthropology of Gīkūyū life, a counter-account deploying ethnographic authority against ethnocentric reductionism.[26]

If Kenyatta was writing before the Mau Mau revolt, Ngũgĩ wa Thiong'o's novel *A Grain of Wheat* (1967) narrativized the experience of villagization. In the novel, hut and village environments are dynamic psychological arenas, theatres of contestation with colonial ways of understanding. Landscape and dwelling are torn by shifts of loyalty and betrayal, as the powers of state and settler, military and

Mark Crinson

FACING
MOUNT KENYA
The Tribal Life of the Gikuyu

by
JOMO KENYATTA

with an Introduction by
B. MALINOWSKI
Ph.D. (Cracow); D.Sc. (London); Hon. D.Sc. (Harvard)
Professor of Anthropology in the University of London

SECKER AND WARBURG
1953

[Frontispiece]   [Photo by Brian Cobbold]
THE AUTHOR

Fig. 14.2 "The Author," frontispiece to Jomo Kenyatta, *Facing Mount Kenya* (1938; repr., London, 1953).

rebel, village and family, come into conflict. Reversing Carothers, the pathologies
in *A Grain of Wheat* are associated with the colonial world and seen as a direct
result of its policies: the sadistic violence of a District Officer, born out of thwarted
idealism and replaying the psychic inversions of Joseph Conrad's Kurtz; and the
emasculation of Gikonyo, a craftsman whose materials and motivations are alienated by the emotional devastations of colonial rule. Ngũgĩ's reading of Fanon's *The
Wretched of the Earth*, usually understood in terms of Fanon's critique of decolonization, may also account for the way the author explicitly tries to link mental
pathologies with the effects of colonialism.[27]

Villagization itself plays a central role in *A Grain of Wheat*. Ngũgĩ understood
land settlement before villagization in Kenyatta-like terms as relatively harmonious; the people are dispossessed but they still recognize the land and revel in it.[28]
Villagization, however, gives this dispossession a wholly new and coercive vicious-
ness, remaking Gĩkũyũ space so that it becomes colonial space: penetrable, know-

able, containable. There is forced ejection, belongings are hurriedly removed, huts burnt in the night.[29] This psychic and spatial violence is especially marked in the case of Mugo, the novel's scapegoat figure, whose serenity is reflected in his hut, "his first big achievement."[30] The act of opening the hut's door after a day in the fields gives him pleasure: "the hut was an extension of himself, his hopes and dreams." He admires the walls and the cone-shaped roof, whistles to himself, cooks his meal and indulges his physical lassitude. But one night this home is ripped open when a fugitive seeks refuge there. Mugo later betrays the fugitive and in contemplating that betrayal his new disassociation is shown as much by his inability to discern the "broken sites" of the old village as by his physical trembling and depression. After the betrayal Mugo becomes completely cut off, his life inarticulate and futile. In a curious ironizing of ethnopsychiatry, his betrayal causes his mental disassociation from the rest of the new village.

New bodily dissociations from land and dwelling culminate in the novel's crucial sexual and political betrayals. The authorities punish the inhabitants for the Mau Mau activities of one of their members by forcing them to dig a ditch around the village. Villagers are beaten and killed while at this labor, their frail relatives and children forced to watch. In a moment of bravery and kindness that soon becomes mythical, Mugo saves a pregnant woman from a beating. The ditch is thus the antonym of the rhyming of body, community, and hut before villagization; it is violently cut through the earth, much as the whips of the soldiers cut the bodies of the villagers working on it. Following Carothers's logic, the ditch's purpose is to contain and control, to sever the villagers from the forest as much as from their communal practices of land tenure. The village as proper community is thus redescribed as a deeply politicized site in Ngũgĩ's novel, part of a larger colonial contest around the home.

Vernacular

The word "vernacular" is not used by Kenyatta or Ngũgĩ, and yet the idea of the vernacular, and associated terms like village and picturesque, played a key role in conceptualizing and justifying the persuasive and coercive functions of colonial architecture. The term had, of course, widespread usage in the metropolis. The vernacular describes the low or common, an unthinking and unchanging dialect of architecture. As a concept it belongs to the master's language, with its Latin roots in *vernaculus* meaning domestic or indigenous. In ancient Rome the *verna* was a household or home-born slave, one favored more than other kinds of slaves.[31] The vernacular's origin defines a subject position only possible within the language of power. To identify the vernacular is thus a performative act creating an asymmetric relationship to something subordinate in status. In Hegelian terms its naming is also a mastering of the other that in the end only makes recognition more

Mark Crinson

difficult; the master sublates or loses himself, because he cannot regard the other as essentially real or different, he can only see himself in the other.[32] The truth of modern self-consciousness is bound up in the servile consciousness of the *vernae*.[33] Naming the vernacular is therefore particularly conflicted and coercive in the immediate contexts of empire. Everywhere, in the spaces of colonialism, the vernacular belonged to the peoples who had been colonized, who were ethnically different from their colonial masters; those who lived on the land but did not determine its future. They were the *vernae* in the colonial house. Wherever it emerges—Europe or the colonies—talking about the vernacular was an attempt to allay or to momentarily forget the effects of modernization. Vernacular discourse usually avoided a deeper political reality; that colonialism would cater for difference, it would license the apparent existence of hetero-temporalities, providing they did not block its own logic of reproduction.[34]

While Kenyatta and Ngũgĩ affirmed the meaningful and layered relations between hut and community, many colonialists were wedded to a racialized understanding of those same things and it was here that vernacular thinking came into its own, helping particularly to disavow the effects of villagization. Relevantly, both in their homes and in their imagining of the Kenya Highlands as "white man's country," colonial settlers had imported ideas of the vernacular taken from a pre-industrial mythology of the English countryside.[35] But the terminology seems even more incongruous when applied to what were effectively detention camps surrounded by barbed-wire. Some colonial officials imagined that villagization was the creation of "a harmonious society of prosperous villages and sturdy yeoman farmers immune to the appeals of political radicalism."[36] It was suggested that "village streets" could still preserve Gĩkũyũ patterns of land holding while presenting reassuring images of "English villages [where] we find blacksmiths, innkeepers, millers and so on as regular members of the community."[37] "The resulting picture," wrote another official, "reminded one of the English medieval manor with its village—though in this case it was a rugged wired-in home guard post on a high knoll with a series of grass roofed mud-walled huts below."[38]

The British architectural culture's response to villagization was more tentative but essentially similar. Architectural culture's very existence, like that of the professional architect, is dependent on maintaining its difference from practices of building deemed vernacular. The liminal or "transitional" condition of much African culture was a trope shared by many architectural commentators.[39] Villagization was only referred to obliquely or in isolated articles, but in those rare instances when the Kenyan emergency was mentioned it was seen instrumentally as an opportunity for architects in what was thought to be a reconstituted vernacular.[40] The following, which appeared in an architecture school journal, may be exemplary: "The simplicity of the early homesteads was retained. . . . The solution answered some of the more immediate problems relative to the emergency and contributed to the overall progress of the native. The African shanty town complex . . . has been avoided."[41] The self-perceived benevolence of late colonialism takes mythical form here, including the separation of high architecture from the activities of policing and coercion. Progress is associated not with the realities of urban change but with securing Africans' proper place within the vernacular, now developed and planned. In all this, the discourse carries its own history of racial subordination inscribed in the very idea of the vernacular.

This extended to "high" architecture too. At the very same moment of villagization, some of the most representative architecture of the colonial state manifested both regionally symbolic and climatically regional responses to Kenya. Contemporary to the new villages, for example, were buildings in Nairobi by Amyas Connell, a pioneering modernist in Britain who came to Kenya in 1941.[42] These included the Crown Law Offices (1960), a generic modernist office block whose major external features were decorative screens using motifs from Indian and Timurid sources pierced with an asymmetrical pattern of windows, including one larger opening framed in a version of Venetian Gothic (figure 14.3). In terms of European modernism, the Crown Law Offices breached the modernist prohibition on ornament, one that Connell had respected in his British buildings. But the breach or "crime" seemed licensed outside European architectural culture and in the context of an "undeveloped" African colony: the Crown Law Offices' screens were a more extensive example of a feature often found in that version of modernism known as "tropical architecture." Whether such ornament was vernacular in any local or general sense is not the point here. Connell and the colonial authorities preferred to conjure up more historically and geographically distant sources (Moorish Spain, Moghul India), perhaps because they were understood as addressing the loyal Muslim population in east Kenya. It was important this symbolically ornamental work was done in the skin of the building while the universalist source of functional authority, the structure and overall spatial form of the building, was unaffected. Departing from its previous adherence to neo-traditionalist expressions of permanence and European association, such as Herbert Baker's interwar neoclassical buildings in Nairobi, high architecture was now allowed to create a scenography of affiliation and difference; it projected the appropriation of a historical architecture, remaking it as vernacular. And in the course of this another imperial tradition was invoked. For it was John Ruskin's "central building of the world," the Ducal Palace in Venice, that the Crown Law Offices simulated and, with it, Ruskin's famous invocation of a hybrid mixture of racial elements, brought together under the paternalist authority of the British empire.

The dynamics of power, cultural form, and racial subordination are complex here, if more gestural than precise in their semiotics, but we need to insist on their

Mark Crinson

Fig. 14.3 Amyas Connell, Crown Law Offices, Nairobi (1960).

entanglement with other spatial politics in contemporary Kenya. While in Nairobi, flamboyant, structurally and ornamentally expressive forms of modernism were declaring the benefits of new policies of welfare and development, just outside the city the coercive intervention of villagization was effectively redefining Gĩkũyũ society. This network of power, with its attendant disavowals and disassociations, was carried across the building cultures and cultural spaces of colonial Kenya.

The antinomies and valences of temporality underpin much of this. The vernacular-high relationship is based on a dialectic between the ahistorical and the ownership of History. Fanon tells us that the colonists' sector is "built to last," or to achieve historical significance by making its claim on time, while the colonized's sector is "prostrate," fixed in an existential present of the body's biological time. The same contrast operates with villagization and high architecture. The latter, whether modernist or historicist, oversees the future (seeking destiny) as much as the past (tracing the plot); it makes a claim on the fullness of time that parallels the European assumption of "a fullness and genericity of being human."[43] The former is always static, always subjected to the discipline of duration, a holding to identity or originality under the threat of violence. In this scheme of things, the isolated hut fails to signify—it has to be brought into the familiar durational time of the vernacular. Simultaneously, it has to be remade as community, with all the accompanying possibility of a disordered community or, worse for colonial power, of a community made assertive by its historical and collective contingency. The vernacular, we might say, becomes the apotropaic figment with which to disavow both the abyss between colonial forms of life and their interdependence. So if villagization seemed like a situation far removed from the concerns of modernism, then that would be to accept modernism's self-mythology as some new universalism, separated from violence and coercion and devoted instead to the ulterior motivations of technological progress and welfarist benevolence.

The paradox, or the built-in incompatibility, is that with two intimately-related architectural modes defined so emphatically by their opposed temporalities, where and how is change allowed to happen? Where is modernity allowed to appear as process, not final object? Offered as resistant, but largely consistent with this, is the anthropological frame of Kenyatta's ontogenetic "integrated culture" and its system of land tenure bound forever by ties of kinship.[44] Even Ngugi's work offers no transitional balm. Here change is registered in acts of violence both on the village and on the body of the villager; the choreography of temporality in the colonized's sector is seen to have failed. Fanon, by contrast, rejects the equally imprisoning constraints of history, declaring instead "invention" as a way of "endlessly creating myself," a "[refiguring] of life as event," a turning to the future as a time invested not with destiny but with new values.[45]

Within the environment and architectures of colonial East Africa, disparate temporalities and architectural-spatial practices thus co-existed in physical and discursive proximity, an interrelated but compartmentalized world. The compartments familiar in the literature on architecture in Kenya at this time are the colonial architecture of the state, indigenous or "vernacular" architecture, and the impact of modernism—including the techno-scientific field of tropical architecture. But these are but slices of space and architecture, and villagization would be seen as outside their compartments, as the province of colonial or military history. Despite geographic and historical proximity, architectural history too easily ignores the insidious and brutal interrelations of land, habitation, and race that cross this compartmentalized world. We do not even have any term for this— "construction sector" and "architectural culture" are clearly inappropriate, while "production of space" says little either about how conceptions of land, skill, home, and race, traverse one territorial entity, or about how space can simultaneously contain hugely variant architectural conceptions of normality and crisis, authority and violence, welfare and warfare.[46] If colonial spaces are typified by abruptly uneven and seemingly contradictory economic modes, then we need to reassert

Mark Crinson

how colonial imaginaries and colonial resource extraction, occupation and resistance, coexist across one differentiated territory.[47] The compartmentalization of the colonial world is strategic; to affirm the distance of coexistence, the inviolability of its separations, it must continue to function especially at moments of crisis in cultural legitimacy.

Blank Space

If the colony is a highly differentiated world as far as architecture is concerned, it is also related by another set of differences and interdependencies to the imperial metropolis. When the Kenya crisis was registered in London there were architectural responses that adopted the idea of racial mixing, attempting to manage difference through the graduated achievement of multiracial community.

In 1953, the same year of Carothers's report, a student at the Architectural Association in London produced a thesis setting out "an environment for multiracial living"—a development plan for the ideal town of Maragua in Kenya (figures 14.4 and 14.5).[48] This was the work of the white East African–raised Richard Hughes (helped by the engineer Terence Powell). Maragua's site was pointedly chosen. It lay on "the boundary between the Kikuyu Reserve and the European alienated land," fifty miles from Nairobi in an area of Murang'a then well known for active anti-colonial protests against land policy.[49] Here Hughes proposed to locate an industrial town and market center, arranging his demographic ingredients—African, Asian, and European—across a main road, backed by a network of minor roads and footpaths. As we know from Ernst May's work in neighboring Uganda, even leftist modernist architects had consolidated the view that Africans and urban life were a fraught conjuncture by formulating African space as strictly divided on lines of racial hierarchy, social hygiene, and what might be called urban pupilage (the idea that Africans must be mentored into city life by passing through the graduated spaces of planning).[50] By contrast, Hughes was concerned with town planning as a way of modelling multiracial cohabitation and even racial integration, through the shaping of residential neighborhoods and the sharing of certain facilities by racial groups. Hughes saw integration as anti-extremist: "The great scourge of the world today," he wrote, "is the rise of militant and uncompromising nationalism."[51] He conceived his town as four neighborhood units, each of 5,000 people (3,500 Africans, 1,000 Asians, and 500 Europeans), each given community facilities, separated from major traffic arteries and set within open spaces both landscaped and recreational.

Race was the governing concern in Hughes's plan. Each racially designated area was given a different density according to supposedly different racial expectations, creating different urban grains.[52] Overlarge single race areas were discouraged by arranging neighborhoods so they were not contiguous with areas of the same race.

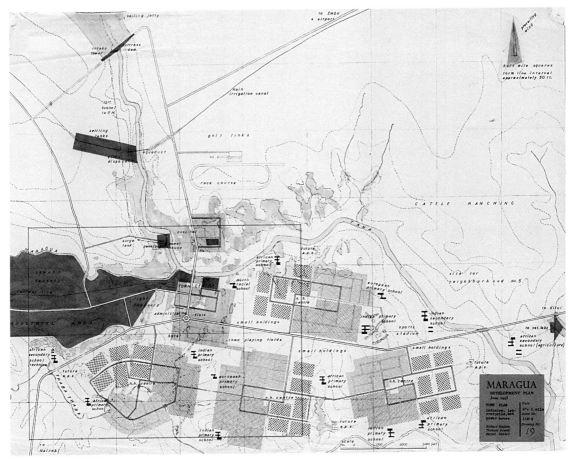

Fig. 14.4 Richard Hughes, Maragua Development Plan, fifth year thesis, Architectural Association (1953)—overall plan. Courtesy of the Architectural Association Archives.

The African neighborhood was given most attention, being further differentiated by arranging houses in short terraces representing family groups, to "soften the impact of modern urban living with its responsibilities and disciplines."[53] To embody the family in a grouping of terraces, the clan by the larger unit of a ten-acre block of such groups, and then the race by the neighborhood, would plan away the impact of modernity, help it to remain outside familiar structures of kinship. Many elements of the plan therefore envisaged race in stable terms, giving the organization a racially restrictive spatial schema whereby phylogenetically limited Kenyans could not advance beyond a certain cosmetic modernity.

Change would occur, or would be registered as having occurred, in two specified areas of the plan. The first is represented in the town center by the plan's finest, most milled-down shading (as opposed to the three racial areas given differently graded shading). Here, in flats and houses "of a fairly high standard," those already prepared would live "amongst those with similar standards." Of these Hughes only

Mark Crinson

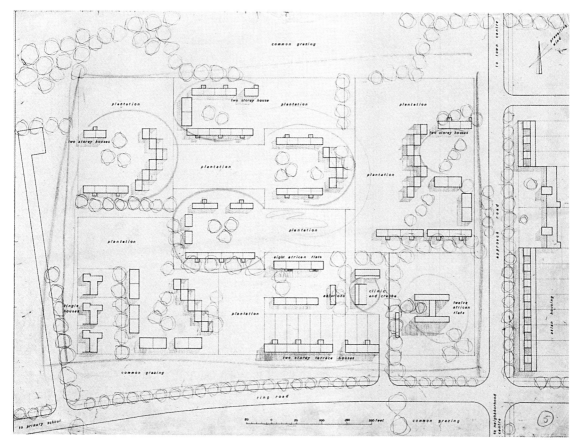

Fig. 14.5 Richard Hughes, Maragua Development Plan, fifth year thesis, Architectural Association (1953)–African neighborhood. Courtesy of the Architectural Association Archives.

singled out the integrated cadres of educated Africans (the *evolué*), who, having already "evolved" (or been routinized into the workplace) elsewhere, would take their rightful place as "leaders of their own community," exemplars of Fanon's sociogenic principle.[54] But while this transculturation activates the most urbanized space of the new town, Europeans and Indians implicitly stay unchanged.

The second area of change consisted of certain designated schools and the central hospital. It was the multiracial nursery schools in the center of each neighborhood that carried the most overt burden of racial mixing. School curricula would expose each child to the cultures of other races through games, folklore, and sharing knowledge about different flora and fauna. The schools were, effectively, distillators of cultural lore, forcing houses of tolerance and respect, racial condensers in which "the lessons of tolerance and respect . . . would be ineradicable."[55]

Beyond such designated areas, however, there are blank unshaded spaces on the plan that are less programmatic, where unsupervised racial integration was possible, but the drifting of the "wretched" more likely. These are found less in the center of neighborhood units, also blank, than in spaces between these units and the town center, such as around a multiracial school. On the outer fringes of the town blank space includes playing fields, small holdings, sports stadiums, and unspecified land. In some blank space, between the shaded areas, racial mixing may be a side effect of avoiding single-race dominance, in others it may be a product of the "blank" hours of nonwork. Similar areas elsewhere—for example in Ernst May's designs and in numerous colonial cities like Nairobi itself—might form *cordons sanitaires*, areas of separation in reality usually populated by "transient" workers. But in Hughes the function of blank space is differently ambiguous; if this is a mixing space, then it is space still determined by and determining of race. Is it space where, in Fanon's terms, "the phenotype undergoes a definitive, an absolute mutation," as it is acted on by sociocultural elements? Is it space where the self becomes a different kind of colonial subject?

A Contrapuntal Relation

There are several contexts in which Maragua's idea of space as a medium for racial mixing had resonance. Its conceptual and visual inspiration, for example, came clearly from those recent prewar and wartime projects, the MARS Plan for London (1938) and Abercrombie and Forshaw's County of London Plan (1943) and Greater London Plan (1944). As well as their elements of zoning these were typified by their cellular conception of neighborhood units. London's postwar integration was based not on the dissolution of classes but a new interclass settlement where class appropriately belonged.[56] The planner had a moral and state-sanctioned right to reshape "inchoate communities" and promote the "greater mingling of the different groups of London's society."[57] Middle class areas would be made accessible to a greater social mix. Class difference would remain, but a more harmonious society would be created by the intricate interpolation of classes across the spaces of the metropolis.[58] And each community would be centered on the primary school as the institution all citizens would value. In fact the very size of a community was defined by the catchment required for such a school (some 6 to 10,000 people).[59] One can conceive of Hughes absorbing these ideas and simply replacing class with race as their governing rationale.

Relations between class and race are not the only link between the politics of spatial planning in London and colonial Kenya. A form of social psychiatry had emerged just before the war and was used by officialdom in Britain after 1945 to reform or control elements of the population deemed socially destabilizing (it would also be used by some of the new "race relations" sociologists of the next decade).[60] The social psychiatrist was a professional of sudden importance, much like the architect and planner of the welfare state; all were experts in the scientific modernism required to heal or reform society, whether as manifest in the decrepit

Mark Crinson

built environment or the ruined social landscape of family structures. The particular focus of this work was the home and its associated dimensions, the "problem family," the "broken home," and the "slum," each treated as formative elements in a subject's environmental history. The sciences leveled at them were motivated in part by the "fear of the crowd . . . the unpredictability of a formless mass" symptomatized at the individual level in terms of "drift."[61] The similarities with the racial symptomatology of Carothers's ethnopsychiatry hardly need spelling out.

Perhaps in Maragua race was more of a difference and less of one, by comparison with the psychopathologies transecting the metropolis. On the one hand, by seeing race as the issue causing colonial revolt, especially the effect of modernity on "the minds of rural people," and by deploying architecture and space as the solution, Hughes was continuing some of the spatio-racial practices that had shaped a colonial city like Nairobi, and even articulating some of the same ideas as Carothers. Maragua, like villagization, was also a response to the "isolated hut" and to the idea of the deracinated urban African; it also shaped new community (urban pupilage here being enacted through racial transition zones). On the other hand, Hughes's thesis embodied the dream of metropolitan postwar planning that architecture would solve inherited social problems as well as those generated by modernity. Maragua was a product of this new moral framework for planning in Britain, as much as or more than it was a statement about Kenya.

While Hughes's thesis made no discernable architectural impact, it did have two links to the emerging postimperial politics of race. The first is in Africa. Hughes joined the Capricorn Africa Society when he returned to Kenya, and later became its historian. This was an organization formed to maintain British economic interests by staving off both white supremacy and black nationalism. It aimed to increase European immigration, and to control the transition from white rule in East Africa to power sharing via a multiracial electorate of the educated, with voting loaded in favor of Europeans via the so-called "plural" or "multiple" vote. The society saw itself as above matters like land tenure, being devoted instead to the issue of political representation, a cohabitation within the suffrage that mirrored the racial cohabitation of Maragua.[62]

The second aspect of postimperial racial politics occurred when Maragua was taken up within the new field of "race relations."[63] This was the official management of cultural difference that developed after the 1948 British Nationality Act, which recognized residents of the empire as British citizens, and the influx of Caribbean immigrants into Britain from that date. Kenya also featured in those new discourses centered on the so-called "problem of color," as sensationalized accounts of Mau Mau violence fused with fears about the effects of immigration.[64] In postwar London Hughes's thesis, presented as "a political programme for a multiracial country," made a splash in the media and especially with the colonial service.[65] Among its admirers were Philip Mason, formerly of the Indian Civil Service and later the first director of the Institute of Race Relations (started in 1958). This context of the empire as a continuing structure of consciousness, rather than the studiously avant-garde circles of the Architectural Association, is where Maragua was best received.[66] For the British reader of the *New Commonwealth* (once the *Crown Colonist*), Maragua seemed to address the central issue of colonial revolt—race—head on, and to deal with it through the means of state planning, the organization of space and facilities, the fantasy of the managed compartmentalized world.

Mark Crinson

15

Style, Race, and a Mosque of the "Òyìnbó Dúdú" (White-Black) in Lagos Colony, 1894

Adedoyin Teriba

In the darkness of early morning on June 6, 1894, a thirty-eight-year-old Englishman thought of the mission that lay before him as he waited in a Liverpool lodging house for the SS *Cabenda* to depart for the British protectorate of Lagos.[1] Less than two months prior, Abdul Hamid II, the sultan of the Ottoman Empire, had conveyed a letter through the Ottoman consul general of Liverpool asking the Briton go to Lagos, in what is now Nigeria, to do two things.[2] First, to bestow the Ottoman Third Class Order of the Medjidie medal on Mohammed Shitta, a Sierra Leonean Muslim immigrant, and second, to deliver a speech on the sultan's behalf at the opening of a mosque in Lagos that Mohammed Shitta had paid for.[3] (The medal was in a parcel from the Ottoman court). The Englishman's name was Abdullah Quilliam, and he was a Victorian Muslim.[4]

It was only natural that Sultan Abdul Hamid had picked Quilliam for these duties: he was the sheikh al-Islam to the sultan, the advisor of Islamic affairs in the British Isles. In 1887, seven years before the inauguration of the mosque in Lagos, to which this essay will soon turn, Quilliam had converted to Islam and founded the Liverpool Islamic Institute. Furthermore, he appointed the kola nut merchant Mohammed Shitta the vice president of the Liverpool organization four

Fig. 15.1 Mohammed Shitta-Bey in the 1890s, from Abdur Rahman I, *Islam in Nigeria* (Zaria, Nigeria: Gaskiya Corp., 1984).

months after the mosque in Lagos opened. After twenty days at sea, Quilliam finally disembarked on the shores of the city, a week before the opening ceremony of the mosque.

Many distinguished guests attended the officiation. King Oyekan I of Lagos was there, as well as Edward Wilmot Blyden, the Trinidadian pan-Africanist and naturalized citizen of Liberia. Sir Gilbert Carter, the British governor general of Lagos sat next to Quilliam during the ceremony. Quilliam delivered a speech on behalf of the sultan of Constantinople and gave Mohammed Shitta the noble Turkish title of "Bey," which was customary for recipients of the Third Class Order of the Medjidie. From that time until Shitta's death in 1895, the financier of the mosque affixed the Ottoman designation to his last name, calling himself Mohammed Shitta-Bey (figure 15.1).

Adedoyin Teriba

The *Lagos Weekly Record* reported at the time that the mosque was the "finest specimen of ecclesiastical architecture in West Africa," and that the edifice should be embraced as an exemplar of what Lagosians could erect.[5] It is worth noting that, at this time, the *Weekly Record* was awash with letters from African immigrants who had debated whether local citizens should wear European-styled clothing and bear English names or cling on to local dress and names.[6] It seems that the *Record*'s coverage of the mosque continued an ongoing quest for a local modernity emerging in different aspects of the Lagosian society.[7] African immigrant readers of the Lagosian newspapers at the turn of the twentieth century had started to debate modernism and constituted a small part of the Lagos populace. The efforts of these settlers to cultivate a local Lagosian elite in print culture and in architecture may have given rise to the term òyìnbó *dúdú* used by locals to describe the immigrants.[8] Translated as "white-black" in English, the term may have been used by local Lagosians to differentiate themselves from the African immigrants who they thought acted and spoke like the British colonialists. Hence, they linked the immigrants' behavior, architecture, and taste in clothing with the European residents in the city: using a physiognomic description (white-black) as a metaphor for the immigrants' activities.

Colonial officials also praised the beauty of Shitta-Bey's mosque and the collaboration of individuals of different religions who executed the project.[9] For example, Sir Gilbert Carter, the British governor-general of Lagos Colony at the time, stated that for Lagos to continue to enjoy peace, the city's population had to emulate the migrant Muslims and Catholics' collaboration on the mosque's construction. This essay will examine how Shitta-Bey's mosque reveals the ways in which the collaborative building efforts of a group of settlers from Brazil and Sierra Leone, as well as Lagosian elites, embodied the enmeshing of architectural style and local notions of race in the colony at the turn of the twentieth century. Moreover, it will also explore how the mosque amplified certain Yorùbá-language concepts like òyìnbó dúdú, which reflected a local racial discourse that tried to decipher the place of African immigrants in the colony.

Before suggesting how Mohammed Shitta's mosque and other structures like it marked a shift in the relations between settlers and locals in Lagos, I will cover a short history of the city as well as a demographic analysis of the African immigrant population and how they related to the rest of Lagos's residents. The region that is now known as Lagos was first settled in the fifteenth century, by King Ògúnfúnminire, who established the fertile area as the kingdom of Èkó.[10] In 1852, Akítóyè, the *oba* (monarch) of Lagos gave the Olówógbówó borough to the Sàró (the Sierra Leonean immigrants).[11] Otherwise called "Sàró Town," it was located in the southwestern part of the city. Portuguese merchants who traded with Akítóyè's ancestors in the fifteenth century had initially named the entire city

"Lago de Curamo"—*lago* meaning lake in Portuguese—which the British later called "Lagos" when they annexed the territory in 1861.[12] Akítóyè had requested the British Crown's aid in order to reclaim his throne, which Kòsókó, his cousin, had usurped in the 1850s. The British drove Kòsókó into exile in the kingdom of Èpé. His banishment also led to a ban on the city's slave trade, because he had exported slaves to Portugal and Brazil. Subsequently the British government in Lagos implemented a policy of "indirect rule," which kept Akítóyè in place as a titular sovereign.

The traditional urban planning of Èkó differed from the other older realms in what is now southwestern Nigeria. For example, in Ifè the palace of the king of lay in the center of the ancient kingdom; chiefs lived in houses that surrounded the Ifè monarch's residence, suggesting that royal power radiated from the center of kingdom outward. The absence of such spatial planning in Lagos alludes to the possibility that Ògúnfúnminire and his descendants ignored the precedent of older urban designs, preferring to conceive the urban landscape differently.[13] For example, the palace in Èkó was an architectural icon to be seen at different angles, and which was not shielded or protected by the houses of chiefs that surrounded it. The British colonialists did not interfere with the layout of the kingdom of Èkó and confined their urban planning to Marina, the seat of the colonial government in Lagos Colony. However, the colonial government also oversaw the allotment of parcels of land to African immigrants in other parts of the colony.[14] Moreover, the colonial government barred most Lagosians from owning property in Marina, only allowing wealthy locals like Chief Conrad Taiwo to purchase land in the vicinity.[15]

The absence of the visual spectacle of chiefs' houses around and concealing the king's palace and Britain's seizure of the Lagos colony in 1861 may have caused native Lagosians to question the power and endurance of the Lagosian monarchy.[16] The appeal to the British of the Sàró and to a lesser extent the Àgùdà (Afro-Brazilian immigrants) who settled in the colony between 1850 and 1900 to annex the kingdom in order to quell the slave trade was another significant event in the history of Lagos.[17] That episode may have worked in tandem with the Sàró and Àgùdà's choices of architectural design and construction to underscore how the British as well as the African immigrants eventually wrested control of the kingdom from the office of the *oba* (king), known for its participation in the slave trade.[18]

The annexation of Lagos saw the emergence of four distinct urban zones at the turn of the twentieth century. The northeast part of the colony—Ìsàlè Èkó—was where the oba of Lagos resided. Consisting of the king's palace and the market, it was also called "Old Lagos."[19] To the north was Pópó Àgùdà, which the oba gave to the Afro-Brazilians.[20] The British settled in and confined their interventions in

Marina, as mentioned earlier, which was east of Olówógbówó, another name for Sàró Town.[21]

Some of the Sàró and the Àgùdà spoke Ìjèbu, Ègbá, and other dialects with common etymological roots, which Ajayi Crowther (1809–1891), a Sàró Protestant clergyman streamlined into a pan-Yorùbá language in the 1840s.[22] Other immigrants spoke the Igbo and Delta-Cross languages that originated in current-day southeastern Nigeria.[23] The Lagosians' connection to the area around the oba's realm shaped their attitudes toward the Sàró and the Àgùdà, and vice versa. Ògúnfúnminire's descendants may have thought of themselves as *omo ilé* (children of the earth) and viewed the new arrivals from Brazil and Sierra Leone as intruders. Consequentially, they would have chosen not to live outside Ìsàlè Èkó. Some Àgùdà and Sàró's contempt for Ifá, the local religion, further soured their already tense relationships with the locals. There were other immigrants, however, who worshipped Yorùbá gods while remaining Muslims or Catholics. In fact, it was not uncommon for some to be devotees of three faiths (Islam, Catholicism, and Ifá) at the same time. Yet the Sàró and the Àgùdà saw this clash of faiths as a distinguishing divide from omo ilé.[24] The Àgùdà also cooked Afro-Brazilian dishes and sang serenades in Portuguese, reminiscing about their past in Brazil.[25] Within this diverse, and often tense, ethnic mix the need to assert one's space in these boroughs became habitual.

The Marina area consisted of the residence of the governor-general, the colonial offices, as well as European and foreign African retail stores. Samuel Pearse's Elephant House of 1907 was an example of how a Sàró's residence conveyed, in the minds of locals, the blurred distinctions between the colonial buildings' facades and those owned by the descendants of Sierra Leonean immigrants. The residential, civic, and commercial buildings of the European residents and colonial officers of Lagos were mostly multistory prefabricated structures or were made out of stone and brick. The height of their architecture alone made a great contrast with the native Lagosians' single-story homes made out of adobe. The Sàró's residences, on the other hand, were as tall as the colonial architecture. Hence, Pearse's name, and two-story Elephant House, as well as his preference for bespoke tailored clothing may have reinforced in the minds of the native Lagosians the blurred distinctions between the Sàró and the European residents.

Born in Lagos in 1866, Pearse was educated in the city's Christian Missionary Society Grammar School. He was the cofounder of a shipping company known as Messrs. Pearse & Thompson, which had offices along the Marina district as well as in Leadenhall Street in London.[26] Additionally, Pearse produced a report on the state of rubber resources in Benin City for the colonial government in 1907. As the secretary of the Lagos Auxiliary of the Anti-Slavery and Aborigines' Rights Protection Society, he led a delegation of Yorùbá chiefs to London to contest the Foreshore decision of the Lagos Supreme Court of 1911, which had granted the British Crown ownership of all the land in Lagos Colony.[27] The Sàró use of ashlar masonry construction—which is specific to European design and construction—also reinforced their desire to be favorably compared with the colonialists. This aspiration to òyìnbó tastes among the Sàró contradicts Níyì Afọlábí's observation that ex-slaves in Brazil and West Africa created artifacts that were solely reconstructions of their "ancestral" pasts.[28] Moreover, the indigenes read the buildings of the Sàró and the Àgùdà as emblems of the visitors' cosmopolitan heritage, which the newcomers had the wherewithal to create. As will be shown, the Sàró and the Àgùdà urban interventions used baroque architectural forms and motifs to reimagine local customs to serve their aspirational goals as "black Europeans."

The Sàró and Àgùdà were part of a large contingent of black Europeans—black immigrants from either Europe or European colonies—who argued that Victorian ideals needed to be embraced to advance the black Lagosian society of the future.[29] The immigrants propagated their agenda through a slew of English-language newspapers they established in the 1880s, such as *Anglo-African* founded by West Indian Robert Campbell in Lagos in 1863.[30] These media outlets also served as platforms for debates over what aspects of Victorian culture and ancestral customs immigrants and natives should emulate or discard. In the case of the *Anglo-African*, about half its readership (roughly three thousand) were Sàró and West Indian, and the remainder were educated indigenes, which indicates the complex configuration of race and class identity in nineteenth-century Lagos. [31]

In literary and dramatic circles within the city, black Lagosian elite often worked with missionaries and European residents to produce concerts and plays and to open the first schools.[32] Within the black Victorian citizenry of Lagos, then, were individuals with varying degrees of influence and relations with their European counterparts and the "uneducated natives." While some immigrants saw themselves as middlemen between the Europeans and the natives in the region, there was a female Sàró whose status ranked even higher than that of the British governor-general of her time.[33] Sarah Forbes Bonetta, whose guardian was Queen Victoria, lived in Lagos from approximately 1863 to 1880 after her marriage to Sàró captain James Davies.[34] Forbes, then Sarah Davies, contributed to the emerging class of educated female natives in the region by teaching in the female institutions in Freetown and Lagos.

The black Victorian class in Lagos also included Muslims who were as committed as their Christian counterparts to "civilizing" the Lagosians—but in an Islamic way. Mohammed Shitta-Bey was one such Sàró Muslim, and his mosque was part of a civilizing project. His endeavor complemented the efforts of the Trinidadian educator Edward Blyden to nurture an Islamic Lagosian elite in the

Adedoyin Teriba

1890s.[35] Mohammed Shitta-Bey's enchantment with the city, its diverse moods, and impressions presented an opportunity to create a lasting legacy for Sàró Muslim immigrants. And since his land was not within view of the ọba's realm, he could build a structure that did not fit into the neighborhood's existing urban fabric. What follows is an account of what prompted Shitta-Bey to build a mosque that changed Lagosians' conceptions of African Islam.

From 1820 to 1899, there was a migration of more than eight thousand ex-slaves of African descent who left northeastern Brazil and settled in Lagos. These migrants left Brazil for a variety of reasons. Salvador, Bahia, in Brazil witnessed nine antislavery uprisings in the nineteenth century.[36] The Malê, a group of Muslim slaves of African descent, were at the forefront of these revolts.[37] There were other Brazilian manumitted slaves who left Brazil because of the diminishing economic opportunities in the city centers—these were carpenters, goldsmiths, blacksmiths, masons, painters. In 1880 alone, Lagos had 3,221 Afro-Brazilians and Afro-Cubans as well as 111 Europeans out of a total population of 37,458 residents.[38]

The Sàró of Sierra Leone were primarily former slaves who had been brought to the colony after the abolition of the British slave trade. Church groups established schools, and even the University of Durham started the Fourah Bay College in Freetown, which taught freedmen. Hence, a number of African residents in Freetown could read and write English. Part of this literate class decided to relocate to southwestern Nigeria, including Mohammed Shitta-Bey. They tended to work as civil servants in the colonial government.

Encoded in the term òyìnbó dúdú, then, was the realization that these newcomers interacted with the British and other European settlers and with each other. Also implicit was the religious aspect of foreign difference, which can be seen in the construction team assembled for Shitta-Bey's mosque. Protestant Christians and Muslims built mosques and churches together in Sierra Leone, so it was no surprise that Mohammed Shitta-Bey hired two Afro-Brazilian Catholics to build his structure in Lagos.[39]

Shitta-Bey's mosque was placed in Sàró Town, in the Olówógbówó district. It was close to the British Government Reserved Area, and the similarity between the stone facing of the pilasters on its front facade and the post office building in Lagos suggests Shitta's taste for the colonial style of building. The symmetrical front facade of Shitta's mosque and the use of oculi echo classical architecture. The pinnacles that crowned the pilasters on both the face of the building and its rear deviate from the design strategies that the local inhabitants employed.

The facade is made out of brick and clad with ceramic tiles (figure 15.2). It is difficult to ascertain whether the building had a dome, as a newspaper article that covered its opening ceremony indicated.[40] Its rectangular square plan and barrel vault suggests that the journalist may have mistakenly called the vault a dome. In

Fig. 15.2 Mosque financed by Mohammed Shitta in colonial Lagos, 1894. Source: British Museum Photographic Archive.

any case, the vault is capped with a gable roof, which is now made of aluminum. Seven stone pilasters laid in ashlar masonry divide the mosque's facade.

A horizontal stone cornice separates the pediment proper from the arcade below, protruding beyond the surface of the pilasters. Intertwining red vine crockets capped with a star under a lunar crescent adorn the pediment's pilasters. The alignment of the pilasters creates a visual continuity despite the difference in surface, alluding to the baroque. The cornice consists of a fillet, cyma recta, cyma reversa, as well as a corona and is devoid of other features found in traditional cornices. Two oculi carved in stone lie side by side with the central pilaster, and a baroque twirl tops the cornice.

The arcade has wooden doors leading to the foyer. Male and female ablution rooms flank the north and south facades (see figures 15.3 and 15.4). Inside, the ceiling is lined with wood. The mihrab, the opening toward Mecca, is located at the center of the qibla wall. The curved staircase to the right of the mihrab serves as a minbar, from where the imam delivers his sermon. The conflation of the mihrab and minbar into a single space in this mosque is an unusual departure from the Islamic architectural canon.

Adedoyin Teriba

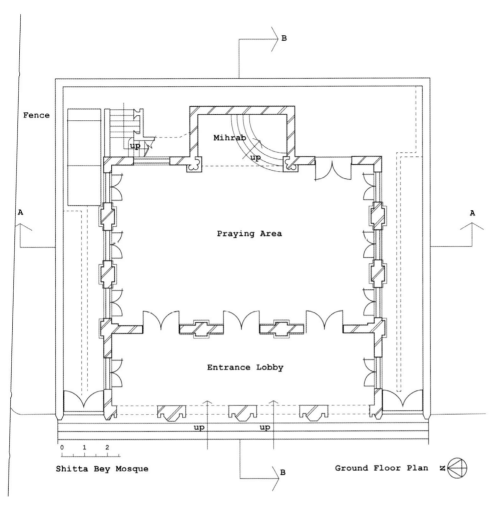

Fence

Mihrab

up

up

Praying Area

Entrance Lobby

up   up

0   1   2

Shitta Bey Mosque

B

B

A   A

Ground Floor Plan   z

Fig. 15.3 Section of mosque. Drawing by Lina Kudinar after original from Marjorie Alonge, "Afro-Brazilian Architecture in Lagos State: A Case for Conservation," PhD diss. (University of Newcastle, 1994).

The symmetry of mosque's front facade was a typology that was common to the Victorian houses in England as well as the Jesuits' ecclesiastical architecture in northeastern Brazil. (The mosque's wooden gates in the arched bays were also a prevalent feature of many houses in northeastern Brazil.) The ashlar pilasters in the broken pediment of the building's facade on the other hand were a feature of Victorian architecture alone and highlight the subtle way that the two Afro-Brazilian master masons who worked on the building appropriated a feature of the colonial buildings in the city. The colorful ornamentation on the pinnacles of the broken pediment—which is dissimilar to the mostly monochromatic pinnacles on Gothic cathedrals—may reveal a continuation of the native Lagosians' propensity to paint icons of spirits on their religious buildings.

The mosque may have been Mohammed Shitta-Bey's most public gesture of elite cosmopolitan taste. Yet his family's Islamic educational causes suggest that

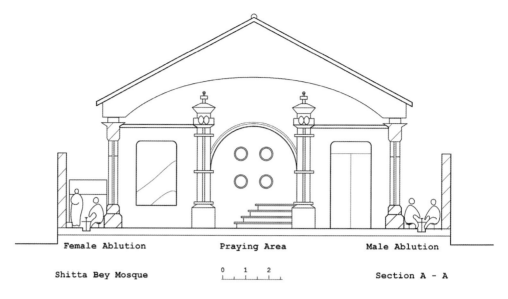

Female Ablution   **Praying Area**   **Male Ablution**

Shitta Bey Mosque   0 1 2   **Section A - A**

Fig. 15.4 Plan of mosque showing north and south ablution rooms. Drawing by Lina Kudinar after original from Marjorie Alonge, "Afro-Brazilian Architecture in Lagos State: A Case for Conservation," PhD diss. (University of Newcastle, 1994).

he may have empathized with local indigenes.[41] Local opinion of him was equally complex. Shitta-Bey was definitely an òyìnbó dúdú. Indigene Lagosians may have gotten this impression when, for example, he was one of the dignitaries who welcomed Princess Helen to Lagos in 1894. Standing side by side with Europeans, he displayed his kinship with the colonialists. His friends included most of the past British consuls of Lagos: John Beecroft, Benjamin Campbell, Henry Grant Foote, and Henry Stanhope Freeman. They affectionately called him William. The locals on their part called him Olówó Pupa, which means "the red man who has money." However, the name Olówó Pupa may have been another way of saying that Shitta-Bey was white, for Lagosians in this era also called Europeans *pupa* because of the pinkish color of their skin.

Additionally, Shitta's exposure to a Victorian worldview differed from the other Muslims in Lagos, further differentiating his aesthetic tastes and the ones of the omo ilé who had become Muslims. Scant evidence exists about what mosques looked like before the Sàró and Àgùdà built their own. Adobe mosques in the British protectorate of Northern Nigeria could have been models Lagosian Muslims relied upon, especially since the emirates of Borno and Sokoto became the spiritual centers of Islam in the northern and southern protectorates of Nigeria.

In conclusion, Mohammed Shitta's mosque was a significant display of local discourses between citizens of various kingdoms in Lagos Colony about race, difference, and foreigners that relied upon a variety of visual markers including architectural styles. The mosque's size, its use of ornament, the status of the architects and patron who built it, as well as the architectural typologies that the mosque drew inspiration from underscore the ọmọ ilé's conception that such material objects, as well as the immigrants' physical features, were proof that the visitors came from a place across the seas. It also serves as evidence for the ways in which colonial power, class difference, and foreignness manifest in architecture aesthetically and materially, complicating an understanding of black and white in Lagos and producing a hierarchical and unstable racial logic.

PART VI

RACE AND URBANISM

16

Black and Blight

Andrew Herscher

In August 2015, volunteers from an organization called Detroit Eviction Defense built a fence in a vacant lot next to the home of Lela Whitfield (figure 16.1).[1] Whitfield was facing eviction. Ten years earlier, her mother took out a reverse mortgage for $25,000 to pay off the home's mortgage and deal with medical bills. Borrowers typically do not pay accrued interest on reverse mortgages while they are alive or occupying the house whose value they are borrowing against. After her mother passed away in 2010, Whitfield inherited a home appraised at $9,000 and a debt of around $60,000 on the reverse mortgage. After refusing Whitfield's attempt to purchase her home for $2,500, the owner of her mortgage, Fannie Mae, foreclosed on her and, in July 2015, a court ordered her to vacate her home.

Whitfield refused to leave. Her neighbors supported her stand and one of them, Myrtle Curtis, cofounder of the Freedom Community Garden across the street from Whitfield's home, referred her to Detroit Eviction Defense. The fence built of pallets and scavenged wood prevented an eviction crew from placing a dumpster next to Whitfield's home and would allow protesters to surround a dumpster more easily. Among the images and messages painted on the fence by members of the neighborhood was the declaration of a "foreclosure-free zone" in which "black homes matter."[2]

Fig. 16.1 Lela Whitfield, Feedom Freedom, Detroit Eviction Defense, and community members' Eviction Defense Fence, Detroit, August 2015. Photo courtesy Detroit Resists.

How can this declaration be translated into histories of architecture and urbanism and what can architectural and urban history offer to its reading? In the following, I will pursue these questions through an examination of the history of "blight" in the American city. While some critical urban histories have addressed blight, these accounts typically neglect the relationship of blight and race, deal with that relationship in passing, or frame that relationship in terms of racial bias or prejudice instead of structural racism or racial capitalism.[3] And yet, in the American city, the definition, discovery, removal, and prevention of blight historically has been coterminous with the displacement and dispossession of non-white communities. As such, the history of blight forms a substantial part of the historical context that produced the declaration that "black homes matter." As one of an ensemble of terms that emerged to know and manage the modern American city, the history of blight is inseparable from the history of race and its inevitable correlate, racism, in American urban modernity.

Andrew Herscher

"Blight Is a Cancer . . ."

"Blight is a cancer. Blight sucks the soul out of everyone who gets near it. . . . Blight is radioactive. Blight is contagious. Blight serves as a venue that attracts criminals and crime. It is a magnet for arsonists. Blight is a dangerous place for firefighters and other emergency workers to perform their duties. Blight is also a symbol . . . of all that is wrong and all that has gone wrong for too many decades in the once-thriving world-class city of Detroit."[4] This was Dan Gilbert, billionaire founder of the online mortgage lender Quicken Loans and self-proclaimed savior of downtown Detroit through real estate development, speaking in 2014 in his new role as cofounder of the Detroit Blight Removal Task Force.[5] The occasion was the release of the *Task Force Plan*, which documented 80,000 buildings in Detroit that were either "blighted" or threatened by what the plan called "future blight": an authentic innovation in the abject annals of blight science. Around 90 percent of these buildings were single-family homes, the predominant repository of wealth for most of Detroit's black families. The plan was to condemn and demolish each and every one of them.

Gilbert's description of blight was, of course, hysterical. But it was also historical. It echoed accounts of urban decay in Detroit from the very moment that such decay came to the attention of municipal officials and the investment class about one hundred years earlier.[6] Indeed, in Detroit, as elsewhere in America, blight removal has functioned identically, efficiently, and racially unevenly as a mechanism of accumulation by dispossession, whether "blight" signified overcrowded working-class neighborhoods or abandoned working-class neighborhoods, whether "blight" was discovered in the industrializing pre–World War II city or the de-industrializing post–World War II city, and whether the definition of "blight" was explicitly racist or seemingly race-neutral.

As such, the conceptualization of blight and practice of blight removal have productively obscured the fundamental needs in capitalism for a population of reserve labor—the underemployed, unemployed, and those working outside the capitalist system—and for urban space to accommodate that population. When defined as blight, the urban spaces that forces of reserve labor occupy are discursively and practically expelled from the system that produced them. These spaces are framed as obstacles to property development, as opposed to products of a disavowed form of de-development premised on maintaining reserve labor in a precarious condition. The pathologization of blight in Detroit and other industrial cities in America thereby occludes a spatial manifestation of a fundamental contradiction between capitalism and democracy—the way in which capitalism requires inequality to productively function.

Race has been the predominant medium of difference that has stabilized and legitimized the hierarchical social order of capitalism.[7] In the American colonies and the United States, "whiteness" and "nonwhiteness" have been consistently conjoined, with these conjunctions structured by historical imperatives for an exploitable population of reserve labor, the enduring effects of exploitation, and ideologies of white supremacy that have rendered exploitation as legitimate, necessary, or nonexistent.

Space, as property, has functioned as a key resource for the production and reproduction of white domination and non-white subordination. In her landmark essay, "Whiteness as Property," Cheryl Harris historicized the inextricable relationship between property and race from the era of enslavement and colonial conquest to the present: "Rights in property are contingent on, intertwined with, and conflated with race. Through this entangled relationship between race and property, historical forms of domination have evolved to reproduce subordination in the present. . . . The evolution of whiteness from color to race to status to property (is) . . . a progression historically rooted in white supremacy and economic hegemony over Black and Native American peoples."[8] Harris's historicizing pushes us to interpret "blight" as an architectural condition that requires the state to take control of property from its seemingly negligent owners. Urban historians have sometimes noted the way in which definitions of blight have vividly changed over time. What has yet to be foregrounded, however, is the way in which those changes have continuously functioned to allow the dispossession and displacement of communities of color in the American city: on the one hand, definitions of blight have consistently applied to property owned or occupied by people of color, while, on the other hand, the remediation of blight has consistently served to transfer property from people of color, through the state, to predominantly white investors, developers, or owners. Property has thereby served as both an instrument and reward of racism; as Harris writes, "Even in the early years of the country, it was not the concept of race alone that operated to oppress Blacks and Indians; rather, it was the interaction between conceptions of race and property that played a critical role in establishing and maintaining racial and economic subordination."[9] Dispossession framed by concepts of "blight" in the modern and contemporary American city can therefore be understood to succeed the dispossession of colonial-era primitive accumulation that Harris and other scholars have described.

A Genealogy of Blight

Emerging in seventeenth-century British agricultural discourse, "blight" referred both to plant diseases of mysterious causes and to the symptoms of those diseases. In either case, blight was often understood to be caused by airborne agents; its geography was one of threats from afar invading unprotected crops and introduc-

Andrew Herscher

ing contagions and epidemics. During the cataclysmic Irish Potato Famine, blight was connected to fungal parasites. The discovery of these parasites, however, did not dispel the mystery of blight. Whether the parasites were its cause or effect, and whether blight was a symptom of a disease or itself a disease, remained topics of dispute into the twentieth century.

In the late nineteenth century, English translations of the Bible began to replace the now-archaic word "blasting" with the word "blight" to describe one of the punishments wreaked by a wrathful god on unbelievers.[10] This biblical employment of blight suggested that the mystery of the disease might be explained by its status as retribution, a connotation that would continue to shape the use of the term as it moved from agriculture to culture and from countryside to city.

These moves took place in the early twentieth century in the context of the industrializing American metropolis. In the United States, early slum reformers did not make much reference to blight; the term does not appear in Jacob Riis's 1890 *How the Other Half Lives*, for example. By 1902, in *The Battle with the Slum*, Riis used the term twice, referring to "the blight of the double-decker" and "the blight of the twenty-five foot lot."[11] Riis's figurative use of "blight" as a name for the tenement's harmful environment corresponded with the simultaneous emergence of the term in the popular press as a metaphor for urban conditions that were undesirable, strange, or threatening to those who spoke on behalf of the city's dominant interests and constituencies. These conditions were connected to poverty, decline, or social difference; cast as "blight," these circumstances were staged as abnormalities—an urban disease that solicited a cure.

Extending blight's agricultural genealogy, early descriptions of urban blight often staged the immigrants who were filling the ranks of the industrial city's reserve armies of labor as agents of this urban disease. These were the same immigrants who were also being portrayed as agents of medical diseases—depictions that reified cultural fears of racial others as biological danger and thereby legitimized the study, management, and control of immigrant bodies and the urban spaces they occupied.[12] Writing about Chinatown, a reporter for the *San Francisco Chronicle* described how the city's "poorer and more vicious classes" were "an eyesore to the municipality and a blight on property."[13] For a reporter at the *Detroit Free Press*, immigrant residents of tenements were a population that would "blight" any city "with the breadth of degradation."[14] These figurations of the socially excluded as agents of blight began to include African Americans in the course of the Great Migration, in which some six million African Americans moved from the rural south to northern cities.[15] As "blight," the impoverishment of the spaces to which the socially excluded were confined became an effect of their inhabitation rather than of urban segregation maintained by zoning, covenants, and violence alike.

Blight Science

"Blight" became a technical term for an urban condition at the same time as it circulated as a metaphor. This happened in the contexts of two newly formed professions: urban planning and real estate development. Each profession recruited "blight" as a name for one of the principal problems that it could solve or capitalize on. The status of blight as a mysterious affliction and metaphorical figure was both traded on and transformed; blight became a problem soliciting the technical solutions of urban planning and opening up challenges and opportunities for real estate development.

In both planning and real estate development, the problem of blight was described in terms of property value. An early reference comes from the Town Planning Institute's Fourth National Conference on City Planning in 1912, in a talk by the Boston architect J. Randolph Coolidge entitled "The Problem of the Blighted District."[16] Already in 1912, Coolidge addressed his audience "as people who know what my definition of a blighted district applies to, each of you in your own city or town."[17] But he then provided his definition, arrogating to city planning the authority and expertise to explain this well-known phenomenon. Coolidge's definition was that "a blighted district is one in which land values after a period of increase are stationary or falling."[18] The suggestion is that increasing property values are a general public good, so that falling values constitute an urban disease—a disease that city planning could defend against and cure. Here, the emerging concept of property value can be located with respect to the venerable Lockean theory of property, with property value posed as a product of what Locke called "cultivation."[19] For the seventeenth-century philosopher, the right to land was commensurate with the ability to till it, in the twentieth, the value of land depended on how it could be made to yield.

As described by Richard M. Hurd in his 1903 book, *Principles of City Land Values*, the real estate market depends on increases in property values, with threats to those increases defined as "nuisances . . . under which name we may class anything tending to depreciate the value of land."[20] As a technical term, "blight" named the spatial product of what Hurd called "nuisances." This placed realtor and planner together in a collaborative project to imagine, in the words of pioneering developer J. C. Nichols, "a future solution of blighted and abandoned areas of urban property of various types which have heretofore been so common in American cities."[21]

In the discussion following Coolidge's presentation on blight, Frank B. Williams, a New York lawyer, zoning advocate, future cofounder of the journal *City Planning*, and future sponsor of the Williams Prize Competition for the Best Essay on Blighted Districts by Students of American City Planning, noted that "a blighted district tends to become an unsanitary district, and where the blight goes far enough in time it may even tend to become a slum district. . . . As soon as health considerations can be urged in connection with this problem the courts allow us a free hand. . . . There is every reason why unsanitary districts or districts blighted in any way should be condemned as a whole, re-planned, and the land sold off so that the city can get all the economic and hygienic advantages."[22] This notion of the slum as "an advanced case of blight" became axiomatic during the Depression.[23] Blight removal as slum prevention provided a symbolic resolution to the actual contradiction between free market real estate development, on the one hand, and social welfare, on the other—the acceleration of social suffering by real estate development. While real estate development failed to promote social welfare in the American city, it could nevertheless be framed as such a promotion by narrating it in terms of blight removal and slum prevention. Blight removal thus came to be an important component of a "reverse welfare state" in which public resources are dedicated to the advancement of corporate welfare, in this case with a rhetoric that masked private interest as public good.[24]

Race, Space, and Blight

As property value was fundamentally shaped by the racial and ethnic definition of its inhabitants, the concept of blight also scientized, spatialized, and monetized white supremacy and racism; the same people of color whose presence depreciated property values became agents of blight. In *City Growth Essentials*, a widely used textbook for students of real estate that replaced Hurd's earlier *Principles of City Land Values*, the authors focused on "colored people" as a particular threat to property value and so a particularly dangerous cause of blight: "Property values have been greatly depreciated by having a single colored family settle on a street formerly occupied exclusively by white residents. . . . Segregation of negroes seems to be the reasonable solution to the problem, no matter how unpleasant or objectional the thought may be to colored residents."[25] The authors go on to implicitly pose white supremacist violence as means to protect threatened property values and thereby prevent blight: "Southern cities have a method of taking care of the problem which is well known, and seems to be entirely effective. . . . Colored people must recognize the economic disturbance which their presence in a white neighborhood causes, and must forego their desire to split off from the established district where the rest of their race lives."[26] Real estate developers and urban planners were assisted in their attempts to define, document, prevent, eliminate, and capitalize on blight by sociological theorizations of the relationship between race and urban space. Particularly relevant was the Chicago School model of urban geography in which the city was described by series of concentric circles marking "the central business district, a zone of transition, a zone of workingmen's homes, a residential area, and a commuter's zone": a system based upon "the tendency of

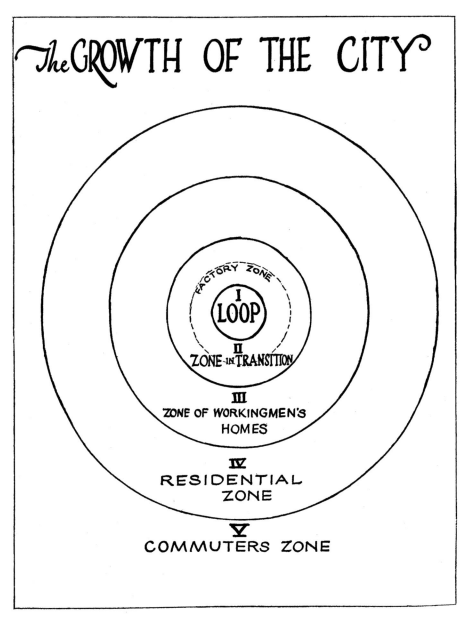

Fig. 16.2 Ernest Burgess, Concentric Zone Model of Urban Growth, 1925. Image from Ernest Burgess, "The Growth of the City: An Introduction to a Research Project," in *The City: Suggestions for Investigation of Human Behavior in the Urban Environment*, ed. Robert E. Park and Ernest Burgess (Chicago: University of Chicago Press, 1925).

each inner zone to extend its area by the invasion of the next outer zone," according to Ernest Burgess, "a process which has been studied in detail in plant ecology" (figure 16.2).[27]

In this model of the city, zones were defined by race, nationality, and class, with invasions representing the movement of a community from its designated zone

Andrew Herscher

into an adjacent zone. In "Residential Segregation in the American City," Burgess described this process of invasion in detail, including a map documenting invasion routes of "immigrants," among which "Negroes" were included with "Irish," "Bohemian," "Poles," and "Jews." For the Chicago School, the American city was a city where only white Anglo-Saxon Americans belonged, so that race and nationality functioned equally as markers of difference.

Following Robert Park's "race relations cycle," Burgess posed the "invasions" of "immigrants" as one phase in a teleological process in which "invasion" would be followed by the resistance—mild or violent—of the invaded community, the "influx" of newcomers and abandonment of the area by old-time residents, and then a "climax," "a new equilibrium of communal stability."[28] The Chicago School model of invasion and assimilation has been criticized for naturalizing and normalizing race and racial inequality, staging racial equality as the result of an evolutionary process of social change, and posing racial prejudice as the root cause of racial conflict. But it was precisely as such that the model provided valuable resources to urban planning and real estate development. In planning and development, the space of invasion was quickly identified as blight, with blight becoming a threatening urban condition that solicited professional expertise to prevent and eliminate it.

And so, by 1930, the causes of blight, according to John Ihlder, executive director of the Washington, DC, Alley Dwelling Authority, included land overcrowding, building obsolescence, the separation of city districts, and "invasion by incompatible uses," including air pollution, heavy traffic, "degenerate" uses of dwellings, and "social or racial groups antipathetic to earlier inhabitants."[29] These invasions were among the causes of the "insidious malady" of blight that attacked urban residential districts and, if left unchecked, yielded slums.[30] In his 1935 book *Rehousing Urban America*, Henry Wright visualized the relationship between invasion and blight in his diagrams of city growth; these diagrams showed the city growing as a series of concentric rings, with the ring of "blight" corresponding to the ring termed "zone of transition" in the Chicago School diagram (figure 16.3).[31]

The continuum between white supremacy, racism, and real estate subtended by blight became governmentalized in the work of economist Homer Hoyt. Hoyt received his PhD at the University of Chicago and was well aware of, and even critical of, Burgess's concentric ring model.[32] At the same time, however, Hoyt also reproduced Chicago School discourse on racial invasion in his work as principal housing economist of the Federal Housing Administration between 1934 and 1946. In *One Hundred Years of Land Values in Chicago*, he ranked "races and nationalities with respect to their beneficial effect upon land values," with "English, Germans, Scotch, Irish, and Scandinavians" having the most favorable effect on land values and "Russian Jews, South Italians, Negroes, and Mexicans" having, in

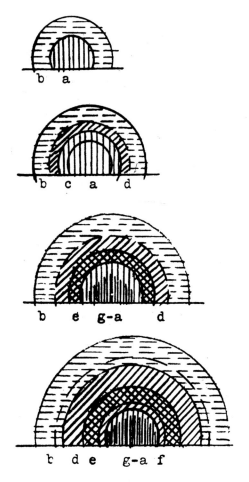

a. Commerce and light industry.

b. Active residential area.

c. Extension of commerce and light industry.

d. Inactive residential area and blight.

e. Actual slum areas. Inactive commerce and light industry.

g. Vertical expansion in high buildings.

2. RINGS OF CITY GROWTH; THE TYPICAL SPREAD OF MODERN AMERICAN CITIES, WITH INCREASING AREAS OF BLIGHT AND SLUMS. *At top,* THE PRIMITIVE CITY; *next,* CONCENTRIC EXPANSION; *third,* ARRESTED GROWTH AT THE CENTER DUE TO VERTICAL EXPANSION; *and last,* SHRINKAGE OF CENTRAL AREAS, AUGMENTED BY LESSENED SPACE NEEDS OF MACHINERY.

Fig. 16.3 Henry Wright, "Typical Spread of Modern American Cities and the Accumulation of Increased Areas of Blight and Slums," in *Rehousing Urban America* (New York: Columbia University Press, 1935).

order, the most detrimental effects.[33] Hoyt wrote that "while the ranking may be scientifically wrong from the standpoint of inherent racial characteristics, it registers an opinion or prejudice that is reflected in land values"; here, what Hoyt specifically calls out as a pseudo-science of racial characteristics is embedded in and consolidated in another pseudo-science—that of "land values"—that Hoyt was central in staging as science-as-such.[34]

The redlining conducted by the Home Owners' Loan Corporation in the 1930s

Andrew Herscher

in its "residential security maps" is one of the well-known results of Hoyt's theorization of land value. These maps were made for mortgage lenders to show the level of security for mortgage loans in a city's various neighborhoods; the presence of people of color in a neighborhood rendered that neighborhood risky for lenders and it would be outlined in red. Historians of redlining have debated its actual role in the loaning activity of the Home Owners' Loan Corporation.[35] What is clear, however, is that the lending of the Home Owners' Loan Corporation involved the federal government in the advancement of residential segregation, racially unequal housing, and racially unequal wealth accumulation.[36]

Segregation confined blight and slums to urban spaces occupied by communities of color. These spaces, however, were still threatening to white communities. As the *Detroit News* reported in 1946, "Slums and civic blight destroy property values—and, because, in doing so, they greatly increase the tax rate for the whole city, they throw an unjust and huge additional tax burden, amounting to tens of millions of dollars annually, on Detroit taxpayers who do not live in the slums and blighted areas. Slums and blighted areas also burden Detroit's taxpayers with still additional millions annually because of the crimes, fires, juvenile delinquency and disease they breed."[37]

As "blight," the effects of segregation, racism, and disadvantage became threats and burdens to the advantaged—a script for further exclusions of the already excluded.

Blight and *Black Metropolis*

In 1945, a doctoral student in anthropology at the University of Chicago, St. Clair Drake, and a former doctoral student in Chicago's sociology department, Horace R. Cayton, published *Black Metropolis*—a book dedicated to their teacher, Robert Park, who had died the previous year. A study of Chicago's South Side, *Black Metropolis* provided the first critical perspective on blight in the context of a professional literature: a perspective immediately signaled by placing the word "blight" in quotation marks whenever it was used in the book.

Drake and Cayton wrote that: "Over half of Black Metropolis lies in that area which the city planners and real-estate interests have designated as 'blighted.' . . . The superficial observer believes that these areas are 'blighted' because large numbers of Negroes and Jews, Italians and Mexicans, homeless men and 'vice' gravitate there. But real-estate boards, city planners, and ecologists know that the Negro, the foreign-born, the transients, pimps, and prostitutes are located there because the area has already been written off as blighted. . . . Black Metropolis has become a seemingly permanent enclave within the city's blighted area."[38] In *Black Metropolis*, blight is no longer an unintended urban anomaly, but a product of the intersection of real-estate development, urban planning, and racism—an intersection whose status as an anomaly was part of the mystification of the economic and ideological structures that produced it.

At the moment when *Black Metropolis* was published, this mystification was becoming ever more pronounced. During and after World War II, racial and ethnic categories began to disappear from definitions of blight—not because race no longer mattered, but because racism was marked as undemocratic in the context of a new racial liberalism.[39] In parallel with antidiscrimination policies advanced in relation to military service and employment in war industries, then, discourse on blight became increasingly race-neutral. In the Federal Housing Administration Underwriting Manual, definitions of neighborhood invasion as changes in "racial occupancy" thereby became changes in "living standards," "user groups," "cultural traditions," "maintenance patterns," and other seemingly race-neutral terms.[40]

Black communities were also named by these terms; the only difference was that now this naming proceeded according to secondary attributes of these communities—attributes that were not targeted in antidiscrimination legislation. That is, to the extent that wealth, privilege and power were unevenly distributed across racial groups, then the project to extract value from property through seemingly race-neutral blight removal also functioned to dispossess black communities.

Race-neutral definitions of blight in the 1950s, then, marked the success of projects and policies to bring race, class, and urban space into correspondence with one another. Race could be explicitly extracted from definitions of blight, and blight removal would still be equivalent to Negro removal. The US Supreme Court famously overturned school segregation in *Brown v. Board of Education* in the summer of 1954 and then famously upheld the use of eminent domain to eliminate blight in *Berman v. Parker* a few months later. The conjunction of these decisions testified to the emergence of urban space—and to the blackness of blight—as the key medium of segregation in a supposedly post-segregation era, an emergence suggested by critical histories of *Brown v. Board of Education*.[41]

Blight Removal

In post–World War II American urban spaces, the discovery of blight was an incentive for urban renewal. As has been amply studied, urban renewal often conjoined the displacement of communities of color with the consolidation of adjacent central business districts and development of other downtown spaces perceived to be deteriorating or depreciating.[42] Racism and segregation were central to both the white beneficiaries of urban renewal and to the communities of color that were displaced by renewal; for the latter, urban renewal carried out as blight removal was the latest instance in a long history of urban dispossession.

In the 1980s and '90s, especially in Rust Belt cities losing population, blight

Andrew Herscher

removal was separated from urban renewal to become a wholly subtractive demolition project, framed in the language of austerity urbanism.[43] Elected officials taught citizens to understand this demolition as a form of progress—a way to "downsize" or "rightsize" shrinking cities, adjusting the supply of houses to the reduced demand for housing, as well as to securitize "intact neighborhoods" from the threats presumably presented by blighted areas.[44] In Detroit, for example, Mayor Dennis Archer pointed out that "when you say you're going to tear down abandoned houses . . . it creates an enormous pride in the city."[45]

Yet rightsizing through blight removal relied upon two elisions. First, "blighted" homes were conflated with "abandoned" and "vacant" homes—a conflation that overlooked the many people who homesteaded in otherwise-empty homes.[46] Second, "depopulation" was conflated with "surplus housing," as if the dramatic drop in the city's population would be correlated with a dramatic increase in housing availability. This conflation overlooked the affordability of housing—the fact that housing is only available if it is affordable. The blight removal policy that developed as a consequence of these two elisions thereby yielded the destruction of increasing numbers of homes precisely at a time when the need for affordable housing was steadily increasing in cities across the United States.

Detroit and "Blight Emergency"

Since the 1950s, Detroit has been shaped by an extremely large outflow of middle-class white and black families to the surrounding metropolitan region—an outflow structured by the decline of auto manufacturing in the city and concurrent movement of industry to Mexico, Canada, and Asia, racial fear on the part of white Detroiters, the postwar development of the metro region, and the global shift from Fordist to post-Fordist production and consumption. Consequently, the city has been the site of ever-expanding demolition projects posed as blight removal. These projects were themselves expanded in the wake of the 2008 financial crisis; for example, Major Dave Bing initiated his tenure in 2010 with the ambition to demolish 10,000 of an estimated 33,000 vacant homes in the city. In his first "State of the City" address, Bing doubled down on the elision of blight and vacancy: "Blight is more than an eyesore. Abandoned and dilapidated buildings are hotspots for crime and a living reminder of a time when the City of Detroit turned a blind eye to owners who neglected their properties. Tonight I am unveiling a plan to demolish 3,000 dangerous residential structures this year and setting a goal of 10,000 by the end of this term."[47] What appeared to be a military-scale program of demolition when it was announced soon appeared to be a merely preliminary effort. After Michigan's governor placed Detroit under "emergency financial management" in 2013, the city's appointed emergency manager declared what may be the first and only "blight emergency" in American urban history.[48] The ensuing program of blight removal was radically expanded, as well as privatized along with many other city services in the context of the emergency manager's austerity urbanism.

The key actor in the privatization of blight removal was Dan Gilbert's Detroit Blight Removal Task Force. In its own words, the task force "brought private, philanthropic, nonprofit, federal and state partners together with the city."[49] Indeed, the bright colors, infographics, highlighted taglines, and other reader-friendly features of the *Task Force Plan*, released in May 2014, were precise registrations of the status of the *Task Force Plan* as a private initiative requiring public advertising, rather than a public initiative to be collectively debated and decided upon.[50]

The *Task Force Plan* radicalized Detroit's historical deployment of blight as a means to raise public fear and render blight removal a management of that fear. According to the task force, its "definition and methodology for classifying property as 'blight' incorporates the concepts of physical blight, economic blight, the public's interest in protecting the health, safety, and general welfare of people in its communities, and the preservation of property values"; these "concepts" were drawn from the State of Michigan's definition of "blighted property" and the City of Detroit's ordinance governing "dangerous buildings."[51] The survey commissioned by the Task Force discovered 84,461 "blighted parcels" among 377,602 surveyed (figure 16.4).

The vast majority of those blighted parcels—72,328—were single-family homes: around 20 percent of the single-family homes in the entire city. The *Task Force Plan* proposed that all blighted parcels in the city be demolished and that existing legal and bureaucratic procedures structuring the administration of those parcels be bypassed in favor of an "expedited foreclosure process" and "aggressive eradication timeline." At the moment when the *Task Force Plan* was published, Detroit's population was approximately 82 percent African American; as the latest stage in the history of blight removal in the American city, the plan once again translated racially based socioeconomic disadvantage into public threat and legal offense.

Taking Back "Blight"

The massive wave of mortgage foreclosures, tax foreclosures, and blight removal currently underway in Detroit has led to the public production of knowledge and solidarity around racially uneven dispossession and displacement. While foreclosures, evictions, and blight removal proceed in race-neutral terms of "renewal," "revitalization," and "redevelopment," communities affected by those policies have consolidated around their racially uneven impact. This has produced a "nobody move" movement dedicated to supporting people who have been delivered eviction notices; a series of anti-foreclosure movements, many led by neighborhood asso-

Scale
0   1   2   4 Miles

**Structures That Meet the
Task Force Definition of Blight**

■ Residential Structures
■ Non-Residential Structures *

* Non-Residential Structures include: Commercial,
Industrial, Institutional, and Unknown

Sources: Motor City Mapping, 2014 (uncertified
results); Detroit Buildings, Safety Engineering, and
Environmental Department; 2014 Historic Resource
Survey; Detroit Parcel Inventory; Wayne County
Register of Deeds; Wayne County Treasurer; Fannie
Mae; Freddie Mac; Valassis VNEF Plus Database;
Data Driven Detroit.
© Michigan Nonprofit Association.
Created April 2014.

Fig. 16.4 Detroit Blight Removal Task Force, "Structures That Meet the Task Force Definition of Blight," in *Detroit Blight Removal Task Force Plan*, Detroit, May 2014.

ciations; and actions to keep individual homeowners in homes after they have received eviction notices for back taxes or mortgage debts.

On a poster from the summer of 2015 advertising a protest to keep Lela Whitfield in her home, it was claimed that "if Lela is evicted, her home will undoubtedly become abandoned and stripped, causing further blight to the community" (figure 16.5). This claim was historical: in the campaign to keep Whitfield in her home, the history of blight in the American city was precisely and strategically reversed. While blight emerged in Detroit, as in other American cities, as a condition produced by the invasion of black bodies into the city, blight here became a condition produced by the expulsion of black bodies from the city. Blighted *homes were thereby reconfigured as* black *homes*.

In Detroit, in the 1960s, advocates of black power proclaimed the city "black man's land" and worked to advance radical self-government by the city's black-majority population.[52] These proclamations were undermined, first by the white

Lela Whitfield has lived in her Detroit home since she was a child. The home belonged to Lela's mother, who took out a reverse mortgage in 2005. Lela's mother passed away in 2010, and the lender foreclosed on the loan. The property has since been deeded to the government-controlled mortgage giant Fannie Mae, which is trying to evict Lela.

Lela is willing and able to buy the home for its market value, Fannie Mae refuses to accept her offer, even though they have already acted illegally by not offering to sell it to a family member. They would rather evict Lela than keep her in her home.

Lela's neighborhood, like so many in Detroit, has been devastated by the foreclosure crisis. If Lela is evicted, her home will undoubtedly become abandoned and stripped, causing further blight on the community.

With support of people on the block, church people, union people, and activists Lela Whitfield plans on staying in her house "by any means necessary."

This is not a new story. Many have experienced and are still going through foreclosures. This fall the biggest tax foreclosure in the history of the U.S. is happening in Detroit. A "new Detroit" is being built while many Detroiter's are losing their home and getting their water shut off. We need to stand with people in our city and neighborhoods to fight the evictions, water shut offs and police brutality.

For Updates, Latest Victories or to Fight Your Eviction:

W: Detroitevictiondefense.org
F: Detroit Eviction Defense
detroitevictiondefense@gmail.com
(313) 740-1073

Free Press Article:
tinyurl.com/pgsd3k8

Lela's Story: youtu.be/C3jKeP0loC8

Detroit Eviction Defense meets every Thursday at 6 p.m Old St. John's church 2120 Russell, Detroit next to Eastern Market

Fig. 16.5 Detroit Eviction Defense, poster protesting eviction of Lela Whitfield, Detroit, July 2015. Image courtesy Detroit Resists.

urban regime and then by the incorporation of subsequent black urban regimes—municipalities led by black officeholders and black elites—in urban development structures that continued to be based on corporate- and investor-centered policies of urban growth and the concurrent predation of working-class communities of color.[53] The reconfiguration of blighted homes as black homes marked a return to the practices and ambitions of radical self-government. Those homes were politicized by the communities who occupied them and transformed from architectural detritus into objects of a political imagination—the imagination of racialized spaces deleted in and by public policy, urban planning, and real estate development alike.

But the reconfiguration of blighted homes as black homes has a historiographical dimension as well as a political one. Resistance opens up repressed and obscured histories; critical architectural and urban histories can articulate architectural and urban dimensions of white supremacy and anti-black racism that resistance emerges from and that conventional histories normalize or ignore. In her analysis of black vernacular architecture, bell hooks argues for what she calls a "subversive historiography" that "connects oppositional practices from the past with forms of resistance in the present, thus creating spaces of possibility where the future can be imagined differently."[54] While histories of blighted homes often mystify the intersections of race and capitalism that yield blight itself, histories of black homes prompted by actions like Lela Whitfield's defense foreground precisely those intersections and might lead into the kind of historiography that hooks calls for.

17

And Thus Not Glowing Brightly

Noah Purifoy's Junk Modernism

Lisa Uddin

A photograph taken at the University of California–Los Angeles in 1966 introduces the junk I will consider in this essay (figure 17.1). Pictured is an installation at the art show *66 Signs of Neon*, curated by Noah Purifoy and Judson Powell and featuring sculptural works sourced from the wreckage of the August 1965 Watts rebellion that was precipitated by the police arrest of Marquette Frye for drunk driving. Frye was a recently discharged military serviceman who, like many black Angelenos, had migrated with his family from the Midwest. The focal piece of the photograph is a 14 in. × 24 in. × 60 in. assemblage work fabricated by Purifoy and composed of an upright wooden railroad crosstie, a rusted flit-gun used to kill mosquitoes, and a shattered car windshield.[1] Behind it stands a boy, peering at the object through another pane of glass that forms the building's exterior wall. Through this composition, the sculpture's title *Sudden Encounter* references at least three distinct moments of impact, each with various degrees of immediacy: the discrete moment that produced the spider-web effects of smashed glass; the event of six days of insurrection by 35,000 "rioters" with 72,0000 "close spectators" resulting in an estimated $200 million in property damage and a body count of

Fig. 17.1 *Sudden Encounter* at UCLA, 1966. Courtesy Noah Purifoy Foundation, 2018.

thirty-four; and the convening of two postwar modernisms that are discernible in the image itself.[2]

Outside the exhibition are signs of one of those modernisms—a spatial imaginary of purity and homogeneity materialized on UCLA's 1960s campus through flat, rectilinear volumes, large windows, and an open staircase with metal railings. The appearance of the clean-cut white boy outside the glass gallery wall accentuates how this particular design vocabulary has nourished specific racial identities and opportunities, functioning not only as aesthetic violence against minoritized people who disidentified with the conventions of white bourgeois hetero-patriarchy, but also as an exercise of biopower.³ Inside the exhibition are signs of another modernism, one calibrated toward a different genre of the human that, following Alexander Wehileye, circulates through "the miniscule movements, glimmers of hope, scraps of food, the interrupted dreams of freedom found in those spaces deemed devoid of full human life."⁴ Life, in this modernism, mani-fests less through a normative ethos of enlightenment agency and more within the condition and form of *Sudden Encounter*—as junk.

"Junk" was a widespread descriptor for Purifoy's work, including by the artist himself. This designation has positioned him within a canon of twentieth century avant-garde art.⁵ In this essay, I show how attention to the modes of Purifoy's junk practice, which spanned art making, teaching, curating, and community arts orga-nizing, illumines the racial dynamics of architectural modernism in and of Los Angeles. Purifoy's intersections with modern architecture were somewhat latent, but nonetheless pose serious challenges to understandings of LA's architecture, design, and urban built environment in the long 1960s that make virtuous and fundamentally human the qualities of, for example, mobility, transparency, infor-mality, simplicity, and indoor-outdoor living. These understandings, and the humanism they reproduced, sidestep how life in Watts, like other segregated spaces for nonwhite Angelenos, was subject to exploitations on which the postwar growth of the region and its primary architectural sensibilities were built, and to which Purifoy's practice spoke.⁶ Re-examining this practice can also add to the social science on Watts' structural poverty and racism in this period by considering how the neighborhood's abstractions into art works, pedagogy, and exhibitions critiqued predominantly white discourses of modern architecture, offering some-thing that I call "junk modernism."

The designation of junk modernism approaches what waste thinker Brian Thill names as "the derelict": "that immense underclass of things that have much more quickly or surreptitiously [than ruins] fallen outside of visibility and desire in our time: the indifferent, the lost, the wayward, the leaking, the ugly, the truly abject and unwanted—all the meddlesome waste caught between the things we've built up in our minds as meaningful and majestic."⁷ Rather than reifying the violent connection between a junk so described and African Americans from South Central Los Angeles, I consider how this community of color was able to with-stand procedures of dereliction that yoked normative architectural modernism to whiteness and ravaged urban sites and objects to blackness. These were the same conflations that fed a logic of looming extinction for people who could not or would not buy into midcentury prosperity and mass consumption. And they are conflations that, more broadly, have helped posit nonhuman waste and "wasted humans" as mounting and interchangeable byproducts of the Good Life. Purifoy's junk modernism aimed to rework that proposition for his community and for those beyond it. Examining how that happened requires some assemblage thinking, mirroring Purifoy's own mode of artistic production and considering the many forces at play in the construction and transformation of any social formation, including race.[8] Geographer Arun Saldanha, reading Gilles Deleuze and Félix Guitarri, asks, "What are the constituent components of race?" and answers, "Potentially everything, but certainly strands of DNA, phenotypical variation, discursive practices (law, media, science), artefacts such as clothes and food, and the distribution of wealth."[9] This linked and lateral formulation acknowledges the racializing power that radiates from material things and sites—in this case, Purifoy's potent compositions, but also the bodies that interacted with them, and the built and unbuilt environment of Watts. Moreover, it helps put stress on the relations *between* the parts of Purifoy's practice rather than fetishizing those parts in ways that loop them back into economies of consumption and the historical fungibility of blackness itself.[10] In approaching the work as assemblage through and through, I sift through a multifaceted urban history that intervened into the racialized matter, and mattering, of disposability and reached for another mode of black humanity.

Before Purifoy had oriented himself to Watts, he was already living the tenuousness of LA modernism for people of color. As the first full-time black student at Chouinard Art Institute in the mid-1950s, he initially chose courses in industrial design to complement his former employment as a high school shop teacher in his home state of Alabama.[11] When the program was discontinued, he moved to fine arts but avoided drawing courses for fear of "being stuck with the human image," which to him did not capture "the essence of being."[12] Still, Purifoy was keyed into midcentury tastes for "ethnic" art and design, making and eventually selling an African ceramic head; a motif he would repeat in later design work through collages inflected with African and Asian overtones.[13]

To support his studies, Purifoy found part-time employment, including night shifts at the Douglas Aircraft defense plant, one of four major companies in the region's booming aviation industry. There he operated a shearing machine that cut metal into templates, connecting him to a staple material in the architecture of both aircraft and modern houses.[14] His subsequent job as a window trimmer found him at Cannell and Chaffin Interior Designs on Wilshire Boulevard, an LA-based firm with a distinguished clientele and an establishment take on the California modern look.[15] Interiors staged for the company's Oasis Model House circa 1954, for example, featured a moderate use of low-profile wood furnishings and floating shelves, but took more liberties with open-space living areas and industrial touches such as a built-in heat lamp over the kitchen counter.[16] Whatever ease and modern comforts were associated with the company's designs, however, did not extend to

Purifoy. Acting on his desire to be an interior designer and salesman on the floor, he took on extra weekend work hours and interacted directly with customers, for which he was eventually terminated.[17]

After graduating, Purifoy continued to struggle in the industry. He was hired at the Angelus Furniture Warehouse to design modern furniture, but the company would not manufacture his work, prompting him to return to machine operation before taking his next job—setting up more furniture for window displays, this time at the Broadway department store where he worked between 1956 and 1964. Off the clock, Purifoy pursued a partnership with fellow Chouinard alumnus and African American John H. Smith, who was the more established of the pair (figure 17.2). The arrangement led to a handful of exhibition opportunities, but ultimately proved too difficult on account of a metonymic character Purifoy called "Mrs. Jones": "I couldn't please Mrs. Jones. You know, I would go and hang the drapery and have the carpet laid and do this and that, tear out this wall and design furniture and have it custom-made and all that. But she'd keep calling me back about something wrong. Now, I couldn't endure that."[18]

Purifoy's flatlined professional trajectory in design was neither unique nor a death knell for his creative capacities. As Wendy Kaplan notes, discriminatory employment practices and attitudes made success in this sector more difficult to achieve for Latinos, Asians, and African Americans than for whites.[19] Purifoy's response was to cultivate his friendships with black Angelenos and begin a small-scale assemblage art practice at his La Brea Avenue home. At the same time, he began to study music and constructed a nine-foot cabinet for his high-fidelity sound system in line with the period craze for domestic sound equipment and its free-standing display. But whereas the latter belonged to an inventory of consumable "must haves" for the modern home, Purifoy understood his hand-built cabinet as a medium for 24-7 community building; a way for familiars and unfamiliars to come and hear "the latest sounds around" and stay until all hours.[20] This ability to bring people together became paramount to the community arts work he assumed with his colleagues in Watts, the 2.12-square-mile neighborhood located on the eastern edge of South Central Los Angeles.

Urbanists have been accustomed to identifying Watts's physical and social isolation in the postwar years, sometimes to the point of reinforcing it in their assessments of Los Angeles. For example, as a parenthetical observation to his 1971 study of LA's built environment, Reyner Banham noted that by the early 1960s "no place was more strategically ill-placed for anything, as the freeways with their different priorities threaded across the plains and left Watts always on one side." This no-place-ness was particularly harmful given that the critic defined LA's freeways and the (auto)mobility they facilitated as the essential feature of the Southern California city, "a special way of being alive" that some locals, despite the daily

Fig. 17.2 Noah Purifoy and a high-fi cabinet designed by Purifoy and John H. Smith, n.d.

irritations of traffic, "find mystical." Watts residents were effectively cut off from such life, and with it, the city's prevailing identity as an "Autopia."[21] In addition to a lack of freeway access, deindustrialization became another mechanism of segregation. Taking their cues from a relocation trend set by the aircraft, aerospace, and electronics industries, other manufacturing firms began leaving the central city for the suburbs as early as 1963. At the same time, residents of Watts witnessed an outmigration of upwardly mobile blacks who were attempting to move into white neighborhoods. Those who were left behind struggled to secure work outside South-Central since more than half, according to one 1964 survey, were without a car.[22] The result was a concentration of black poverty that historians have characterized as a process of ghettoization familiar to other American cities.[23]

The narrative of ghettoization relies on an image of postwar Watts as a wasteland lying on the margins of a healthy modernist society. Evidence of that pathology has been well-documented and deserves some recapitulation in order to detail how the antiblackness of LA modernism took spatial form and catalyzed Purifoy's oppositional pedagogy. Poor housing conditions were part of that spatialization. During the war African Americans left the South in high numbers for the West, and with the rapid uptick in population garages and woodsheds became dwelling units minus running water, toilets, and occasionally windows. Beginning in the mid-1950s, city officials identified these and other residential structures as sub-standard and razed many of them, reducing the overall housing stock. What remained were often small one-family dwellings rented at high rates to more than one family without any attention to maintenance.[24] A longtime Watts resident and activist Sonora McKeller related in 1967 that these were "rat-, roach-, and termite-infested homes—poor structures at best; houses as old as Watts with plumbing of the same vintage, and electrical fixtures and wiring so fragile that they are virtual firetraps."[25] Public housing was no better. In the postwar years, the area became, in historian Josh Sides's terms, "a dumping ground" for developments that were unwelcome in other parts of Los Angeles. These included the 184 one-story units of Hacienda Village, completed in 1942 with design credits to African American architect Paul R. Williams and Richard Neutra. Between 1953 and 1955, the Housing Authority of the City of Los Angeles built three more projects in Watts, including the massive 1,110-unit and 69-acre Nickerson Gardens. These develop-ments were initially well-functioning and racially mixed, but soon transformed into the overcrowded crime-ridden complexes that became synonymous with Watts residency.[26] Nonresidential Watts was likewise marked by a notion of waste, including inadequate schools and health care facilities, and degrading encounters with local law enforcement. More concretely, residents could point to the plentiful vacant lots, the junkyards that purchased scavenged scrap, and the heaps of metal that had accumulated outside defunct foundries as signs of the city's economic restructuring. There were accumulations of household waste as well, piled on the curbs when the city's garbage trucks were slow to pick up or when they bypassed certain streets entirely.

The artist became part of this geography, and it showed in his teaching. As a cofounder and director of the Watts Towers Arts Center from 1964 to 1966, Purifoy helped establish a vibrant art education program for children and youth who lived in the community. They performed street cleanups, painted houses with supplies collected from paint stores, and practiced "being concerned about the next-door neighbor" adjacent to and across from the center's 107th Street location. Teachers also took children on walking trips to find discarded materials and objects that could be made into assemblages, emulating Purifoy's own work (figure 17.3). As he recalled, "We learned that is was rather natural and instinctive for the kids to assemble and disassemble an object, with the idea of counting the parts and so forth."[27] However innate the ability, it was honed through Purifoy's own attentiveness to the mutability of physical things and the already disassembled environment that shaped young lives in Watts. The neighborhood, in this sense, was rife with potential for how to re-present the conditions of postwar blackness in urban LA, be it through a coat of fresh paint or attention to how things are both taken apart and can come together.

Lisa Uddin

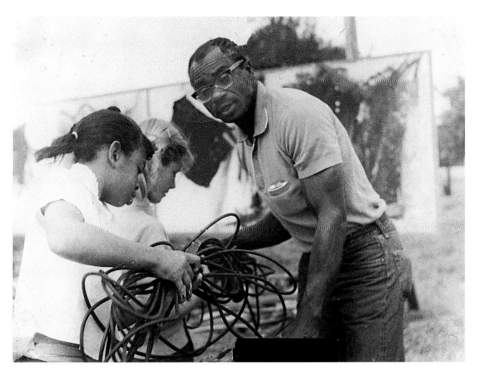

Fig. 17.3 Noah Purifoy making work with students, n.d. Photo by Irene Rosenfeld, courtesy Noah Purifoy Foundation, 2018.

As a pedagogical philosophy, Purifoy often framed junk art making as a pragmatic means to becoming more recognizably human in the wider social field: "It improved [the children's] self-image, and this would make a great deal of difference in terms of their ability and capacity to grasp whatever the objectives were, whether it was in school or out of school."[28] Stronger versions of this outlook emerged when the artist exported his curriculum to predominantly white settings. In local coverage of a two-week course at the University of California, Santa Cruz, Purifoy related that: "In junk art we take two unlike objects and put them together. . . . And you can transfer this to human experience. For two supposedly unlike human beings can come together and find they can communicate with each other contrary to what they have always been taught." The newspaper massaged this postwar picture of racial integration, commenting that Purifoy was using wood, metal, and glass in his own sculpture, having "stopped discriminating along the way."[29] While the question of which object or material stood for which human remains open, what is more certain is that teaching with junk made sense given its prevalence in the LA neighborhood that was lived and known *as* junk, and whose genres of the human were thereby obscured.

Purifoy's intimate connection to the waste of Watts intensified in the immediate aftermath of the August 1965 rebellion, beginning at the back door of the Watts Towers Arts Center. When the upheaval began, the artist and his colleagues had unobstructed sightlines to the epicenter of the destruction: a three-block stretch of 103rd Street where forty-one buildings occupied primarily by food, liquor, furniture, and clothing stores were demolished, and which became known as "Charcoal Alley."[30] They also received direct accounts of what was happening when youth returned to the center to stash their loot.[31] After amassing three tons of debris in the form of "hunks of melted neon signs, medicine bottles embedded in the molten remains of colorful plastic raincoats, twisted bits of metal, charred wood, pieces of smashed automobiles," the process of eventually working with it was multisensory and open-ended.[32] As Purifoy recounted in the exhibition catalogue, he and Powell "gave much thought to the oddity of our found things. Often the smell of debris, as our work brought us into the vicinity of the storage area, turned our thoughts to what were and were not tragic times in Watts, and to what to do with the junk we had collected, which had begun to haunt our dreams."[33] Consider the force of the junk in this reflection. Echoing aspects of what Jane Bennett calls "thing power," the collection exceeded its assigned role as inert or useable stuff and flashed itineraries of mattering that were independent from human ones.[34] Through a pungency that was odd unto itself, the debris of the rebellion solicited the artists' attention, entering into a working relationship between (at minimum) Purifoy and Powell's bodies, work spaces, sleep spaces, and the conjugations of Watts as waste-scape. Through these relations, the artists were able to help redefine rather than reinforce Watts's "tragic times" and work on the recurrent question of how the material could reconstitute in form and significance. Purifoy pondered the same process in a poem that was issued in conjunction with *66 Signs of Neon*. Entitled "Seeing," the text expressed the mystery of the junk that occupied his environs and outlined modes of perception particular to postwar LA blackness: "But there was junk—piles of junk / All bundled up and neatly packaged / Scattered out down the railroad track / Glowing brightly in the absence of sunlight / And thus not glowing brightly." The power of these piles lay neither in their ubiquity nor tidiness, but in their capacity to shine without a light source and against reason; a riddle that may have read less so for people estranged from ideologies of endless sunshine and clear visibility. The poem continued: "Neat bright bundles pressed hard, piled high / Beer cans, shattered glass, bottle tops flat-out / Foreign objects lying there without relationship / To self or any other, aged forms/ Banked up inactivity, meaningless existence?" The non-relation of the objects, first framed as a kind of opaque autonomy, resisted points of interaction and inscriptions of meaning, but not indefinitely. Seen anew, the objects could join an amalgam of creative possibility without entirely sacrificing their initial force: "If I could see it differently / For what it is or is not / Still flat out and piled up / In another way yet the same way / I'd offer it up."[35] Thus, what might have read to some exhibition-goers as esoteric musings on artistic process was also an account of junk modernism as a collaboration between oddly vibrant things and black ways of seeing that reconfigured the modalities of disposability.

The gymnasium of Watts's Markham Junior High School at 1650 E. 104th Street became the first location of *66 Signs of Neon*, featuring the work of eight artists experimenting with refuse from the uprising.[36] The show ran in early April as part of the Simon Rodia Commemorative Watts Renaissance of the Arts Festival with more than a thousand other pieces by mostly Watts-based makers, a performance of Handel's "Israel in Egypt," readings of Malcolm X's writing, and a poetry recitation by LeRoi Jones. As Kellie Jones has observed, curating *66 Signs* in this and other institutionally precarious settings marked Purifoy as a community arts organizer of exceptional strength, and Watts as a place of make-do creativity.[37] Coverage of the festival in the *Los Angeles Times* opened instead with a juxtaposition of art worldliness and the black ghetto: "It could be a scene in Beverly Hills or Pasadena: smartly-dressed people milling around displays of painting, sculpture and photography. But on Thursday this was the scene in Watts." About three thousand people attended in the first four days.[38]

Later that year, Purifoy installed *66 Signs* at the Annual Los Angeles Home Show in a sports complex, exhibiting alongside modernist furnishings and prefabricated homes in what Yael Lipschutz has interpreted as Purifoy's "most calculated attempt to critique the overblown and alienating society that surrounded him."[39] That critique hinged on an assemblage's appropriation of its modernist source material. In *Breath of Fresh Air*, for example, two joints of a stovepipe stood at thirty-six inches tall, topped with part of a roof of tar paper and tin. A metal brace held the composition up, making a parabolic arc. Richard Cándida Smith has argued that the piece formed graceful shapes associated with aluminum or other modern, high-tech materials and their state-of-the-art manipulation. In so doing, it challenged notions that "only certain materials can be sleek or that junk must be nostalgic."[40] The work's title, moreover, played on modernist mantras of space-age aesthetics as a vehicle for healthy living, while the sculpture's reproduction on the cover of the show's catalogue, collaged into and against a sepia-toned junkyard, highlighted the decidedly earthbound afterlives of those space-age materials (figure 17.4).

As *66 Signs* travelled to universities across California, including UCLA, UC Santa Cruz, and UC Berkeley, visitors' responses to the show in the exhibition guest books attested to the sense of an architectural modernism out of joint. Many expressed their frustration over what was on display. That the show was allocated to student union halls and other multipurpose spaces instead of university galleries fanned the flames.[41] In the tradition of the avant-garde, the pieces perverted the concept of art and the experience of consuming art in and of the modern city. "'Junk' is right," one person wrote, while another noted the display "definitely

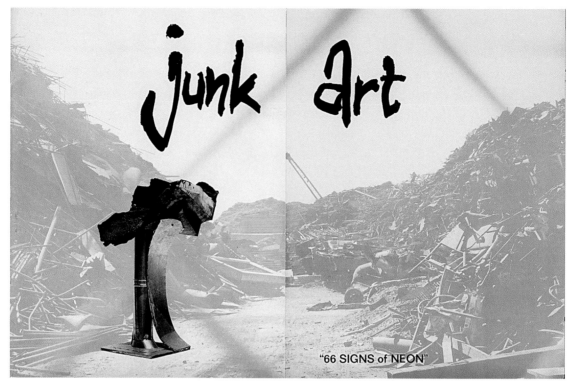

Fig. 17.4 Cover of *66 Signs of Neon* catalogue, featuring *Breath of Fresh Air*. Courtesy Noah Purifoy Foundation, 2018.

degrades and ridicules 'art.'" Viewers criticized the works from their inappropriate prices ("you're kidding of course!") to their lack of skill ("Any one can go to a junk dealer and pick up all the junk that you have here.") to their sheer ugliness ("frankly, I wouldn't want many of the exhibits in my home.") One visitor felt lied to: "a normal fire doesn't melt and distort metal like that—looks more like something that might be found after an A bomb." Another put it more succinctly: "Excellent example of 'artistic deception.'" Of the few people who identified their residency in the guest books, Earnest Freeman of Watts gave a different interpretation of the exhibition, which recognized its status as rudimentary junk but was less judgmental in the assessment: "That all it can be call because that all it is, junk art. It could not be call [*sic*] anything but junk." Other respondents rejected the term entirely and its disruptive possibility by filtering the work through fantasies of liberal democratic equality ("If people could only realize that we are but people and none better than other, each doing their best") and aesthetics ("Some objects a little bitter, but its better to show it in art than in riots").[42] A handful of visitors were unhinged in their anti-black racism, including one visitor who penned a panoramic description of the show's other-than-humanness: "Scrap metal salad. Shredded newspapers. 400 frenzied orangutans hurling paint cans. Demented junkman's paradise." What these and similar reactions indicate is how Purifoy's

Lisa Uddin

waste-based assemblage practice harnessed and was harnessed to a highly racialized iteration of urban Los Angeles; one enacted through, in this particular configuration, borrowed exhibition spaces, predominantly white viewing subjects, anti-junk affects, and built things that were, according to one visitor, "very expressive." This expressivity was perhaps the most potent nodal point of the show's modernist dislocations, asking visitors to consider how materials from the rubble of Watts may well have had their own truths to tell.

Additional exhibitions of Purifoy's work suggest other versions of junk modernism, each a pointed response to LA modernism's anti-blackness, but increasingly uncertain as feasible forms of black humanity. For example, the American Cement Corporation of Los Angeles hosted *66 Signs* at their 1966 annual meeting. As per usual, Purifoy mounted documentary photographs of the rebellion's outbreak and aftermath as backdrops to the assemblages, setting up his terms for discussion. The corporation set up its terms as well. In his address, President James P. Giles forecasted steep growth for US cities and conveyed urgency for an urban plan and building schedule that would accommodate it. Anything less meant letting cities continue on their own: "and be forever damned by the unfortunate millions who inherit our shapeless, aimless, non-cities, 'our slurbs—our sloppy, sleazy, slovenly, slipshod, semi-cities,' as Professor Wheaton of the Institute of Urban and Regional Development, University of California, calls them."[43] Near this industrial-academic discourse of urban dystopia, whose vocabulary pulled from older anxieties over slums and slum dwellers, stood—quite literally—sculptures of damaged materials and objects from South Central Los Angeles. At a narrow angle, the projects were similar. Like Purifoy, with his openness to the dormant capacities of metal and glass, Giles shared the immediate goal "to probe the basic nature of cement in search for ways to make it an even more versatile construction material." But any affinities were fleeting, given his expressed interest in coordinating efforts of "the presently fragmented elements of our society indispensable to building better cities—those in government at all levels, the building and planning professions, higher education and private industry." Not surprisingly, organizations like the Watts Towers Arts Center were not included in the sectors identified as instrumental to urban improvement, nor was Purifoy's practice cited as a model for this agenda. Instead, American Cement leadership praised the space program for accomplishing "a well-defined objective desired by the bulk of the population," and in an act of social conscience, financed the publication of the *66 Signs* catalogue.[44]

After the university and American Cement Corporation shows, the uncertainties of how Purifoy's practice might prompt critique and reinvention only escalated. In 1971, the artist turned his focus to an installation at the Brockman Gallery, the LA art space dedicated to African American artists since 1967. Purifoy had exhibited there previously with David Hammons, and in a group show run out of a high-end furniture store in Central LA.[45] By contrast, the 1971 exhibition replicated a squalid apartment in the upstairs section of the gallery. Purifoy culled from the junk pile to construct an "environmental experience" that chewed up and spit out any inkling of a livable midcentury modernist interior (figure 17.5). *Art Magazine*'s description of the work is worth quoting at length:

> The viewer climbs the back stairs and enters the living quarters through the back hall, stepping around overflowing trash cans, and dirty brooms and mops, past a filthy bathroom sink and toilet, and stockings dangling overhead. The array in the next room is even more appalling. In every corner dirty clothes are piled high. Greasy food in take-out containers mingles with styrofoam cups and cigarette butts. Seemingly holding the walls together is a patchwork pastiche of wallpaper samples and newspapers. Huddled beneath blankets on mattresses on the floor, approximately eight bodies lie motionless beneath the staring eye of a blank but turned on TV screen. Meanwhile on the bed behind the TV, two bodies mechanically writhe up and down. The bedside table is adorned with empty bottles; a red light is near the window. Above the bed a calendar Christ at the Last Supper surveys the scene. A recording of a variety of ghetto noises, from children fighting to a telephone ringing without response, complete the tableau.[46]

Against ideals of domestic Southern California as light-filled, straightforward, and clean, Purifoy's installation, with its malfunctioning, dirty people and things, re-spatialized the abject underbelly of middle-class whiteness to convey "the very essence of poverty and the way black people live."[47]

Although enlisting visitors into provocative three-dimensional spaces was a common practice in the art world of the 1970s, it was not a popular strategy in the efforts to regenerate Watts after 1965. For example, the Watts Summer Festival launched in 1966 as a hybrid of black revolutionaries who understood the event as a precursor to armed revolt and a moderate strand of community workers invested in cultural revitalization.[48] Some of those moderates intersected with the HUD-funded Urban Workshop aimed at, according to one participant, "transform[ing] a despairing community into a landmark of human progress" via projects like landscape development, debris cleanup, and playground construction.[49] Purifoy made his contributions on this front as well. In 1968, he and Powell assisted an urban antipoverty plan by constructing a model for a library and art gallery, to be attached to a pilot community center in Watts.[50] These projects, whether self-consciously radical or more modest versions of urban-environmental reform, were antithetical to Purifoy's Brockman Gallery piece, which carried the bleakest of titles: *Niggers Ain't Never Ever Gonna Be Nothin'—All They Want to Do is Drink + Fuck.* This was another junk-centric co-mingling with LA anti-blackness, a dwell-

Fig. 17.5 Material used in *Niggers Ain't Never Ever Gonna Be Nothin'—All They Want to Do is Drink + Fuck,* 1971. Courtesy Noah Purifoy Foundation, 2018.

ing within it, but now without suggestions on how to translate wastedness into something else.

The absence of translation made it difficult for the audience to connect with Purifoy's work in the way the artist had hoped. *Los Angeles Times* art critic William Wilson, for instance, refused to comply with the bleakness, maintaining that Purifoy's "ghetto apartment" was "less an art work than a desperate fact" and, therefore, "the most effective piece of black protest art" he had seen thus far; a willful, recuperative reading of an artist who understood protest as secondary to the creative process.[51] Other visitors, meanwhile, declined the total environmental experience. As Purifoy recalled, most people did not move through the length of the space, preferring to turn around somewhere near the midpoint. Even Alonzo Davis, codirector of the gallery, "behaved like everyone else, in a way" by avoiding the installation and keeping others away until it was completely assembled.[52]

The critical and creative prospects for junk modernism were further strained when Purifoy's work was solicited by the US Office of Information for an exhibition at the 1972 German Industries Fair in Berlin. The show highlighted the varied possibilities of garbage for an international audience. Purifoy submitted four sculptures. Art by Edward Kienholz, Robert Rauchenberg, and John Chamberlain was also on view. Rounding out the exhibition were informational displays and live demonstrations about waste management and sustainable furniture. Southern California was heavily represented therein, with designs by Gere Kavanaugh, LA-based companies Environmental Concepts and Huddle Environments, and the Easy Edges furniture line of corrugated cardboard chairs by Frank Gehry.[53]

This was odd and difficult company for Purifoy's work, partly because of the design world he had abandoned a decade prior and partly because of the exhibition's indeterminate framing of garbage. English translations of the organizing theme ranged from "Garbage—the Need to Recycle" to "Garbage Needs Recycling" to "Garbage Is Beautiful."[54] In all versions, garbage took center stage, emphasized by the accumulation of junk that occupied the central exhibition space. The third translation, however, suggests ways in which the focal issue could be racialized for English speakers familiar with the rallying cry "Black Is Beautiful," by substituting "black" for "garbage" and letting the connotations fly. Even without the slippage, Purifoy's pieces were the only works attributed to a black Angeleno and as such were differently located from those of his peers. Not all garbage was created equal nor equally. Purifoy's assemblages emerged from his sustained experience of a disposability whose forms and intensities were distinct from those evoked in Kienholz's countercultural commentaries on the inhumanities of modern life or in Gehry's playful, low-risk explorations with cheap, plentiful cardboard from the comforts of his Santa Monica office. It was a disposability underscored by one report that headlined "U.S. Exhibition at Berlin Fair is Trash," and published six equally sized photographs of Purifoy's junk art. One of those photographs pictured the smashed windshield of *Sudden Encounter*, and through it, the artist's portrait in three-quarter view, as if to suggest that trash, however striking, was an epistemological frame for Purifoy.[55] Even the deployment of beauty as an aesthetic to re-know and re-value waste was a no-win scenario for his art, with its ties to an anti-beauty assemblage tradition. More significantly, Purifoy's versatile practice was an expression of the ongoing living conditions of postwar Watts for which black activists had already argued beauty was small recompense.[56]

Given its myriad vulnerabilities, what then can be said of junk modernism as a viable genre of black humanity? To what extent did Purifoy's multiple movements contra the whiteness of architectural modernism lose their promise in the long shadows of postwar Los Angeles and a postmodern turn to junk that would have and produce different stakes?[57] In a 1973 letter to Sue Welch, a close friend and colleague from the Watts Towers Arts Center's early years, the artist reflected on the struggle to improve black lives in the city. Eight years had passed since the Watts rebellion. The letter expressed frustration with the absence of change in the neighborhood, its enduring status as America's archetypal ghetto, and a post-rebellion LA divided between "art for art's sake" and gang warfare. Purifoy's balm

Lisa Uddin

was the community of makers who had ties to the center and a sense that art's contribution to the struggle lay in its process more than its marketable product. Then, in a moment of reckoning with his racial position, he wrote: "I am a long ways from resolving my blackness. I am still body oriented. And to whatever extent we are, it is to this extent we are unable. My solution to this problem (personal) is a strange one. But I think ultimately it is the solution to the whole problem of human relation."[58] For Purifoy, a resolved and flourishing blackness meant getting over the human figure and continuing a practice of making with the stuff of urban waste, which was the work of becoming differently human and our work of learning how to know it.

18

Open Architecture, Rightlessness, and Citizens-to-Come

Esra Akcan

In 1973, *Der Spiegel* referred to Berlin's immigrant borough Kreuzberg as the Harlem of Germany. The federal housing minister Hans-Jochen Vogel had called the area "a small Harlem" and politicians often warned about the "Turkish ghetto." And so, summarizing the general sentiment of such figures, *Der Spiegel* reported: "Ghettos are developing, and sociologists are prophesying the downfall of the cities, increased criminality, and social misery like those found in Harlem. . . . The first Harlem symptoms are already visible. In the eroding sectors of German cities, 'a new subproletariat is growing in which the seed of social diseases is sown.'"[1] This analogy between Kreuzberg and Harlem invites us to excavate the overlooked relation between race and citizenship. How did a New York neighborhood known for racism against its African American population become a metaphor to describe a district renowned for its Turkish guest workers in Berlin? What does this collapse of categories related to the socially constructed notion of race and the legally constructed definition of citizenship indicate? Given that a "nation" has been historicized as a constructed, imagined, and limited category by scholars, does this comparison imply that the same applies to the category of "race"?[2] If a noncitizen could be so commonly characterized as belonging to another race, was it also common that a citizen perceived to be belonging to a marginalized race was treated as a noncitizen?

The category of race has not translated into the German context easily. During the postwar period many authors were careful to avoid the term race due to its association with the anti-Semitic ideology of their country's recent past. Others identified the collapse of race and anti-Semitism as problematic, and criticized mapping an influential category in one context onto another. Such conceptual indeterminacy reveals the historically constructed nature and usually unjustified foundations of these categories. Writing in 1993, for instance, German writer Lothar Baier said, "There are countries in which the expression *racism* is not merely a vague ideological accusation. It possesses a precisely circumscribed meaning, for 'race' in such contexts signifies something specific. In the United States for example, 'race' is an administrative category like religious affiliation. . . . This concept of racism cannot be transferred to German circumstances. . . . I do not believe that Hitler's proclamation of genocide had anything to do with racial-biological concepts."[3] Recently however, scholars have noted the explanatory power of racism in historicizing the discrimination against people who came to Germany through the guest worker program in the 1960s and '70s. The socially constructed category of race implies a hierarchy and stark segregation, in contrast to other markers of difference such as ethnicity and religion—which have been used more often in Germany when referring to immigrants of this period, but whose conceptual boundaries with race are nonetheless fluid and unstable.[4] As Ruth Mandel put it, in the context of Germany, "'ethnic' is deployed to equalize and relativize peoples, groups and statuses. Instead, such deployment backfires, as 'ethnic' becomes the euphemism for what a generation ago would have been called 'race.'"[5] In the words of Rita Chin, "If we are to understand German conceptions of difference through apparently neutral terms such as guest worker, foreigner and migrant, it is important to absorb the crucial lessons that have come out of critical race theory. . . . Such work helps us see that these categories—like their more obvious 'racial' counterparts—operate as ideological constructs with very particular implications for how social hierarchy is developed and regulated."[6] Urban discourse often referred to city areas whose populations had a high percentage of noncitizens as ghettos, in the sense of sources of trouble, crime, and chaos.[7] Countless examples abound to exemplify the racialization of and discrimination against guest workers during this period, who were referred to as foreigners (*Ausländer*), as opposed to, for instance, architects from other countries invited to build for Germany who were referred to as "international architects." Toilet decrees explaining how to handle human waste, foreigner classes segregating the education of German and Turkish children, newspaper advertisements that made it clear that foreigners were not eligible to rent apartments, and other measures all made clear the social sep-

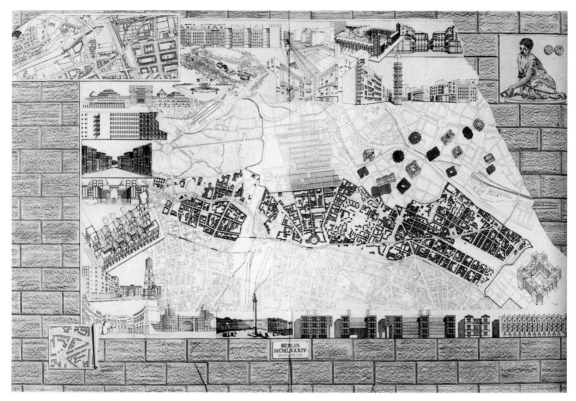

Fig. 18.1 IBA-1984/87 (Internationale Bauausstellung-Berlin). Site plan and drawings of buildings on the plate presented at the seventeenth Triennial of Milan. Drawing by Giovannella Bianchi, Ebe Gianotti, Werner Oeschlin, Luca Ortelli. Private collection of Werner Oeschlin, Luca Ortelli.

aration and othering of guest workers. Civil society groups protecting the rights of immigrants from Turkey saw themselves as organizations against racism and fascism. Rather than drawing sharp categorical lines between race and other constructed identity markers, this paper argues that the interchangeability of race, nation, ethnicity, and religion in the public eye, and their association with citizenship status, in Germany makes evident the partialities related to these categories, and their historically and geographically changing effects.

This paper contributes to this discussion by reviewing some of the issues of my book *Open Architecture* that explores how socially and geopolitically constructed hierarchies about immigrants operated in and through architecture, particularly by focusing on the urban renewal of Kreuzberg, known as IBA-1984/87 (Internationale Bauausstellung-Berlin, 1979–1987).[8] This book gives voice to not only architects and policy makers, but also noncitizen habitants through oral history and storytelling. It does so not by accepting a priori the identity markers, but by registering the words and level of importance that are assigned to these categories by the subjects involved themselves. An astonishingly large number of cutting-edge "international architects" from Europe and the United States were

Esra Akcan

invited to design for the rundown Kreuzberg, including Mario Botta, Peter Cook, Peter Eisenman, John Hejduk, Vittorio Gregotti, Zaha Hadid, Rob Krier, Rem Koolhaas, Martorell-Bohigas-Mackay Architects, Aldo Rossi, Alvaro Siza, James Stirling, Oswald Mathias Ungers, and many others (figure 18.1). This makes IBA-1984/87 not only a microcosm of the postmodernist, participatory, and poststructuralist architectural debates of its time, but also an exemplary subject in analyzing the relation between housing, social citizenship, and race. Kreuzberg at the time was as an area that had been heavily destroyed during World War II but, unlike other parts of Berlin, left to decay afterward. It was also a borough where some sections had a population composed of almost 50 percent noncitizens, predominantly from Turkey, who had arrived as "guest workers" since 1961, and as refugees after the coup d'état and subsequent violence since 1980 (figure 18.2).

IBA was divided into *Neubau* and *Altbau* sections, directed by Josef Paul Kleihues and Hardt-Waltherr Hämer respectively, which differed not only geographically—one was in West, the other in East Kreuzberg—and the nature of their architectural work—one constructed new buildings, the other renovated existing ones—but also with respect to their approaches to noncitizens. IBA Neubau's fresh formal ideals were complicated by its immigration politics that exposed the unpreparedness of architectural discourse to issues of latent racism. Despite the detailed historical research of Kreuzberg's urban development and rigorous theorization of the team's urban renewal approach, competition briefs and publications surprisingly ignored the area's noncitizen residents.

Historically, socially constructed racial identities have been built and maintained through architecture in a few modes. The first has been representation and symbolism. While there was no shortage of identity symbolism during this period, at the height of postmodernism, it would also be shortsighted to think that race operates in architecture through identity symbolism alone. Segregated cities, whether the colonial cities of North Africa or modern cities of North America, have justifiably been at the forefront of critical race studies. It might be harder to notice, however, the smoother ways that discriminatory housing laws and regulations are reflected in urban planning and architectural programs. In the case of postwar West Berlin, the government implemented discriminatory policies in the name of desegregation, rather than segregation. Between 1975 and 1978, the Berlin Senate passed a series of housing laws and regulations such as the "ban on entry and settlement" (*Zuzugssperre*, 1975*)*, and the "desegregation regulations" (1978), which had serious consequences for the guest workers. While the former prohibited the movement of additional foreign families to Kreuzberg, Wedding, and Tiergarten (three of the twelve boroughs in the city), the latter suggested that only 10 percent of residential units be rented to noncitizens all over West Berlin. Justified as an "integration of foreigners" into German society by their forced

Fig. 18.2 View of Kreuzberg, photographed by Heide Moldenhauer Berlin, ca. 1981. Private collection of Heide
Moldenhauer.

dispersal evenly throughout the city, the restrictions were presented as a de-ghettoizing initiative, but were also meant to prevent Turkish families from inhab-iting dwellings close to their relatives and to reserve the new buildings for citi-zens.[9] Namely, the Berlin Senate, IBA's employer, had assessed that there were too many noncitizens from Turkey living in IBA's areas, and the new urban renewal project would regulate what they named as desegregation. During the time that these regulations were put in place, it was procedurally impossible for guest employees to have fulfilled the immigration requirements and become naturalized, which meant that the laws and regulations easily targeted the immigrant popula-tion from Turkey by taking advantage of the citizenship law. The collapsibility of race and noncitizen conveniently served to exert discrimination under the pretext of law.

In addition to being an urban design tool for social control, it is possible to observe how these housing laws were transposed into the functional program of the IBA-Neubau buildings. For example, the percentage of big flats that would accommodate the stereotypical big Turkish family was tightly regulated. Even though the percentage of immigrants reached 50 percent in many areas of East Kreuzberg, the Senate mandated that only 5 percent or a maximum of 10 percent of new units would be big (four or more bedroom) apartments; and that no more than 10 percent of foreigners could live in any building. Coupled with the "ban on entry" law, the Senate's restrictions were meant to diminish Turkish families' chances to move into the IBA-Neubau buildings and consequently to change the percentage of the foreigner population in the area. Unlike many cases of urban renewal that causes gentrification, IBA remained a public housing project, but one through which the Senate devised other means of citizen and noncitizen separa-tion in the city. While reducing noncitizens' chances to move into the new build-ings, IBA designated some formal experiments specifically as guest worker and refugee zones, such as Block 1, designed by Ungers.

Most architects in IBA-Altbau approached the noncitizen issue less as a matter of national or racial identity symbolism, but more as a matter of rights to the city; they concentrated precisely on subverting these Senate-imposed housing regula-tions for immigrants. Instead of master plans implemented from above, the Altbau director Hämer promoted what he called "gentle urban renewal without displace-ment," insisting that the population directly affected by the buildings' renovation should become the decision makers. The Altbau team declared twelve principles, such as the democratization of the process, the consideration of the current resi-dents' needs and interests, the protection of their rights and financial security through settling legal measures, and the protection of the "Kreuzberg mixture" (the mix of work and residential spaces).[10] The team pursued a laborious participatory design process on a unit-by-unit basis, organized regular *Hausverssamlung*—

tenant meetings—for each building, went door to door to every apartment to communicate with residents in order to determine the best distribution of rooms between families, and to discuss the necessary renovations in each unit. Architects avoided over-modernization that would have raised the rents and displaced the current residents. Civil rights organizations and tenant advisory services were mobilized to gain public support for protecting Kreuzberg as a noncitizen neighborhood. As a result, no single family was displaced, and consequently, the Senate's 10 percent foreigner rule and ban on entry law were broken by a team that was employed by the Senate itself (figure 18.3). Álvaro Siza's housing was a unique endeavor in this sense, because it was a new building, yet in the Altbau areas where the Senate's discriminatory rules were relatively subverted.[11] This participatory process was not without its contradictions, however, especially in the context of the radical or plural democracy debates of its time.[12] Acknowledging the plurality of social struggles and the open-ended possibilities that need to be present for the perpetually changing subjects add several layers of complexity to participatory design. For example, some in the Altbau team tried to accommodate seemingly incommensurable demands in a few cases (such as tabs in living rooms for ablution), but it was exposed at some occasions that IBA-Altbau's participatory model welcomed the participants only as long as they had requests commensurable with its own values, setting a limit beyond which the noncitizen participants could not speak. It was also unclear who the democratically legitimate participants of the urban renewal process needed to be. It is therefore problematic to idealize the unresolved participatory design process as a synonym of democracy.[13]

A similar cautionary remark might be added about idealizing the victim of racism as the synonym of the good. Friedrich Nietzsche was the first to warn that the victim—the slave, in his case—is not necessarily the embodiment of the good, simply by virtue of being the opposite of the master.[14] Similarly, being a target of racism is not a guarantee of immunity toward exerting racism over others. In the case of Kreuzberg, multiple layers of race and ethnicity functioned as categories of exclusion, including those between German and Turkish, Turkish and Kurdish, Turkish and Arab, and so on. An ethno-lingual analysis might expose further layers of latent racism, but even during my interviews, I witnessed that there was no shortage of manifest intolerance voiced by individuals who complained about racial discrimination against themselves.

Precisely on this topic, among the many examples of IBA-1984/87, Peter Eisenman and Jaquelin Robertson's design submitted to IBA's most prestigious "Kochstrasse/Friedrichstrasse Competition" at Checkpoint Charlie merits further examination.[15] Given the historical connections between racism and anti-Semitism in Germany, this project provides an opportunity to discuss the triangulation between German, Jewish, and Turkish populations in relation to discrimination.

Fig. 18.3 Views of Kreuzberg after urban renewal, photographed by Esra Akcan, ca. 2010.

Not yet totally immersed in his collaboration with Jacques Derrida and the post-structural turn toward the referential impossibility of architecture, and not yet having published about his search for a *non*classical, and therefore nonrepresentational (autonomous), artificial (arbitrary), and timeless (originless and endless) architecture,[16] Eisenman questioned some of the basic constructed values of modernity with this project.

There were at least three versions of the explanation report for this project, "The City of Artificial Excavations," written during 1980 and 1981.[17] All three versions stated the architects' intention to respond to the symbolic location of the site along the Berlin Wall and to "excavate all" of its historical layers:

> History is not continuous. It is made up of stops and starts, of presences and absences. . . . The European city today is a manifestation of such a memory void. As such it presents a crisis not only of history but of architecture itself. . . .
>
> The city of Berlin offers a potential alternative to these processes. For it is in itself a record not just of the continuity but of the end of the history of the Enlightenment. In this sense it is a unique object: the locus of a historical void. The wall that runs around and through it already makes it *almost* a museum-city . . . it is nothing more nor less than the memory of its own *interrupted* history. The competition site, the intersection of the Friedrichstrasse and the Berlin Wall is the paradigmatic locus of this notion of memory. . . . By the middle of this century ~~all of~~ this *chain of* history was rudely ~~interrupted~~ broken. In 1945, bombing left Friedrichstadt in ruins. Three buildings remained on ~~the~~ our site, their scarred walls a standing reminder of their beginning and their end ~~of their history~~. Then the imposition of the Berlin Wall in 1961 felled ["crushed" in the shorter version] the Angel of History ~~for good~~ *forever*.[18]

The choice of words here warrant a closer analysis. It was not very common at the time in architectural circles to think of the present as a culmination of the Enlightenment, nor to declare that this period had ended with World War II. Eisenman's identification of Berlin as the standing metaphor of the "end of the history of Enlightenment" was similar to the ideas of Frankfurt School members, who had suggested that this war had cast doubt on the promises and values of the Enlightenment.[19] Eschewing the perception of the Enlightenment as the beholder of reason, freedom and equality, the authors had argued that myth and the Enlightenment, reason and instrumentality, and freedom and the triumphalist will to control nature and society were so entangled with each other that the Enlightenment, which had promised emancipation, delivered domination. The last chapter—"Elements of Anti-Semitism," written after the war—"dealt with the reversion of enlightened civilization to barbarism."[20] In "The End of Reason," Max Horkheimer had defined the end of reason as both the intention, or the telos, of the Enlightenment and the manifestation of its failure, thus asking whether there was something inherent in modernity that unavoidably carried humanity toward irrationality and fascism.[21] Moreover, Eisenman's choice of the words "Angel of History," the title of a drawing by Paul Klee, was a clear reference to Walter Benjamin, who had written, "There is no document of civilization which is not at the same time a document of barbarism" in the essay he penned just before killing himself to avoid being captured by the Gestapo during his attempted escape from the Nazis.[22]

Eisenman's frequent use of the concepts of memory and history might seem less surprising at first sight, given the overwhelming interest in the past among architects of this period. However, Eisenman's interest in memory voids seems more akin to this concept's connotation in literary criticism than architecture. In *Twilight Memories* and *Present Pasts*, Andreas Huyssen argued that memory had become a cultural preoccupation during the Cold War, largely due to the growing sense that "the major required task of any society today is to take *responsibility for its past.*"[23] The term "void" that Eisenman frequently uses provided an inspiring metaphor for literary critics and philosophers, who described Berlin as a city that had been "written, erased and rewritten throughout that violent century."[24] Memorials to the victims of state brutality were at the forefront of the public debate about commemoration during the 1980s and 1990s, and Holocaust memorials—as testimonials to the voids carved into cities by the absence of the Jewish population—were the most instructive.[25] Even though the word "Holocaust" never appeared in Eisenman's reports, and even though the IBA team never saw or discussed this project as a memorial that raised consciousness about the Holocaust,[26] given Eisenman's intellectual sources and the history of Berlin, it is not too unthinkable that if "The City of Artificial Excavations" had been built, it would have been an avant la lettre memorial to the Holocaust.

In their unbuilt project, Eisenman and Robertson translated these ideas into physical space in the form of the cut and the void. Like a scar in memory, the void became an index of the absence of the Jewish population in Berlin, the rupture of Jewish history in the city. Eisenman and Robertson refused to simply ignore the traumas of history and to build social housing on this site or to reconstruct Berlin's nineteenth-century urban fabric as IBA-1984/87 required. Instead, the construction on this site needed to remind viewers of the city's disrupted history and take notice of its gaps in memory. "An archeological earthwork"[27] built artificial indexes of the layers of Berlin's history: "Thus the absent wall of the eighteenth century, the foundation walls of the nineteenth century, the remnants of the twentieth century grid as projected upward in the vertical walls of the existing buildings, and finally the Berlin Wall, a monument to the erosion of the unity of the city and the world, form a nexus of wall[s] at different levels which become a composite datum of memory."[28] While these layers embraced Berlin's memory, one more layer, the Mercator grid (used to depict the geometry of the globe), was superimposed on the city grid as an embodiment of anti-memory, and as an indication of no-place (figure 18.4). If it had been built, people would have walked on limestone walls as high as the Berlin Wall that followed the Mercator grid and perceived the layers of Berlin's history as if they were in an archeological excavation.[29] In all three versions of the explanation report, Eisenman emphasized the "inaccessibility of the earthwork."[30] What Eisenman calls inaccessibility could well have been the translation of the concept of unrepresentability into physical space. The unrepresentability and unspeakability of the Holocaust, and the impossibility of creating a victim's experience of it, would become one of the central concepts in Holocaust studies in the 1980s and 1990s.[31]

Throughout the whole process, from competition to construction of a revised project, the one point that seems to have remained constant in Eisenman's argument was that time was at a standstill. Humanity had never worked through or moved past the trauma of 1945, which was only confirmed by the construction of the Berlin Wall in 1961: "Since 1945 there is both a memory of a time that has been lost forever and an immanence of a time which may be again. This submission deserves recognition because it presents an architecture suspended in this new time as an archeological moment."[32] While attempting to come to terms with Berlin's disrupted past, and while constructing the artificial traces of the city's past two hundred years, Eisenman's history stopped at 1961, the year when the wall was constructed and when the first labor recruitment contract was signed between Germany and Turkey, after which guest workers started moving into the area. While writing the history of Berlin's traumatic past and erasures, implying that the finale was a consequence of anti-Semitism, Eisenman's historical narrative identified 1961 as the end of history. The present violence occurring in the area was hence not acknowledged in a project that sought to raise consciousness about the many incidents of historical violence on this very site.

In *Cosmopolitan Anxieties*, Ruth Mandel identified the time of Berlin as a chronotope: "continually stretched, pulled between an unbearable memory and contested visions of its future." The city's troubled memories were like "a palimpsest. Whichever layer one looks at, be it the Weimar political polarization and artistic efflorescence, the thirteen years of the Nationalist Socialist capital, or as the puppet like city-state of the Allied powers in the dangerous games of [the] Cold War, it is ultimately impossible to escape these multiple temporalities when imagining the future."[33] However, Mandel also identified the racism against guest workers from Turkey as one of the major layers of this palimpsest, deserving the most attention in theorizing Berlin's present, where "the discussion [shifted] from biologically based racism to racism derived from cultural determinism."[34] Eisenman's

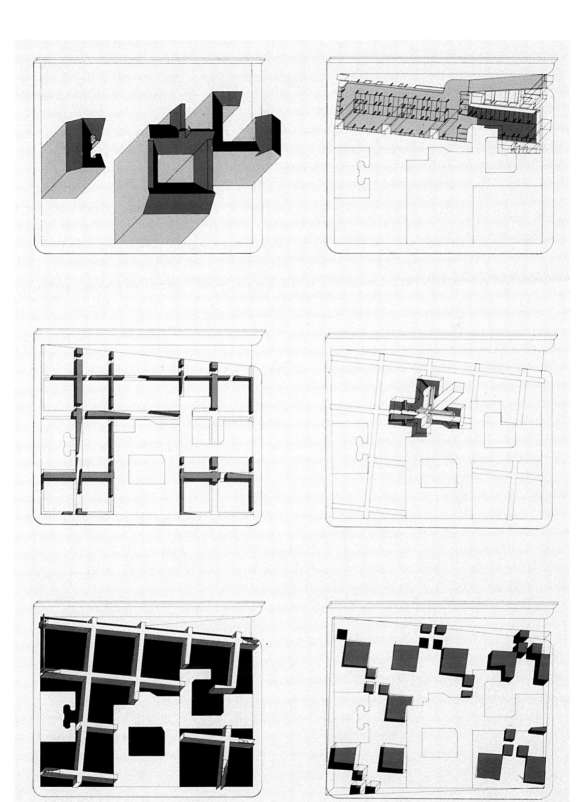

Fig. 18.4 Peter Eisenman and Jaquelin Robertson, "Kochstrasse/Friedrichstrasse Competition" project, IBA-1984/87, Berlin. Peter Eisenman Papers, Canadian Center for Architecture (DR1991_0018_723).

reaction against building public housing on this site and his narrative that froze time in 1961 make one question whether he was so intellectually invested in building an avant la lettre memorial to the Holocaust that he remained oblivious to the traumas currently being enacted in the area. But these traumas were in plain sight during this time. These were the days when Semra Ertan set herself on fire to protest xenophobia in Germany (on May 26, 1982) and the asylum seeker Cemal Altun jumped out of the window of West Berlin's administrative court to avoid being deported (August 30, 1983). I already mentioned the racialization of guest workers, and the Senate's housing laws that discriminated against noncitizens.

The complex and changing relations between Holocaust memory, xenophobia, and the reception of noncitizens in Germany from the 1970s into the 2010s has been a topic of recent scholarly work. The common view during the 1970s, especially in the fields of political science and anthropology, was that "the Turks are the Jews of today."[35] Mandel, Gökçe Yurdakul, and Michael Bodemann have shown how immigrants from Turkey compared racism against them to anti-Semitism, especially after the neo-Nazis' deadly attacks in Mölln (1992) and Solingen (1993), and took the German-Jewish trope as a model for their own cooperative unions, associations, and demands for rights.[36] In literary studies, Huyssen and Leslie Adelson have analyzed Holocaust consciousness and accountability in German-Turkish immigrant literature after Germany's reunification, further complicated by its Armenian counterpart, through the work of authors such as Zafer Şenocak, whose words best summarize this situation: "In today's Germany, Jews and Germans no longer face one another alone."[37] Michael Rothberg and Yasemin Yıldız have reread Holocaust memory in Germany by taking into account immigrant artists' work, as well as discussions in community organizations.[38] Esra Özyürek has argued that the situation changed in the 2000s, when "the interconnected commitments of European leaders to remember the Holocaust and fight anti-Semitism became one of the grounds for legitimizing racialization of immigrants, and specifically Muslims, by signaling them out as the main contemporary anti-Semites."[39] Matti Bunzl has analyzed the emerging relationship between Islamophobia and anti-Semitism.[40] For our purposes, it might be fitting to quote Michael Brenner in reference to my cautionary remark about idealizing the consciousness against one racism as a guarantee against racism itself or other types of violence toward the other: "It would be mistaken to view the treatment of the Jewish minority in Germany today as representative of the interaction with other religious and ethnic minorities. Fortunately, anti-Semitism is still widely considered a social taboo. However, opinions and ordinances against other religious minorities and foreigners are, on the contrary, socially acceptable. There was a time when politicians could express wonderful sentiments about their Jewish fellow citizens and in the same breath warn about the danger of foreign infiltration in Germany."[41] Not having yet lived through the postunification debates about Holocaust memory and their intersections with postwar migration, Eisenman's avant la lettre memorial to the Holocaust nonetheless is an early indicator of the uneasy triangulation between German, Jewish, and Turkish constructed identities, designed at a time when those on the democratic left did indeed draw connections between historical and contemporary discriminations against the Jewish and Turkish population, respectively.

Social inequalities constructed by using race and citizenship categories are twin problems, given that the exclusion from citizenship has been enduring throughout the history of citizenship: slaves, women, colonial subjects, guest workers, legal aliens, illegal immigrants, refugees—all have been identified as noncitizens at one point in the past, and some continue to be so in the present. The Jewish population was deprived of their German citizenship as they were subject to National Socialist horror. This is a needless reminder of the bond between citizenship and social rights. Ever since the first declaration of rights, natural and civil rights have been collapsed into each other; an unsubstantiated link between "man" and "citizen," birth and nationhood has defined human rights. This has made citizenship the necessary condition to have rights, denying many rights to noncitizens and making refugees completely rightless. The hitherto noncitizens continue to be denied social citizenship, in T. H. Marshall's sense,[42] as the former exclusion of slaves, guest workers, and refugees in the past is projected onto the present in the form of class difference and white supremacy. Étienne Balibar also theorizes on the relation between *internal* and *external exclusions* from citizenship, in order to understand the mechanism that denies legal citizens the "right to have rights"—a concept from Hannah Arendt's groundbreaking texts on the refugee phenomenon. In Balibar's words, "In its most general definition, it means that an 'external' border is mirrored by an 'internal' border, or that the condition of foreignness is projected within a political space or national territory to create an inadmissible alterity (as was the case with slaves and is the case with immigrants), or, on the contrary, an additional element of interiority and belonging is introduced into an anthropological category, in such a way to as to push the foreigner out."[43] It is a similar mirroring between race and citizenship status that collapses Harlem and Kreuzberg, and moreover, that turns citizenship into a "club" in Balibar's metaphor, where one is admitted or refused regardless of one's legal rights (which are already very limited or nonexistent for the noncitizen). "It is always citizens 'knowing' and 'imagining' themselves as such, who exclude from citizenship and who, thus, 'produce' non-citizens in such way as to make it possible for them to represent their own citizenship to themselves as a 'common' belonging."[44]

Public housing and housing as a human right continue to be at the forefront of discussions about social citizenship, as the decline of the welfare system around the world today with the advance of global capitalism puts public housing and with it the idea of social citizenship even at further risk. For this reason, working on a public housing and urban renewal project in an immigrant city district has carried me to a theory of open architecture in my aforementioned book. I define open architecture as the translation of a new ethics of hospitality into architecture, and elaborate on it as collectivity, democracy, and multiplicity. Differentiating it from the neoliberal ethos of the open market that actually closes boundaries for the majority, I suggest thinking on the concept of openness by bringing forth open borders more than the open market, collectivity more than individuality, the openness of society more than the free circulation of consumer products, user participation more than the author-architect, the collaborative more than the egoistic designer. A new hospitality would be at its best when directed toward the noncitizen, because nothing exposes the unresolved contradictions of modern international law and current human rights regime as effectively as the concept of the noncitizen. The stateless puts into question the very limits of the human rights that are defined under the precondition of being a citizen of a state in the first place. In Giorgio Agamben's words, "The paradox here is that the very figure who should have embodied the rights of man par excellence—the refugee—signals instead the concept's radical crisis."[45] When citizenship rights disappear, so do human rights. The urban renewal of Kreuzberg exposes the historical consequences of this human rights paradox as it is reflected in housing and urbanism. The legal distinctions between different types of noncitizens such as guest workers and refugees lose their relevance in this context, as all noncitizens from Turkey were subject to the same housing laws. Let us not forget that in her texts about the loss of human rights, Arendt was quick to specify housing as the first major human right lost to the refugee.[46] If the conventional notion of hospitality that informs the current international laws and human rights regime is conditional and limited, the new hospitality toward the noncitizen has to be left open and in the making, "always to come." The concept of citizenship has historically been in constant evolution precisely by virtue of the hospitality toward the hitherto noncitizen, as former slaves, women, and colonial subjects gained rights. It ought to remain changing even perhaps more comprehensively as refugees and global migrants continue to remain rightless.

Esra Akcan

Notes

Introduction

1. Race is ignored in most of the classic histories of the period, for example Leonardo Benevolo, *History of Modern Architecture*, 2 vols. (Cambridge, MA: MIT Press, 1971); Henry-Russell Hitchcock, *Architecture: Nineteenth and Twentieth Centuries* (Baltimore: Penguin Books, 1958); and Sigfried Giedion, *Space, Time and Architecture: The Growth of a New Tradition*, 5th ed. (Cambridge, MA: Harvard University Press, 2009). Race is also absent from Marxist critical histories of the 1980s, for example Manfredo Tafuri and Francesco Dal Co, *Modern Architecture* (New York: Harry N. Abrams, 1979); and Kenneth Frampton, *Modern Architecture: A Critical History* (New York: Oxford University Press, 1980).

2. Hanno-Walter Kruft, *A History of Architectural Theory from Vitruvius to the Present* (New York: Princeton Architectural Press, 1994), 285. On recent scholarship that challenges Kruft's view, see note 21 below.

3. For examples of histories that address nineteenth-century architecture's rapprochement with biology and ethnography yet remarkably downplay race, see Philip Steadman, *The Evolution of Designs: Biological Analogy in Architecture and the Applied Arts* (London: Routledge, 2008) and Alina Payne, *From Ornament to Object: Genealogies of Architectural Modernism* (New Haven, CT: Yale University Press, 2012).

4. See, among others, Dipesh Chakrabarty, *Provincializing Europe: Postcolonial Thought and Historical Difference* (Princeton, NJ: Princeton University Press, 2000); Denise Ferreira da Silva, *Toward a Global Idea of Race* (Minneapolis: University of Minnesota Press, 2007); Walter D. Mignolo, *Local Histories/Global Designs: Coloniality, Subaltern Knowledges, and Border Thinking*, rev. ed. (Princeton, NJ: Princeton University Press, 2012); and Sylvia Wynter, "Unsettling the Coloniality of Being/Power/Truth/ Freedom: Towards the Human, After Man, Its Overrepresentation—An Argument," *CR: The New Centennial Review* 3, no. 3 (2003): 257–337.

5. See Sven Beckert, *Empire of Cotton: A Global History* (New York: Alfred A. Knopf, 2014); Susan Buck-Morss, *Hegel, Haiti, and Universal History* (Pittsburgh, PA: University of Pittsburgh Press, 2009); Paul Gilroy, *The Black Atlantic: Modernity and Double Consciousness* (Cambridge, MA: Harvard University Press, 1993); Uday Singh

Mehta, *Liberalism and Empire: A Study in Nineteenth-Century British Liberal Thought* (Chicago: University of Chicago Press, 1999); and Cedric J. Robinson, *Black Marxism: The Making of the Black Radical Tradition* (Chapel Hill: University of North Carolina Press, 2000).

6. Mignolo, *Local Histories/Global Designs*, 22.

7. David Bindman, *Ape to Apollo: Aesthetics and the Idea of Race in the 18th Century* (London: Reaktion Books, 2002), 83.

8. Mitchell Schwarzer, "Origins of the Art History Survey Text," *Art Journal* 54, no. 3 (1995): 24.

9. Bindman, *Ape to Apollo*, 92, 208.

10. Edward Augustus Freeman, *A History of Architecture* (London: Joseph Masters, 1849), 11–19.

11. Theodore Koditschek, "A Liberal Descent? E. A. Freeman's Invention of Racial Traditions," in *Making History: Edward Augustus Freeman and Victorian Cultural Politics*, ed. G. A. Bremner and Jonathan Conlin (Oxford: Oxford University Press, 2015), 199–216.

12. Banister Fletcher, *A History of Architecture on the Comparative Method* (London: Batsford, 1905), 4.

13. Gülsüm Baydar Nalbantoğlu, "Toward Postcolonial Openings: Rereading Sir Banister Fletcher's 'History of Architecture,'" *Assemblage* 35 (1998): 6–17.

14. Quoted in Leslie Herman, "Building Narratives of the Irish 'Colonial Period' in American Architectural History" (PhD diss., Columbia University, 2020); also see William H. Pierson Jr., *American Buildings and their Architects: The Colonial and Neoclassical Styles* (New York: Oxford University Press, 1970), 3.

15. See John Michael Vlach, *Back of the Big House: The Architecture of Plantation Slavery* (Chapel Hill: University of North Carolina Press, 1993); Dell Upton, "White and Black Landscapes in Eighteenth-Century Virginia," *Places* 2, no. 2 (1984), 59–72; and Dell Upton, ed., *America's Architectural Roots: Ethnic Groups That Built America* (New York: John Wiley and Sons, 1986).

16. Zeynep Çelik, *Displaying the Orient: Architecture of Islam at Nineteenth-Century World's Fairs* (Berkeley: University of California Press, 1992); Mark Crinson. *Empire Building: Orientalism and Victorian Architecture* (London and New York: Routledge, 1999); Patricia A. Morton, *Hybrid Modernities: Architecture and Representation at the 1931 Colonial Exposition, Paris* (Cambridge, MA: MIT Press, 2000); and Mabel O. Wilson, *Negro Building: Black Americans in the World of Fairs and Museums* (Berkeley: University of California Press, 2012).

17. The literature is by now too vast for us to name all the important contributions, but the following are some representative examples: Tom Avermaete, Serhat Karakayali, and Marion von Osten, *Colonial Modern: Aesthetics of the Past, Rebellions for the Future* (London: Black Dog, 2010); Zeynep Çelik, *Empire, Architecture, and the City: French–*

Ottoman Encounters, 1830–1914 (Seattle: University of Washington Press, 2008); Crinson, *Empire Building*; Itohan Osayimwese, *Colonialism and Modern Architecture in Germany* (Pittsburgh, PA: University of Pittsburgh Press, 2017); and Gwendolyn Wright, *The Politics of Design in French Colonial Urbanism* (Chicago: University of Chicago Press, 1991).

18. Martin A. Berger, *Sight Unseen: Whiteness and American Visual Culture* (Berkeley: University of California Press, 2005), 1–2.

19. Simon Gikandi, *Slavery and the Culture of Taste* (Princeton, NJ: Princeton University Press, 2011), x.

20. Anne Anlin Cheng, "Skins, Tattoos, and Susceptibility," *Representations* 108, no. 1 (2009): 101.

21. Laurent Baridon, *L'imaginaire scientifique de Viollet-le-Duc* (Paris: Éditions L'Harmattan, 1996); Martin Bressani, *Architecture and the Historical Imagination: Eugène-Emmanuel Viollet-le-Duc, 1814–1879* (London: Ashgate, 2014); Charles L. Davis II, "Viollet-le-Duc and the Body: The Metaphorical Integrations of Race and Style in Structural Rationalism," *Architectural Research Quarterly* 14, no. 4 (2010), 341–48; and Lauren M. O'Connell, "A Rational, National Architecture: Viollet-le-Duc's Modest Proposal for Russia," *JSAH* 52, no. 4 (Dec. 1993), 436–52.

22. Dianne Harris, *Little White Houses: How the Postwar Home Constructed Race in America* (Minneapolis: University of Minnesota Press, 2013).

23. See Darell Wayne Fields, *Architecture in Black* (London: Athlone Press, 2000), and the work published in the journal *Appendx* (1993–1995). Fields's work has been influenced by the work of critical race studies scholar Henry Louis Gates.

24. See Tommy L. Lott and John P. Pittman, eds., *A Companion to African-American Philosophy* (Malden, MA: Blackwell, 2003), 3–7.

25. See Henry Louis Gates Jr. and Kwame Anthony Appiah, eds., *"Race," Writing, and Difference* (Chicago: University of Chicago Press, 1986); and Houston A. Baker Jr., *Modernism and the Harlem Renaissance* (Chicago: University of Chicago Press, 1987).

26. Toni Morrison, *Playing in the Dark: Whiteness and the Literary Imagination* (Cambridge, MA: Harvard University Press, 1992).

27. See Kimberlé Crenshaw, Neil Gotanda, Gary Peller, and Kendall Thomas, *Critical Race Theory: The Key Writings That Formed the Movement* (New York: New Press, 1995).

28. Michael Omi and Howard Winant, *Racial Formation in the United States: From the 1960s to the 1990s* (New York: Routledge, 1994).

29. Edward W. Said, *Orientalism* (New York: Vintage Books, 1979).

30. See Gayatri Chakravorty Spivak, "Can the Subaltern Speak," in *Marxism and the Interpretation of Culture*, ed. Cary Nelson and Lawrence Grossberg (Urbana: University of Illinois Press, 1988), 271–313; and Homi Bhabha, *The Location of Culture* (New York: Routledge, 1994).

31. See Amy Kaplan and Donald E. Pease, *Cultures of United States Imperialism* (Durham, NC: Duke University Press, 1993); and Amy Kaplan, *The Anarchy of Empire in the Making of U.S. Culture* (Cambridge, MA: Harvard University Press, 2005).

32. Ferreira da Silva, *Toward a Global Idea of Race.*

33. Jodi Melamed, *Represent and Destroy: Rationalizing Violence in the New Racial Capitalism* (Minneapolis: University of Minnesota Press, 2011).

34. See Sara Ahmed, "A Phenomenology of Whiteness," *Feminist Theory* 8, no. 2 (Aug. 2007): 149–68; and Linda Martín Alcoff, *The Future of Whiteness* (Cambridge: Polity Press, 2015).

35. Saidiya V. Hartman, *Scenes of Subjection: Terror, Slavery, and Self-Making in Nineteenth-Century America* (New York: Oxford University Press, 1997); Fred Moten, "The Case of Blackness," *Criticism* 50, no. 2 (Spring 2008): 177–218; and Hortense J. Spillers, "Mama's Baby, Papa's Maybe: An American Grammar Book," *Diacritics* 17, no. 2 (Summer 1987): 64–81.

36. Donna Haraway, "Situated Knowledges: The Science Question in Feminism and the Privilege of Partial Perspective," *Feminist Studies* 14, no. 3 (Autumn 1988): 589.

37. Walter D. Mignolo, "Delinking," *Cultural Studies* 21, no. 2 (2007): 451. Also see Aníbal Quijano, "Coloniality and Modernity/Rationality," *Cultural Studies* 21, no. 2 (2007): 168–78.

1. Notes on the Virginia Capitol

My thanks to colleagues at the National Gallery of Art's Center for Advanced Study in the Visual Arts and the Chrysler Museum of Art for their generous feedback on earlier versions of this essay.

1. Immanuel Kant, *Observations on the Feeling of the Beautiful and the Sublime* (1764), ed. Patrick Frierson and Paul Guyer (Cambridge: Cambridge University Press, 2011), 58–59.

2. David Bindman, *Ape to Apollo* (London: Reaktion Books, 2002).

3. Sylvia Wynter, "Unsettling the Coloniality of Being/Power/Truth/Freedom: Towards the Human, After Man, Its Overrepresentation—An Argument," *CR: The New Centennial Review* 3, no. 3 (Fall 1993): 263–64.

4. Wynter, "Unsettling the Coloniality of Being," 263–64.

5. Anibal Quijano, "Coloniality of Power, Eurocentrism, and Latin America," *Neplantla: Views from South* 1, no. 3 (2000).

6. Walter D. Mignolo, *The Darker Side of the Renaissance: Literacy, Territoriality, and Colonization* (Ann Arbor: University of Michigan Press, 2010), 259–60.

7. Denise Ferreira da Silva, *Toward a Global Idea of Race* (Minneapolis: University of Minnesota Press, 2007).

8. See Mignolo, *Darker Side of the Renaissance*, 264; Keith Weheliye, *Habeus Viscus: Racializing Assemblages, Biopolitics, and Black Feminist Theories of the Human* (Durham,

NC: Duke University Press, 2014), 24; and Wynter, "Unsettling the Coloniality of Being," 310.

9. Barry Bergdoll, *European Architecture 1750–1890* (Oxford: Oxford University Press, 2000), 1–5.

10. Fiske Kimball, "Jefferson and the Public Buildings of Virginia: II Richmond, 1779–1780," *Huntington Library Quarterly* 12, no. 3 (May 1949): 303.

11. Ferreira da Silva, *Toward a Global Idea of Race*, 97.

12. Mark Wenger, "Thomas Jefferson and the Virginia State Capitol," *Virginia Magazine of History and Biography* 101, no. 1 (January 1993): 82.

13. Thomas Jefferson, *Notes on the State of Virginia* (Richmond, VA: J. W. Randolph, 1853), 164.

14. Fiske Kimball, "Jefferson and the Public Buildings of Virginia: I Williamsburg, 1770–1776," *Huntington Library Quarterly* 12, no. 2 (Feb. 1949): 115.

15. Wenger, "Thomas Jefferson and the Virginia State Capitol," 99.

16. Wenger, "Thomas Jefferson and the Virginia State Capitol," 88.

17. William Hay and James Buchanan to Thomas Jefferson, March 20, 1785, folder 12, box 7, Capitol Square Data, vol. 2, Grounds (Original), 1776–1931, Archives and Maps Research Rooms, Library of Virginia.

18. "To Thomas Jefferson from Patrick Henry," September 10, 1785, *The Papers of Thomas Jefferson Digital Edition*, ed. Barbara B. Oberg and J. Jefferson Looney (Charlottesville: University of Virginia Press, 2008–2016).

19. William Bainter O'Neal, *Jefferson's Fine Arts Library for the University of Virginia: With Additional Notes on Architectural Volumes Known to Have Been Owned by Jefferson, Issue 1* (Charlottesville: University of Virginia Press, 1956), 71–78.

20. Wenger, "Thomas Jefferson and the Virginia State Capitol," 96–99.

21. "To James Madison," September 20, 1785, *The Papers of Thomas Jefferson Digital Edition*, ed. Barbara B. Oberg and J. Jefferson Looney (Charlottesville: University of Virginia Press, 2008–2016).

22. "To James Madison," September 20, 1785, *The Papers of Thomas Jefferson Digital Edition*.

23. "To James Buchanan and William Hay," June 13, 1786, *The Papers of Thomas Jefferson Digital Edition*.

24. "To James Madison," September 20, 1785, *The Papers of Thomas Jefferson Digital Edition*.

25. "To James Madison," September 20, 1785, *The Papers of Thomas Jefferson Digital Edition*.

26. "To James Madison," September 20, 1785, *The Papers of Thomas Jefferson Digital Edition*.

27. Simon Gikandi, *Slavery and the Culture of Taste* (Princeton, NJ: Princeton University Press, 2014), 17.

28. Jefferson, *Notes on the State of Virginia*, 48.

29. Jefferson, *Notes on the State of Virginia*, 47–48.

30. Jefferson, *Notes on the State of Virginia*, 47–48.

31. Jefferson, *Notes on the State of Virginia*, 63–66.

32. Jefferson, *Notes on the State of Virginia*, 68.

33. Jefferson, *Notes on the State of Virginia*, 70.

34. Jefferson, *Notes on the State of Virginia*, 70.

35. Jefferson, *Notes on the State of Virginia*, 149.

36. Jefferson, *Notes on the State of Virginia*, 145.

37. Fred Moten, "The Case of Blackness," *Criticism* 50, no. 2 (Spring 2008): 180.

38. Jefferson, *Notes on the State of Virginia*, 151.

39. Jefferson, *Notes on the State of Virginia*, 152.

40. Jefferson, *Notes on the State of Virginia*, 152.

41. Jefferson, *Notes on the State of Virginia*, 148.

42. Jefferson, *Notes on the State of Virginia*, 149.

43. Jefferson, *Notes on the State of Virginia*, 149.

44. Jefferson, *Notes on the State of Virginia*, 149.

45. Jefferson, *Notes on the State of Virginia*, 149.

46. Jefferson, *Notes on the State of Virginia*, 155.

47. Jefferson, *Notes on the State of Virginia*, 155.

48. Jefferson fathered several mixed-raced children with his enslaved concubine Sally Hemings. See Annette Gordon Reed, *Thomas Jefferson and Sally Hemings: An American Controversy* (Charlottesville: University of Virginia Press, 1998).

49. Jefferson officially freed Robert and James Hemings before he died; after his death, John Hemings, Burwell Colbert, Joseph Fosset, along with Jefferson's two sons with Sally Hemings, Madison and Eston Hemings, were set free. See Lucia Stanton, *"Those Who Labor for My Happiness": Slavery at Thomas Jefferson's Monticello* (Charlottesville: University of Virginia Press, 2012).

50. Marie Tyler-McGraw, *At the Falls: Richmond, Virginia, and its People* (Chapel Hill: University of North Carolina Press, 1995), 65.

51. "To James Buchanan and William Hay," August 13, 1785, *The Papers of Thomas Jefferson Digital Edition.*

52. Virginia Census and Tax List, Richmond, 1791, http://www.binnsgenealogy .com/VirginiaTaxListCensuses/CityRichmond/1791Personal/09.jpg.

53. Virginia Census and Tax List, Richmond, 1791, http://www.binnsgenealogy .com/VirginiaTaxListCensuses/CityRichmond/1791Personal/05.jpg.

54. "Gentlmn, Please Pay to Robt Goode," October 9, 1788, folder 1, Capitol Building Vouchers, box 2, Capitol Square Data Records, Library of Virginia Archives.

55. Virginia Census and Tax List, Richmond, 1791, http://www.binnsgenealogy .com/VirginiaTaxListCensuses/CityRichmond/1791Personal/12.jpg; and Virginia

Census and Tax List, Orange, 1790, http://www.binnsgenealogy.com/VirginiaTax ListCensuses/Orange/1790PersonalB/16.jpg.

56. "The Directors of the Capitol to Dabney Minor," February 27, 1790, and "State of contracts made and executed in 1788 by the undertakers of work on the Capitol and paid for by the Directors viz.," n.d., folder 1, Capitol Building and Receipts, 1786–1790, box 1, Capital Square Data Records, Library of Virginia Archives.

57. "Explore Advertisements," Geography of Slavery, accessed June 13, 2017, http://www2.vcdh.virginia.edu/gos/browse/browse_ads.php?year=1794&month=9&page=0.

58. "Laborer Fortune waits for you," July 2, 1788, folder 15, box 1, "Dr. W. Samuel Dobie in Account," n.d., folder 1, box 1; and "Labr. Fortune work'd at clearing," October 1788, folder 1, box 1, Capital Square Data Records, Library of Virginia Archives.

59. Jefferson, *Notes on the State of Virginia*, 149.

2. American Architecture in the Black Atlantic

1. W. E. B. Du Bois, *The Souls of Black Folk: Essays and Sketches* (Chicago: A. C. Mclurg, 1903); Paul Gilroy, *The Black Atlantic: Modernity and Double Consciousness* (New York: Verso, 1993).

2. Charles M. Harris offers a thorough biography of Thornton. C. M. Harris, introduction to *The Papers of William Thornton: Volume 1, 1781–1802* (Charlottesville: University Press of Virginia, 1995), xxxi–lxxv.

3. Sven Beckert, *Empire of Cotton: A Global History* (New York: Knopf, 2014).

4. Gavin Wright, *Slavery and American Economic Development* (Baton Rouge: Louisiana State University Press, 2006), 72–73.

5. Gaillard Hunt has collected many of Thornton's writing on African colonization. Gaillard Hunt, *William Thornton and Negro Colonization* (Worcester: The American Antiquarian Society, 1921). Harris has collected much of Thornton's writing and correspondences. *Papers of William Thornton: Volume 1, 1781–1802*, ed. C. M. Harris (Charlottesville: University Press of Virginia, 1995). Harris also discusses Thornton's colonization scheme; see Harris, introduction.

6. Simon Schama offers a compelling account of the life and works of Granville Sharp. Simon Schama, *Rough Crossings: Britain, the Slaves, and the American Revolution* (London: BBC Books, 2005).

7. Hunt, *William Thornton and Negro Colonization*, 11–13; William Thornton to John Coakley Lettsom, Philadelphia, November 15, 1788, in Harris, *Papers of William Thornton*, 77–79.

8. Harris, introduction, xlvi.

9. William Thornton to John Coakley Lettsom, New York, November 18, 1786, in Harris, *Papers of William Thornton*, 34.

10. Sharp maintained an atavistic English medievalism for the settlement and proposed a revival of the English medieval frankpledge, where the settlement would be

divided into small kinship units—numbering ten to twelve households—that jointly held responsibility for each of its members. Granville Sharp to John Coakley Lettsom, October 13, 1788, in Harris, *Papers of William Thornton*, 90–97; David Brion Davis, *The Problem of Slavery in the Age of Revolution, 1770–1823* (Ithaca, NY: Cornell University Press, 1975), 394–95. We might trace a line from the medievalism of Sharpe's frank-pledge, through that of the English arts and crafts movement, to reactionary revivalist and neo-vernacular planning proposals of the Thatcher era. In each case the return to a premodern past sought to resolve social crises, and in each case these projects were performed in the aesthetic plane while ultimately maintaining the social order. Their legacies are the modern garden city movement and postmodern new urbanism that solidified social alienation and racial discrimination in space. Today these terms find renewed currency in Western neofascist and white nationalist movements that seek to recall a racially homogenous past (medieval Europe was *not* racially homogenous) as a pretense to exploit and exclude nonwhites.

11. William Thornton, "General Outlines of a Settlement on the Tooth or Ivory Coast of Africa [1786]," in Harris, *Papers of William Thornton*, 39.

12. William Thornton to John Coakley Lettsom, New York, November 18, 1786, 32–33.

13. Michael Hardt, "Jefferson and Democracy," *American Quarterly* 59, no. 1 (2007): 41–78; Jefferson discusses his theories on white supremacy and the necessity for the removal of freed slaves in Thomas Jefferson, *Notes on the State of Virginia* (London: John Stockdale, 1787), 204–6.

14. See, for instance, William Thornton to John Coakley Lettsom, Philadelphia, November 15, 1788, 77–80.

15. Granville Sharp to John Coakley Lettsom, October 13, 1788, 90–97.

16. Granville Sharp to William Thornton, Leadonhall Street, London, October 5, 1791, in Harris, *Papers of William Thornton*, 158–61.

17. William Thornton, *Cadmus, or, A Treatise on the Elements of Written Language, Illustrating, by a Philosophical Division of Speech, the Power of Each Character, Thereby Mutually Fixing the Orthography and Orthoepy* (Philadelphia: R. Aitken and Son, 1793).

18. Thornton, *Cadmus*, 17–18.

19. Thornton, *Cadmus*, 63.

20. Thornton, *Cadmus*, v–vii.

21. Thornton, *Cadmus*, 28.

22. On Spence's land reform: T. M. Parssinen, "Thomas Spence and the Origins of English Land Nationalization," *Journal of the History of Ideas* 34, no. 1 (1973): 135–41; and Joan Beal, "A Radical Plan for the English Language: Thomas Spence's 'New Alphabet,'" *Miranda*, no. 13 (2016).

23. Thomas Spence, *A Supplement to the History of Robinson Crusoe* (Newcastle: Thomas Saint, 1782); quoted in Beal, "Radical Plan for the English Language," 5.

24. William Thornton to the President and Members of the Council of the Virgin Islands, Tortola, February 22, 1791, in Harris, *Papers of William Thornton*, 129.

25. William Thornton to John Coakley Lettsom, November 26, 1795, in Harris, *Papers of William Thornton*, 340.

26. William Thornton to John Coakley Lettsom, November 26, 1795, 340.

27. One could think of this politics of translation in terms of an untranslatable that disrupts the normative systems of meaning. Emily Apter, *Against World Literature: On the Politics of Untranslatability* (New York: Verso, 2013).

28. Charles M. Harris, "William Thornton (1759–1828)," Biographies and Essays (Center for Architecture, Design, and Engineering), Library of Congress Prints and Photographs Reading Room, last revised October 2015, https://www.loc.gov/rr/print/adecenter/essays/B-Thornton.html.

29. For a discussion of Hallet's scheme: Pamela Scott, "Stephen Hallet's Designs for the United States Capitol," *Winterthur Portfolio* 27, no. 2/3 (1992): 145–70.

30. Fiske Kimball and Wells Bennett argue that Thornton's rendering of a Georgian complex represents his "Tortola Scheme" for the US Capitol Building. Fiske Kimball and Wells Bennett, "William Thornton and the Design of the United States Capitol," *Art Studies* (1923): 76–92. Charles M. Harris argues that the architectural drawings that Thornton brought back from Tortola are lost and that the drawings labeled as Thornton's "Tortola Scheme" in the Prints and Photographs Division of the Library of Congress are better attributed to George Turner in his own preliminary design that he subsequently shared with Thornton. C. M. Harris, "Editorial Note: Preliminary Designs for the United States Capitol," in *Papers of William Thornton*, 211–12.

31. For a discussion of Thornton's scheme: Pamela Scott, *Temple of Liberty: Building the Capitol for a New Nation* (New York: Oxford University Press, 1995), 42–43, 50–51; Bates Lowry, *Building a National Image: Architectural Drawings for the American Democracy, 1789–1912* (Washington, DC: National Building Museum, 1985), 20–25; Damie Stillman, "The United States Capitol: Icon of the Republic," in *Capital Drawings: Architectural Designs for Washington, D.C., from the Library of Congress*, ed. C. Ford Peatross (Baltimore: Johns Hopkins University Press, 2005), 62–65; C. M. Harris, "Editorial Note: The Premiated Design for the United States Capitol," in *Papers of William Thornton*, 239–42.

32. David Cannadine, ed., *The Houses of Parliament: History, Art, Architecture* (London: Merrell, 2000); and Jean-Philippe Heurtin, "The Circle of Discussion and the Semicircle of Criticism," in *Making Things Public: Atmospheres of Democracy*, ed. Bruno Latour and Peter Weibel (Cambridge, MA: MIT Press, 2005), 754–69.

33. We might take this configuration—and the emergence of the president's house as the seat of executive power—simply within the realpolitik of the emerging struggle between the Republicans and the Federalists. Benjamin Henry Latrobe's plans for the Capitol and the White House after 1800 certainly speak to this.

34. The present monumental cluster configured by the addition of the Supreme Court and Library of Congress buildings to the east of the Capitol was never part of L'Enfant's original plans. L'Enfant expressly sought to distribute such institutions around the city in order to spur real estate development.

35. William Allen discusses the various proposals submitted for the US Capitol Building: William C. Allen, *History of the United States Capitol: A Chronicle of Design, Construction, and Politics* (Washington, DC: US Government Printing Office, 2001), 13–18.

36. Harris, "Editorial Note: The Premiated Design for the United States Capitol," 241.

37. C. M. Harris relates L'Enfant's plan for Washington, DC, to a Hamiltonian monarchism: C. M. Harris, "Washington's Gamble, L'Enfant's Dream: Politics, Design, and the Founding of the National Capital," *William and Mary Quarterly* 56, no. 3 (July 1999).

38. Raymond Williams, "The New Metropolis," in *The Country and the City* (New York: Oxford University Press, 1973), 279–88.

39. De Wailly built Montmusard between 1765 and 1769; it was partially demolished in 1795, but images of the building circulated widely through the print culture of the late eighteenth century. Two oil paintings of Montmusard by Jean-Baptiste Lallemand were exhibited in the Salon of 1771. These served as models for a set of engravings of Montmusard by Marie-Alexandre Duparc published in the second volume of Benjamin de la Borde's 1784 *Voyage pittoresque de la France*. Duparc's engravings were widely reproduced as postcards and appeared in several publications, most notably in S. Sparrow's etching *The Palace of Montmusard with a Distant View of the City of Dijon*, executed sometime between 1784 and the early 1790s. Yves Beauvalot, "À propos de documents inédits, la construction du château de Montmusard à Dijon," *Bulletin de la Société de l'Histoire de l'Art français*, March 3, 1984, 119–67.

40. There is a great deal of literature on the central role of slavery in the economic development of the United States; this largely focuses on slavery and agricultural wealth production. See Eric Williams, *Capitalism and Slavery* (Chapel Hill: University of North Carolina Press, 1994). I follow Gavin Wright in discussing slavery as property that can secure investments; Wright, *Slavery and American Economic Development*. Bonnie Martin offers a case study of slavery as investment property in colonial Louisiana; Bonnie Martin, "Slavery's Invisible Engine: Mortgaging Human Property," *Journal of Southern History* 76, no. 4 (November 2010): 817–66. Jonathan Levy and Sven Beckert discuss the transfer and consolidation of southern agricultural wealth in northern financial networks; Jonathan Levy, *Freaks of Fortune: The Emerging World of Capitalism and Risk in America* (Cambridge, MA: Harvard University Press, 2012); Beckert, *Empire of Cotton*.

41. Davis, *Problem of Slavery*, 382.

42. Cheryl Harris discusses this under the rubric of a possessive individualism: Cheryl I. Harris, "Whiteness as Property," *Harvard Law Review* 106, no. 8 (1993): 1707–91.

43. William Thornton, "Thornton's Outlines of a Constitution for United North and South Columbia [1815]," ed. N. Andrew and N. Cleven, *Hispanic American Historical Review* 12, no. 2 (May 1932): 198–215.

44. Thornton, "Thornton's Outlines of a Constitution," 215.

45. Thornton, "Thornton's Outlines of a Constitution," 210.

3. Drawing the Color Line

1. Max Horkheimer and Theodor W. Adorno, *Dialectic of Enlightenment: Philosophical Fragments*, trans. Edmund Jephcott (Stanford, CA: Stanford University Press, 2002).

2. Manfredo Tafuri, "The Ashes of Jefferson," in *The Sphere and the Labyrinth: Avant Gardes and Architecture from Piranesi to the 1970s*, trans. Pellegrino d'Acierno and Robert Connolly (Cambridge, MA: MIT Press, 1987), 291–303. Tafuri does not actually discuss Thomas Jefferson in this chapter. In what follows, I am referring both to his allegorical use of Jefferson above and to his earlier treatment of Jefferson's "agrarian idealism" in *Architecture and Utopia: Design and Capitalist Development*, trans. Barbara Luigia La Penta (Cambridge, MA: MIT Press, 1976), 24–40.

3. For a nuanced critical analysis of Jefferson's architecture specifically in relation to slavery and racial ideology, see Irene Cheng, "Race and Architectural Geometry: Thomas Jefferson's Octagons, *J19: The Journal of Nineteenth Century Americanists* 3, no. 1 (Spring 2015): 121–30. See also Dell Upton, *Architecture in the United States* (New York: Oxford University Press, 1998), 20–37. Even the revised edition of Richard Guy Wilson's exhibition catalogue, *Thomas Jefferson's Academical Village: The Creation of an Architectural Masterpiece*, rev. ed. (Charlottesville: University of Virginia Press, 2009), touches only lightly on the use of slave labor to build the University of Virginia, in Joseph M. Lasala, Patricia C. Sherwood, and Richard Guy Wilson, "Architecture for Education: Jefferson's Design of the Academical Village," 38–39.

4. George M. Fredrickson emphasizes the continuity between eighteenth-century racial or ethnological typologies, and the explicit racial hierarchies proposed by later white supremacist ideologies. Intriguingly, Fredrickson also suggests different forms of modernization as a possible explanation for distinctions between European anti-Semitism and American ideologies of white supremacy at the end of the nineteenth century. George M. Fredrickson, *Racism: A Short History* (Princeton, NJ: Princeton University Press, 2002), 49–95.

5. On race as lineage prior to 1800, see Michael Banton, *The Idea of Race* (London: Tavistock Publications, 1977), 18–22. On what Ivan Hannaford calls the "first stage in the development of an idea of race" during the European eighteenth century, which includes Johann Friedrich Blumenbach's anthropological classification of racial "vari-

eties," and the philosophical discourse on the "character" of races and nations in David Hume, Immanuel Kant, and Johann Gottlieb Fichte, see Hannaford, *Race: The History of an Idea in the West* (Washington, DC: Woodrow Wilson Center Press, 1996), 187–233. On the institutionalization of race as a category in natural and social sciences in France popularized in the work of Arthur de Gobineau and by the "Gobineau myth" in Germany, see Carole Reynaud-Paligot, "Construction and Circulation of the Notion of 'Race' in the Nineteenth Century," in *The Invention of Race: Scientific and Popular Representations*, ed. Nicolas Bancel, Thomas David, and Dominic Thomas (New York: Routledge, 2014), 87–99. On the passage from history as a "conflict among races" to a historico-biological discourse of degeneration, and subsequently to "the rise of the race-state," see Hannaford, *Race*, 235–76 and 277–324, respectively. For the American context, an important early source is Thomas F. Gossett, *Race: The History of an Idea in America* (Dallas: Southern Methodist University Press, 1963).

6. Ann Laura Stoler, *Race and the Education of Desire: Foucault's History of Sexuality and the Colonial Order of Things* (Durham: Duke University Press, 1995).

7. Michel Foucault, *The History of Sexuality, Volume 1: An Introduction*, trans. Robert Hurley (New York: Random House, 1978), esp. part 5: "Right of Death and Power over Life," 133–59; and in more detail, Michel Foucault, *"Society Must Be Defended": Lectures at the Collège de France, 1975–1976*, trans. David Macey (New York: Picador, 2003).

8. W. E. B. Du Bois, *The Souls of Black Folk*, ed. Henry Louis Gates Jr. and Terri Hume Oliver (New York: W. W. Norton, 1999), 5. As an editorial footnote to this edition explains, Du Bois first made this statement in an address delivered at the first Pan-African Conference in London in 1900 (5n1).

9. W. E. B. Du Bois, "The Conservation of Races," American Negro Academy, *Occasional Papers* 2 (1897), reprinted in Du Bois, *Souls of Black Folk*, 176–77.

10. Du Bois, "Conservation of Races," 178.

11. Du Bois, "Conservation of Races," 178.

12. Kwame Anthony Appiah, "The Uncompleted Argument: Du Bois and the Illusion of Race," in *The Idea of Race*, ed. Robert Bernasconi and Tommy L. Lott (Indianapolis: Hackett, 2000), 118–35. The quote is from W. E. B. Du Bois, "Races," *The Crisis* 2, no. 4 (August 1911): 158, cited in Appiah, "Uncompleted Argument," 130.

13. Du Bois, "Conservation of Races," 181.

14. Alexander Crummell, "Civilization, the Primal Need of the Race," American Negro Academy inaugural address, March 1897, reprinted in Du Bois, *Souls of Black Folk*, 173.

15. Crummell, "Civilization, the Primal Need of the Race," 174.

16. Mabel O. Wilson, *Negro Building: Black Americans in the World of Fairs and Museums* (Berkeley: University of California Press, 2012), esp. 84–190.

17. Crummell, "Civilization, the Primal Need of the Race," 175.

18. See for example the essays and addresses collected in W. E. B. Du Bois, *The*

Education of Black People: Ten Critiques, 1906–1960, ed. Herbert Aptheker (New York: Monthly Review Press, 1973).

19. Alfred L. Brophy, *University, Court, and Slave: Pro-Slavery Thought in Southern Colleges and Courts and the Coming of Civil War* (New York: Oxford University Press, 2016); and Craig Steven Wilder, *Ebony and Ivy: Race, Slavery, and the Troubled History of America's Universities* (New York: Bloomsbury Press, 2013).

20. Du Bois, *Souls of Black Folk*, 127.

21. Friedrich A. Kittler, *Discourse Networks, 1800/1900*, trans. Michael Metteer, with Chris Cullens (Stanford, CA: Stanford University Press, 1990), 370. Du Bois was enrolled as a doctoral student at the University of Berlin from 1892 to 1894, where he was also associated with the Verein für Socialpolitik. On Du Bois's interest in German political history, see Kenneth Barkin, "W. E. B. Du Bois and the Kaiserreich," *Central European History* 31, no. 3 (1998): 155 69. On the German intellectual context, see also Andrew Zimmerman, *Alabama in Africa: Booker T. Washington, the German Empire, and the Globalization of the New South* (Princeton, NJ: Princeton University Press, 2010), 104–11.

22. In his notebooks, Jefferson described a device for installing a system of moveable gilt stars on the dome's interior surface. The stars would be positioned on a blue interior surface by means of a pivoting arc that would accurately plot their position onto the dome's curvature at any given time in the night sky, based on printed astronomical charts. Had it been constructed, the device would have converted the dome into a teaching planetarium through a read-write mechanism that translated two-dimensional information, recorded in the charts, into a three-dimensional model of the celestial sphere on the dome's interior surface. Thomas Jefferson, "Notes and Specifications," pocket memorandum book, University of Virginia, July 18, 1819, page 2, recto and verso, Thomas Jefferson Papers, 38–163, Special Collections, University of Virginia Library, http://ead.lib.virginia.edu/vivaxtf/view?docId=uva-sc/viu00007 .xml#series1.

23. On slavery at the University of Virginia, see the resources collected by the President's Commission on Slavery and the University at http://slavery.virginia.edu/.

24. Thomas Jefferson, *Notes on the State of Virginia* [1785] (New York: Penguin, 1999), 150. See also Peter S. Onuf, "Thomas Jefferson, Race, and National Identity," in Peter S. Onuf, *The Mind of Thomas Jefferson* (Charlottesville: University of Virginia Press, 2007), 205–12.

25. Horkheimer and Adorno, *Dialectic of Enlightenment*, 35–62.

26. On the dumbwaiters at Monticello, see Susan R. Stein, *The Worlds of Thomas Jefferson at Monticello* (New York: Harry N. Abrams, 1993), 60–61, 282–83. On Jefferson's likely encounter with the dumbwaiters at the Café Mécanique, a popular restaurant at the recently transformed Palais Royal, see the editorial note in Thomas Jefferson, *Jefferson's Memorandum Books: Accounts, with Legal Records and Miscellany,*

1767–1826, Volume 1, ed. James A. Bear Jr. and Lucia C. Stanton (Princeton, NJ: Princeton University Press, 1997), 562–63n91. See also Howard C. Rice, *Thomas Jefferson's Paris* (Princeton: Princeton University Press, 1976), 14–18. On Jefferson's devices as intermediary, hybridized "servants" belonging to a media history of "quasi-objects," see Markus Krajewski, *Der Diener: Mediengeschichte einer Figur zwischen König und Klient* (Frankfurt: S. Fischer Verlag, 2010), 436–38. I am grateful to Bernhard Siegert for calling the latter reference to my attention.

27. Immanuel Kant, "An Answer to the Question: What Is Enlightenment? (1784)," trans. James Schmidt, in *What Is Enlightenment? Eighteenth-Century Answers and Twentieth-Century Questions*, ed. James Schmidt (Berkeley: University of California Press, 1996), 63.

28. Margaret Bayard Smith, *The First Forty Years of Washington Society, Portrayed by the Family Letters of Mrs. Samuel Harrison Smith (Margaret Bayard)*, ed. Gaillard Hunt (New York: Charles Scribner's Sons, 1906), 387–88.

29. Information on the provenance of standalone dumbwaiters at Monticello is available at https://www.monticello.org/site/house-and-gardens/dumbwaiters.

30. Isaac Jefferson, *Memoirs of a Monticello Slave, Dictated to Charles Campbell in the 1840s by Isaac, One of Thomas Jefferson's Slaves* (Charlottesville: University of Virginia Press, 1951), 27.

31. Thomas Jefferson, "79. A Bill for the More General Diffusion of Knowledge, 18 June 1779," *Founders Online*, National Archives, https://founders.archives.gov/documents/Jefferson/01-02-02-0132-0004-0079. Also in Julian P. Boyd, ed., *The Papers of Thomas Jefferson*, vol. 2, *1777–18 June 1779* (Princeton, NJ: Princeton University Press, 1950), 526–35. Roy J. Honeywell, *The Educational Work of Thomas Jefferson* (Cambridge, MA: Harvard University Press, 1931), 7–25.

32. Honeywell, *Educational Work of Thomas Jefferson*, 7–25.

33. On Mumford as a historian of technology, see the essays collected in Thomas P. Hughes and Agatha C. Hughes, eds., *Lewis Mumford: Public Intellectual* (New York: Oxford University Press, 1990), in particular, Arthur P. Molella, "Mumford in Historiographical Context," 21–42, and Rosalind Williams, "Lewis Mumford as a Historian of Technology in *Technics and Civilization*," 43–65.

34. Lewis Mumford, *Technics and Civilization* (New York: Harcourt, Brace, 1934), 60.

35. Mumford, *Technics and Civilization*, 63.

36. Mumford, *Technics and Civilization*, 64.

37. Mumford, *Technics and Civilization*, 290.

38. Mumford, *Technics and Civilization*, 408.

39. Harold E. Stearns, ed., *Civilization in the United States: An Inquiry by Thirty Americans* (New York: Harcourt, Brace, 1922).

40. Harold E. Stearns, "Preface," in *Civilization in the United States: An Inquiry by Thirty Americans*, ed. Harold E. Stearns (New York: Harcourt, Brace, 1922), iii.

41. Stearns, "Preface," vii; and Geroid Tanquary Robinson, "Racial Minorities," in *Civilization in the United States: An Inquiry by Thirty Americans*, ed. Harold E. Stearns (New York: Harcourt, Brace, 1922), 351.

42. Robinson, "Racial Minorities," 371.

43. Lewis Mumford, "The City," in *Civilization in the United States: An Inquiry by Thirty Americans*, ed. Harold E. Stearns (New York: Harcourt, Brace, 1922), 3–20.

44. Mumford, "The City," 19.

45. Mumford, "The City," 16.

46. Stearns, "Preface," vii.

47. Charles Flint Kellogg, *NAACP: A History of the National Association for the Advancement of Colored People*, vol. 1, *1909–1920* (Baltimore: Johns Hopkins University Press, 1967), 61.

48. Marshall van Deusen, *J. E. Spingarn* (New York: Twayne Publishers, 1971), 60–62.

49. W. E. B. Du Bois, *The Amenia Conference: An Historic Negro Gathering* (New York: Troutbeck Press, 1925), 13.

50. Lewis Mumford, "The Domain of Troutbeck," in *Sketches from Life: The Autobiography of Lewis Mumford, the Early Years* (New York: Dial Press, 1982), 480–92.

51. Lewis Mumford to Catherine Bauer, August 20, 1933, in Lewis Mumford, *My Works and Days: A Personal Chronicle* (New York: Harcourt Brace Jovanovich, 1979), 310.

52. Mumford to Bauer, August 20, 1933, 310.

53. A full and fascinating account of the second Amenia conference is given in Eben Miller, *Born along the Color Line: The 1933 Amenia Conference and the Rise of a National Civil Rights Movement* (New York: Oxford University Press, 2012), 105–41; on Du Bois's contribution, see 136–37. On tensions between Spingarn and Du Bois, see Van Deusen, *J. E. Spingarn*, 71–72.

54. In 1979 Mumford appended a note to his published correspondence with Bauer that said of Spingarn, "Though he did not in the least share the communism of W. E. B. Du Bois, the outstanding leader of the Negro intellectuals, [Spingarn] admired the quality of his mind." In Mumford, *My Works and Days*, 311.

55. For an excellent summary of Johnson's political activities during this period, see Joan Ockman, "The Figurehead: On Monumentality and Nihilism in Philip Johnson's Life and Work," in *Philip Johnson: The Constancy of Change*, ed. Emmanuel Petit (New Haven, CT: Yale University Press, 2009), 82–109, esp. 85–88. In 1934, Johnson traveled to Baton Rouge in support of the demagogic senator from Louisiana, Huey Long; by September 1939, he was in Poland bearing enthusiastic witness to the German invasion as a correspondent for *Social Justice*, a far-right, anti-Semitic magazine published by the Michigan-based Roman Catholic priest Father Charles Coughlin. A more detailed account that includes the German invitation is found in Franz Schulze, *Philip Johnson:*

Life and Work (New York: Alfred A. Knopf, 1994), 102–46; and on Johnson's relationship with Jimmie Daniels, 93–94. Mark Lamster also describes Johnson's visit to Poland, which included other more skeptical journalists, in *The Man in the Glass House: Philip Johnson, Architect of the Modern Century* (New York: Little, Brown, 2018), 171–80.

56. On Mumford, Bauer, and the MoMA exhibition, see *The International Style: Exhibition 15 and the Museum of Modern Art*, ed. Terence Riley and Stephen Perrella (New York: Rizzoli, 1992), 60–61. On Mumford's view of the exhibition, see Robert Wojtowicz, *Lewis Mumford and American Modernism: Eutopian Theories for Architecture and Urban Planning* (Cambridge, MA: Cambridge University Press, 1996), 91–96; on the housing section, 129–30.

57. Lewis Mumford, "Housing," in *Modern Architecture: International Exhibition* (New York: Museum of Modern Art, 1932), 179, 182. A brief appreciation by Johnson of the German architect Otto Haessler's work in Kassel is appended to Mumford's essay that does not repudiate the latter's social progressivism so much as give it an aesthetic gloss. Though Mumford and Johnson held drastically opposed political views, they did share an interest in the cultural pessimism of thinkers like Werner Sombart and Oswald Spengler.

58. Lewis Mumford, *The South in Architecture* (New York: Harcourt, Brace, 1941), 41.

59. Mumford, *South in Architecture*, 54.

60. Mumford, *South in Architecture*, 55–56.

61. Friedrich Hertz, *Race and Civilization*, trans. A. S. Levetus and W. Entz (London: Kegan Paul, Trench, Trubner, 1928), 1–2.

4. From "Terrestrial Paradise" to "Dreary Waste"

I am grateful to the editors, and my colleagues Diana Martinez, Ginger Nolan, Victoria Bugge Øye, and Eva Schreiner, for their perceptive and incisive commentary.

1. Garnet Joseph Wolseley, *Narrative of the War with China in 1860* (London: Longman, Green, Longman, and Roberts, 1862), 280.

2. On the emergence of race in Western thought and aesthetics, see *Race and the Enlightenment: A Reader*, ed. Emmanuel Chukwudi Eze (Malden, MA: Blackwell, 1997); David Bindman, *Ape to Apollo: Aesthetics and the Idea of Race in the 18th Century* (London: Reaktion Books, 2002); and the present volume. On China specifically, see Walter Demel, "How the Chinese became Yellow: A Contribution to the Early History of Race Theories," in *China in the German Enlightenment*, ed. Bettina Brandt and Daniel Purdy (Toronto: University of Toronto Press, 2016), 20–59.

3. Erik Ringmar, *Liberal Barbarism: The European Destruction of the Palace of the Emperor of China* (New York: Palgrave Macmillan, 2013), 12–13; Marie-Julie Frainais-Maitre, "The Edifying and Curious Letters: Jesuit China and French Philosophy," in *The Chinese Chameleon Revisited: From the Jesuits to Zhang Yimou*, ed. Zheng Yangwen

(Newcastle upon Tyne: Cambridge Scholars Publishing, 2013); Raymond Dawson, *The Chinese Chameleon: An Analysis of European Conceptions of Chinese Civilization* (London: Oxford University Press, 1967), 9–34; William W. Appleton, *A Cycle of Cathay: The Chinese Vogue in England during the Seventeenth and Eighteenth Centuries* (New York: Columbia University Press, 1951), 4–8; and Zhang Longxi, "The Myth of the Other: China in the Eyes of the West," *Critical Inquiry* 15, no. 1 (1988): 116–18.

4. E.g., Spinoza, Leibniz, Voltaire. See Frainais-Maitre, "Edifying and Curious Letters," 38–40, 48–49; Dawson, *Chinese Chameleon*, 44–46, 54–56; and David Porter, *Ideographia: The Chinese Cipher in Early Modern Europe* (Stanford: Stanford University Press, 2001), especially ch. 2.

5. Johann Bernhard Fischer von Erlach, *Entwurf* [*sic*] *Einer Historischen Architektur* (Dortmund: Harenberg Kommunikation, 1978). I rely also on the 1737 English translation by Thomas Lediard, *A Plan of Civil and Historical Architecture* (London: self-published, 1737); and Esther Gordon Dotson, *J. B. Fischer von Erlach: Architecture as Theater in the Baroque Era* (New Haven: Yale University Press, 2012).

6. Fischer von Erlach, *Entwurf*, front matter, n.p.; and Joseph Rykwert, *On Adam's House in Paradise: The Idea of the Primitive Hut in Architectural History* (New York: Museum of Modern Art, 1972).

7. Dotson, *Fischer von Erlach*, 135, 142.

8. It is possible some exclusions stem from rushed production or serve to reduce the conceptual distance between ancient Rome and Fischer's imperial patrons. See Dotson, *Fischer von Erlach*, 142.

9. Fischer von Erlach, *Plan of Civil and Historical Architecture*, A2.

10. Lydia Liu, "Robinson Crusoe's Earthenware Pot," *Critical Inquiry* 25, no. 4 (1999): 749–56; Dotson, *Fischer von Erlach*, 151, 155.

11. Johannes Nieuhof, *Het gezantschap der Neêrlandtsche Oost-Indische Compagnie, aan den grooten Tartarischen Cham, den tegenwoordigen keizer van China* (Amsterdam: Jacob van Meurs, 1665).

12. Fischer von Erlach, *Plan of Civil and Historical Architecture*, A3.

13. Denise Ferreira da Silva, *Toward a Global Idea of Race* (Minneapolis: University of Minnesota Press, 2007).

14. Peter Fenves, "Imagining an Inundation of Australians; or, Leibniz on the Principles of Grace and Race," in *Race and Racism in Modern Philosophy*, ed. Andrew Valls (Ithaca, NY: Cornell University Press, 2005); Longxi, "Myth of the Other," 119–21. On universal-language projects, see Porter, *Ideographia*, ch. 1, and Appleton, *Cycle of Cathay*, 21–30.

15. Jean Denis Attiret, "A Description of the Emperor of China's Gardens and Pleasure Houses near Pe-King," in *Miscellaneous Pieces Relating to the Chinese*, ed. Thomas Percy (London: R. and J. Dodsley, 1762), 154, 159, 167, 192.

16. Attiret, 179–81, 198.

17. Appleton, *Cycle of Cathay*, 14–16, 91–94, 151–53; Liu, "Robinson Crusoe's Earthenware Pot," 731–32; Longxi, "Myth of the Other," 122; David Porter, "Monstrous Beauty: Eighteenth-Century Fashion and the Aesthetics of the Chinese Taste," *Eighteenth-Century Studies* 35, no. 3 (2002): 396, 400; and Porter, *Ideographia*, ch. 4.

18. On chinoiserie, see Dawn Jacobson, *Chinoiserie* (London: Phaidon, 1993); Hugh Honour, *Chinoiserie: The Vision of Cathay* (London: J. Murray, 1961); David Porter, *The Chinese Taste in Eighteenth-Century England* (Cambridge, MA: Cambridge University Press, 2010); and Porter, *Ideographia*, ch. 3. On Chambers, see Honour, *Chinoiserie*, 154–56; R. C. Bald, "Sir William Chambers and the Chinese Garden," *Journal of the History of Ideas* 11, no. 3 (1950); and Porter, *Ideographia* and *Chinese Taste*.

19. William Chambers, preface to *Designs of Chinese Buildings, Furniture, Dresses, Machines, and Utensils* (London: published for the author, 1757), n.p. Possible sources date back to the 1680s; see Honour, *Chinoiserie*, 145–47; and John Harris's introduction to the 1972 edition of William Chambers's *A Dissertation on Oriental Gardening* (Farnborough: Gregg, 1972).

20. Chambers, preface to *Designs*, n.p.; and Appleton, *Cycle of Cathay*, 146.

21. Chambers, *Designs*, 17–19; and Bindman, *Ape to Apollo*, 58–60. On "nature" in readings of China, see Porter, *Ideographia*, 170–71.

22. William Chambers, *A Dissertation on Oriental Gardening* (London: W. Griffin, 1772), ii, iv-viii, x, 105–6.

23. See Bald, "Sir William Chambers and the Chinese Garden," 308.

24. Chambers, *Dissertation*, 39–43, 75–76.

25. Chambers, *Dissertation*, 31–37, 104.

26. Jean-François de Bastide, "The Little House: An Architectural Seduction" (New York: Princeton Architectural Press, 1995); and G. B. Piranesi, "Parere su L'architettura" [1765], *Oppositions*, no. 26 (1984).

27. Porter, "Monstrous Beauty," 403–5.

28. Ferreira da Silva, *Toward a Global Idea of Race*.

29. Johann Friedrich Blumenbach, *The Anthropological Treatises* (Boston: Longwood Press, 1978), 71–73, 81, 98–100, 107, 119.

30. Bindman, *Ape to Apollo*, 197–201. The absence of "slanting eyes" is debatable.

31. Catherine Pagani, "Chinese Material Culture and British Perceptions of China in the Mid-Nineteenth Century," in *Colonialism and the Object: Empire, Material Culture, and the Museum*, ed. T. J. Barringer and Tom Flynn (London: Routledge, 1998), 33, 38; and Jacobson, *Chinoiserie*, 178, 183, 199.

32. Ringmar, *Liberal Barbarism*; Wolseley, *Narrative*, 278–81; and Robert James Leslie McGhee, *How We Got to Pekin: A Narrative of the Campaign in China of 1860* (London: Richard Bentley, 1862), 289.

33. Ringmar, *Liberal Barbarism*, 18.

34. Johann Gottfried von Herder, *Reflections on the Philosophy of the History of*

Mankind, trans. T. O. Churchill (Chicago: University of Chicago Press, 1968), xxiv, xvii–xxi, 99, 103; and Johann Gottfried von Herder, *On World History: An Anthology*, ed. Hans Adler and Ernest A. Menze, trans. Ernest A. Menze and Michael Palma (Armonk, NY: M. E. Sharpe, 1997), 231–34.

35. Georg Wilhelm Friedrich Hegel, "Lectures on the Philosophy of History" [1822–28], in *Race and the Enlightenment: A Reader*, ed. Emmanuel Chukwudi Eze, 110–11, 121, 143–46. This same supposed isolation was seen as an asset in the Jesuit era; see Porter, *Ideographia*, 47–48, or Chambers's discussion in the *Designs* of how the Chinese "formed their own manners," from Chambers, preface to *Designs*, n.p.

36. See Ferreira da Silva, *Toward a Global Idea of Race*, 69–90. On trade ambitions, see Porter, *Ideographia*, 245.

37. Dawson, *Chinese Chameleon*, 65–71.

38. Johann Gottfried von Herder, *Outlines of a Philosophy of the History of Man*, trans. T. O. Churchill (London, 1800), 296.

39. Robert Fortune, *Three Years' Wanderings in the Northern Provinces of China* (London: J. Murray, 1847), 5; G. N. Wright, preface to *The Chinese Empire Illustrated* (London: London Printing and Pub. Co., ca. 1858), n.p.

40. See Porter, *Ideographia*, 240.

41. McGhee, *How We Got to Pekin*, 283–89; and Attiret, "Description of the Emperor of China's Gardens," 181, 185. McGhee's account does not describe him as directly participating in any arson or looting. However, even if he only served as a witness, he might still be viewed as a participant for his role in providing support to the soldiers who set the fires.

42. Fortune, *Three Years' Wanderings*, 9.

43. Fortune, 280–83, 287–88; and Herder, *On World History*, 235. Wolseley would become famous for leading the Third Anglo-Ashanti War (1873–1874), which involved the similar burning of Kumasi.

44. See Ringmar, *Liberal Barbarism*, 9, 82.

5. Henry Van Brunt and White Settler Colonialism in the Midwest

Epigraph. Henry Van Brunt, "Architecture in the West," *Atlantic Monthly*, December 1889, 772.

1. Previous studies tended to use European architectural theory as a starting point for constructing a narrative of the growth and development of a bona fide indigenous style of modern architecture in the United States. See, for example, David Watkin's early monograph *A History of Western Architecture* (London: Laurence King, 2015); Alan Colquhoun's *Modern Architecture* (Oxford: Oxford University Press, 2002); Kenneth Frampton's *Modern Architecture: A Critical History* (London: Thames and Hudson, 1985); and Panayotis Tournikiotis's *The Historiography of Modern Architecture* (Cambridge, MA: MIT Press, 1999).

2. Martin Berger, *Sight Unseen: Whiteness and American Visual Culture* (Berkeley: University of California Press, 2005).

3. Berger, *Sight Unseen*, 42–80.

4. Henry Van Brunt, "Architecture in the West," in *Architecture and Society: Selected Essay of Henry Van Brunt*, ed. William A. Coles (Cambridge, MA: Harvard University Press, 1969), 181.

5. Viollet-le-Duc pioneered an ethnographical history of architectural style in the 1870s; his *Histoire de l'Habitation Huamine* (1876) illustrated the parallel historical development of racial typologies and vernacular typologies through time. This narrative visualizes the physiognomic effects of the universal principles of nature that Viollet-le-Duc believed structured the evolution of all vernacular forms in cultural history. See Charles L. Davis, "Viollet-le-Duc and the Body: The Metaphorical Integrations of Race and Style Theory in Structural Rationalism," *Architectural Research Quarterly* 14, no. 4 (2010): 341–48.

6. Eugène-Emmanuel Viollet-le-Duc, *Discourses on Architecture*, trans. Henry Van Brunt (Boston: James R. Osgood, 1875).

7. See Charles N. Glaab, *Kansas City and the Railroads: Community Policy in the Growth of a Regional Metropolis* (1962; repr., Lawrence: University Press of Kansas, 1993); and Terry Lynch, *The Railroads of Kansas City* (Boulder, CO: Pruett Publishing, 1984).

8. Thomas L. Karnes, *William Gilpin: Western Nationalist* (Austin: University of Texas Press, 1970), 104.

9. William Gilpin, *The Cosmopolitan Railway: Compacting and Fusing Together All the World's Continents* (San Francisco: The History Company, 1890).

10. Gilpin, *Cosmopolitan Railway*, 125.

11. Gilpin, *Cosmopolitan Railway*, 127.

12. Van Brunt's essays discussed in this chapter have been reprinted in Henry Van Brunt, *Architecture and Society: Selected Essays of Henry Van Brunt*, ed. William A. Coles (Cambridge, MA: Harvard University Press, 1969); "On the Present Condition and Prospects of Architecture" (1886) appears on pages 150–58; "Architecture of the West" (1889) appears on pages 180–94; and "Two Interpreters of National Architecture" (1897) appears on pages 359–73.

13. Van Brunt, *Architecture and Society*, 158.

14. Van Brunt, *Architecture and Society*, 159.

15. Van Brunt, *Architecture and Society*, 160.

16. Van Brunt, *Architecture and Society*, 160–66.

17. Van Brunt, *Architecture and Society*, 160.

18. Van Brunt, *Architecture and Society*, 161.

19. Van Brunt, *Architecture and Society*, 164: "These revivals, as I have said, have found a large and by no means an unintelligent expression in the United States. But the

national genius of our architects and their freedom from the tyranny of historic precedent have encouraged them to a far wider range of experiment in architectural forms.
Out of these experiments hitherto there have as yet come no definite promises for art."

20. Van Brunt, *Architecture and Society*, 181.

21. Van Brunt, *Architecture and Society*, 181.

22. Van Brunt, *Architecture and Society*, 182.

23. Van Brunt, *Architecture and Society*, 187.

24. Van Brunt, *Architecture and Society*, 176. Van Brunt suggests that Richardson's
interpretation of the Romanesque style departed from any known European style of
the day. He states, "He was fortunate enough to hit upon an undeveloped style, full of
capacity, picturesque, romantic; its half-savage strength beguiled by traces of refinement inherited from the luxury of the late Roman Empire."

25. James F. O'Gorman, *H. H. Richardson: Architectural Forms for an American Society*
(Chicago: University of Chicago Press, 1987).

26. Thomas Hubka, "The Picturesque in the Design Method of H. H. Richardson,"
in *H. H. Richardson: The Architect, His Peers, and Their Era*, ed. Maureen Meister
(Cambridge, MA: MIT Press, 1999), 2–35.

27. Janet Greenstein Potter, *Great American Railroad Stations* (New York: John
Wiley and Sons, 1996), 9–13.

28. See a description and illustration of this station in Potter, *Great American
Railroad Stations*, 326–27.

29. The placement of a clock tower was especially prominent in Van Brunt's design
for the Ogden, Utah, station; the only other high point in the town was a clock tower
at city hall.

30. "Our New Depot," *Cheyenne Daily Sun*, June 14, 1885.

31. See William John Hennessey, "The Architectural Works of Henry Van Brunt,"
PhD diss., Columbia University, 1979, 188–213.

32. See Joanna Merwood-Salisbury, "Western Architecture: Regionalism and Race
in the Inland Architect," in *Chicago Architecture: Histories, Revisions, Alternatives*, ed.
Charles Waldheim and Katerina Ruedi Ray (Chicago: University of Chicago Press,
2005), 3–14.

33. "A Historical Society," *Kansas City Journal*, December 27, 1896, 3.

6. The "New Birth of Freedom"

1. Kirk Savage, *Standing Soldiers, Kneeling Slaves: Race, War, and Monument in
Nineteenth-Century America* (Princeton NJ: Princeton University Press, 1997), 3.

2. Melissa Dabakis, "Ain't I a Woman? Anne Whitney, Edmonia Lewis, and the
Iconography of Emancipation," in *Seeing High and Low: Representing Social Conflict in
American Visual Culture*, ed. Patricia A. Johnston (Berkeley, CA: University of
California Press, 2006), 84–102. On the context of Whitney's work, see Wayne Craven,

Sculpture in America (Newark: University of Delaware Press, 1984); and Charmaine A. Nelson, *The Color of Stone: Sculpting the Black Female Subject in Nineteenth-Century America* (Minneapolis: University of Minnesota Press, 2007).

3. Ronald G. Walters, *The Antislavery Appeal: American Abolitionism after 1830* (Baltimore: Johns Hopkins University Press, 1976); Timothy McCarthy and John Stauffer, eds., *Prophets of Protest: Reconsidering the History of American Abolitionism* (New York: New Press, 2006); and Mark A. Noll, *The Civil War as a Theological Crisis* (Chapel Hill: University of North Carolina, 2006).

4. Dabakis, "Ain't I a Woman?," 90.

5. On nineteenth-century stereotypes of blackness and whiteness, see George M. Frederickson, *The Black Image in the White Mind: The Debate on Afro-American Character and Destiny, 1817–1914* (New York: Harper and Row, 1971); Alexander Saxton, *The Rise and Fall of the White Republic: Class Politics and Mass Culture in Nineteenth-Century America* (London: Verso, 1990); Reynolds J. Scott-Childress, ed., *Race and the Production of Modern American Nationalism* (New York: Garland, 1999).

6. "A Word about the Statues," *New Path* 2, no. 6 (June 1865): 104.

7. Quoted in Dabakis, "Ain't I a Woman?," 92.

8. In the wake of these criticisms, Whitney reworked the face, hands, and feet of the statue, making the cheekbones and nose broader and the lips fuller. However, she was not satisfied with the result, and the statue was never realized in marble. The plaster model was destroyed sometime after 1874.

9. "Association for the Advancement of Truth in Art," *New Path* 1, no. 1 (May 1863): 11–12; *North American Review* 98, no. 202 (January 1864): 303. On the Ruskinian Gothic tradition in the United States, see Roger B. Stein, *John Ruskin and Aesthetic Thought in America, 1840–1900* (Cambridge, MA: Harvard University Press, 1967); Linda S. Ferber and William H. Gerdts, *The New Path: Ruskin and the American Pre-Raphaelites* (Brooklyn, NY: Brooklyn Museum, 1985); Michael W. Brooks, "Ruskin's Influence in America," in *John Ruskin and Victorian Architecture* (New Brunswick: Rutgers University Press, 1987), 277–97; and Lauren Weingarden, "Gothic Naturalism and the Ruskinian Critical Tradition in America," in *Louis H. Sullivan and a Nineteenth-Century Poetics of Naturalized Architecture* (London: Ashgate Press, 2009), 71–96.

10. "Miss Hosmer's Statue of Zenobia," *New Path* 2, no. 4 (April 1865): 49.

11. "The National Academy of Design—Fortieth Annual Exhibition," *New Path* 2, no. 6 (June 1865): 97.

12. "Miss Hosmer's Statue of Zenobia," *New Path* 2, no. 4 (April 1865): 54.

13. James Fergusson, "Ethnography as Applied to Architectural Art: North America," *History of Architecture in All Countries from the Earliest Times to the Present Day*, 4 vols. (London, 1862–1867), 436.

14. Fergusson, "Ethnography as Applied," 436.

15. Publication of the *Crayon* was supported by the National Academy of Design; with William J. Stillman, Asher B. Durand's son John Durand was the editor. Stephen L. Dyson, *The Last Amateur: The Life of William J. Stillman* (Albany: State University of New York Press, 2014).

16. "Manufacturing Interests," *Crayon* 2 (July–December 1855): 136.

17. On the history of the National Academy of Design, see Thomas S. Cummings, *Historic Annals of the National Academy of Design, New York Drawing Association, etc., With Occasional Dottings by the Way-side, from 1825 to the Present Time* (Philadelphia: G. W. Childs, 1861); "The National Academy of Design National Academy Notes Including the Complete Catalogue of the Spring Exhibition," *National Academy of Design*, no. 4 (1884), 127–38; and Eliot Candee Clark, *History of the National Academy of Design, 1825–1953* (New York: Columbia Press, 1954).

18. Clark, *History of the National Academy of Design*, 68–75.

19. On the Gothic Revival in the United States, see Leland M. Roth, "Age of Enterprise 1865–1885," in *A Concise History of American Architecture* (New York: Harper and Row, 1979), 126–37; "Victorian Gothic," in *American Architecture, Volume 2: 1860–1976*, ed. Marcus Whiffen and Frederick Koeper (Cambridge, MA: MIT Press, 1983): 212–15; and Michael J. Lewis, *The Gothic Revival* (New York: Thames and Hudson, 2002), 73–106.

20. "Church of All Souls," *Crayon* 5 (1858): 20. On Mould, see David Van Zanten, "Jacob Wrey Mould: Echoes of Owen Jones and the High Victorian Styles in New York, 1853–1865," *Journal of the Society of Architectural Historians* 28, no. 1 (March 1969): 41–57.

21. "National Academy of Design," *Architects and Mechanics Journal*, March 23, 1861, 245. See also Cummings, *Historic Annals of the National Academy of Design*, 335–36; Clark, *History of the National Academy of Design*, 75–87; and Sarah Bradford Landau, *P. B. Wight, Architect, Contractor, and Critic, 1835–1925* (Chicago: Art Institute of Chicago, 1981), 9–18.

22. "New National Academy of Design; Laying of the Corner Stone with Special Ceremonies," *New York Times*, October 22, 1863. See also "Our Streets in an Architectural Point of View: The New Academy of Design," *New York Weekly Review*, January 14, 1865, 3; "National Academy of Design," *New York Times*, April 28, 1865; and "The National Academy of Design," *Harper's Weekly*, June 3, 1865.

23. Review of *National Academy of Design*, by P. B. Wight, *North American Review* 103, no. 213 (October 1866): 587.

24. "Medieval Gothic," *Crayon* 3 (1856): 288; and Leopold Eidlitz, "Christian Architecture," *Crayon* 5 (1858): 53.

25. Horatio Greenough, "American Architecture," *Crayon* 2 (1855): 224–26. On the racial basis of nineteenth-century organic theories of architecture, see Charles L. Davis II, "Viollet-le-Duc and the Body: The Metaphorical Integrations of Race and Style in

Structural Rationalism," *Architectural Research Quarterly* 14, no. 4 (2010): 341–48; and Irene Cheng, "Structural Racialism in Modern Architectural Theory" in this volume.

26. See for example, Steven Hoelscher, "The White Pillared Past: Landscapes of Memory and Race in the American South," in *Landscape and Race in the United States*, ed. Richard H. Schein (London: Routledge, 2006), 139–61.

27. On the centrality of the Aryan myth in nineteenth-century America, see Reginald Horsman, *Race and Manifest Destiny: The Origins of American Racial Anglo-Saxonism* (Cambridge, MA: Harvard University Press, 1981); and Richard Slotkin, *The Fatal Environment: The Myth of the Frontier in the Age of Industrialization, 1800–1890* (New York: Atheneum, 1985).

28. Theodore Roosevelt, *The Winning of the West*, 4 vols. (New York: G. P. Putnam's Sons, 1889–1896).

29. I have described the Chicago architect William Le Baron Jenney's explicit references to theories of Aryanism in Joanna Merwood-Salisbury, *Chicago 1890: The Skyscraper and the City* (Chicago: University of Chicago Press, 2009), 24–28.

30. Martin Berger, "Museum Architecture and the Imperialism of Whiteness," in *Sight Unseen: Whiteness and American Visual Culture* (Berkeley: University of California Press, 2005), 81–121.

31. Berger, *Sight Unseen*, 97–98.

32. On the growth of New York City in the early nineteenth century and its dependence on the southern cotton economy, see Edward K. Spann, *The New Metropolis: New York City, 1840–1857* (New York: Columbia University Press, 1981); Edwin G. Burrows and Mike Wallace, *Gotham: A History of New York City to 1898* (New York: Oxford University Press, 1999); David M. Scobey, *Empire City: The Making and Meaning of the New York City Landscape* (Philadelphia: Temple University Press, 2002); and Sven Beckert, "Slavery Takes Command," in *Empire of Cotton: A Global History* (New York: Alfred A. Knopf, 2014).

33. "Dr. Cheever at Home," *Independent*, vol. 13, no. 668, September 19, 1861, 4.

34. "Theory and Practice—A Negro in Dr. Cheever's Church," *New York Herald*, January 15, 1860; and "Religious Intelligence. City Churches," *New York Herald*, February 19, 1860, 5 (asterisks in the original).

35. On the public opinion of New Yorkers during the Civil War, see Philip Forner, *Business and Slavery: The New York Merchants and the Irrepressible Conflict* (Chapel Hill: University of North Carolina Press, 1941); Ernest McKay, *The Civil War and New York City* (New York: Syracuse University, 1990); Edward K. Spann, *Gotham at War: New York City, 1860–65* (New York: Scholarly Resources, 2002); and Steven H. Jaffe, *New York at War: Four Centuries of Combat, Fear, and Intrigue in Gotham* (New York: Basic Books, 2012), 141–76.

36. Iver Bernstein, *The New York City Draft Riots: Their Significance for American Society and Politics in the Age of Civil War* (New York: Oxford University Press, 1990).

37. On the formation of this social and political class, see Sven Beckert, *The Monied Metropolis: New York City and the Consolidation of the American Bourgeoisie, 1850–96* (Cambridge: Cambridge University Press, 1993). The Union League Club was formed in 1863 with the explicit aim of providing leadership for the Unionist cause in New York City. The Rev. Henry Bellows, minister of All Souls Unitarian Church, was one of the founding members. On the Union League Club and the performance of anti-slavery civic ceremonies in Union Square during the Civil War, see Joanna Merwood-Salisbury, *Design for the Crowd: Patriotism and Protest in Union Square* (Chicago: University of Chicago Press, 2019), 52–69.

38. *The National Academy of Design. Ceremonies on the Occasion of Laying the Cornerstone, October 21st 1863 and the Inauguration of the Building April 27th 1865* (New York: Miller and Matthews, 1865), 25.

39. "An Important Gothic Building," *New Path* 2, no. 2 (June 1864): 18.

40. "An Important Gothic Building," *New Path*, 29–30.

41. "Architecture (The Oxford Museum)," *Crayon* 6, no. 8 (August 1859), 251. Calvert Vaux and Jacob Wrey Mould later employed a more sedate version of the Gothic Revival style for the American Museum of Natural History on Central Park West (1874–1877).

42. "An Important Gothic Building," *New Path*, 30.

43. Anthony E. Kaye, "Nationalism and Abolitionist Politics in Great Britain and the United States," *Fernand Braudel Center Review* 35, no. 2 (2012): 158.

44. Karl Marx, *Capital*, vol. 1 (1867, reprint; New York: Penguin Books, 1990), 415. Marx saw the results of the war close up, as the New York–based correspondent for an Austrian newspaper. He was vocal in his belief that the end of slavery in the United States, and the destruction of the power of the slave-owning class, would lead to fur-ther revolutions advancing the cause of workers. See Karl Marx and Frederick Engels, *The Civil War in the United States*, ed. Richard Enmale (New York: International Press, 1937).

45. Frederick Jackson Turner, "The Significance of the Frontier in American History. A Paper Read at the Meeting of the American Historical Association in Chicago, July 12, 1893," in *The Significance of the Frontier in American History* (New York: Henry Holt, 1920); and Roosevelt, *Winning of the West* (1889–1896).

46. David Roediger, *Colored White: Transcending the Racial Past* (Berkeley: University of California Press, 2003).

47. I explore this later phase of Wight's career in Joanna Merwood-Salisbury, "The Gothic Revival and the Chicago School: From Naturalistic Ornament to Constructive Expression," in *Skyscraper Gothic: Medieval Style and Modernist Buildings*, ed. Kevin D. Murphy and Lisa Reilly (Charlottesville: University of Virginia Press, 2017), 88–111.

7. Structural Racialism in Modern Architectural Theory

1. See, for example, Esra Akcan, *Architecture in Translation: Germany, Turkey, and the Modern House* (Durham: Duke University Press, 2012); Tom Avermaete, Serhat Karakayali, and Marion von Osten, *Colonial Modern: Aesthetics of the Past—Rebellions for the Future* (London: Black Dog, 2010); and Itohan Osayimwese, *Colonialism and Modern Architecture in Germany* (Pittsburgh, PA: University of Pittsburgh Press, 2017).

2. A few important exceptions should be noted, including Mark Crinson, *Empire Building: Orientalism and Victorian Architecture* (London: Routledge, 1996) and Charles L. Davis II, "Tracing the Integrations of Race and Style Theory in Nineteenth-Century Architectural Style Debates: E. E. Viollet-Le-Duc and Gottfried Semper, 1834–1890" (PhD diss., University of Pennsylvania, 2009). On "racialism" versus racism, see Kwame Anthony Appiah, "Racisms," in *Anatomy of Racism*, ed. David Theo Goldberg (Minneapolis: University of Minnesota Press, 1990), 3.

3. On nineteenth-century historicism, see Alan Colquhoun, "Three Kinds of Historicism," in *Theorizing a New Agenda for Architecture: An Anthology of Architectural Theory, 1965—1995*, ed. Kate Nesbitt (New York: Princeton Architectural Press, 1997), 202–9; Barry Bergdoll, *Leon Vaudoyer: Historicism in the Age of Industry* (Cambridge, MA: MIT Press, 1994); and Mari Hvattum, *Gottfried Semper and the Problem of Historicism* (Cambridge: Cambridge University Press, 2004).

4. By "race science" I mean not just studies exclusively focused on race, but also work in the fields of philology, ethnography, biology, and physical anthropology that took race as a central organizing paradigm.

5. For a general overview on the history of race, see George Fredrickson, *Racism: A Short History* (Princeton, NJ: Princeton University Press, 2002). On the period under examination here, see Hannah Augstein, *Race: The Origins of an Idea, 1760–1850* (Bristol: St. Augustine's Press, 2000).

6. Johann Friedrich Blumenbach, "On the Natural Variety of Mankind," in *The Idea of Race*, ed. Robert Bernasconi and Tommy Lee Lott (Indianapolis: Hackett Publishing, 2000), 27.

7. Winthrop D. Jordan, *White over Black: American Attitudes toward the Negro, 1550–1812* (Chapel Hill: University of North Carolina Press, 1968), 243.

8. Nancy Stepan, *The Idea of Race in Science: Great Britain, 1800–1960* (London: Macmillan, 1982), 4. See also Jennifer Pitts, *A Turn to Empire: The Rise of Imperial Liberalism in Britain and France* (Princeton, NJ: Princeton University Press, 2006), 12–21.

9. In contrast, in Germany (which arrived late to the imperial contest) anthropology was more liberal and tended to focus on material archaeology and culture rather than racial classification, at least in the period before the twentieth century. H. Glenn Penny, "Traditions in the German Language," in *A New History of Anthropology*, ed. Henrika

Kuklick (London: Blackwell, 2008), 79–95. This emphasis on material archaeology is reflected in the work of German architects who most closely engaged with anthropology, such as Gottfried Semper. On Semper's relation to nineteenth-century ethnography, see Harry Francis Mallgrave, "Gustav Klemm and Gottfried Semper: The Meeting of Ethnological and Architectural Theory," *RES: Journal of Anthropology and Aesthetics* 9 (Spring 1985): 69–79; and Davis, "Tracing the Integrations," chapter 3.

10. Hannah Arendt, *The Origins of Totalitarianism*, 1st ed. (New York: Harcourt, Brace, Jovanovich, 1973), 159–61.

11. Sylvia Lavin, *Quatremère de Quincy and the Invention of a Modern Language of Architecture* (Cambridge, MA: MIT Press, 1992), 63.

12. Antoine-Chrysostome Quatremère de Quincy, "Architecture," in *Encyclopédie Méthodique d'Architecture* (1788). Translated and excerpted in "Extracts from the *Encyclopédie Méthodique d'Architecture*," *9II 7* (1985). 28–29.

13. On the racial themes in Freeman, see Alex Bremner and Jonathan Conlin, "History as Form: Architecture and Liberal Anglican Thought in the Writings of E. A. Freeman," *Modern Intellectual History* 8, no. 2 (2011): 299–326; and Crinson, *Empire Building*, 39–42.

14. Edward A. Freeman, *A History of Architecture* (London: J. Masters, 1849), 15. Freeman probably adapted his typology from Quatremère de Quincy through reading Thomas Hope's *An Historical Essay on Architecture* (London: J. Murray, 1835). However Hope emphasized the transmission of these inherited types by "habit" rather than instinct.

15. Freeman, *History*, 12.

16. Freeman, *History*, 150, 212, 298–99. Although Freeman believed the Gothic embodied the genius of the Teutonic Northman, he did allow that the style had multiple origins: He believed, for instance, that the pointed arch was probably adapted by the "Teutonic races" from Arabic sources—but whereas in the hands of the Arabs, the pointed arch remained in a "dead unproductive state," the Northmen enabled it to attain perfection of expression by endowing it with "true life and vigour" (313, 27).

17. Quoted in Martin Bressani, *Architecture and the Historical Imagination: Eugène-Emmanuel Viollet-le-Duc, 1814–1879* (London: Ashgate, 2014), 119.

18. On Winckelmann as a proto-racial-aesthetic theorist, see David Bindman, *Ape to Apollo: Aesthetics and the Idea of Race in the 18th Century* (Ithaca, NY: Cornell University Press, 2002), chapter 1.

19. Eric Michaud, "Barbarian Invasions and the Racialization of Art History," *October* (January 1, 2012): 69.

20. I mean liberal in the broad sense of embracing reform and progress, though one could also speculate on the relationship between Jones's aesthetic reformism and the political liberalism being articulated simultaneously by John Stuart Mill and others. On liberal philosophy and race, see Uday Singh Mehta, *Liberalism and Empire: A Study*

in Nineteenth-Century British Liberal Thought (Chicago: University of Chicago Press, 1999); and Pitts, *Turn to Empire*.

21. Owen Jones, *The Grammar of Ornament* (London: Bernard Quaritch, 1868), plate 36, 2.

22. On Viollet-le-Duc's engagement with race science and anthropology, see Bressani, *Architecture*, chapter 10; Laurent Baridon, "Anthropologie," in *L'imaginaire scientifique de Viollet-le-Duc* (Paris: Editions L'Harmattan, 1996); Davis, "Tracing the Integrations," chapter 4; and Charles L. Davis II, "Viollet-Le-Duc and the Body: The Metaphorical Integrations of Race and Style in Structural Rationalism," *Architectural Research Quarterly* 14, no. 4 (2010): 341–48.

23. Eugène-Emmanuel Viollet-le-Duc, *The Habitations of Man in All Ages*, trans. Benjamin Bucknall (Boston: J. R. Osgood, 1875), 69.

24. Viollet-le-Duc, *Habitations*, 45, 122–23.

25. The term "racial signature" is from Lauren M. O'Connell, "A Rational, National Architecture: Viollet-Le-Duc's Modest Proposal for Russia," *Journal of the Society of Architectural Historians* 52, no. 4 (1993): 442.

26. Viollet-le-Duc, *Cours d'esthétique appliquée à l'histoire de l'art* (1864), quoted in Baridon, "Anthropologie", 54.

27. Viollet-le-Duc, *Habitations*, 392, 394.

28. Viollet-le-Duc, *Habitations*, 393.

29. Viollet-le-Duc, *L'art russe; ses origines, ses éléments constitutifs, son apogée, son avenir* (Paris: Ve A. Morel, 1877. See O'Connell, "Rational, National Architecture," 436–52.

30. Viollet-le-Duc, "Style," 246.

31. Sir George Gilbert Scott, *Lectures on the Rise and Development of Mediæval Architecture* (London: John Murray, 1879): 14, 17.

32. Eugène-Emmanuel Viollet-le-Duc, *The Foundations of Architecture: Selections from the Dictionnaire Raisonné*, trans. Kenneth D. Whitehead (New York: G. Braziller, 1990), 71.

33. On the rise of various Nordic myths in the nineteenth century and earlier, see Jacques Barzun, *Race: A Study in Superstition* (New York: Harper & Row, 1965), chapter 2; Leon Poliakov, *The Aryan Myth: A History of Racist and Nationalist Ideas in Europe* (New York: Barnes & Noble Books, 1996); Reginald Horsman, *Race and Manifest Destiny: Origins of American Racial Anglo-Saxonism*, reprint edition (Cambridge, MA: Harvard University Press, 1981).

34. Stepan, *Race Science*, 93.

35. For a summary, see Barzun, *Race*, chapter 2.

36. Michaud, "Barbarian Invasions," 60.

37. Gobineau, *Inequality*, 25. Gobineau allowed that intermixing of races could lead to artistic achievement. On beneficial fusions, see Stepan, *Race Science*, 105.

38. Michaud, "Barbarian Invasions," 60.

39. James Fergusson, *A History of Architecture in All Countries from the Earliest Times to the Present Day*, vol. 1 (London: John Murray, 1865), 73.

40. Fergusson, *History*, 212.

41. Tapati Guha-Thakurta, *Monuments, Objects, Histories: Institutions of Art in Colonial and Post-Colonial India* (New York: Columbia University Press, 2004), 16–17.

42. Bressani, *Architecture*, 345–65.

43. Quoted in Bressani, *Architecture*, 354.

44. "[T]he Aryan-Hellenes, Semitized in Greece, found themselves in conditions of such intermingling as to have produced arts superior to what the world had seen or will ever see again." Viollet-le-Duc, eighth *Entretien*, quoted in Bressani, *Architecture*, 350.

45. Baridon, "Anthropologic," 52.

46. Bressani cites precedents for these ideas not only in Gobineau but also Michelet, Renan, and Ramée. Bressani, *Architecture*, 355.

47. Viollet-le-Duc, *Habitations*, 121, 182.

48. Regarding the reception of Viollet-le-Duc's *L'art russe*, where he analyzed the racial composition of the Russian population in order to argue for a style that would be true to its national origin, Lauren M. O'Connell writes that Viollet-le-Duc's racial argument was roundly criticized in the French press. See O'Connell, "Rational, National Architecture," 442n27.

49. Joanna Merwood-Salisbury, "Western Architecture: Regionalism and Race in the Inland Architect," in *Chicago Architecture: Histories, Revisions, Alternatives*, ed. Charles Waldheim and Katerina Ruedi Ray (Chicago: University of Chicago Press, 2005), 3–14.

50. Johannes Fabian has argued that nineteenth-century anthropologists transposed the spatial dispersal of human groups onto a temporal model adopted from the natural scientists. Past and living cultures "were irrevocably placed on a temporal slope, a stream of Time—some upstream, others downstream." Fabian locates this temporalization at the origin of anthropologists' ideas about civilization, evolution, development, modernization, and acculturation. Johannes Fabian, *Time and the Other: How Anthropology Makes Its Object* (New York: Columbia University Press, 1983), 11–17.

51. On this point, see Pitts, *Turn to Empire*, 17–18.

52. Fergusson, *History*, 76–77.

53. Fergusson, *History*, 76, 52.

54. Robert J. C. Young, *Colonial Desire: Hybridity in Theory, Culture and Race* (London: Routledge, 1995), 52.

55. Jones, *Grammar*, 2.

56. David Theo Goldberg, *The Racial State* (Malden, MA: Wiley-Blackwell, 2001).

57. Adolf Loos, "Ornament and Crime," in *Programs and Manifestoes on 20th-Century*

Architecture, ed. Ulrich Conrads, trans. Michael Bullock (Cambridge, MA: MIT Press, 1970), 19. On the publication details of Loos's essay, see Christopher Long, "The Origins and Context of Adolf Loos's 'Ornament and Crime,'" *Journal of the Society of Architectural Historians* 68, no. 2 (June 1, 2009): 200–223. On the influence of criminal anthropology, especially the work of Cesare Lombroso, on Loos, see Jimena Canales and Andrew Herscher, "Criminal Skins: Tattoos and Modern Architecture in the Work of Adolf Loos," *Architectural History* 48 (January 2005): 235–56. Canales and Herscher suggest Max Nordau as one source for Loos's language of degeneration.

58. Loos, quoted in Janet Stewart, *Fashioning Vienna: Adolf Loos's Cultural Criticism* (London: Routledge, 2000), 65.

59. Loos, in his journal *Das Andere: A Journal for the Introduction of Western Culture into Austria*, 1903, quoted in Stewart, *Fashioning*, 48–49.

60. Stewart notes that Loos is relatively silent about the two largest minorities in Austria-Hungary: Jews and Czechs. See Stewart, *Fashioning*, 67.

61. Stewart, *Fashioning*, 49.

62. Loos, "Plumbers," in *Plumbing: Sounding Modern Architecture,* ed. Nadir Lahiji and D. S. Friedman (New York: Princeton Architectural Press, 1997), 19.

63. Mark Crinson, *Rebuilding Babel: Modern Architecture and Internationalism* (London: I. B. Tauris, 2017).

64. Henry Russell Hitchcock and Philip Johnson, *The International Style*, rev. ed. (1932; New York: W. W. Norton, 1997), 35.

65. This is a simplification. In Europe, modernism was variously associated with German culture, with cosmopolitan rootlessness, and with Jewish and Mediterranean–North African cultures. See Paul Overy, "White Walls, White Skins: Cosmopolitanism and Colonialism in Inter-War Modernist Architecture," in *Cosmopolitan Modernisms*, ed. Kobena Mercer (Cambridge, MA: MIT Press, 2005), 50–67.

8. Race and Miscegenation in Early Twentieth-Century Mexican Architecture

Epigraph. Sybil Moholy-Nagy, "Mexican critique," *Progressive Architecture* 34 (November 1953): 175–76.

1. It would be historically and theoretically inaccurate to apply Nestor García-Canclini's ideas of "hybrid cultures" or Angel Rama's theories of "transculturation" in discussing the hybrid or transcultural condition of miscegenation presented here. First of all, García-Canclini's ideas of hybridity suggest that always and already pure identities are impossible. Expressions of "pure" identities, as the architectural discussion that follows will show, had been ideologically established as a way to propel and explain the transformative nature of early twentieth-century nationalism in Mexico. Second, since the notion of transculturation is based on the premise of choice and amount of choice in accepting and rejecting culture or traditions, to use this in the case of race

would amount to some form of controlled racial eugenics, which, as we will see, was not central to the project of nationalism.

2. Étienne Balibar, "The Nation Form" in *Race, Nation, Class: Ambiguous Identities* (New York: Verso, 1991), 96.

3. Gamio studied with Boas between 1908 and 1910, at the time that Boas was working on his ideas that would be published as *The Mind of the Primitive Man* (1911). Boas travelled with Gamio to Mexico and stayed there between 1910 and 1912.

4. Denise Ferreira da Silva, *Toward a Global Idea of Race* (Minneapolis: University of Minnesota Press, 2007), 140–42.

5. Manuel Gamio, *Forjando Patria: Pro Nacionalismo* (Mexico: Editorial Porrua, 1916), 85–86.

6. Gamio, *Forjando Patria*, 92.

7. Gamio, *Forjando Patria*, 325, emphasis in original.

8. Juan Antonio Siller, "Semblanza: Manuel Amábilis (1883–1966)," *Cuadernos de Arquitectura Mesoamericana* 9 (January 1987): 95–96.

9. This text appeared at the same time that Amábilis was working on the design and construction of the Mexican Pavilion in Seville. For this, he received the gold medal from the Spanish Real Academia de Bellas Artes de San Fernando for the advancement in the study of pre-Hispanic art and architecture. Amábilis's work was highly valued since it narrowly defeated Ignacio Marquina's now seminal *Estudio Arquitectónico Comparativo de los Monumentos Arqueológicos de México* for the prize.

10. Manuel Amábilis, "Conferencia en la Sociedad de Arquitectos Mexicanos—9 de Noviembre 1933," in *Pláticas sobre Arquitectura* (1934; repr., Mexico: INBA, 2001), 8.

11. Manuel Amábilis, *La Arquitectura Precolombina de México* (1929; repr., Mexico: Editorial Orion, 1956), 35.

12. While Amábilis does not make any mention or reference to either Boas or Gamio, it is very likely that he encountered *Forjando Patria* as it was an important text after the revolution; he most likely encountered Boas's works as a result of his archeological investigations. These works would have informed his understanding of race.

13. Manuel Amábilis, *Donde* (Mexico: Imp. E. Gómez, 1933), 11.

14. Amábilis, *Donde*, 45.

15. Amábilis, *Donde*, 46.

16. Amábilis, *La Arquitectura Precolombina de México*, 31.

17. Allan Knight, "Racism, Revolution, and *Indigenismo*: Mexico, 1910–1940," in *The Idea of Race in Latin America, 1870–1940*, ed. Richard Graham (Austin: University of Texas Press, 1990), 73.

18. Kelley Swarthout, *"Assimilating the Primitive": Parallel Dialogues on Racial Miscegenation in Revolutionary Mexico* (New York: Peter Lang International Academic Publishers, 2004), 69.

19. Francisco Bulnes, one of Díaz's "cientificos," "espoused explicit eugenic policies

. . . and developed his own form of Spencerian Darwinism by combining it with a theory about diet, culture, and racial superiority." See Eduardo Mendieta, "The Death of Positivism and the Birth of Mexican Phenomenology," in *Latin American Positivism: New Historical and Philosophic Essays*, ed. Gregory D. Gilson and Irving W. Levinson (Lanham, MD: Lexington Books, 2013), 5.

20. Leopoldo Zea, *El Positivismo en México: Nacimiento, Apogeo y Decadencia* (Mexico: Fondo de Cultura Económica, 1968).

21. Jesús Acevedo, "La Arquitectura Colonial en México," in *Disertaciones de un Arquitecto* (Mexico: Ediciones México Moderno, 1920), 90–91.

22. Acevedo, "Arquitectura Colonial en México," 90–91.

23. Jesús Acevedo, "Apariencias Arquitectónicas," in *Disertaciones de un Arquitecto* (Mexico: Ediciones México Moderno, 1920), 45.

24. Acevedo, "Apariencias Arquitectónicas," 50.

25. Hanno-Walter Kruft, *A History of Architectural Theory: From Vitruvius to the Present* (New York: Princeton Architectural Press, 1994), 284–85.

26. For more on the relationship between Viollet-le-Duc and Gobineau, see Martin Bressani, "Instinct and Race," in *Architecture and the Historical Imagination: Eugène-Emmanuel Viollet-le-Duc, 1814–1879* (New York: Routledge, 2016), 333–80.

27. Acevedo, "Arquitectura Colonial en México," 94.

28. Federico E. Mariscal, *La Patria y la Arquitectura Nacional: Resúmenes de las Conferencias dadas en la Casa de la Universidad Popular Mexicana* (Mexico: Imprenta Stephan y Torres, 1915), 10.

29. Mariscal, *La Patria y la Arquitectura Nacional*, 10.

30. José Vasconcelos, *El Monismo Estético: Ensayos*, in *Obras Completas*, vol. 4 (1918; repr., Mexico: Libreros Mexicanos Unidos, 1961), 46.

31. José Vasconcelos, "Hay que Construir," *Boletín de la Secretaría de Educación Pública* 1, no. 4 (First Semester 1923): 4. The reference to the "wooden house" could be a direct critique of Gobineau's assertion that "the 'pure Aryan dwelling' was built of wood." See Bressani, "Instinct and Race," 346.

32. José Vasconcelos, *La Raza Cósmica: Misión de la Raza Iberoamericana* (1925; repr., Mexico: Epasa-Calpe, 1992), 9.

33. Vasconcelos, *Raza Cósmica*, 52–53.

34. Sylvia Calles, trans., "A Declaration of Social, Political, and Aesthetic Principles" (orig. Manifiesto del Sindicato de Obreros, Técnicos, Pintores y Escultores), in *Art and Theory, 1900–1990: An Anthology of Changing Ideas*, ed. Charles Harrison and Paul Wood (Cambridge: Basil Blackwell, 1992), 388.

35. Vasconcelos, *Raza Cósmica*, 3.

36. Vasconcelos, *Raza Cósmica*, 49–50.

37. Marissa K. López, *Chicano Nations: The Hemispheric Origins of Mexican American Literature* (New York: New York University Press, 2011), 130.

9. Modern Architecture and Racial Eugenics at the Esposizione Universale di Roma

1. Marcello Piacentini, "Bilancio del razionalismo," *Il Giornale d'Italia* 38, no. 165 (July 13, 1938): 3.

2. See Regio decreto-legge (R.D.L.), 17 novembre 1938-XVII, n. 1728, "Provvedimenti per la difesa della razza italiana," in *Gazzetta Ufficiale del Regno* 79, no. 264 (November 19, 1938): 4794–96.

3. Aaron Gillette, *Racial Theories in Fascist Italy* (London: Routledge, 2002).

4. Charles L. Davis II, "Viollet-le-Duc and the Body: The Metaphorical Integrations of Race and Style in Structural Rationalism," *Architectural Research Quarterly* 14, no. 4 (2010): 341–48.

5. Mabel O. Wilson, *Negro Building: Black Americans in the World of Fairs and Exhibitions* (Berkeley: University of California Press, 2012), 172–74.

6. Benito Mussolini, "Al popolo di Reggio Emilia," in *Opera Omnia di Benito Mussolini, Volume XXII, Dall'attentato Zaniboni al discorso dell'Ascensione (5 novembre 1925–26 maggio 1927)*, ed. Edoardo and Duilio Susmel (Florence: La Fenice, 1951–1962), 246.

7. Aaron Gillette, "Racial Theory and Fascism, 1915–1935," in *Racial Theories in Fascist Italy*, 35–49.

8. See Benito Mussolini, "Al Consiglio Nazionale del P.N.F.," October 25, 1938, from *Popolo d'Italia*, 298, October 26, 1938, in *Opera Omnia di Benito Mussolini, Volume XXIX*, ed. Edoardo and Duilio Susmel (Florence: La Fenice, 1951–1962), 185–96.

9. Gillette, *Racial Theories in Fascist Italy*, 55. See also Alexander De Grand, "Mussolini's Follies: Fascism in Its Imperial and Racist Phase, 1935–1940," *Contemporary European History* 13, no. 2 (May 2004): 127–47.

10. Emilio Gentile, *Fascismo di pietra* (Rome: Giuseppe Laterza & Figli, 2007), 224–25. Other exceptions include Richard Etlin's *Modernism in Italian Architecture, 1890–1940* (Cambridge, MA: MIT Press, 1991); and Joshua Arthurs's *Excavating Modernity: The Roman Past in Fascist Italy* (Ithaca: Cornell University Press, 2012).

11. Michel Foucault, *"Society Must Be Defended": Lectures at the Collège de France, 1975–76*, trans. David Macey (New York: Picador, 2003), 240.

12. Foucault, *"Society Must Be Defended,"* 256.

13. Giuseppe Casazza, "Giuseppe Pensabene e il «mal di Parigi»," in *«La Difesa della Razza» Politica, ideologia e immagine del razzismo fascista* (Turin: Giulio Einaudi Editore, 2008), 252–69.

14. See especially Giuseppe Pensabene, "Sopratutto in Italia è importante la questione della razza," *Quadrivio* 6, no. 14 (January 30, 1938): 2; and Giuseppe Pensabene, *La razza e le arti figurative* (Roma: Cremonese, 1939).

15. Giuseppe Pensabene, "Arte nostra e deformazione ebraica," *Difesa della Razza* 1, no. 6 (October 20, 1938): 55.

16. Pensabene, "Arte nostra e deformazione ebraica," 55.

17. Telesio Interlandi, "La questione dell'arte e la razza," *Il Tevere*, November 14, 1938, 3. Interlandi was editor of the daily *Il Tevere* (1924–1943), the weekly *Il Quadrivio* (1933–1943), and the biweekly *Difesa della Razza* (1938–1943).

18. Interlandi, "La questione dell'arte e la razza," 3.

19. Filippo Tommaso Marinetti, "Italianità dell'arte moderna," *Il Giornale d'Italia* 38, no. 279 (November 24, 1938): 3.

20. Marinetti, "Italianità dell'arte moderna," 3.

21. Giuseppe Bottai, *La Politica delle Arti, scritti degli anni 1918–1943*, ed. Alessandro Masi (Rome: Istituto Poligrafico dello Stato, 2009). See also Giordano Bruno Guerri, "Chapter 7. Scuola, Arte, Razza," in *Giuseppe Bottai, fascista* (Milan: Mondadori, 1996), 134–58.

22. "Discussioni sull'arte moderna," *Le Arti* 1, no. 3 (February–March 1939): 170–73, II-V.

23. "Discussioni sull'arte moderna," *Le Arti*, 170.

24. Giuseppe Bottai, "Modernità e tradizione nell'arte italiana d'oggi," *Le Arti* 1, no. 3 (February–March 1939): 230–31.

25. Marla Susan Stone, "Italian Fascist Culture Wars," in *The Patron State: Culture and Politics in Fascist Italy* (Princeton, NJ: Princeton University Press, 1998), 177–221. See also Sileno Salvagnini, *Il sistema delle arti in Italia, 1919–1943* (Bologna: Minerva Edizioni, 2000).

26. Giorgio Ciucci, "Razionalismo di forme assolute," in *Gli architetti e il fascismo. Architettura e città 1922–44* (Turin: Piccolo Biblioteca Einaudi, 1989), 69–76. See also Dennis P. Doordan, *Building Modern Italy: Italian Architecture, 1914–1936* (New York: Princeton Architectural Press, 1988), 45–52.

27. Marcello Piacentini, "Prima internazionale architettonica," *Architettura e Arti Decorative* 6, no. 12 (August 1928): 544–62.

28. Piacentini, "Prima internazionale architettonica," 548.

29. Marcello Piacentini, "Dove è irragionevole l'architettura razionale," *Dedalo* 10, no. 11 (January 1931): 535.

30. "Per l'architettura italiana moderna: Comunicato ufficiale," *Architettura: Supplemento sindacale della rivista el Sindacato Nazionale Fascista Architetti* 8 (June 30, 1934): 79.

31. Giuseppe Pagano, "Mussolini salva l'architettura italiana," *Casabella* 78 (June 1934): 2–3.

32. Quoted in Pagano, "Mussolini salva l'architettura italiana," 3.

33. Piacentini, "Bilancio del razionalismo," 3.

34. Piacentini, "Bilancio del razionalismo," 3.

35. Marcello Piacentini, "Nuova rinascità," *Il Giornale d'Italia* 38, no. 167 (July 15, 1938): 3.

36. Piacentini, "Nuova rinascità," 3.

37. Etlin, *Modernism in Italian Architecture*, 594.

38. Gruppo 7, "Architettura," *Rassegna Italiana* 18, no. 103 (December 1926): 852.

39. See "Concorso per il Palazzo degli edifici delle forze armate," in Archivio Centrale dello Stato (ACS)—E42, b. 904, fascicolo 7885, sottofascicolo 3; and press release, October 11, 1937, in ACS—E42, b. 49, fascicolo 212, n. 16.

40. Charles Rydell, *All the World's a Fair: Visions of Empire at the American International Expositions, 1876–1916* (Chicago: University of Chicago Press, 1984), 5.

41. Giuseppe Bottai, "Progetto di massima per una Esposizione Universale di Roma, 23 marzo 1939 o 1942," April 1935, 3, ACS—Segreteria Particolare del Duce-Carteggio Ordinario: 509.832.

42. Karen Fiss, *The Grand Illusion: The Third Reich, the Paris Exposition, and the Cultural Seduction of France* (Chicago: University of Chicago Press, 2009), 65.

43. Marcello Piacentini, "Architettura del tempo di Mussolini," *Illustrazione Italiana* 65, no. 51 (December 18, 1938): 1034.

44. Ente Autonomo Esposizione Universale di Roma (Ente E42), "Bando di concorso per il progetto del Palazzo dei ricevimenti e dei congressi," 3 (Rome, 1937), in ACS—E42, b. 49, f. 212.

45. Ente E42, "Bando di concorso per il Progetto degli edifici delle forze armate," 3 (Rome, 1937), in ACS—E42, b. 132, f. 718, sf. 1.

46. Ente E42, "Bando di concorso per il Progetto degli edifici delle forze armate," 7.

47. "Relazione della Commissione Giudatrice del Concorso per il Progetto degli Edifici delle Forze Armate," ACS—E42, b. 132, f. 718, sf. 6, ssf. 1.

48. "Relazione della Commissione Giudatrice del Concorso per il Progetto degli Edifici delle Forze Armate," 10.

49. Letter from Cipriano Efisio Oppo to Gino Pollini, July 7, 1938, in ACS—E42, b. 917, f. 8038. See also Letter from Cipriano Efisio Oppo, Ente E42, to Mario De Renzi, July 7, 1938, in ACS—E42, b. 920, f. 8145.

50. Ente E42, "Bando del Concorso per il Progetto degli Edifici delle Forze Armate," 4.

51. Letter to Cipriano Efisio Oppo from Il Capo Servizio Architettura, parchi e giardini, October 18, 1938, in ACS—E42, b. 904, f. 7885, sf. 3.

52. Servizio Architettura Parchi e Giardini, "Programma di progettazione," July 5, 1938, in ACS—E42, b. 878, f. 7722, Attività 1938.

53. Marla Susan Stone, *The Patron State: Culture and Politics in Fascist Italy* (Princeton, NJ: Princeton University Press, 1998), 220.

54. Benito Mussolini, "Il Piano regolatore della nuova economia italiana," March 23, 1936, in *Opera Omnia di Benito Mussolini, Volume XXVII*, ed. Edoardo and Duilio Susmel (Florence: La Fenice, 1951–1962), 242–43.

55. Gillette, *Racial Theories in Fascist Italy*, 83.

56. Stone, *Patron State*, 180.

57. "Aspetti del problema dell'autarchia nel campo edile," *Rassegna di Architettura* 9, no. 12 (December 1937): 476–77.

58. Carlo Enrico Rava, "Architettura di razza italiana," *L'Architettura Italiana* 34, no. 1 (January 1939): 37.

59. Rava, "Architettura di razza italiana," 45.

60. Giuseppe Pagano, "Variazioni sull'autarchia architettonica," *Casabella* (September 1938): 2–3; and Giuseppe Pagano, "Variazioni sull'autarchia architettonica II," *Casabella* (October 1938): 2–3.

61. Pagano, "Variazioni sull'autarchia architettonica," 2.

62. Letter from Direttore dei Servizi architettura parchi e giardini to Architetti Di Renzi e Pollini, May 17, 1939, in ACS—E42, b. 904, f. 7885, sf. 2.

63. Letter from Vittorio Cini to Benito Mussolini, September 11, 1939, in ACS—SPD-CO—509.832.

64. Letter from De Renzi and Pollini to Vittorio Cini, undated (July 1940), in ACS—E42, b. 904, f. 7885, sf. 2.

65. A. C., "Il Palazzo dell'autarchia, del corporativismo e della previdenza ed assicurazione all'Esposizione Universale di Roma," *Civiltà* 3, no. 9 (April 21, 1942): 30.

66. Alberto Francini, "Marmi e marmo raro all'Esposizione Universale di Roma," *Civiltà* 2, no. 6 (July 21, 1941): 37–41.

67. Ente E42, "Servizio Tecnici, Relazione sull'attività svolta nel trimestre aprile-Giugno 1942–XX," 21–23, in ACS—E42, b. 53, f. 214, sf. 6.

68. Servizi Tecnici, "Relazione sull'attività svolta nel 1942," in ACS—E42 b. 53, f. 214, sf. 6. See also Ente E42, "Rapporto, 31 dicembre, 1942–XX," in ACS—E42, b. 39, f. 27, Rapporti al Duce, sf. 10. Rapporto 31/12/1942.

69. Foucault, *"Society Must Be Defended,"* 254–55.

10. The Invention of Indigenous Architecture

1. "Eine deutsche Dorf-Anlage in den Ostmarken," *Deutsche Kunst und Dekoration*, 18 (April–September 1906): 533–37.

2. On invented traditions, see Eric Hobsbawm and Terence Ranger, *The Invention of Tradition* (Cambridge: Cambridge University Press, 1983). On architecture and whiteness, see Martin Berger, *Sight Unseen: Whiteness and American Visual Culture* (Berkeley: University of California Press, 2005).

3. See Maiken Umbach and Bernd Hüppauf, eds., *Vernacular Modernism: Heimat, Globalization, and the Built Environment* (Stanford: Stanford University Press, 2005).

4. Alan Knight has shown for Mexico how *indigenismo* represented "yet another non-Indian formulation of the 'Indian problem.'" Similarly, Prita Meier has shown that for the Swahili Coast, the concept was integral to attempts to fix in place societies that were in fact essentially trans-local and cosmopolitan. See Alan Knight, "Racism,

Revolution, and Indigenismo: Mexico, 1910–1940," in *The Idea of Race in Latin America, 1870–1940*, ed. Richard Graham (Austin: University of Texas Press, 1990), 71–113; and Prita Meier, *Swahili Port Cities: The Architecture of Elsewhere* (Bloomington: Indiana University Press, 2016).

5. Kenny Cupers, "Bodenständigkeit: The Environmental Epistemology of Modernism," *Journal of Architecture* 21, no. 8 (2017): 1226–52.

6. Verband Deutscher Architekten und Ingenieur-Vereine, *Das Bauernhaus im Deutschen Reiche und in seinen Grenzgebieten* (Dresden: Verlag von Gerhard Kühtmann, 1906).

7. See Anita Aigner, ed., *Vernakulare Moderne: Grenzüberschreitungen in der Architektur um 1900: Das Bauernhaus und seine Aneignung* (Bielefeld: Transcript, 2010).

8. Barbara Miller Lane, *National Romanticism and Modern Architecture in Germany and the Scandinavian Countries* (Cambridge: Cambridge University Press), 4.

9. Celia Applegate, *A Nation of Provincials: The German Idea of Heimat* (Berkeley: University of California Press, 1990)

10. Wilhelm Heinrich Riehl, *Die Naturgeschichte des Volkes als Grundlage einer deutschen Sozial-Politik: Bd. 1: Land und Leute* (Stuttgart: J. G. Cotta, 1854). On anti-urban ideology and romantic approaches to German agricultural landscapes, see Klaus Bergmann, *Agrarromantik und Großstadtfeindschaft* (Meisenheim am Glan: Verlag Anton Hain, 1970).

11. The term is defined in a contribution to a Festschrift for Albert Schäffle in 1901: "Der Lebensraum: Eine biogeographische Studie," in K. Bücher, K. V. Fricker, et al., *Festgaben für Albert Schäffle zur siebenzigsten Wiederkehr seines Geburtstages am 24. Februar 1901* (Tübingen, 1901), 101–89.

12. Ulrike Jureit, *Das Ordnen von Räumen. Territorium und Lebensraum im 20. Jahrhundert* (Hamburg: Hamburger Edition HIS Verlag, 2012).

13. Woodruff D. Smith, "Friedrich Ratzel and the Origins of Lebensraum," *German Studies Review* 3, no. 1 (1980): 51–68.

14. Geheimes Staatsarchiv Preußischer Kulturbesitz, I.HA Rep. 90A, 2246, Jahresberichte der Ansiedlungskommission für Westpreußen und Posen, Denkschriften über die Ausführung des Ansiedlungsgesetzes vom April 26, 1886, bd. 4 (Denkschrift 1919–1920).

15. Gesetz, betreffend die Beförderung deutschr Ansiedlungen in den Provinzen Westpreußen und Posen, vom April 26, 1886 (art 1), in Geheimes Staatsarchiv Preußischer Kulturbesitz, VI. HA, Nl Braun, O., A nr. 40, Gesetze und Ausführungsbestimmungen für die Ansiedlungskommission, Berlin.

16. Hans-Joachim Corvimus, "Die Tätigkieit der Ansiedlungskommission in der ehemals preußischen Provinz Posen in national- und wirtschaftspolitischer Hinsicht" (PhD diss., Universität Greifswald, 1926), 36. Also see Gesetz über Maßnahmen zur Stärkung des Deutschtums in den Provinzen Westpreußen und Posen, vom 20.03.1908,

Geheimes Staatsarchiv Preußischer Kulturbesitz, I.HA Rep. 90A, 4205, Grundsätze für die Ansiedlung deutscher Arbeiter in den gemischtsprachigen östlichen Landesteilen.

17. Mark Tilse, *Transnationalism in the Prussian East: From National Conflict to Synthesis, 1871–1914* (Basingstoke: Palgrave MacMillan, 2011), 39.

18. See Sebastian Conrad, *Deutsche Kolonialgeschichte* (München: Verlag C. H. Beck, 2008), 99.

19. Resettlement in Prussia was strongly supported by the National Liberals, who championed this ethnolinguistic conception of nationality in the east. See Tilse, *Transnationalism in the Prussian East*, 34.

20. See Ausführungsvorschriften zu den Besitzfestigungesgesetze vom Juni 26, 1912, and Vorordnung über sein Anwendungsgebiet vom März 12, 1913, Geheimes Staatsarchiv Preußischer Kulturbesitz, VI. HA, Nl Braun, O., A nr. 40, Gesetze und Ausführungsbestimmungen für die Ansiedlungskommission, Berlin 1908.

21. Elizabeth B. Jones, "The Rural 'Social Ladder': Internal Colonization, Germanization and Civilizing Missions in the German Empire," *Geschichte und Gesellschaft: Zeitschrift für Historische Sozialwissenschaften* 40, no. 4 (2014): 457–92.

22. See Paul Fischer, "Landschaftsbild und Ansiedlung," in *25 Jahre Ansiedlung 1886–1911*, ed. Georg Minde-Pouet (Lissa i.P.: Oskar Euliß' Verlag, 1911); and Paul Fischer, *Ländliches Bauwesen* (Stuttgart: Bauzeitungs-Verlag Karl Schuler, 1915).

23. Jahresbericht 1896, 11–13, in Geheimes Staatsarchiv Preußischer Kulturbesitz, I.HA Rep. 90A, 4188. Jahresberichte der Ansiedlungskommission für Westpreußen und Posen. Denkschriften über die Ausführung des Ansiedlungsgesetzes vom April 26, 1886, bd. 2, 1892–1901. See also Königliches Staatsministerium / Haus der Abgeordneten, ed., *Zwanzig Jahre deutscher Kulturarbeit, 1886–1906: Tätigkeit und Aufgaben neupreußischer Kolonisation in Westpreußen und Posen* (Berlin: W. Moeser, 1907), 63.

24. See Jahresbericht 1902, in Geheimes Staatsarchiv Preußischer Kulturbesitz, I. HA Rep. 90A, 2245. Jahresberichte der Ansiedlungskommission für Westpreußen und Posen. Denkschriften über die Ausführung des Ansiedlungsgesetzes vom April 26, 1886, bd. 3, 1902–1911; and Heinrich Sohnrey, *Eine Wanderfahrt durch die deutschen Ansiedelungsgebiete in Posen und Westpreußen* (Berlin: Th. Schoenfeldt, 1897), 86.

25. See, for example, Paul Fischer (Regierungs- und Baurat), *Ansiedlungsbauten in den Provinzen Posen und Westpreußen (im Autrage der Königl. Ansiedlungskommission in Posen)* (Halle a.S.: Ludwig Hofstetter Verlag, 1904).

26. See Marion Wallace, *A History of Namibia: From the Beginning to 1990* (London: Hurst, 2011).

27. See Hannes Raath, "Die Begrip Hartbeeshuis," *South African Journal of Cultural History* 17, no. 1 (2003): 72–90.

28. Notizen für Ansiedler in DSWA (April 1893), p. 6. R 8023/600a: Syndikat für südwestafrikanische Siedlung, bd. 2

29. See Esmé Berman, *Art and Artists of South Africa* (Western Cape: Southern Book Publishers, 1996): 279–80.

30. For example, the Woermann farmstead, built for Hamburg shipping company owner Adolph Woermann, and designed by architect Friedrich Höft.

31. Walter Peters, *Baukunst in Südwestafrika, 1884–1914: Die Rezeption deutscher Architektur in der Zeit von 1884 bis 1914 im ehemaligen Deutsch-Südwestafrika (Namibia)* (Windhoek: Vorstand der SWA Wissenshaftlichen Gesellschaft, 1981), 113–15.

32. Curfews were in place in many towns, including Usakos: Verordnung betreffend das betreten der Eingeborenen Werften in Usakos vom Otkober 27, 1908, in R 1001/1912: Polizeivorschriften in Deutsch-Südwestafrika (Nov. 1907–Juni 1925).

33. For Windhoek, see, for example, Namibian National Archives, BAU/52 B78: Bau eines Aufseher-Wohnhauses auf der Eingeborenenwerft, Windhoek, 1913–14.

34. Jürgen Zimmerman and Joachim Zeller. *Genocide in German South-West Africa: The Colonial War of 1904–1908 and Its Aftermath* (Monmouth: Merlin Press, 2008).

35. Giorgio Miescher, *Namibia's Red Line: The History of a Veterinary and Settlement Border* (New York: Palgrave MacMillan, 2012).

36. For example, the Zehnmannhaus in Windhoek, or Duwisib Castle, designed by Wilhelm Sander. Before he left for German Southwest Africa in 1901, Sander studied in Höxter, Westfalen, where he was likely inspired by its medieval architecture. See Peters, *Baukunst in Südwestafrika, 1884–1914*, 85–90, 303–8.

37. See Namibian National Archives, BAU/13 A21: Gefängnisbau Swakopmund, 1905–1909.

38. The quotation in the original reads: "Als material sollen den örtlichen klimatischen Verhältnissen entsprechend nur Bruchsteine bzw. Cementsandziegel in verlängertem Cementmörtel vermauert, zur Anwendung kommen." Namibian National Archives, BAU/13 A21: Gefängnisbau Swakopmund, 1905–1909, p. 84.

11. Erecting the Skyscraper, Erasing Race

1. The subject of Mohawk labor on skyscrapers would not become a topic of popular interest until the late 1940s, when the famed *New Yorker* writer Joseph Mitchell began writing about Mohawk workers' legacy within the business; the topic would reemerge later in the 1960s in Edmund Wilson's *Apologies to the Iroquois.* Joseph Mitchell, "The Mohawks in High Steel," *New Yorker*, September 17, 1949, 38; and Edmund Wilson, *Apologies to the Iroquois* (New York: Farrar, Straus and Cudahy, 1960).

2. In 1908, African American sociologist Kelly Miller wrote that "the city Negro grows up in shade . . . completely overshadowed by his overtowering environment. As one walks along the streets of our great cities and views the massive buildings and

sky-seeking structures, he finds no status for the Negro above the cellar floor." And even the cellar remained a questionable space for black employment. Mary White Ovington, white sociologist and a cofounder of the NAACP, details the labor situation of African Americans in Manhattan in her 1911 study, *Half a Man: The Status of the Negro in New York*. She notes that while elevator operation in residential buildings was mostly an "occupation [that] is given over to the Negro," within spaces such as "office buildings, large stores and hotels"—building uses often associated with downtown skyscrapers—blacks were rarely hired." Kelly Miller, *Race Adjustment [and] the Everlasting Stain* (New York: Arno Press, 1968), 129; and Mary White Ovington, *Half a Man: The Status of the Negro in New York* (New York: Negro Universities Press, 1969).

3. Anne Anlin Cheng, *Second Skin: Josephine Baker & the Modern Surface* (New York: Oxford University Press, 2010).

4. William A. Gleason, *Sites Unseen: Architecture, Race, and American Literature* (New York: New York University Press, 2011), 3.

5. Dianne Harris, *Little White Houses: How the Postwar Home Constructed Race in America* (Minneapolis: University of Minnesota Press, 2013), 13.

6. Henry James, *The American Scene* (London: Chapman and Hall, 1907), 89.

7. In *The Black Skyscraper: Architecture and the Perception of Race* (Baltimore: Johns Hopkins Press, 2017), I examine texts by writers such as W. E. B. Du Bois, Nella Larsen, William Dean Howells, F. Scott Fitzgerald, and Louis Sullivan that approach the skyscraper as newly shaping the experience of race.

8. The most comprehensive history of skyscraper labor is Jim Rasenberger, *High Steel: The Daring Men Who Built the World's Greatest Skyline* (New York: HarperCollins, 2004). See also Grace Palladino's *Skilled Hands, Strong Spirits: A Century of Building Trades History* (Ithaca, NY: Cornell University Press, 2005). Mike Cherry's 1974 memoir *On High Steel: The Education of an Ironworker* (New York: Quadrangle, 1974) also provides an insightful glimpse into the rhythms, frustrations, and socialities of being a unionized ironworker.

9. Faith Baldwin, *Skyscraper* (New York: Dell Murray Hill, 1931), 2.

10. "Watching a Skyscraper Grow out of a Hole," *New York Times*, February 17, 1929.

11. Stevedoring, or the loading and unloading of cargo ships, was the only other potential type of labor that both required massive amounts of laborers and was visually accessible to the public. However, stevedores' labor was segregated within Manhattan to its outskirts along the shores, out of sight of the daily traffic of commuters. For a fictional account of longshoreman work, see Ernest Poole's Pulitzer-winning novel from 1915, *The Harbor* (New York: Macmillan, 1915).

12. See John Tauranac's *The Empire State Building: The Making of a Landmark* (New York: Scribner, 1995) and Carol Willis's *Building the Empire State* (New York: W.W. Norton, 1998).

13. Mary Borden, *Flamingo: A Novel* (Garden City: Doubleday, Page, 1927), 113.

14. Borden, *Flamingo*, 113.

15. See Rasenberger, *High Steel*, 190, for more on this typing of the ironworker. The term *nigger-head* was generally used in the early twentieth century to refer to an assortment of objects, tools, or places alleged to resemble African Americans largely due to being dark in color. Here, the usage is ambiguous, seemingly referring to men who used such tools on skyscraper worksites but also perhaps suggesting the inferior nature of the men tasked with this job.

16. Anne Anlin Cheng makes this point in a reading of zebra print in modernist style, reading it as both primitive, and mechanistic. Here is the quote in full: "The animal, the human, and the mechanical—the three foundational, distinctive categories that underpin Modernism—themselves turn out to provide the preconditions for their distinction from each other, in a series of disavowals that are, however, perfectly legible on the surface. In short, the categories of the animal, the human, and the machine, while ideologically segregated, are stylistically identical." Anne Anlin Cheng, "Skins, Tattoos, and Susceptibility," *Representations* 108 (2009): 98–121.

17. Edmund Wilson, *The American Earthquake: A Documentary of the Twenties and Thirties* (Garden City: Doubleday, 1958), 293; and *New Masses* 7, no. 1 (June 1931), 9.

18. Tauranac, *Empire State Building*, 220.

19. Besides *Skyscrapers and the Men Who Build Them*, the text I primarily deal with in this section, also see Paul Starrett's 1938 memoir, *Changing the Skyline* (New York: McGraw-Hill, 1938) and critic Jeffrey Cody's book *Exporting American Architecture, 1870–2000*, detailing William Starrett's 1919 trip to Japan as an emissary of the George A. Fuller Construction Company, bringing American engineering know-how to help corporate clients build four "monuments to the god of business and trade" (London: Routledge, 2003).

20. Starrett was the youngest of five brothers, all of whom eventually worked in some aspect of the business of building. With his brother Paul, he founded Starrett Bros. & Eken in 1922 and worked on a number of Manhattan buildings in the 1920s. William Starrett would die in early 1932 at age fifty-four, less than a year after Empire State's completion.

21. William A. Starrett, *Skyscrapers and the Men Who Build Them* (New York: Scribner's, 1928), 4.

22. Starrett, *Skyscrapers*, 75.

23. Starrett, *Skyscrapers*, 1.

24. Starrett, *Skyscrapers*, 1.

25. Starrett, *Skyscrapers*, 2.

26. Starrett, *Skyscrapers*, 2.

27. Starrett, *Skyscrapers*, 2.

28. Starrett, *Skyscrapers*, 4.

29. Starrett, *Skyscrapers*, 6, 7.

30. For more on white appropriations of the vanishing Indian in the early twentieth century, see Walter Benn Michaels, *Our America: Nativism, Modernism, and Pluralism* (Durham, NC: Duke University Press, 1997).

31. Originating from the Canadian community of Kahnawake in the 1850s, Mohawk ironworkers eventually "boomed out" to work on skyscrapers across the United States and Canada into the present day. While never making up more than 15 percent of the ironworkers in New York, Mohawks worked on most of the major buildings of the twentieth century including Empire State, Chrysler, RCA, the Bank of Manhattan, and eventually the World Trade Center Towers, to name only a few. See Rasenberger, *High Steel*, 33–34. Moreover, Joanna Merwood-Salisbury has noted the practice of early Chicago skyscrapers taking Native American names: "The common practice of naming the skyscraper after a Native American tribe or mountain range (the Tacoma, Monadnock, Katahdin, and Wachusett to name but a few) is a testament to building developers' efforts to promote their construction as native and organic objects." Joanna Merwood-Salisbury, "The First Chicago School," in *Architecture and Capital: 1845 to the Present*, ed. Peggy Deamer (New York: Routledge, 2013), 25–39, quotation on p. 39.

32. Starrett, *Skyscrapers*, 63, 144.

33. Starrett, *Skyscrapers*, 144.

34. Arno Dosch, "Just Wops," *Everybody's Magazine* 25.5, November 1911, 579–89, quotation on p. 579.

35. For more on this film see Charles Musser, *The Emergence of Cinema: The American Screen to 1907, Volume 1* (Berkeley: University of California Press, 1994), 454; Willa Cather, "Behind the Singer Tower," *Colliers Magazine* 18, May 1912, 16–17, 41.

36. The Hughes poems are "Negro" and "Being Old." See Langston Hughes, *The Collected Poems of Langston Hughes* (New York: Vintage, 1995), 24, 109.

37. Arthur B. Reeve, "Men Monkeys Who Build Our Towers," *Scrap Book*, vol. 5, May 1908, 759–67.

38. Journalists Margaret Norris and Brenda Ueland in 1931 enact a similar pattern of noting Indian labor to further reify white laboring power. Published in the *Saturday Evening Post* alongside Lewis Hines's photographs, the article "Riding the Girders" notes that "ironworkers are recruited from all over our own country and most parts of Europe, though one rarely finds Jews or Italians or Poles or Negroes among them." Briefly recognizing the presence of some "half-breed Indians" and recounting a story about a rare Italian ironworker who, upon almost falling to his death, reacted with hysterics allows Norris and Ueland to stabilize the predominantly Anglo heritage of the ironwork. On these grounds, they can ultimately assert the ironworker as agent: "So, though theorists lament that the machine age is making robots and automatons of all men, here is one type of workman, the steel man, the very spirit of the skyscraper, a direct product of the Power Age, whose personality the machine age exalts" (98).

39. Adolf Loos, *Ornament and Crime: Selected Essays* (Riverside: Ariadne Press, 1998), 167.

40. Starrett, *Skyscrapers*, 125.

12. Modeling Race and Class

1. "Blueprint for Modern Living" telecast, December 4, 1956. The Illinois Institute of Technology broadcast this program on Chicago educational television as part of a fifteen-part series. The series' December 4 program was moderated by Bill Dunlap (an associate partner at SOM), and featured the architect A. Quincy Jones, and the owners of the steel house in the U.S. Gypsum Research Village (Mr. and Mrs. John Reindel). Jones's associate, James Bort, who prepared the house's contract documents, also appeared on the program. Dunlap spoke of home building in the present age of technology and technological advance—the idea that factory-produced materials would appear with greater frequency in the design of houses. A. Quincy Jones, FAIA, Architecture Archive, Text Files (003.0 454), courtesy the late Elaine Sewell Jones. The A. Quincy Jones Archive now resides in UCLA's Library Special Collections, Charles E. Young Research Library.

2. Hugh Stubbins Collection, E029, Tri-fold publicity folio for Research Village, Special Collections, Frances Loeb Library, Harvard Design School.

3. For more on those prescriptions, see Dianne Harris, *Little White Houses: How the Postwar Home Constructed Race in America* (Minneapolis: University of Minnesota Press, 2013).

4. Fredie Flore and Mil De Kooning, "Postwar Model Homes: Introduction," *Journal of Architecture* 9 (Winter 2004): 411.

5. Susan Sontag famously wrote about the camera's work as voyeuristic and as inscribing power relations between the viewer/photo maker and the viewed subject. See Susan Sontag, *On Photography* (New York: Dell, 1977), 10.

6. Timothy Mennel, "Miracle House Hoop-La: Corporate Rhetoric and the Construction of the Postwar American House," *Journal of the Society of Architectural Historians* 64, no. 3 (Sept. 2005): 340.

7. This sales decline was first anticipated and then felt across the country. J. G. Maynard, who was president of the advertising agency in charge of publicity for the U.S. Gypsum Research Village, wrote to builder Leonard Frank: "With the approaching recession in new home sales and volume, it appears that new ideas can help to maintain a volume level of low-cost home building if they are effectively promoted and publicized." Letter dated June 22, 1953, Hugh Stubbins Collection, F155.07, Special Collections, Frances Loeb Library, Harvard Design School. On fluctuations in housing sales during the 1950s, see also Dianne Harris, "The House I Live In: Architecture, Modernism, and Identity in Levittown," in *Second Suburb: Levittown, Pennsylvania,*

ed. Dianne Harris (Pittsburgh: University of Pittsburgh Press, 2010), 237–38; and Harris, *Little White Houses*, 43–44.

8. On the idea of a neoliberal spatial imaginary conveyed through images, see Ned O'Gorman, introduction and chapter 1, in *The Iconoclastic Imagination: Image, Catastrophe, and Economy in America from the Kennedy Assassination to September 11* (Chicago: University of Chicago Press, 2016).

9. For more on the representation of whites in connection to postwar housing, see Harris, *Little White Houses*, chapters 1–3. The literature on the construction of whiteness/critical studies of whiteness has grown in recent decades and is now quite substantial. For an introduction, see the following: Richard Dyer, *White: Essays on Race and Culture* (New York: Routledge, 1997); David Roediger, *The Wages of Whiteness: Race and the Making of the American Working Class* (New York: Verso, 2007); Nell Irvin Painter, *The History of the White People* (New York: W. W. Norton, 2011); Thomas Guglielmo, *White on Arrival: Italians, Race, Color, and Power in Chicago, 1890–1945* (Oxford: Oxford University Press, 2004); Matthew Frye Jacobsen, *Whiteness of a Different Color: European Immigrants and the Alchemy of Race* (Cambridge, MA: Harvard University Press, 1999); Mike Hill, ed., *Whiteness: A Critical Reader* (New York: NYU Press, 1997); and Richard Delgado and Jean Stefancic, eds., *Critical White Studies: Looking Behind the Mirror* (Philadelphia: Temple University Press, 1997).

10. Elspeth H. Brown, *The Corporate Eye: Photography and the Rationalization of American Commercial Culture, 1884–1929* (Baltimore: Johns Hopkins University Press, 2005), 1.

11. Brown, *Corporate Eye*, 5–6, 16.

12. Brown, *Corporate Eye*, 22.

13. On the history of depicting tortured black bodies, see Saidiya Hartman, *Scenes of Subjection: Terror, Slavery, and Self-Making in Nineteenth-Century America* (Oxford: Oxford University Press, 1997); Karen Haltunnen, "Humanitarianism and the Pornography of Pain in Anglo-American Culture," *American Historical Review* 100, no. 2 (April 1995): 303–34; and Grace Hall, *Making Whiteness: The Culture of Segregation in the South, 1890–1940* (New York: Vintage, 1999).

14. Christine Harold and Kevin Michael DeLuca, "Behold the Corpse: Violent Images and the Case of Emmett Till," in *Visual Rhetoric: A Reader in Communication and Culture*, ed. Lester C. Olson, Cara A. Finnegan, and Diane S. Hope (Los Angeles: Sage, 2008), 258.

15. Martin Berger has demonstrated that the Till story "grew into the most important news story" of the black press in the 1950s. While coverage in the white press was less extensive, Berger shows that northern white newspaper coverage increased after Till's funeral but tended to focus on the trial rather than on the murder itself, so that most whites experienced the murder as "a sad, impersonal event" that was detached

from the horrors of the violence associated with the corporal mutilation, "the visual evidence of the crime" itself. Berger insists further that "failure to publish (images of the corpse) signified a failure to grapple with the race-based killing of blacks." See Martin Berger, *Seeing through Race: A Reinterpretation of Civil Rights Photography* (Berkeley: University of California Press, 2011), 126–27, 129, 133.

16. My thanks to Charles Davis for helping me to consider the deeper relationships that exist between the Till photograph and the Hedrich Blessing photographs.

17. For example, it is possible to find photographs of black families and their homes in *Ebony* from the 1950s. However, their number is few, and they tended to accompany features of extraordinarily prominent black families or celebrities rather than the countless images of ordinary whites that appeared with housing images during the same period in (again) countless publications. For more on this, see Harris, *Little White Houses*, 61, 85, 95, 101.

18. James Loewen, *Sundown Towns: A Hidden Dimension of American Racism* (New York: Touchstone, 2006), 125.

19. Loewen, *Sundown Towns.*

20. J. G. Maynard, "Program Information for Designing Architects, United States Gypsum's Research Village of Low Cost Homes," Hugh Stubbins Collection, F155.08, Special Collections, Frances Loeb Library, Harvard Design School. It should be noted that in this program, the firm of Keyes, Smith, and Satterlee is listed as one of the six participating architects instead of Lethbridge. Francis Lethbridge was a partner in this firm. The architectural advisory panel consisted of L. Morgan Yost, John Root, and Richard Bennett, and a builder advisory panel consisting of Rodney Lockwood, Leonard Frank, Martin Bartling, Nathan Manilow, Andrew Place, Richard Hughes, and Ned Cole.

21. The pairing of builders with architects was as follows: Leonard Frank worked with Hugh Stubbins; Joseph Eichler worked with A. Quincy Jones; Alex Simms worked with Gilbert Coddington; Eli Luria with Francis Lethbridge; Don Drummond with Harris Armstrong; and Frank Robertson with O'Neil Ford. "Research Village," *Arts + Architecture*, March 1954, p. 24.

22. Author unknown, *Business of Building*, 1955, p. 2.

23. "Data on United States Gypsum Research Village: Purpose of Program," typed manuscript, no date, p. 2. Hugh Stubbins Collection, F155.09, Special Collections, Frances Loeb Library, Harvard Design School.

24. "Research Village: Architect-Builder Collaboration," *Progressive Architecture*, March, 1954, p. 10. In cases where architects used products that were manufactured by direct competitors of USG, the architects were asked to substitute a USG product. See letter from L. Morgan Yost to Hugh Stubbins, December 24, 1953, Hugh Stubbins Collection, F155.07, Special Collections, Frances Loeb Library, Harvard Design School.

25. Hugh Stubbins Collection, letter dated May 25, 1955, F155.03, Special Collections Department, Frances Loeb Library, Harvard Design School. On prices for houses in Levittown, Pennsylvania, see Harris, "The House I Live In," 200–242.

26. Author unknown, *Business of Building*, 1955, p. 2.

27. Again, I wish to thank Charles Davis for his thoughtful advice in this section.

28. The models in the photographs may or may not have been professionals, but it appears the photography firm used the same people to pose as family members and house occupants for the various houses, perhaps instructing them to change clothing and wigs in order to give the appearance of multiple families occupying the various model homes. I am grateful to Steve Hall from Hedrich Blessing for making time to talk with me about this in a telephone conversation on October 27, 2015. Hall noted that the models may well have been Hedrich Blessing friends or family members since hiring models was expensive, and using relatives or friends as models was a fairly common practice. Ironically, this made the photographs even more akin to the family snapshot genre discussed in the next paragraphs.

29. Susan Sontag, *On Photography* (New York: Picador, Farrar, Straus & Giroux, 1973), 8.

30. Diane S. Hope, "Memorializing Affluence in the Postwar Family: Kodak's Colorama in Grand Central Terminal (1950–1990)," in *Visual Rhetoric: A Reader in Communication and American Culture*, ed. Lester C. Olson, Cara A. Finnegan, and Diane S. Hope, 313–26 (Los Angeles: Sage, 2008), 323.

31. See O'Gorman as noted above, and Nicholas Mirzoeff, *The Right to Look: A Counterhistory of Visuality* (Durham, NC: Duke University Press, 2011), 3, 6.

32. See Kimberlé Williams Crenshaw, *On Intersectionality: Essential Writings* (New York: New Press, forthcoming); and Patricia Hill Collins and Sirma Bilge, *Intersectionality (Key Concepts)* (Cambridge: Polity Press, 2016).

33. U.S. Gypsum, *Operative Remodeling: The New Profit Frontier for Builders*, with National Association of Home Builders (Chicago: U.S. Gypsum, 1956), 118.

34. Albert Cole, frontispiece, in U.S. Gypsum, *Operative Remodeling*. Albert Cole was an administrator for the Housing and Home Finance Agency.

35. U.S. Gypsum, *Operative Remodeling*, 11.

36. Hugh Stubbins Collection, Press Release from A. J. Watt, General Merchandise Manager, April 6, 1955. F.E029, Special Collections, Frances Loeb Library, Harvard Design School.

37. On the relationship between family snapshots, advertising, and capitalism, see Diane S. Hope, "Memorializing Affluence in the Postwar Family: Kodak's Colorama in Grand Central Terminal (1950–1990)," in *Visual Rhetoric: A Reader in Communication and American Culture*, ed. Lester C. Olson, Cara A. Finnegan, Diane S. Hope (Los Angeles: Sage Publications, 2008), 316–21.

38. A. Nordstrom, "Dreaming in Color," in *Colorama: The World's Largest Photographs*,

ed. A. Nordstrom and P. Roalf (New York: Aperture Foundation, 2004), 5. Cited in Hope, "Memorializing Affluence," 317.

39. Lorna Roth, "Looking at Shirley, the Ultimate Norm: Colour Balance, Image Technologies, and Cognitive Equity," *Canadian Journal of Communication* 34 (2009): 111–36. Accessed online July 12, 2017, at http://www.cjc-online.ca/index.php/journal/article/view/2196/3069.

40. Marsha Ackerman, "What Should Women (and Men) Want? Advertising Home Air Conditioning in the Fifties," *Columbia Journal of American Studies* 3, no. 1 (1998): 12.

41. Tony Chapman, "Stage Sets for Ideal Lives: Images of Home in Contemporary Show Homes," in *Ideal Homes? Social Change and Domestic Life*, ed. Tony Chapman and Jenny Hockey (London: Routledge, 1999), 45, 48.

42. On the rhetorical power of documentary photography, see Reginald Twigg, "The Performative Dimension of Surveillance: Jacob Riis' 'How the Other Half Lives,'" in *Visual Rhetoric: A Reader in Communication and Culture*, ed. Lester C. Olson, Cara A. Finnegan, and Diane S. Hope (Los Angeles: Sage, 2008), 23.

13. Race and Tropical Architecture

Special thanks to Irene Cheng, T. K. Sabapathy, and especially Lim Chong Keat for their insights. Research for this chapter is supported by a Ministry of Education Academic Research Fund (Tier 1) for "Agents of Modernity: Pioneer Builders, Architecture and Independence in Singapore, 1890s–1970s," WBS no. R-295–000–127–112.

1. Following Sibel Bozdoğan, I use "visible politics" to foreground how architecture was deployed to outwardly project certain forms of political ideology. See Sibel Bozdoğan, *Modernism and Nation Building: Turkish Architectural Culture in the Early Republic* (Seattle: University of Washington Press, 2001).

2. Quoted in Udo Kultermann, "Architecture in South-East Asia, 4: Malaysia," *Mimar* 26 (1987): 68. This is confirmed in an interview with Tay Kheng Soon, July 29, 2004.

3. Tay Kheng Soon, *Mega-Cities in the Tropics: Towards an Architectural Agenda for the Future* (Singapore: Institute of Southeast Asian Studies, 1989), 10.

4. Tay, *Mega-Cities in the Tropics*, 10.

5. Abidin Kusno, *Behind the Postcolonial: Architecture, Urban Space and Political Cultures in Indonesia* (London: Routledge, 2000), 199.

6. The other four were Teoh Ong Tuck, Lee Seng Long, Liew Peng Leong, and Wee Chwee Heng. "Five to Help 'Malayanise' Designs in Architecture," *Malay Mail*, August 24, 1963.

7. Harry Chia, "A Malayan Style of Architecture Is at Last on the Way," *SFP*, June 23, 1960.

8. Tay Kheng Soon, "Neo-Tropicality or Neo-Colonialism?," *Singapore Architect* 211 (2001): 21.

9. See Jiat-Hwee Chang, *A Genealogy of Tropical Architecture: Colonial Networks, Nature and Technoscience* (London: Routledge, 2016).

10. Hannah Le Roux, "The Networks of Tropical Architecture," *Journal of Architecture* 8 (2003).

11. Chang, *Genealogy of Tropical Architecture*; and David Arnold, *The Problem of Nature: Environment, Culture and European Expansion* (Oxford: Blackwell, 1996).

12. Raymond Honey, "An Architecture for Malaya," *PETA* 3, no. 2 (1960). The battle for the "hearts and minds" was not limited to architecture. It was even evident in other cultural realms, such as fine art. See Yu Jin Seng, "Curator's Notes," in *From Words to Pictures: Art during the Emergency* (Singapore: Singapore Art Museum, 2007).

13. J. S. Furnivall, *Colonial Policy and Practice* (New York: New York University Press, 1956), 304–5.

14. Tan Jing Quee, "The Politics of a Divided National Consciousness," in *The May 13 Generation*, ed. Tan Jing Quee, Tan Kok Chiang, and Hong Lysa (Petaling Jaya: Strategic Information and Research Development Centre, 2011).

15. Anthony J. Stockwell, "The White Man's Burden and Brown Humanity: Colonialism and Ethnicity in British Malaya," *Asian Journal of Social Science* 10, no. 1 (1982): 54.

16. Stockwell, "White Man's Burden," 54; Charles Hirschman, "The Making of Race in Colonial Malaya: Political Economy and Racial Ideology," *Sociological Forum* 1, no. 2 (1986); Charles Hirschman, "The Meaning and Measurement of Ethnicity in Malaysia: An Analysis of Census Classifications," *Journal of Asian Studies* 46, no. 3 (1987); and Daniel P. S. Goh, "From Colonial Pluralism to Postcolonial Multiculturalism: Race, State Formation and the Question of Cultural Diversity in Malaysia and Singapore," *Sociology Compass* 2, no. 1 (2008).

17. Stockwell, "White Man's Burden," 57. See also Sandra Khor Manickam, *Taming the Wild: Aborigines and Racial Knowledge in Colonial Malaya* (Singapore: NUS Press, 2015), 121–22.

18. C. M. Turnbull, *A History of Modern Singapore* (Singapore: NUS Press, 2005), 90–91, 247; and Joe Conceicao, *Singapore and the Many-Headed Monster: A Look at Racial Riots against a Socio-Historical Ground* (Singapore: Horizon, 2007).

19. Embong Abdul Rahman, "Revisiting Malaya: Envisioning the Nation, the History of Ideas and the Idea of History," *Inter-Asia Cultural Studies* 16, no. 1 (2015).

20. See Mark Ravinder Frost and Yu-Mei Balasingamchow, *Singapore: A Biography* (Singapore: Editions Didier Millet, 2009), 327–32.

21. Sy Ren Quah, "Imagining Malaya, Practising Multiculturalism: The Malayan Consciousness of Singapore Chinese Intellectuals in the 1950s," *Inter-Asia Cultural Studies* 16, no. 1 (2015); Chen Chong Swee, *Unfettered Ink: The Writings of Chen Chong*

Swee, trans. Chow Teck Seng, Goh Ngee Hui, and Ng Kum Hoon (Singapore: National Gallery, 2017); Tan Jing Quee, Tan Kok Chiang, and Hong Lysa, eds., *The May 13 Generation* (Petaling Jaya: Strategic Information and Research Development Centre, 2011).

22. My use of "creolized" here draws from Brian Bernards, *Writing the South Seas: Imagining the Nanyang in Chinese and Southeast Asian Postcolonial Literature* (Seattle: University of Washington Press, 2015).

23. Stockwell, "White Man's Burden," 62.

24. Zuraini Md Ali, "Tan Sri Dato' Dr Mubin Sheppard: Pioneer in the Conservation of Historical Buildings in Malaysia, 1950–1994," *Journal of the Malaysian Branch of the Royal Asiatic Society* 83, no. 2 (2010). For the publications of Sheppard, see H. S. Barlow, "Bibliography of Tan Sri Dato Dr Haji Mubin Sheppard," *Journal of the Malaysian Branch of the Royal Asiatic Society* 68, no. 2 (1995).

25. Zuraini, "Tan Sri Dato' Dr Mubin Sheppard," 58.

26. Mark Crinson, "Singapore's Moment: Critical Regionalism, Its Colonial Roots and Profound Aftermaths," *Journal of Architecture* 13, no. 5 (2008).

27. He restored and converted the old Malay istana at Ampang Tinggi into the State Museum of Negeri Sembilan during the early 1950s.

28. Ho was probably also selected because he was the president (1954–1968) of the Singapore Art Society and had experience working closely with the British colonial government to promote Malayan culture through art. See Seng, "Curator's Notes."

29. Lai Chee Kien, *Building Merdeka: Independence Architecture in Kuala Lumpur, 1957–1966* (Kuala Lumpur: Gelari Petronas, 2007), 72.

30. J. de V. Allen, "Two Imperialists: A Study of Sir Frank Swettenham and Sir Hugh Clifford," *Journal of the Malaysian Branch of the Royal Asiatic Society* 37, no. 1 (1964).

31. J. M. Gullick, "Mubin Sheppard," *Journal of the Malaysian Branch of the Royal Asiatic Society* 68, no. 2 (1995).

32. Allen, "Two Imperialists," 60, 61.

33. 莫美颜, "年轻建筑学者看南大华族传统复兴式建筑," 联合早报, October 22, 2010. Mo Meiyan, "A young architectural scholar's view of Chinese traditional revival architecture," *Lianhe Zaobao*, October 22, 2010.

34. Delin Lai, "Searching for a Modern Chinese Monument: The Design of the Sun Yat-Sen Mausoleum in Nanjing," *Journal of the Society of Architectural Historians* 64, no. 1 (2005).

35. Delin Lai, "Idealizing a Chinese Style: Rethinking Early Writings on Chinese Architecture and the Design of the National Central Museum in Nanjing," *Journal of the Society of Architectural Historians* 73, no. 1 (2014).

36. Based on an unpublished lecture by Ho Puay Peng, son of Ho Beng Hong, which was delivered on August 2, 2014, at Chung Cheng High. The senior Ho (1919–1986)

received his architectural education at the National Central University, Chongqing, from 1943 to 1947. As a student of Liu Dunzhen, he was trained to design Chinese traditional revival architecture.

37. Tan, Tan, and Hong, eds., *The May 13 Generation*.

38. Sikko Visscher, *The Business of Politics and Ethnicity: A History of the Singapore Chinese Chamber of Commerce and Industry* (Singapore: NUS Press, 2007).

39. A series of articles appeared in *PETA, Journal of the Federation of Malaya Society of Architects (FMSA)*, from 1955 to 1960, under the theme of "Towards a Malayan Architecture." The series culminated in "Discussion on 'What Is Malayan Architecture,'" *PETA* 3, no. 4 (1961).

40. See especially "Discussion on 'What Is Malayan Architecture,'" *PETA* 3, no. 4 (1961).

41. For the modernist faith in fundamental principles and climatic design, see chapter 6 of my book, *A Genealogy of Tropical Architecture*. The most articulate advocate for tropical architecture as Malayan architecture among the expatriate architects was Julius Posener, a German architect and architectural historian who was teaching at the Technical College in Kuala Lumpur in the 1950s. See Julius Posener, "Architecture in Malaya: Impressions of a Newcomer," *PETA* 2, no. 1 (1957).

42. All twenty-three members and ten associate members of the Society of Malayan Architects in 1958–1959 were Chinese. Of the thirty-six student members, only three were non-Chinese. "The Society of Malayan Architects," *Journal of the Society of Malayan Architects* 1, no. 1 (1958).

43. *Kampong* or *kampung* is the Malay word for village or urban squatter settlement, although historically it also denoted an urban district and a compound, or a unit of enclosure. Imran bin Tajudeen, "From 'Kampong' to 'Compound': Retracing the forgotten connections," *Singapura Stories* website, accessed July 3, 2017, http://singapura stories.com/kampungcompound-houses/kampungcampongcompound/.

44. Eu Jin Seow, "The Malayan Touch," *Rumah: Journal of the Society of Malayan Architects* 3 (1960): 15, 18, 20.

45. Lim Chong Keat, "Courses in Architecture at the Singapore Polytechnic," *Rumah: Journal of the Society of Malayan Architects* 2 (1959): 33.

46. Eu Jin Seow's mother was a descendent of Tan Tock Seng, one of the early revenue farmers and philanthropists in the Straits Settlements, and his father was a general manager at the Overseas Chinese Bank, one of the oldest local banks. Alfred Wong is a descendant of Wong Ah Fook, a revenue farmer, building contractor, and philanthropist of Johor and Singapore between the second half of nineteenth century and early twentieth century. Lim Chong Keat and William Lim likewise came from prominent families, distinguished less, comparative speaking, by their wealth than by the political and social standings of their members. Lim Chong Keat's uncle is Sir Lim Han Hoe, a physician and politician who was the second Malayan to be knighted, and

his brother is Lim Chong Eu, a former chief minister of Penang. William Lim's father is Richard Chuan Hoe Lim, a lawyer, Labour Front politician, and deputy speaker of the Legislative Assembly in the 1950s. See Alfred Hong Kwok Wong, *Recollections of Life in an Accidental Nation* (Singapore: Select Books, 2016); Patricia Pui Huen Lim, *Wong Ah Fook: Immigrant, Builder and Entrepreneur* (Singapore: Times, 2002); and Eu Jin Seow, "Oral History Interview," ed. Jannie Poh Hoon Lim (Singapore: National Archives of Singapore, 1980).

47. Chua Ai Lin, "Imperials Subjects, Straits Citizens: Anglophone Asians and the Struggle for Political Rights in Inter-War Singapore," in *Paths Not Taken: Political Pluralism in Post-War Singapore*, ed. Carl Trocki and Michael Barr (Singapore: NUS Press, 2008).

48. Chang, *Genealogy of Tropical Architecture*, 188–91.

49. Lim Chong Keat, "Book Review," *Rumah: Journal of the Singapore Institute of Architects* 4 (1961). Oakley was a British architect who had worked in Kuwait and Jamaica and done research at the Colonial Liaison Unit at the Building Research Station by the time he wrote the book. For an account of his career, see Robert Home, "Knowledge Networks and Postcolonial Careering: David Oakley (1927–2003)," *ABE Journal: European Architecture beyond Europe [Online]* 4 (2013).

50. Its function as the Trade Union House ceased in 2000, when the National Trades Union Congress moved out of the building.

51. "An Afro-Asian Common Market," *Straits Times*, October 26, 1965.

52. *Souvenir Brochure for the Opening of the Singapore Conference Hall & Trade Union House on 15th October, 1965* (Singapore: Singapore Government, 1965); and "A Hall of International Standing and Unique in Many Ways," *Straits Times*, October 15, 1965.

53. Tan Kok Meng, "Critical Weave: Interwoven Identities in the Singapore Conference Hall," *Journal of South East Asian Architecture* 4, no. 1 (2000): 21.

54. Tay Kheng Soon, "Trade Union House and Singapore Conference Hall at Shenton Way," *Singapore Architect* 212 (2001). This is high praise indeed from Tay, who had tried to develop a vocabulary of modern tropical architecture for several decades. See Jiat-Hwee Chang, "Deviating Discourse: Tay Kheng Soon and the Architecture of Postcolonial Development in Tropical Asia," *Journal of Architectural Education* 63, no. 3 (2010); and Tay Kheng Soon, "The Architectural Aesthetics of Tropicality," in *Line, Edge & Shade : The Search for a Design Language in Tropical Asia; Tay Kheng Soon & Akitek Tenggara*, ed. Robert Powell and Tay Kheng Soon (Singapore: Page One, 1997).

55. Carl Alexander Gibson-Hill, "Malay Hats and Dish-Covers," *Journal of the Malayan Branch of the Royal Asiatic Society* 24, no. 1 (1951): 136.

56. Lim has a lifelong interest in vernacular houses of not just Malaya but of the southeast Asian region. He was the honorary project director of the Southeast Asia

Culture Research Project (SEACRP), 1981 to 1984, based at the Institute of Southeast Asia Studies (ISEAS) in Singapore, and funded by Toyota Foundation, Japan. The project was initiated to photographically document the "fast disappearing" traditional buildings in Southeast Asia that were "irretrievably altered in the modernisation process." Lim curated a number of photographic exhibitions of these traditional buildings. *Documentation of Traditional Architecture and Built Form: Southeast Asian Cultural Research Programme* (Singapore: Institute of Southeast Asia, 1983); and Lim Chong Keat, "Introduction," in *Habitat in Southeast Asia: A Pictorial Survey of Folk Architecture* (Kuala Lumpur: National Art Gallery, 1986).

57. Lim Chong Keat, "The International Context for Southeast Asian Architecture," in *Architecture and Identity: Proceedings of the Regional Seminar*, ed. Robert Powell (Singapore: Concept Media, 1983).

58. Lim, "International Context," 25.

59. Fuller's view of Southeast Asia as a cradle of early human civilization is most clearly articulated in chapter 1, "Speculative Prehistory of Humanity," in R. Buckminster Fuller, *Critical Path* (New York: St. Martin's Press, 1981), 1–24.

60. Fuller, chapter 1 in *Critical Path*, 5.

61. Fuller, chapter 1 in *Critical Path*, 5, 6, 13.

14. "Compartmentalized World"

1. Frantz Fanon, *The Wretched of the Earth* (1963), trans. Richard Philcox (New York: Grove Press, 2004), 3–5.

2. Frantz Fanon, *Black Skin White Masks* (1952), trans. C. L. Markmann (London: Pluto, 1986), 4.

3. "The architecture of this work is rooted in the temporal": Fanon, *Black Skin*, 5. "The future should be an edifice supported by living men": Fanon, *Black Skin*, 6.

4. Sylvia Wynter, "Towards the Sociogenic Principle: Fanon, Identity, and the Puzzle of Conscious Experience, and What It Is Like to Be 'Black,'" *National Identity and Socio-Political Changes in Latin America*, ed. Mercedes F. Durán-Cogan and Antonio Gómez-Moriana (New York: Routledge, 2001), 31. On Fanon's social therapy, see Adam Shatz, "Where Life Is Seized," *London Review of Books*, January 19, 2017, 19–27.

5. Fanon, *Black Skin*, 18, 120. Carothers's work was endorsed by the World Health Organization and the likes of Margaret Mead and even Marshall McLuhan: Fanon, *Wretched*, 226–27.

6. J. C. Carothers, "Frontal Lobe Function and the African," *Journal of Mental Science* 97 (1951), 41.

7. J. C. Carothers, *The African Mind* (Geneva: World Health Organization, 1953).

8. Peter Hudis, *Frantz Fanon—Philosopher of the Barricades* (London: Pluto, 2015), 25–26, 35.

9. Quoted in Hudis, *Frantz Fanon*, 59.

10. David Macey, *Frantz Fanon—A Biography* (London: Verso, 2012), 320.

11. On the many etymologies of Mau Mau, see Brendon Nicholls, *Ngugi wa Thiong'o, Gender, and the Ethics of Postcolonial Reading* (Farnham: Ashgate, 2010), 61–62.

12. The chronology is tight. By March 1953 some villagization had been introduced, but it was not until June 1954 that it was adopted as "full-scale policy": Caroline Elkins, *Britain's Gulag: The Brutal End of Empire in Kenya* (London: Jonathan Cape, 2005), 409n3.

13. Carothers's predecessor, H. L. Gordon, saw urbanization as key to African mental illness: Jock McCulloch, *Colonial Psychiatry and "the African Mind"* (Cambridge: Cambridge University Press, 1995), 46–47.

14. J. C. Carothers, *The Psychology of Mau Mau* (Nairobi: Colony and Protectorate of Kenya, 1951), 5–6.

15. Carothers, *Psychology*, 15.

16. For a contemporary anthropological account ascribing primitive qualities to isolated dwellings, see Robert Redfield, *The Primitive World and Its Transformation* (Ithaca, NY: Cornell University Press, 1953), xi, 7–8.

17. Carothers, *Psychology*, 22–23.

18. Carothers, *Psychology*, 25.

19. T. N. Harper, *The End of Empire and the Making of Malaya* (Cambridge: Cambridge University Press, 1999).

20. Elkins, *Britain's Gulag*.

21. For more on Kenyatta and his book, see Carolyn Marvin Shaw, *Colonial Inscriptions: Race, Sex and Class in Kenya* (Minneapolis: University of Minnesota Press, 1995), 118–48; and Barbara Celarent, book review "*Facing Mount Kenya* by Jomo Kenyatta," *American Journal of Sociology* 116 (September 2010): 722–28.

22. Jomo Kenyatta, *Facing Mount Kenya* (London: Secker & Warburg, 1938), 21.

23. Kenyatta, *Facing*, 27.

24. Kenyatta, *Facing*, 47.

25. Kenyatta, *Facing*, 79.

26. See James Clifford, *The Predicament of Culture: Twentieth-Century Ethnography, Literature, and Art* (Cambridge, MA: Harvard University Press, 1988), 21–22, 25–32, 45–46.

27. Simon Gikandi, *Ngugi wa Thiong'o* (Cambridge: Cambridge University Press, 2000), 98–100.

28. Ngũgĩ Wa Thiong'o, *A Grain of Wheat* (1967) (London: Penguin, 2002), 98.

29. Ngũgĩ, *Grain*, 136.

30. Ngũgĩ, *Grain*, 182.

31. Christer Bruun, "Greek or Latin? The Owner's Choice of Names for *Vernae* in Rome," in *Roman Slavery and Roman Material Culture*, ed. Michele George (Toronto: University of Toronto Press, 2013), 25–26.

32. G. W. F. Hegel, *Phenomenology of Spirit*, trans. by A. V. Miller (Oxford: Oxford University Press, 1977), 111 para. 179.

33. Hegel, *Phenomenology*, 117 para. 193.

34. Vivek Chibber, *Postcolonial Theory and the Specter of Capital* (London: Verso, 2013), 238–39.

35. G. A. Myers, *Verandahs of Power: Colonialism and Space in Urban Africa* (Syracuse, NY: Syracuse University Press, 2002), 34–37.

36. Bruce Berman, "Bureaucracy and Incumbent Violence: Colonial Administration and the Origins of the 'Mau Mau' Emergency," in *Unhappy Valley: Conflict in Kenya and Africa*, ed. Bruce Berman and John Lonsdale (London: James Currey, 1992), 254.

37. G. B. Masefield, "A Comparison Between Settlement in Villages and Isolated Homesteads," *Journal of African Administration* 7 (April 1955): 65, 67.

38. O. E. B. Hughes, "Villages in the Kikuyu Country," *Journal of African Administration* 7 (October, 1955): 172.

39. Betty Spence and Barrie Biermann, "M'Pogga," *Architectural Review* 116 (July 1954): 36–40.

40. "African Housing in Kenya," *Colonial Building Notes* 25 (1954): 3; Hamzah-Sendut, "Planning Resettlement Villages in Malaya," *Planning Outlook* 1 (December 1966): 58–70; and Ian Marshall, "Letter from Nairobi," *Architect & Building News* 215 (February 18, 1959): 210–11.

41. Terry Ward, "Kenya Landscape," *244 Journal of the University of Manchester Architectural and Planning Society* (Spring 1960): 17.

42. On Connell's African career see Dennis Sharp, "The Modern Movement in East Africa," *Habitat International* 7:5/6 (1983): 311–26.

43. Wynter, "Towards," 40.

44. Kenyatta, *Facing*, 309. See also Wynter, "Towards," 35.

45. Fanon, *Black Skin*, 229; and David Marriott, "Inventions of Existence: Sylvia Wynter, Frantz Fanon, Sociogeny and 'the Damned,'" *CR: Centennial Review* 11 (Winter 2011): 46.

46. Henri Lefebvre's "production of space" tends to emphasize the "unity of the productive process," and not compartments, referring space back to its rationality within an economic mode of production: Henri Lefebvre, *The Production of Space*, trans. D. Nicholson-Smith (Oxford: Basil Blackwell, 1991), 42.

47. On the colony as state of exception, see Achille Mbembe, "Necropolitics," *Public Culture* 15, no. 1 (2003): 11–40.

48. Richard Hughes, "Maragua Development Plan," 1, Fifth Year Thesis (1953), Architectural Association Archives. See also Rhodri Windsor Liscombe, "Modernism, Multi-Racial Community and Mau Mau," in *The Scaffolding of Empire*, ed. Peter Scriver (Adelaide: CAMEA, 2007), 17–42.

49. Richard Hughes, "Town Plan to Facilitate Racial Integration," *New Commonwealth* 26, no. 6 (September 14, 1953): 287.

50. Regina Göckede, "The Architect as Colonial Technocrat of Dependent Modernisation: Ernst May's Plans for Kampala," in *Afropolis—City Media Art*, ed. Kerstin Pinther, Larissa Forster, and Christian Hanussek (Auckland Park: Jacana Media, 2012), 54–65.

51. Hughes, "Maragua," 1. On nationalists' relegation of the integration issue, see Ngũgĩ Wa Thiong'o, *Dreams in a Time of War—A Childhood Memoir* (London: Vintage Books, 2011), 204.

52. 1:1.2:4.5 in numbers, or two houses per acre, five houses per acre, and twelve houses per acre.

53. Hughes, "Town Plan," 287.

54. Hughes, "Maragua," 6.

55. Richard Hughes, *Capricorn—David Stirling's Second African Campaign* (London: Radcliffe Press, 2003), 28; and Hughes, "Maragua," 12.

56. David Matless, "Appropriate Geography: Patrick Abercrombie and the Energy of the World," *Journal of Design History* 6, no. 3 (1993): 167.

57. J. H. Forshaw and Patrick Abercrombie, *County of London Plan* (London: Macmillan, 1943), 20.

58. Richard Hornsey, *The Spiv and the Architect: Unruly Life in Postwar London* (Minneapolis: University of Minnesota Press, 2010), 46.

59. Forshaw and Abercrombie, *County of London Plan*, 122.

60. See, for instance, Michael Banton, *The Coloured Quarter: Negro Immigrants in an English City* (London: Jonathan Cape, 1955).

61. Gillian Swanson, *Drunk with Glitter: Space, Consumption and Sexual Instability in Modern Urban Culture* (London: Routledge, 2007), 48.

62. Hughes, *Capricorn*, 70–73, 82.

63. On the new type of race relations expert, see Chris Waters, "'Dark Strangers' in our Midst: Discourses of Race and Nation in Britain, 1947–73," *Journal of British Studies* 36 (April 1997): 209.

64. Frank Mort, *Capital Affairs: London and the Making of the Permissive Society* (New Haven, CT: Yale University Press, 2010), 136. I am grateful to Lynda Nead for letting me see her chapter "30,000 Colour Problems" from her forthcoming book *The Tiger in the Smoke.*

65. Hughes, *Capricorn*, 70; Hughes, "Town Plan," 287–89; and *Daily Mail*, July 28, 1953.

66. Mark Crinson, "Imperial Modernism," *Architecture and Urbanism in the British Empire*, ed. G. A. Bremner (Oxford: Oxford University Press, 2016), 211–14.

15. Style, Race, and a Mosque of the "Òyìnbó Dúdú" (White-Black) in Lagos Colony, 1894

1. Ron Geaves, *Islam in Victorian Britain: The Life and Times of Abdullah Quilliam* (Leicestershire: Kube Publishing, 2010), 75.

2. "The Consecration of Mr. Shitta's Mosque," *Lagos Weekly Record*, July 7, 1894. Additionally, see "The Sultan of Turkey and West African Muslims: Mohammed Shitta Bey," *Lagos Weekly Record*, May 19, 1894, for an earlier journalistic piece that informed the Lagosian populace of Quilliam's impending visit.

3. "The Consecration of Mr. Shitta's Mosque," *Lagos Weekly Record*, July 7, 1894.

4. For more on Quilliam, see Geaves, *Islam in Victorian Britain*, 2–3.

5. "The Consecration of Mr. Shitta's Mosque," *Lagos Weekly Record*, July 7, 1894.

6. Michael Echeruo, "The Intellectual Context," in *Victorian Lagos: Aspects of Nineteenth Century Lagos Life* (London: Macmillan, 1977), 37–39.

7. Echeruo, "The Intellectual Context," 37–39.

8. R. C. Abraham, "Òyìnbó," in Dictionary of Modern Yoruba (London: University of London Press, 1958), 459. "Òyìnbó" means the person whose skin has been peeled off due to the harshness of the sun, and was a word used to define Caucasians who Lagosians met. The word may have originated in the fifteenth century when Portuguese traders bought slaves from the king of Lagos, as well as from wealthy merchants in this region.

9. "Address of His Excellency Sir Gilbert T. Carter K.C.M.G.," *Lagos Weekly Record*, July 7, 1894.

10. A. B. Adéribigbé, *Lagos: The Development of an African City* (Ìkeja: Longman Nigeria, 1975), 1–3. In the Òyọ́ dialect, Ògúnfúnminire means the "god of iron has given me success." Additionally, see Liora Bigon, *A History of Urban Planning in Two West African Colonial Capitals: Residential Segregation in British Lagos and French Dakar (1850–1930)* (Lewiston, NY: Edwin Mellen Press, 2009).

11. Spencer Brown, "A History of the People of Lagos State, 1852–1886" (PhD diss., Northwestern University, 1964). Olówógbówó meant "the rich take money" in Yorùbá. The term "Sàró" was a term that described the origins of a particular African immigrant population in Lagos who resettled in the colony from Sierra Leone. In fact, "Sàró" was a conflation of "Sierra Leone." "Sàró" also spoke to the ability of such individuals to behave like Englishmen and to cultivate Victorian customs.

12. Brown, "History of the People," 9. However, the natives called the town Èkó or Oko, which means "farm" in Yorùbá, since their ancestors had moved to the location to grow food. Èkó was originally comprised of the king's palace and the market located south of it. Historically, markets have had a religious function among the Yorùbá. Kings situate markets south of their palaces.

13. Lower-ranking ọba in other parts of the city like the king of Oto recognized the

supremacy of Ògúnfúnminire's throne. Nevertheless, these kings presided over smaller kingdoms, which present-day Lagosians refer to as towns. See O. A. Akinyeye, *Eko: Landmarks of Lagos, Nigeria* (Lagos: Mandilas Group, 1999), 65. The king of one of these kingdoms, Oto, built his palace in 1805.

14. Marianno Carneiro da Cunha, *From Slave Quarters to Town Houses: Brazilian Architecture in Nigeria and the People's Republic of Benin* (Sao Paulo: Livraria Nobel-Edusp, 1985), 52.

15. Carneiro da Cunha, *Slave Quarters to Town Houses*, 42.

16. The urban historian Liora Bigon gently inveighs against the criticism of British colonial urban planners who stated that the nineteenth-century layout of some parts of Lagos was "freestyle." Bigon asks if there was a logic to the meandering nature and lack of clearly defined edges of the urban corridors in Lagos. Chieftain architecture, with its "irregular plans" protruding out in different directions and which varied along the sides of each king's palace in other kingdoms, may have given more fodder to the colonial planners' prejudice against local urban design. The sight of the oba's palace in Lagos protruding in different directions because it had many rooms around numerous courtyards may have given the colonial planners the idea that local urban designing was devoid of thinking. See Liora Bigon, "Sanitation and Street Layout in Early Colonial Lagos: British and Indigenous Conceptions, 1851–1900," *Planning Perspectives*, no. 20 (2005), 253–54; and David Aradeon, "Architecture," in *The Living Culture of Nigeria*, ed. Saburi Biobaku (Lagos, Nigeria: Thomas Nelson, 1976), 44. Evidence to support this fact is based on the Nigerian architect David Aradeon's discovery of adages for secular buildings in the 1970s. Examples of such sayings were "Ile Awosifila," which means, "The house that makes you lose your cap when admiring its height." That proverb highlighted the grandiosity of the structure.

17. Robert S. Smith, *The Lagos Consulate, 1851–1861* (Berkeley: University of California Press, 1979), 40–181.

18. Smith, *Lagos Consulate*, 40.

19. "Ìsàlè Èkó" literally means "the bottom of Èkó" or metaphorically the origins of Èkó in Yorùbá. Èkó is the Yorùbá name of the original town that eventually became Lagos.

20. "Pópó Àgùdà" literally meant the "Area of the Àgùdà" in Yorùbá. It could also mean "Àgùdà Street."

21. Historically Lagosians had left Marina empty because it had served as a burial ground for outcast individuals. See Liora Bigon, "Tracking Ethno-Cultural Differences: The Lagos Steam Tramway, 1902–1933," *Journal of History Geography*, no. 33 (2007), 607. Additionally, see Bigon, "Sanitation and Street Layout," 247–69, for a discussion of how British colonialists criticized local urban planning strategies in Lagos, as well as the colonists' lackadaisical efforts to extend their urban design strategies beyond Marina.

22. Crowther published a Yorùbá Bible in 1840 and a dictionary in 1843. Both were critical to the creation of a written language that was lucid to natives who spoke similar dialects in southwestern Nigeria.

23. Mac Dixon-Fyle, "The Saro in Political Life of Early Port-Harcourt, 1913–49," *Journal of African History* 30, no. 1 (1989), 126.

24. An explanation needs to be provided regarding how the terms "omọ ilé," "indigene," and "Lagosians" are being used here. These categories serve, in this essay, to define the locals who lived in the Èkó kingdom. Citizens of other realms such as Èpé, which presently is in Lagos State, but which in the 1890s was not part of Lagos Colony, may not have called themselves omọ ilé. Instead, they probably associated with Èpé—possessing a different dialect that underscored their difference from the citizens of Èkó. Members of different kingdoms such as Èkó and Èpé may have seen each other as outsiders, belonging to different civilizations, and speaking distinct dialects. Hence, for both communities "race" may not have been as important a concept as the location of an individual's ancestral homeland. Yet the use of the word *òyìnbó* does suggest that an awareness of a racial other entered into the minds of some omọ ilé as a way to account for their difference from the European residents in the colony. The Sàró bishop Samuel Ajayi Crowther listed *òyìnbó* in his dictionary of Yorùbá in 1852, which shows its usage among the omọ ilé population at that time. In his dictionary, the term is translated as the individual who "came from across the sea." Thus, òyìnbó conveyed a sense of difference that emphasized distance, and the proof to the locals that the Europeans lived across the sea was the ships they arrived on and their fairer complexions. The addition of dúdú to òyìnbó, on the other hand, suggests that the omọ ilé's language to describe foreigners became more precise in an ironic way: not only were there òyìnbó, but there were also other settlers from "across" the waters who spoke and dressed like the òyìnbó but who had complexions similar to the omọ ilé. Therefore, one may say that the racial pronouncements of the omọ ilé in the nineteenth century emerged from their interactions with other civilizations in Lagos Colony and with various immigrants settling in the colony in the nineteenth century. See Samuel Ajayi Crowther, "Oyibo," in *A Vocabulary of the Yoruba Language* (London: Seeleys, 1852), 210.

25. The Àgùdà introduced dishes such as feijão de leite and mingao in Lagos. In Antonio Olinto, *The Water House* (New York: Carrol and Graf, 1986), 77, one female Àgùdà boasted that the Afro-Brazilians taught the locals numerous construction trades and introduced cassava and cashew nuts into Lagos Colony.

26. Olinto, *Water House*, 77.

27. Rina Okonkwo, "The Lagos Auxiliary of the Anti-Slavery and Aborigines Rights Protection Society: A Re-Examination," *International Journal of African Historical Studies* 15, no. 3 (1982), 427.

28. Níyì Afọlábí, *Afro-Brazilians: Cultural Production in a Racial Democracy* (Rochester, NY: University of Rochester Press, 2009), 240.

29. Michael Echeruo, *Victorian Lagos: Aspects of Nineteenth Century Lagos Life* (London: Macmillan, 1977), 1–3.

30. Echeruo, *Victorian Lagos*, 3–4. Almost twenty years after Robert Campbell founded the *Anglo-African*, other Sàró established five more newspapers. These were the *Lagos Times and Gold Coast Advertiser* (1880), *Lagos Observer* (1882), *Eagle and Lagos Critic* (1883), the weekly *Mirror* (1887), and the *Weekly Record* (1891).

31. Echeruo, *Victorian Lagos*, 30.

32. Michael Echeruo, "The Musical Culture," in *Victorian Lagos: Aspects of Nineteenth Century Lagos Life* (London: Macmillan, 1977), 73–76. In 1882, the Brazilian Dramatic Company, which most likely consisted of Àgùdà, staged a play in honor of Queen Victoria's Jubilee. The company's patron was the German consul of Lagos, Heinrich Bey. In 1884, the Lagos Melodramatic Society organized a concert in Faji. Echeruo suggests that the society consisted of Sàró members. Furthermore, the Sàró former seaman and entrepreneur James Pinson Labulo Davies financed the Church Missionary Society Grammar School in Lagos, which opened in 1859. For more about the school, see Adéyẹmọ Elébuté, *The Life of James Pinson Labulo Davies: A Colossus of Victorian Lagos* (Lagos, Nigeria: Kachifo, 2013), 190. Elébuté is a former professor of surgery at the Lagos University Teaching Hospital and an alumnus of the Grammar School.

33. Echeruo, "Intellectual Context," 35. The author cites a letter from a Sàró (John Craig) to the English Rev. Henry Townsend stating that Sàrós were middlemen between people like Townsend and the Egbas.

34. Walter Myers, *At Her Majesty's Request: An African Princess in Victorian England* (New York: Scholastic Press, 1999); and Elébuté, *Life of James Pinson Labulo Davies*, 41–81. The second Sàró was Bishop Samuel Ajayi Crowther. The British naval commander Frederick Forbes rescued four-year-old Sarah Forbes from King Gezo of Dahomey and presented her before Queen Victoria in England. The ruler then supported Sarah Forbes financially for the next fifteen years of her life—asking the commander to raise her. Sarah Forbes eventually married the Sàró captain James Davies and lived in Freetown, Sierra Leone, before settling in Lagos. Sarah received private lessons within the Forbes household in England and later, briefly, at the Church Missionary Society Female Institution in Sierra Leone in 1851. She continued her education when Queen Victoria recalled her to England in 1855. Even when Sarah resettled as a married woman in Lagos in 1867, she was one of two Sàrós that Queen Victoria ordered her royal navy to evacuate if a state of emergency was ever declared in the city. The British queen also became godmother to Sarah's first child, Victoria. Sarah was also one of the bridesmaids in Princess Alice's wedding in 1862. Princess Alice was Queen Victoria's second-oldest daughter.

35. Echeruo, *Victorian Lagos*, 84–87. According to Echeruo, Blyden had published a book entitled *Christianity, Islam and the Negro Race* in 1887, which many black immigrants and educated natives in Lagos read. Blyden also established a Muslim school

system in Lagos that the colonial government sponsored. He also founded in Lagos a Muslim school in 1899. The ratio of Muslim to Christian conversions among Lagosian natives was 20:1 in the 1880s.

36. Pierre Verger, *Trade Relations between the Bight of Benin and Bahia from the 17th Century to the 19th Century* (Ibadan: University of Ibadan Press, 1968), 294–309. The main source is João Reis, *Slave Rebellion in Brazil: The Muslim Uprising of 1835 in Bahia* (Baltimore: Johns Hopkins University Press, 1993), 73–129.

37. Reis, *Slave Rebellion in Brazil*, 73–129.

38. Bọ́lánlé Awẹ́, "The Cultural Contribution of the Blacks of the Diaspora to Africa with Special Emphasis on Nigeria," in *Proceedings of Meeting of the Experts on the Cultural Contribution of the Blacks of the Diaspora to Africa* (Paris: UNESCO, 1983), 7.

39. Nothing else is known about the two builders beyond the mention of their first names in "The Consecration of Mr. Shitta's Mosque," *Lagos Weekly Record*, July 7, 1894.

40. "The Consecration of Mr. Shitta's Mosque," *Lagos Weekly Record*, July 7, 1894.

41. Hollis Lynch, *Edward Wilmot Blyden: Pan-Negro Patriot, 1832–1912* (London: Oxford University Press, 1967), 235. One of Shitta's relatives started an Islamic school with the Trinidadian pan-Africanist Edward Blyden.

16. Black and Blight

1. See Bill Laitner, "Activists, Neighbors Hope to Block Detroiter's Eviction," *Detroit Free Press*, August 15, 2015.

2. These particular messages were painted by Wayne Curtis, cofounder of Feedum Freedom with his wife, Myrtle.

3. See, for example, Mark Gelfand, "The Road to Urban Redevelopment: 1933–1949," in *A Nation of Cities: The Federal Government and Urban America, 1933–1965* (New York: Oxford University Press, 1975), 105–56; M. Christine Boyer, "Must American Cities Decay?," in *Dreaming the Rational City: The Myth of American City Planning* (Cambridge, MA: MIT Press, 1986), 203–32; Robert A. Beauregard, "On the Verge of Catastrophe," in *Voices of Decline: The Postwar Fate of U.S. Cities* (Cambridge: Blackwell, 1993), 103–23; Robert M. Fogelson, "Inventing Blight: Downtown and the Origins of Urban Redevelopment," in *Downtown: Its Rise and Fall, 1880–1950* (New Haven, CT: Yale University Press, 2001), 317–80; Colin Gordon, "Blighting the Way: Urban Renewal, Economic Development, and the Elusive Definition of Blight," *Fordham Urban Law Journal* 31 (2003–2004); Robert Bruegmann, "Early Remedies: From Anti-Blight to Anti-Sprawl," in *Sprawl: A Compact History* (Chicago: University of Chicago Press, 2005), 169–72; Colin Gordon, "Fighting Blight: Urban Renewal Policies and Programs, 1945–2000," in *Mapping Decline: St. Louis and the Fate of the American City* (Philadelphia: University of Pennsylvania Press, 2008); Jennifer Light, "The City Is a National Resource," in *The Nature of Cities: Ecological Visions and the American Urban Professions, 1920–1960* (Baltimore: Johns Hopkins University Press,

2009), 6–36; and Joshua Akers, "A New Urban Medicine Show: On the Limits of Blight Remediation," in *Why Detroit Matters: Decline, Renewal, and Hope in a Divided City*, ed. Brian Doucet (Bristol, UK: Policy Press, 2017).

4. Detroit Blight Removal Task Force, *Detroit Blight Removal Task Force Plan*, 2014, 1.

5. Gilbert spoke at the launch of the *Detroit Blight Removal Task Force Plan* on May 27, 2014, in Detroit.

6. "Nothing can so effectually destroy a city's future as the disproportionate increase of homes that are unsanitary, damp, dark, unclean, unattractive, unventilated, overcrowded and immoral. And this disproportionate growth is exactly what is taking place today.... The cancer is spreading." "Housing Plans Are Mapped Out: Slum Paramount Curse of Every Large City," *Detroit Free Press*, December 9, 1910.

7. In Cedric J. Robinson's decisive framing, as "the development, organization, and expansion of capitalist society pursued essentially racist directions, so too did social ideology. As a material force, then, it could be expected that racialism would inevitably permeate the social structures emergent from capitalism"; see *Black Marxism: The Making of the Black Radical Tradition* (1983; repr., Chapel Hill, NC: University of North Carolina Press, 2000), 2.

8. Cheryl I. Harris, "Whiteness as Property," *Harvard Law Review* 106:8 (1993), 1714.

9. Harris, "Whiteness as Property," 1716.

10. See Deuteronomy 28:22 in King James Bible, Cambridge Edition: 1769, and in English Revised Version Bible, Oxford Edition: 1885.

11. See Jacob A. Riis, *The Battle with the Slum* (New York: Macmillan, 1902), 37 and 76. See also Jacob A. Riis, "The Tenement House Blight," *Atlantic Monthly*, June 1899, 760–70.

12. See, for example, Alan M. Kraut, *Silent Travelers: Germs, Genes, and the "Immigrant Menace"* (Baltimore: Johns Hopkins University Press, 1994); Howard Markel, *Quarantine! East European Jewish Immigrants and the New York City Epidemics of 1892* (Baltimore: Johns Hopkins University Press, 1997); Nayan Shah, *Contagious Divides: Epidemics and Race in San Francisco's Chinatown* (Berkeley: University of California Press, 2001); and Natalia Molina, *Fit to Be Citizens? Public Health and Race in Los Angeles, 1878–1939* (Berkeley: University of California Press, 2006).

13. "Chinatown's Doom Is Foreshadowed," *San Francisco Chronicle*, September 25, 1898, 9.

14. M. Quad, "New York's Worst Side," *Detroit Free Press*, May 19, 1895, 25.

15. Len G. Shaw, "Detroit's New Housing Problem," *Detroit Free Press*, June 3, 1917, E1.

16. J. Randolph Coolidge, "The Problem of the Blighted District," *Proceedings of the Fourth National Conference on City Planning* (Boston: Town Planning Institute, 1912).

17. Coolidge, "The Problem of the Blighted District," 100.

18. Coolidge, "The Problem of the Blighted District," 101.

19. John Locke, "On Property," in *Two Treatises on Government*, ed. Peter Laslett (1689; repr., Cambridge: Cambridge University Press, 1988).

20. Richard M. Hurd, *Principles of City Land Values* (New York: Record and Guide, 1903), 117.

21. J. C. Nichols, "The Responsibility of Realtors in City Planning," *City Planning* 1, no. 1 (1925): 36.

22. Frank. B. Williams, "Discussion," *Proceedings of the Fourth National Conference on City Planning* (Boston: Town Planning Institute, 1912), 110–11.

23. See, for example, Edith Elmer Wood, *Slums and Blighted Areas in the United States* (Washington, DC: Federal Emergency Administration of Public Works, 1935); Mabel L. Walker, *Urban Blight and Slums* (Cambridge, MA: Harvard University Press, 1938); and Clarence Arthur Perry, *The Rebuilding of Blighted Areas* (New York: Regional Plan Association, 1938).

24. On the "reverse welfare state," see Roy Lubove, *Twentieth Century Pittsburgh: Government, Business, and Environmental Change* (Pittsburgh: University of Pittsburgh Press, 1996).

25. Stanley McMichael and Robert F. Bingham, *City Growth Essentials* (Cleveland: Stanley McMichael Publishing Organization, 1928), 343.

26. McMichael and Bingham, *City Growth Essentials*, 343.

27. Ernest Burgess, "The Growth of the City: An Introduction to a Research Project," in *The City*, ed. Ernest Burgess, Robert Park, and R. D. McKenzie (Chicago: University of Chicago Press, 1925), 73.

28. Ernest Burgess, "Residential Segregation in American Cities," *Annals of the American Academy of Political and Social Science* 140 (1928), 112.

29. John Ihlder, "Rehabilitation of Blighted Areas: The Part of City Planning," *City Planning* 6, no. 2 (1930): 110.

30. Clarence Perry, *The Rebuilding of Blighted Areas* (New York: Regional Plan Association, 1935), 1.

31. Henry Wright, *Rehousing Urban America* (New York: Columbia University Press, 1935), 8.

32. Hoyt reviews and criticizes Burgess's model in a number of his writings: see, for example, *The Structure and Growth of Residential Neighborhoods in American Cities* (Washington, DC: Federal Housing Administration, 1939), 17–23; and "Recent Distortions of the Classical Models of Urban Structure," *Land Economics* 40, no. 2 (1964): 282–95.

33. Homer Hoyt, *One Hundred Years of Land Values in Chicago* (Chicago: University of Chicago Press, 1933), 314.

34. Hoyt, *One Hundred Years of Land Values in Chicago*, 314.

35. Kenneth T. Jackson, "Race, Ethnicity, and Real Estate Appraisal: The Home Owners Loan Corporation and the Federal Housing Administration," *Journal of Urban History* 6, no. 4 (1980); Amy Hillier, "Redlining and the Home Owners Loan Corporation," *Journal of Urban History* 29, no. 4 (2003); David M. P. Freund, *Colored Property: State Policy and White Racial Politics in Suburban America* (Chicago: University of Chicago Press, 2007), 111–18; and Jennifer S. Light, "Nationality and Neighborhood Risk at the Origins of FHA Underwriting," *Journal of Urban History* 36, no. 5 (2010).

36. See Richard Rothstein, *The Color of Law: A Forgotten History of How Our Government Segregated America* (New York: Liveright, 2017).

37. James Sweinhart, "Lack of Civic Vision Is Breeder of Slums," *Detroit News*, November 27, 1946.

38. St. Clair Drake and Horace R. Cayton, *Black Metropolis: A Study of Negro Life in a Northern City* (Chicago: University of Chicago Press, 1945), 206.

39. See Jodi Melamed, *Represent and Destroy: Rationalizing Violence in the New Racial Capitalism* (Minneapolis: University of Minnesota Press, 2011), 25.

40. "Incompatible racial and social groups" are referenced in the Federal Housing Authority *Underwriting Manual* of 1936; "living standards" are referenced in the Federal Housing Authority *Handbook on Urban Redevelopment for Cities in the United States* of 1941; and "user groups" are referenced in the Federal Housing Authority *Underwriting Manual* of 1947.

41. Harris, for example, writes that "*Brown I's* dialectical contradiction was that it dismantled an old form of whiteness as property while simultaneously permitting its reemergence in a more subtle form. White privilege accorded as a legal right was rejected, but de facto white privilege not mandated by law remained unaddressed"; see "Whiteness as Property," 1753.

42. See, for example, Martin Anderson, *The Federal Bulldozer: A Critical Analysis of Urban Renewal, 1949–1962* (Cambridge, MA: MIT Press, 1964); Arnold Hirsch, *Making the Second Ghetto: Race and Housing in Chicago, 1940–1960* (Cambridge: Cambridge University Press, 1983); John Bauman, *Public Housing, Race, and Renewal: Urban Planning in Philadelphia, 1920–1974* (Philadelphia: Temple University Press, 1987); June Manning Thomas, *Redevelopment and Race: Planning a Finer City in Postwar Detroit* (1997; repr., Detroit: Wayne State University Press, 2013); and Samuel Zipp, *Manhattan Projects: The Rise and Fall of Urban Renewal in Cold War New York* (New York: Oxford University Press, 2010).

43. See Jason Hackworth, "Rightsizing as Spatial Austerity in the American Rust Belt," *Environment and Planning A* 47 (2015).

44. On "downsizing" and "rightsizing," see Andrew Highsmith, "Demolition Means Progress: Urban Renewal, Local Politics, and State-Sanctioned Ghetto Formation in Flint, Michigan," *Journal of Urban History* 35:3 (2009); and Hackworth, "Rightsizing as Spatial Austerity in the American Rust Belt."

45. Dennis Archer, quoted in Jennifer Dixon and Darci McConnell, "HUD Hands Detroit a $160-Million Gift Days Before Election," *Detroit Free Press*, October 29, 1997.

46. Homeless advocates in Detroit have estimated this number in the tens of thousands; for a recent estimate of homesteading in Detroit, see *2013 State of Homelessness Annual Report for the Detroit Continuum of Care* (Detroit: Homeless Action Network of Detroit, 2013). On homesteading in Detroit, see also Claire S. W. Herbert, "Property Rights in the Context of Urban Decline: Informality, Temporality, and Inequality" (PhD dissertation, University of Michigan, 2016).

47. "Bing State of the City Address," March 24, 2010, http://archive.freep.com /article/20130213/NEWS01/130213094/Full-text-Mayor-Dave-Bing-s-State-City -address.

48. The blight emergency was declared in the fine print of an emergency order allowing wrecking crews to bid for contracts without certification: Emergency Manager, City of Detroit, "Order No. 15: Suspending Certain City Wrecking Requirements to Address Blight," August 29, 2013. The declaration of the blight emergency was not publically recognized for two weeks: see Nolan Finley, "Blight Rises to Emergency Status," *Detroit News*, September 12, 2013.

49. Detroit Blight Removal Task Force, *Detroit Blight Removal Task Force Plan*, 2014.

50. The Detroit Blight Removal Task Force Plan lists its "Book Design Director" as Rock Ventures—the real estate development company owned and led by Dan Gilbert.

51. Detroit Blight Removal Task Force, *Detroit Blight Removal Task Force Plan*, 45–49.

52. See, for example, Grace and James Boggs, "The City Is the Black Man's Land," *Monthly Review*, April 1966.

53. In the words of Adolf Reed Jr., "The dynamics that make possible the empowerment of black regimes are the same as those that produce the deepening marginalization and dispossession of a substantial segment of the urban black population": see "The Black Urban Regime: Structural Origins and Constraints," in *Stirrings in the Jug: Black Politics in the Post-Segregation Era* (Minneapolis: University of Minnesota Press, 1999), 88.

54. bell hooks, "Black Vernacular: Architecture as Cultural Practice," in *Art on My Mind: Visual Politics* (New York: New Press, 1995), 151.

17. And Thus Not Glowing Brightly

The author thanks Jennifer Montooth, Kelly Quinn, Susan Haller, Matthew Reynolds, Michael B. Gillespie, and the interlocutors of R+MAP for their generous assistance with this research.

1. *African-American Artists of Los Angeles: Noah Purifoy, Interviewed by Karen Anne*

Mason, Oral History Program, Collection 300/383, Center for Oral History Research, Library Special Collections, University of California, Los Angeles, 1992, p. 84.

2. Gerald Horne, *Fire This Time: The Watts Uprising and the 1960s* (Charlottesville: University of Virginia Press, 1995), 3.

3. My analysis of midcentury architectural modernism draws from several sources, including George Lipsitz, "The Racialization of Space and the Spatialization of Race: Theorizing the Hidden Architecture of Landscape," *Landscape Journal* 26, no. 1 (2007): 10–23; Eric Avila, *Popular Culture in the Age of White Flight: Fear and Fantasy in Suburban Los Angeles* (Berkeley: University of California Press, 2006); Eric Avila, *The Folklore and the Freeway: Race and Revolt in the Modernist City* (Minneapolis: University of Minnesota Press, 2014); Dianne Harris, *Little White Houses: How the Postwar Home Constructed Race in America* (Minneapolis: University of Minnesota Press, 2012); Rashad Shabazz, *Spatializing Blackness: Architectures of Confinement and Black Masculinity in Chicago* (Champaign: University of Illinois Press, 2015); José Esteban Muñoz, *Disidentifications: Queers of Color and the Performance of Politics* (Minneapolis: University of Minnesota Press, 1999); Michel Foucault, *The History of Sexuality, vol. 1: An Introduction*, trans. Robert Hurley (New York: Vintage, 1978); and Michel Foucault, *"Society Must Be Defended": Lecture at the Collège de France 1975–76*, ed. Mauro Bertani and Alessandro Fontana (New York: Picador, 2003).

4. Alexander G. Weheliye, *Habeas Viscus: Racializing Assemblages, Biopolitics, and Black Feminist Theories of the Human* (Durham, NC: Duke University Press, 2014), 12.

5. See, for example, Yael Lipschutz, "66 Signs of Neon and the Transformative Art of Noah Purifoy," in *L.A. Object & David Hammons Body Prints*, ed. Connie Rogers Tilton and Lindsay Charlwood (New York: Tilton Gallery, 2011); *Noah Purifoy: Junk Dada*, ed. Franklin Sirmans and Yael Lipschutz (New York: Prestel, 2015); Richard Cándida Smith, *The Modern Moves West: California Artists and Democratic Culture in the Twentieth Century* (Philadelphia: University of Pennsylvania Press, 2009); and Kellie Jones, *South of Pico: African American Artists in Los Angeles in the 1960s and 1970s* (Durham and London: Duke University Press, 2017).

6. Philip Ethington, "The Deep Historical Morphology of the Los Angeles Metropolis," in *Overdrive: L.A. Constructs the Future, 1940–1990*, ed. Wim de Wit and Christopher James Alexander (Los Angeles: Getty Research Institute, 2013), 19.

7. Brian Thill, *Waste* (New York: Bloomsbury, 2015), 7.

8. Ben Anderson, Matthew Kearnes, Colin McFarlane, and Dan Swanton, "On assemblages and geography," *Dialogues in Human Geography* 2, no. 2 (2012): 172.

9. Arun Saldanha, "Reontologising Race: The Machinic Geography of Phenotype," *Environment and Planning D: Society and Space* 24 (2006): 19.

10. On blackness as the fungible terms of objecthood, commodity, and property, see, for example, Franz Fanon, *Black Skin White Masks*, trans. Charles Lam Markmann

(New York: Grove, 1967); Fred Moten, *In the Break: The Aesthetics of the Black Radical Tradition* (Minneapolis: University of Minnesota Press, 2003); and Saidiya Hartman, *Scenes of Subjection: Terror, Slavery, and Self-Making in Nineteenth-Century America* (New York: Oxford University Press, 1997), respectively.

11. Jones, *South of Pico*, 73.

12. *African-American Artists of Los Angeles*, 31.

13. Wendy Kaplan, "Introduction: 'Living in a Modern Way,'" in *Living in a Modern Way: California Design 1930–1965*, ed. Wendy Kaplan (Los Angeles: Los Angeles County Museum of Art, 2012), 51; *African-American Artists of Los Angeles*, 56–57; and Jones, *South of Pico*, 74.

14. Vanessa R. Schwartz, "LAX: Designing for the Jet Age," in *Overdrive*, 163; and Dana Hutt, "Experimental Jet Set: Aerospace and the Modern House in Los Angeles" in *Overdrive*, 149–51.

15. Lipschutz, "66 Signs of Neon," 224. The company had been in business since 1919.

16. See, for example, "Oasis Model, Kitchen, Los Angeles, CA," Maynard L. Parker negatives, photographs, and other material, Huntington Library Photo Archives, accessed Nov. 30, 2017, https://calisphere.org/collections/14167/?rq=oasis.

17. *African-American Artists of Los Angeles*, 33.

18. *African-American Artists of Los Angeles*, 37.

19. Kaplan, "Introduction," 51.

20. Pat Kirkham, "At Home with California Modern, 1945–65," in *Living in a Modern* Way, 163; *African-American Artists of Los Angeles*, 40.

21. Banham further revealed his own distance from the struggles of Watts in his argument that LA's dream of urban homesteading—via the car, house, and "unlimited land"—could not be abated by Watts's dereliction and the riots that took place therein. Reyner Banham, *Los Angeles: The Architecture of Four Ecologies* (1971; repr., Los Angeles: University of California Press, 1999), 155, 159, 196–77.

22. Josh Sides, *L.A. City Limits: African American Los Angeles from the Great Depression to the Present* (Los Angeles: University of California Press, 2003), 179–80.

23. Paul Robinson, "Race, Space, and the Evolution of Black Los Angeles," in *Black Los Angeles: American Dreams and Racial Realities*, ed. Darnell Hunt and Ana-Christina Ramón (New York: New York University Press, 2010), 41–45; Horne, *Fire This Time*, 27; and Sides, *L.A. City Limits*, 95–120.

24. Robinson, "Race, Space, and the Evolution," 38; and Horne, *Fire This Time*, 214, 218.

25. Sonora McKeller, "Watts—Little Rome," in *From the Ashes: Voices of Watts*, ed. Budd Schulberg (New York: New American Library, 1967), 215.

26. Sides, *L.A. City Limits*, 117, 120; and "Hacienda Village, Los Angeles, CA," The Paul R. William Project, accessed August 15, 2016, http://www.paulrwilliamsproject .org/gallery/hacienda-village-los-angeles-ca/.

27. *African-American Artists of Los Angeles*, 60, 70, 141.

28. *African-American Artists of Los Angeles*, 64.

29. Mildred Ann Smith, "Junk Art Takes Shape at UCSC," *Santa Cruz Sentinel*, n.d., n.p., Scrapbook, 1935–1976, Noah Purifoy papers, 1935–1998, Archives of American Art, Smithsonian Institution.

30. Horne, *Fire This Time*, 3.

31. *African-American Artists of Los Angeles*, 64–66.

32. Art Berman, "Junk from First Watts Riot Turned Into Works of Art," *Los Angeles Times*, March 28, 1966, 3.

33. Noah Purifoy cited in *66 Signs of Neon* catalogue, n.p.

34. Given its historical conflations with blackness, the extent to which the junk in Purifoy and Powell's purview could achieve the degree autonomy necessary for "thing power" is an open question. Jane Bennett, *Vibrant Matter: A Political Ecology of Things* (Durham, NC: Duke University Press, 2010).

35. Noah Purifoy poem republished in Lipschutz, "66 Signs of Neon," 241.

36. In addition to Purifoy and Powell, the participating artists in the show were Ruth Saturensky, Debby Brewer, Gordon Wagner, Max Neufeldt, Arthur Secunda, and Leon Sulter. Lipschutz, "66 Signs of Neon," 230–32, 247.

37. Jones, *South of Pico*, 85–86.

38. Art Berman, "Watts Easter Week Arts Festival Puts Riot Debris to Cultural Uses," *Los Angeles Times*, April 8, 1966, A1. A history of who attended the first run of the exhibit in Watts and how they responded to it is still unwritten.

39. Lipschutz, "66 Signs of Neon," 247.

40. Cándida Smith, *Modern Moves West*, 134.

41. *African-American Artists of Los Angeles*, 90–91.

42. Exhibit guest books, Noah Purifoy papers 1935–1998, Archives of American Art, Smithsonian Institution.

43. "The President's Address to Shareholders," Scrapbook, 1935–1976, Noah Purifoy papers 1935–1998, Archives of American Art, Smithsonian Institution.

44. *Modern Art in Los Angeles: Harry Drinkwater oral history interview, 2010*, Getty Research Institute, Los Angeles, Accession Number 2012.IA.101, p. 23.

45. Brockman Gallery Press Release, cited in Dale Davis, "Brockman Gallery," in *L.A. Object & David Hammons Body Prints*, 83, 84–85.

46. Melinda Terbell, "Los Angeles," *Arts Magazine*, May 1971, 48.

47. *African-American Artists of Los Angeles*, 51.

48. Bruce M. Tyler, "The Rise and Decline of the Watts Summer Festival, 1965 to 1986," *American Studies* 31, no. 2 (Fall 1990): 61–81.

49. Robert Ballard, "Watts's Urban Workshop," in *Everything Loose Will Land: 1970s Art and Architecture of Los Angeles*, ed. Sylvia Lavin (West Hollywood: MAK Center for Art and Architecture, 2013), 143, 144.

50. Jack Jones, "New Neighborhood Antipoverty Plan Will Begin Jan. 1," *Los Angeles Times*, December 22, 1968, E1.

51. Henry J. Seldis and William Wilson, "Art Walk: A Critical Guide to the Galleries," *Los Angeles Times*, March 26, 1971, F8; and *African-American Artists of Los Angeles*, 119–120.

52. *African-American Artists of Los Angeles*, 51–52.

53. Lipschutz, "66 Signs of Neon," 217. "U.S. Exhibition at Berlin Fair is Trash," Scrapbook, 1935–1975, Noah Purifoy papers, 1935–1998, Archives of American Art, Smithsonian Institution; Noah Purifoy, Oral history interview, 46.

54. "U.S. Exhibition at Berlin Fair is Trash"; *African-American Artists of Los Angeles*, 46; and Lipschutz, "66 Signs of Neon," 247. The exhibit's German title "Müll Macht's Möglich" is more strictly translatable as "garbage makes it possible."

55. "U.S. Exhibition at Berlin Fair is Trash."

56. Bobby Seale's famous remark that "power for the people doesn't grow out of the sleeve of a dashiki" captures some of this critique. Seale quoted in Erika Doss, "Revolutionary Art Is a Tool for Liberation: Emory Douglas and Protest Aesthetics at the *Black Panther*," in *Liberation, Imagination, and the Black Panther Party*, ed. Kathleen Cleaver and George Katsiaficas (New York: Routledge, 2001), 180.

57. Where, for example, can we locate the convergences of blackness and junk within Rem Koolhaas's account of "Junkspace"? Rem Koolhaus, "Junkspace," *October*, vol. 100, Obsolescence (Spring 2002): 175–90.

58. Noah Purifoy letter to Sue Welch, p. 3, dated Thursday A.M., Noah Purifoy papers, 1935–1998, Archives of American Art, Smithsonian Institution.

18. Open Architecture, Rightlessness, and Citizens-to-Come

1. "Die Türken kommen: Rette sich wer kann," *Der Spiegel*, July 30, 1973. Translated as "The Turks Are Coming! Save Yourself If You Can!" trans. David Gramling, in *Germany in Transit: Nation and Migration*, ed. Deniz Göktürk, David Gramling, and Anton Kaes (Berkeley: University of California Press, 2007), 110–11; quotations: 110, 111.

2. Benedict Anderson, *Imagined Communities: Reflections on the Origins and Spread of Nationalism*, rev. ed. (London: Verso, 1991).

3. Lothar Baier, "Die Gnade der richtigen Geburt," in *Die verleugnete Utopie* (Berlin: Aufbau Tachenbuch Verlag, 1993). Translated as "The Grace of the Right Birth," trans. Tes Howell, in *Germany in Transit: Nation and Migration*, ed. Deniz Göktürk, David Gramling, and Anton Kaes (Berkeley: University of California Press, 2007), 123–26; quotation: 124.

4. Rita Chin and Heide Fehrenbach, "What's Race Got to Do with It? Postwar German History in Context," in *After the Nazi Racial State: Difference and Democracy*

in Germany and Europe, ed. Rita Chin, Geoff Eley, Heide Fehrenbach, and Atina Grossmann (Ann Arbor: University of Michigan Press, 2009), 1–29.

5. Ruth Mandel, *Cosmopolitan Anxieties: Turkish Challenges to Citizenship and Belonging in Germany* (Durham, NC: Duke University Press, 2008), 99.

6. Rita Chin, *The Guest Worker Question in Postwar Germany* (Cambridge: Cambridge University Press, 2007), 16.

7. Ayhan Kaya, *Sicher in Kreuzberg: Constructing Diasporas: Turkish Hip Hop Youth in Berlin* (Bielefeld, Germany: Transcript Verlag, 2001); Mandel, *Cosmopolitan Anxieties*; and Carla Elizabeth MacDougall, "Cold War Capital: Contested Urbanity in West Berlin, 1963–1989" (PhD diss., Rutgers University, 2011).

8. For more comprehensive discussion of some of the passages included here, see Esra Akcan, *Open Architecture: Migration, Citizenship and the Urban Renewal of Berlin-Kreuzberg through IBA 1984/87* (Basel: Birkhäuser, 2018).

9. Cihan Arın, "Analyse der Wohnverhältnisse ausländischer Arbeiter in der Bundesrepublik Deutschland—mit einer Fallstudie über türkische Arbeiterhaushalte in Berlin Kreuzberg" (PhD diss., Technische Universität, 1979);and Cihan Arın, "The Housing Market and the Housing Policies for the Migrant Labor Population in West Berlin," in *Urban Housing Segregation of Minorities in Western Europe and the United States*, ed. E. Huttman (Durham, NC: Duke University Press, 1991).

10. Wulf Eichstädt, "Die Grunsätze der behutsamen Stadterneureung," *Idee, Prozeß, Ergebnis. Die Reparatur und Rekonstruktion der Stadt*, 111–13. For the condensed declaration, see *Deutsche Bauzeitung* 122, no. 9 (Sept. 1988): 15.

11. Akcan, *Open Architecture*, chapter 5. Also see Esra Akcan, "A Building with Many Speakers: Turkish 'Guest Workers' and Alvaro Siza's *Bonjour Tristesse* Housing for IBA-Berlin," in *The Migrant's Time*, ed. Saloni Mathur (New Haven, CT: Yale University Press, 2011), 91–114.

12. See, for instance, Ernesto Laclau, and Chantal Mouffe, *Hegemony and Socialist Strategy: Towards a Radical Democratic Politics* (London: Verso, 1985).

13. For more discussion, see Akcan, *Open Architecture*, chapter 4.

14. Friedrich Nietzsche, *On the Genealogy of Morals*, ed. Walter Kaufmann (New York: Random House, 1967; originally published in 1887).

15. For a more comprehensive discussion, see Akcan, *Open Architecture*, chapter 6.

16. Peter Eisenman, "The End of the Classical. The End of the Beginning. The End of the End," *Perspecta* 21 (1984): 154–73.

17. Peter Eisenman, "The City of Architectural Excavation." I will cite them as Version 1 (Competition Report) undated, Version 2 "1/12/81," Version 3 "27 January 1981" (with handwritten corrections). DR1991:0018:939, Eisenman Papers, CCA. Selections from the first version were published in *Erste Projekte: Internationale Bauausstellung Berlin 1984/87 Die Neubaugebiete Dokumente Projekte*, vol. 2 (Berlin:

Quadriga Verlag, 1981), 284. The third version was published as Peter Eisenman and Jaquelin Robertson, "Koch-/Friedrichstrasse, Block 5," *AD* 53, nos. 1–2 (1983): 91–93.

18. Eisenman, Version 3 "27 January 1981," 1, 2, and 3. Deletions are differentiated with overstrikes, additions with italics font.

19. Max Horkheimer and Theodor Adorno, *Dialectic of Enlightenment: Philosophical Fragments*, trans. Edmund Jephcott (Stanford, CA: Stanford University Press, 2002; first published1944), xiv.

20. Horkheimer and Adorno, *Dialectic of Enlightenment*, xix.

21. Max Horkheimer, "The End of Reason," in *The Essential Frankfurt School Reader*, ed. Andrew Arato and Eike Gebhardt (New York: Continuum, 1985), 26–48.

22. Walter Benjamin, "Theses on the Philosophy of History," in *Illuminations*, ed. Hannah Arendt, trans. Harry Zohn (New York: Schocken Books, 1968), 256.

23. Andreas Huyssen, *Present Pasts: Urban Palimpsests and the Politics of Memory* (Stanford, CA: Stanford University Press, 2003), 94. See also Andreas Huyssen, *Twilight Memories: Marking Time in a Culture of Amnesia* (New York: Routledge, 1995).

24. Huyssen, *Present Pasts*, 51

25. James Young, *Texture of Memory: Holocaust Memorials and Meaning* (New Haven, CT: Yale University Press, 1993).

26. Günter Schlusche interview by the author, November 8, 2016, Berlin, in English, 02:32:00–02:34:45. Both audio and video recordings of this interview are in the author's collection.

27. The term appeared in the competition report, but was dropped in the later versions, Eisenman, version 1.

28. Eisenman, version 3, 6.

29. Peter Eisenman, "Kochstrasse Housing," *Architectural Review* 181, no. 1082 (1987): 60.

30. Eisenman, version 1, 4.

31. Saul Friedlander, *Probing the Limits of Representation: Nazism and the "Final Solution"* (Cambridge, MA: Harvard University Press, 1992).

32. Peter Eisenman, Manuscript. Undated. Probably 1988, written for AIA Award application.

33. Mandel, *Cosmopolitan Anxieties*, 35.

34. Mandel, *Cosmopolitan Anxieties*, 90.

35. Leslie Adelson, *The Turkish Turn in Contemporary German Literature: Toward a New Critical Grammar of Migration* (New York: Palgrave Macmillan, 2005), 84–86; and Jeffrey Peck, "Turks and Jews: Comparing Minorities after the Holocaust," in *German Cultures/Foreign Cultures: The Politics of Belonging*, ed. Jeffrey Peck, Harry Gray, and Helen Gray (Washington: American Institute of Contemporary Studies, 1997), 1–6.

36. Mandel, *Cosmopolitan Anxieties*, 109–40; and Gökçe Yurdakul and Michael

Bodemann, "'We Don't Want to Be the Jews of Tomorrow': Jews and Turks in Germany after 9/11," *German Politics and Society* 24, no. 2 (2006): 44–67.

37. Zafer Şenocak, *Gefährliche Verwandtschaft* (Munich: Babel, 1998), 89. See also Adelson, *Turkish Turn in Contemporary German Literature*, 79–122; and Andreas Huyssen, "Diaspora and Nation: Migration into Other Pasts," *New German Critique* 88 (2003): 47–164.

38. Michael Rothberg and Yasemin Yıldız, "Memory Citizenship: Migrant Archives of Holocaust Remembrance in Contemporary Germany," *Parallax* 17, no. 4 (2011): 32–48.

39. Esra Özyürek, "Export-Import Theory and the Racialization of Anti-Semitism: Turkish- and Arab-Only Prevention Programs in Germany," *Comparative Studies in Society and History* 58, no.1 (2016): 40–65; quotation: 41.

40. Matti Bunzl, *Anti-Semitism and Islamophobia: Hatreds Old and New in Europe* (Chicago: Prickly Paradigm Press, 2007).

41. Michael Brener, "No Place of Honor," trans. Tes Howell, in *Germany in Transit: Nation and Migration*, ed. Deniz Göktürk, David Gramling, and Anton Kaes (Berkeley: University of California Press, 2007), 216–19; quotation: 217.

42. Much has been said about T. H. Marshall's tripartite definition of citizenship as civil, political, and social citizenship, challenging him on numerous fronts, especially for his account on the concept's historical evolution, and assumption of a unitary process tied to the British context. Nonetheless, his insight into three types of rights have continued to have an explanatory power. According to this framework, social citizenship rights are those tied to economic welfare and security, such as insurance against unemployment, rights to healthcare, education, and pension. T. H. Marshall, *Social Policy in the Twentieth Century* (London: Hutchinson, 1965); Bryan Turner, "Outline of a Theory of Citizenship," in *Dimensions of Radical Democracy: Pluralism, Citizenship, Community*, ed. Chantal Mouffe (London: Verso, 1992), 33–62; and Richard Bellamy, *Citizenship* (Oxford: Oxford University Press, 2008).

43. Étienne Balibar, *Citizenship*, trans. Thomas Scott-Railton (Cambridge: Polity Press, 2015), 69–70.

44. Balibar, *Citizenship*, 76.

45. Giorgio Agamben, "We Refugees," *Symposium* 1995, no. 49(2) (Summer): 114–19, English trans. Michael Rocke. For a revised version, see Giorgio Agamben, "Biopolitics and the Rights of Man," *Homo Sacer: Sovereign Power and Bare Life*, trans. Daniel Heller-Roazen (Stanford: Stanford University Press, 1998), 126–35; quotation: 126.

46. Hannah Arendt, "The Perplexities of the Rights of Man," *Origins of Totalitarianism* (Orlando: Harcourt, 1976; first published 1951).

Bibliography

This list is designed to serve both as a general introduction to the study of race in architecture and to expand upon the subjects covered in individual chapters. As such, this bibliography begins with a list of general references on histories and theories of race, followed by thematic subheadings that correspond to the main sections of the book. The works listed include secondary sources that offer valuable analytical frameworks for studying race, as well as selected primary texts that provide key examples of the phenomena examined within this book.

General: Theory/Background/Method

Ahmed, Sara. "A Phenomenology of Whiteness." *Feminist Theory* 8, no. 2 (2007): 149–68.

Alcoff, Linda Martín. *The Future of Whiteness*. Cambridge: Polity Press, 2015.

Alexander, Michelle. *The New Jim Crow: Mass Incarceration in the Age of Colorblindness*. New York: New Press , 2010.

Augstein, Hannah Franziska, ed. *Race: The Origins of an Idea, 1760–1850*. Bristol, England: Thoemmes Press, 1996.

Back, Les, and John Solomos, eds. *Theories of Race and Racism: A Reader*. London: Routledge, 2000.

Balibar, Ètienne, and Immanuel Wallerstein. *Race, Nation, Class: Ambiguous Identities*. Trans. Chris Turner. London: Verso, 1991.

Barrett, Lindon W. *Racial Blackness and the Discontinuity of Western Modernity*, Urbana, IL: University of Illinois Press, 2014.

Barton, Craig E., ed. *Sites of Memory: Perspectives on Architecture and Race*. New York: Princeton Architectural Press, 2001.

Barzun, Jacques. "Race and the Fine Arts." In *Race: A Study in Modern Superstition*, 110–34. New York: Harcourt, Brace, 1937.

Baydar, Gülsüm. "The Cultural Burden of Architecture." *Journal of Architectural Education* 57, no. 4 (2004): 19–27.

Beckert, Sven. *Empire of Cotton: A Global History*. New York: Alfred A. Knopf, 2014.

Berger, Martin A. *Sight Unseen: Whiteness and American Visual Culture.* Berkeley: University of California Press, 2005.

Bernasconi, Robert, and Tommy L. Lott, eds. *The Idea of Race.* Indianapolis: Hackett, 2000.

Chakrabarty, Dipesh. *Provincializing Europe: Postcolonial Thought and Historical Difference.* Princeton: Princeton University Press, 2000.

Cheng, Irene, Charles L. Davis II, and Mabel O. Wilson. "Field Note: Racial Evidence." *Journal of Society of Architectural Education* 76, no. 4 (December 2017): 440–42.

Crenshaw, Kimberlé, Neil Gotanda, Gary Peller, and Kendall Thomas, eds. *Critical Race Theory: The Key Writings That Formed the Movement.* New York: New Press, 1995.

da Silva, Denise Ferreira. *Toward a Global Idea of Race.* Minneapolis: University of Minnesota Press, 2007.

Delgado, Richard, and Jean Stefancic. *Critical Race Theory: An Introduction.* New York: New York University Press, 2001.

Du Bois, W. E. B. *Black Reconstruction in America.* New York: Harcourt, Brace, 1935.

Du Bois, W. E. B . "The Conservation of Races." 1897. Reprinted in *The Souls of Black Folk.* New York: W. W. Norton, 1999.

Du Bois, W. E. B. *The Souls of Black Folk.* Oxford: Oxford University Press, 2007.

Eigen, Sara, and Mark Larrimore, eds. *The German Invention of Race.* Albany, NY: State University of New York Press, 2006.

Fields, Darell Wayne. *Architecture in Black: Theory, Space, and Appearance.* Updated edition. London: Bloomsbury Academic, 2015.

Fredrickson, George M. *Racism: A Short History.* Princeton, NJ: Princeton University Press, 2002.

Gates, Henry Louis, Jr., and Kwame Anthony Appiah, eds. *"Race," Writing, and Difference.* Chicago: University of Chicago Press, 1986.

Gilroy, Paul. *The Black Atlantic: Modernity and Double Consciousness.* London: Verso, 1993.

Harney, Stefano, and Fred Moten. *The Undercommons: Fugitive Planning & Black Study.* Wivenhoe: Minor Compositions, 2013.

Harris, Cheryl. "Whiteness as Property." *Harvard Law Review.* Vol. 106, no. 8 (June 1993): 1707–1791.

Hartman, Saidiya V. *Scenes of Subjection: Terror, Slavery, and Self-Making in Nineteenth-Century America.* New York: Oxford University Press, 1997.

Horsman, Reginald. *Race and Manifest Destiny: The Origins of American Racial Anglo-Saxonism.* Cambridge, MA: Harvard University Press, 1981.

Johnson, Walter. *River of Dark Dreams: Slavery and Empire in the Cotton Kingdom.* Cambridge, MA: Belknap Press, 2013.

Kim, Claire Jean. "The Racial Triangulation of Asian Americans." *Politics & Society* 27, no. 1 (March 1999): 105–38.

Lipsitz, George. *How Racism Takes Place*. Philadelphia: Temple University Press, 2011.

Lipsitz, George. *The Possessive Investment in Whiteness: How White People Profit from Identity Politics*. Philadelphia: Temple University Press, 1998.

Lokko, Lesley Naa Norle, and Araya Asgedom, eds. *White Papers, Black Marks: Architecture, Race, Culture*. Minneapolis: University of Minnesota Press, 2000.

Lowe, Lisa, *Intimacies of Four Continents*. Durham, NC: Duke, 2015.

Lott, Tommy L., and John P. Pittman, eds. *A Companion to African-American Philosophy*. Malden, MA: Blackwell, 2003.

Mignolo, Walter. *The Darker Side of the Renaissance: Literacy, Territoriality, and Colonization*. Ann Arbor: University of Michigan Press, 1995.

Mignolo, Walter. *Local Histories/Global Designs. Coloniality, Subaltern Knowledges, and Border Thinking*. Princeton, NJ: Princeton University Press, 2000.

Mills, Charles W. *The Racial Contract*. Ithaca, NY: Cornell University Press, 1997.

Morrison, Toni. *Playing in the Dark: Whiteness and the Literary Imagination*. New York: Vintage Books, 1992.

Omi, Michael, and Howard Winant. *Racial Formation in the United States: From the 1960s to the 1990s*. New York: Routledge, 1994.

Painter, Nell Irvin. *The History of White People*. New York: W. W. Norton, 2010.

Robinson, Cedric J. *Black Marxism: The Making of the Black Radical Tradition*. Chapel Hill: University of North Carolina Press, 2000.

Roediger, David. C*olored White: Transcending the Racial Past*. Berkeley: University of California Press, 2002.

Saldanha, Arun. "Reontologising Race: The Machinic Geography of Phenotype." *Environment & Planning D: Society and Space* 24 (2006): 9–24.

Said, Edward W. *Culture and Imperialism*. New York: Vintage Books, 1993.

Said, Edward W. *Orientalism*. New York: Vintage Books, 1979.

Spillers, Hortense. "Mama's Baby, Papa's Maybe: An American Grammar Book." *Diacritics* 17, no. 2 (Summer 1987): 64–81.

Spivak, Gayatri Chakravorty. "Can the Subaltern Speak?" In *Marxism and the Interpretation of Culture*, edited by Cary Nelson and Lawrence Grossberg, 271–313. Urbana: University of Illinois Press, 1988.

Stocking, Jr., George W. "The Spaces of Cultural Representation: Reflections on Museum Arrangement and Anthropological Theory in the Boasian and Evolutionary Traditions." In *The Architecture of Science*, edited by Peter Galison and Emily Thompson, 165–80. Cambridge, MA: MIT Press, 1999.

Valls, Andrew, ed. *Race and Modern Philosophy*. Ithaca, NY: Cornell University Press, 2005.

West, Cornel. "A Note on Race and Architecture." In *Keeping Faith: Philosophy and Race in America*, 45–54. New York: Routledge, 1993.

Wynter, Sylvia. "Unsettling the Coloniality of Being/Power/Truth/Freedom: Towards the Human, after Man, Its Overrepresentation—An Argument." *CR: New Centennial Review* 3, no. 3 (Fall 1993): 263–64.

Race and Enlightenment

Anthony, Carl. "The Big House and the Slave Quarters: Part I, Prelude to New World Architecture." *Landscape* 20, no. 3 (Spring 1976): 8–19.

Anthony, Carl. "The Big House and the Slave Quarters: Part II, African Contributions to the New World." *Landscape* 21, no. 1 (Autumn 1976): 9–15.

Anthony, Carl. "The Big House and the Slave Quarter: Prelude to New World Architecture." University of California, Berkeley. Dept. of Architecture. Working Paper 3. Berkeley, Calif., 1975.

Baucom, Ian. *Specters of the Atlantic: Finance Capital, Slavery, and the Philosophy of History.* Durham, NC: Duke University Press, 2005.

Bindman, David. *Ape to Apollo: Aesthetics and the Idea of Race in the 18th Century.* London: Reaktion, 2002.

Buck-Morss, Susan. *Hegel, Haiti and Universal History.* Pittsburgh, PA: University of Pittsburgh Press, 2009.

Cairns, Stephen. "Notes for an Alternative History of the Primitive Hut." In *Primitive: Original Matters in Architecture,* edited by Jo Odgers, Flora Samuel, and Adam Sharr, 86–95. London: Routledge, 2006.

Cheng, Irene. "Race and Architectural Geometry: Thomas Jefferson's Octagons." *J19: The Journal of Nineteenth-Century Americanists* 3, no. 1 (Spring 2015): 121–30.

Ellis, Clifton, and Rebecca Ginsburg, eds. *Cabin, Quarter, Plantation: Architecture and Landscapes of North American Slavery.* New Haven, CT: Yale University Press, 2010.

Eze, Emmanuel Chukwudi. *On Reason: Rationality in a World of Cultural Conflict and Racism.* Durham, NC: Duke University Press, 2008.

Eze, Emmanuel Chukwudi, ed. *Race and the Enlightenment: A Reader.* Malden, MA: Blackwell, 1997.

Gikandi, Simon. *Slavery and the Culture of Taste.* Princeton, NJ: Princeton University Press, 2011.

Muthu, Sankar. *Enlightenment against Empire.* Princeton, NJ: Princeton University Press, 2003.

Nelson, Louis. *Architecture and Empire in Jamaica.* New Haven, CT: Yale University Press, 2016.

Nelson, Louis. "The Architectures of Black Identity: Buildings, Slavery and Freedom in the Caribbean and the American South." *Winterthur Portfolio* 45, no. 2/3 (2011): 177–93.

Nelson, Louis. "Architectures of West African Enslavement." *Buildings & Landscapes* 21, no. 1 (Spring 2014): 88–124.

Quatremère de Quincy, Antoine-Chrysostome. "Architecture" and "Character" (1788). *9H*, no. 7 (1985): 25–35.

Upton, Dell. "White and Black Landscapes in Eighteenth-Century Virginia." *Places* 2, no. 2 (1984): 59–72.

Wright, Gwendolyn. "The 'Big House' and the Slave Quarters." In *Building the Dream: A Social History of Housing in America*, 41–57. New York: Pantheon Books, 1981.

Vlach, John Michael. *Back of the Big House: The Architecture of Plantation Slavery*. Chapel Hill: University of North Carolina Press, 1993.

Vlach, John Michael. "The Shotgun House: An African Architectural Legacy." *Common Places: Readings in American Vernacular Architecture*, edited by Dell Upton and John Michael Vlach, 58–78. Athens: University of Georgia Press, 1986.

Race and Organicism

"Anthological Excerpts from Gottfried Semper to Henri Focillon." *Rassegna* 12, no. 41 (1990): 76–89.

Baridon, Laurent. *L'imaginaire scientifique de Viollet-le-Duc*. Paris: Éditions L'Harmattan, 1996.

Blumenbach, Johann Friedrich. *On the Natural Varieties of Mankind* (1776).

Bressani, Martin. *Architecture and the Historical Imagination: Eugène-Emmanuel Viollet-Le-Duc, 1814–1879*. Farnham, Surrey: Ashgate, 2014.

Canales, Jimena, and Andrew Herscher. "Criminal Skins: Tattoos and Modern Architecture in the Work of Adolf Loos." *Architectural History* 48 (2005): 235–56.

Cogdell, Christina. "Breeding Ideology: Parametricism and Biological Architecture." In *The Politics of Parametricism: Digital Technologies in Architecture*, edited by Matthew Poole and Manuel Shvartzberg, 23–137. London: Bloomsbury Academic, 2015.

Cogdell, Christina. *Eugenic Design: Streamlining America in the 1930s*. Philadelphia: University of Pennsylvania Press, 2004.

Davis II, Charles L. *Building Character: The Racial Politics of Modern Architectural Style*. Pittsburgh, PA: University of Pittsburgh Press, 2019.

Davis II, Charles L. "Viollet-Le-Duc and the Body: The Metaphorical Integrations of Race and Style in Structural Rationalism." *Architectural Research Quarterly* 14, no. 4 (2010): 341–48.

Gubler, Jacques. "In Search of the Primitive." In *Eugène Emmanuel Viollet-le-Duc, 1814–1879*, edited by Penelope Farrant, Brigitte Hermann, and Ian Latham, 80–83. Architectural Design Profiles. London: Academy Editions, 1980.

Loos, Adolf. "Plumbers" (1898)" and "Ornament and Crime" (1908/1929). In *Ornament and Crime: Selected Essays*, translated by Michael Mitchell, edited by Adolf Opel, 82–88, 167–76. Riverside, CA: Ariadne Press, 1998.

Loos, Adolf. "Architecture" (1910. In *On Architecture*, translated by Michael Mitchell, edited by Adolf and Daniel Opel, 73–85. Riverside, CA: Ariadne Press, 2002.

Mallgrave, Harry Francis. "Gustav Klemm and Gottfried Semper: The Meeting of Ethnological and Architectural Theory." *RES: Anthropology and Aesthetics* 9 (1985): 68–79.

Merwood, Joanna. "Western Architecture: Regionalism and Race in the Inland Architect." In *Chicago Architecture: Histories, Revisions, Alternatives*, edited by Katerina Rüedi-Ray and Charles Waldheim, 3–14. Chicago: University of Chicago Press, 2005.

Mitchell, Timothy. "Orientalism and the Exhibitionary Order." In *Colonialism and Culture*, edited by Nicholas Dirks, 289–318. Ann Arbor: University of Michigan Press, 1992.

Mitchell, W. J. T., ed. "Imperial Landscape." In *Landscape and Power*, 5–30. 2nd edition. Chicago: University of Chicago Press, 2002.

Semper, Gottfried. "The Four Elements of Architecture: A Contribution to the Comparative Study of Architecture" (1851). *The Four Elements of Architecture and Other Writings*, translated by Harry Francis Mallgrave and Wolfgang Herrmann, 74–129. Cambridge: Cambridge University Press, 1989.

Sullivan, Louis. "Characteristics and Tendencies of an American Architecture" (1885). In *Kindergarten Chats and Other Writings*, edited by Isabella Athey, 177–81. New York: Wittenborn, Schultz, 1947.

Teyssot, Georges. *A Topology of Everyday Constellations*. Cambridge, MA: MIT Press, 2013.

Viollet-le-Duc, Eugène-Emmanuel. *The Habitations of Man in All Ages (Histoire de l'habitation humaine, depuis les temps préhistoriques jusqu'à nos jours)*. Translated by Benjamin Bucknall. Boston: J. R. Osgood, 1876 (1875).

Race and Nationalism

Arthurs, Joshua. "Empire, Race and the Decline of Romanità, 1936–1945." In *Excavating Modernity: The Roman Past in Fascist Italy*, 125–50, 187–94. Ithaca, NY: Cornell University Press, 2012.

Etlin, Richard. "Italian Rationalism and Anti-Semitism." In *Modernism in Italian Architecture*, 569–97, 670–78. Cambridge, MA: MIT Press, 1991.

Gillette, Aaron. "The Implementation of Nordic Racism in Italy, 1936–1938." In *Racial Theories in Fascist Italy*, 50–99, 197–207. London: Routledge, 2002.

Knight, Alan. "Racism, Revolution, and Indigenismo: Mexico, 1910–1940." In *The Idea of Race in Latin America*, 1870–1940, edited by Richard Graham, 71–113. Austin: University of Texas Press, 1990.

Horsman, Reginald. *Race and Manifest Destiny: The Origins of American Racial Anglo-Saxonism*. Cambridge, MA: Harvard University Press, 1981.

Lane, Barbara Miller. *Architecture and Politics in Germany, 1918–1945*. Cambridge, MA: Harvard University Press, 1985.

O'Connell, Lauren M. "A Rational, National Architecture: Viollet-le-Duc's Modest Proposal for Russia." *Journal of the Society of Architectural Historians* 52, no. 4 (1993): 436–52.

Poliakov, Léon. *The Aryan Myth*, trans. Edmund Howard. London: Sussex University Press, 1974.

Race and Colonialism

Akcan, Esra. "Postcolonial Theories in Architecture." In *A Critical History of Contemporary Architecture (1960–2010)*, edited by Elie Haddad and David Rifkind, 115–36. London: Ashgate, 2014.

Avermaete, Tom. "Framing the Afropolis: Michel Ecochard and the African City for the Greatest Number." *OASE* no. 82 (2010): 77–99.

Avermaete, Tom, Serhat Karakayali, and Marion von Osten, eds. *Colonial Modern: Aesthetics of the Past, Rebellions for the Future.* London: Black Dog, 2010.

Baydar, Gülsüm, and Nalbantoğlu. "Toward Postcolonial Openings: Rereading Sir Banister Fletcher's 'History of Architecture.'" *Assemblage* 35 (1998): 6–17.

Bennett, Tony. "The Exhibitionary Complex." *New Formations* 4 (Spring 1988).

Bhandar, Brenna. *Colonial Lives of Property: Law, Land, and Racial Regimes of Ownership.* Durham, NC: Duke University Press, 2018.

Bremner, G. A., ed. *Architecture and Urbanism in the British Empire.* Oxford: Oxford University Press, 2016.

Çelik, Zeynep. *Displaying the Orient: Architecture of Islam at Nineteenth-Century World's Fairs.* Berkeley: University of California Press, 1992.

Çelik, Zeynep. *Empire, Architecture, and the City: French-Ottoman Encounters, 1830–1914.* Seattle: University of Washington Press, 2008.

Çelik, Zeynep. *Urban Forms and Colonial Confrontations: Algiers under French Rule.* Berkeley, CA: University of California Press, 1997.

Césaire, Aimé. *Discourse on Colonialism.* New York: MR, 1972.

Chattopadhyay, Swati. "Blurring Boundaries: The Limits of 'White Town' in Colonial Calcutta." *Journal of the Society of Architectural Historians* 59, no. 2 (June, 2000): 154–79.

Coetzer, Nicholas. *Building Apartheid: On Architecture and Order in Imperial Cape Town.* Farnham, UK: Ashgate, 2013.

Crane, Sheila. "The Shantytown in Algiers and the Colonization of Everyday Life." In *Use Matters: An Alternative History of Architecture*, edited by Kenny Cupers, 103–19. London: Routledge, 2013.

Crinson, Mark. *Empire Building: Orientalism and Victorian Architecture.* London: Routledge, 1996.

Fanon, Frantz. *Black Skin, White Masks.* New York: Grove Press, 2008.

Fanon, Frantz. *The Wretched of the Earth.* New York: Grove Press, 1963.

Fry, Maxwell, and Jane Drew. "Introduction" and "Climate." In *Tropical Architecture in the Dry and Humid Zones*, 17–25. Huntington, NY: R. E. Krieger, 1964.

Glover, Will. *Making Lahore Modern: Constructing and Imagining a Colonial City.* Minneapolis: University of Minnesota Press, 2007.

Göckede, Regina. "The Architect as Colonial Technocrat of Dependent Modernisation: Ernst May's Plans for Kampala." In *Afropolis—City Media Art*, edited by Kerstin Pinther, Larissa Forster, and Christian Hanussek, 54–65. Auckland Park: Jacana Media, 2012.

Guha-Thakurta, Tapati. *Monuments, Objects, Histories: Institutions of Art in Colonial and Postcolonial India.* New York: Columbia University Press, 2004.

Jaschke, Karin. "Mythopoesis of Place and Culture: Aldo Van Eyck, Herman Haan, and the Dogon." In *Team 10: Keeping the Language of Modern Architecture Alive*, edited by Pablo Allard, 110–125. Delft: Delft University, 2006.

Liscombe, Rhodri Windsor, "Modernism in Late Imperial British West Africa: The Work of Maxwell Fry and Jane Drew, 1946–56." *Journal of the Society of Architectural Historians* 65, no. 2 (2006): 188–215.

Mbembe, Achille. *Critique of Black Reason.* Trans. Laurent Dubois. Durham, NC: Duke University Press, 2017.

Mbembe, Achille. *Necropolitics.* Durham, NC: Duke University Press, 2019.

Meier, Prita. *Swahili Port Cities: The Architecture of Elsewhere.* Bloomington: Indiana University Press, 2016.

Metcalf, Thomas R. *An Imperial Vision: Indian Architecture and Britain's Raj.* Berkeley: University of California Press, 1989.

Morton, Patricia A. *Hybrid Modernities: Representation and Architecture at the 1931 International Colonial Exposition in Paris.* Cambridge, MA: MIT Press, 2000.

Osayimwese, Itohan. *Colonialism and Modern Architecture in Germany.* Pittsburgh, PA: University of Pittsburgh Press, 2017.

Rydell, Robert. *All the World's a Fair: Visions of Empire at the American International Expositions, 1876–1916.* Chicago: University of Chicago Press, 1984.

Silverman, Debora L. "Art Nouveau, Art of Darkness: African Lineages of Belgian Modernism." *West 86th: A Journal of Decorative Arts, Design History, and Material Culture* 18, no. 2 (2011): 139–81.

Wright, Gwendolyn. *The Politics of Design in French Colonial Urbanism.* Chicago: University of Chicago Press, 1991.

Race and Representation

Brown, Adrienne. *The Black Skyscraper: Architecture and the Perception of Race.* Baltimore: John Hopkins University Press, 2017.

Cheng, Anne Anlin. *Second Skin: Josephine Baker and the Modern Surface.* New York: Oxford University Press, 2011.

Gleason, William. *Sites Unseen: Architecture, Race, and American Literature*. New York: New York University Press, 2011.

Gooden, Mario. *Dark Space: Architecture, Representation, Black Identity*. New York: Columbia Books on Architecture and the City, 2016.

Harris, Dianne. *Little White Houses: How the Postwar Home Constructed Race in America*. Minneapolis: University of Minnesota Press, 2013.

Harris, Dianne. "Seeing the Invisible: Reexamining Race and Vernacular Architecture." *Perspectives in Vernacular Architecture* 13, no. 2 (2006–2007): 96–105.

hooks, bell. "Black Vernacular: Architecture as Cultural Practice." In *Art on My Mind: Visual Politics*, 145–51. New York: New Press, 1995.

Savage, Kirk. *Standing Soldiers, Kneeling Slaves: Race, War, and Monument in Nineteenth-Century America*. Princeton, NJ: Princeton University Press, 1999.

Sheehan, Tanya. "Comical Conflations: Racial Identity and the Science of Photography." *Photography & Culture* 4, no. 2 (July 2011): 133–55.

Sheehan, Tanya. "Looking Pleasant, Feeling White: The Social Politics of the Photographic Smile." In *Feeling Photography*, edited by Elspeth Brown and Thy Phu, 127–57. Durham, NC: Duke University Press, 2014.

Upton, Dell. *What Can and Can't Be Said: Race, Uplift, and Monument Building in the Contemporary South*. New Haven, CT: Yale University Press, 2015.

Wilkins, Craig L. *The Aesthetics of Equity: Notes on Race, Space, Architecture, and Music*. Minneapolis: University of Minnesota Press, 2007.

Wilson, Mabel O. "Dancing in the Dark: The Inscription of Blackness in Le Corbusier's Radiant City." In *Places Through the Body*, edited by Heidi J. Nast and Steve Pile, 133–52. New York: Routledge, 1998.

Wilson, Mabel O. *Negro Building: Black Americans in the World of Fairs and Museums*. Berkeley: University of California Press, 2012.

Race and Urbanism

Barron, Mark. "Adequately Re-Housing Low Income Families: A Study of Class and Race in the Architecture of Public Housing, Marietta, Georgia, 1938–1941." *Perspectives in Vernacular Architecture*, vol. 11 (2004): 54–70.

Bristol, Katharine. "The Pruitt Igoe Myth." *Journal of Architectural Education* 44, no. 3 (1991): 163–71.

Brown, Adrienne, and Valerie Smith. *Race and Real Estate*. Oxford: Oxford University Press, 2016.

Coates, Ta-Nehisi. "The Case for Reparations." *Atlantic*, June 2014.

Connolly, N. D. B. *A World More Concrete: Real Estate and the Remaking of Jim Crow South Florida*. Chicago: University of Chicago Press, 2014.

Drake, St. Claire, and Horace Clayton. *Black Metropolis: A Study of Negro Life in a Northern City*. New York: Harcourt, Brace, 1945.

Freund, David M. P. *Colored Property: State Policy and White Racial Politics in Suburban America.* Chicago: University of Chicago Press, 2007.

Goldstein, Brian D. *The Roots of Urban Renaissance: Gentrification and the Struggle over Harlem.* Cambridge, MA: Harvard University Press, 2017.

Gutman, Marta. "Race, Place and Play: Robert Moses and the WPA Swimming Pools in New York City." *Journal of the Society of Architectural Historians* 67, no. 4 (December 2008): 532–61.

Hock, Jennifer. "Bulldozers, Busing and Boycotts: Urban Renewal and the Integrationist Project." *Journal of Urban History* 39, no. 3 (May 2013): 433–53.

Hunter, Marcus Anthony, Mary Pattillo, Zandria F. Robinson, and Keeanga-Yamahtta Taylor. "Black Placemaking: Celebration, Play, and Poetry." *Theory, Culture & Society* 33, no. 7–8 (December 1, 2016): 31–56.

Judin, Hilton, and Ivan Vladislavić, eds. *Blank: Architecture, Apartheid and After.* Rotterdam: NAi Publishers, 1998.

Knoblauch, Joy. "Defensible Space and the Open Society." *Aggregate.* http://we -aggregate.org/piece/defensible-space-and-the-open-society.

Kurgan, Laura. "Million-Dollar Blocks." In *Close Up at a Distance: Mapping, Technology, and Politics*, 187–206. New York: Zone Books, 2013.

Lasner, Matthew Gordon. "Segregation by Design: Race, Architecture, and the Enclosure of the Atlanta Apartment." *Journal of Urban History*. May 2017. doi:10.1177/0096144217704316.

Le Corbusier. *When the Cathedrals Were White.* Translated by Francis Hyslop. New York: McGraw-Hill, 1964 (1947).

Lipsitz, George. "The Racialization of Space and the Spatialization of Race: Theorizing the Hidden Architecture of Landscape." *Landscape Journal* 26, no. 1 (2007): 10–23.

Massey, Douglas S., and Nancy A. Denton. *American Apartheid: Segregation and the Making of the Underclass.* Cambridge, MA: Harvard University Press, 1993.

McKittrick, Katherine and Clyde Woods, eds. *Black Geographies and the Politics of Place.* Cambridge, MA: South End Press, 2007.

Nemser, Daniel. *Infrastructures of Race: Concentration and Biopolitics in Colonial Mexico.* Austin: University of Texas Press, 2017.

Nightingale, Carl H. *Segregation: A Global History of Divided Cities.* Chicago: Chicago University Press, 2012.

Park, Robert Ezra, Ernest W. Burgess, and Roderick D. McKenzie. "The City" (1915). In *The City*, 1–46. Chicago: University of Chicago Press, 1925.

Rothstein, Richard. *The Color of Law: A Forgotten History of How Our Government Segregated America.* New York: Liveright Publishing, 2017.

Schein, Richard, ed. *Landscape and Race in the United States.* London: Routledge, 2006.

Shabazz, Rashad. *Spatializing Blackness: Architectures of Confinement and Black Masculinity in Chicago.* Urbana: University of Illinois Press, 2015.

Shah, Nayan. *Contagious Divides: Epidemics of Race in San Francisco's Chinatown.* Berkeley: University of California Press, 2001.

Taylor, Keeanga-Yamahtta. *Race for Profit: How Banks and the Real Estate Industry Undermined Black Homeownership.* Chapel Hill: University of North Carolina Press, 2019.

Wiltse, Jeff. *Contested Waters: A Social History of Swimming Pools in America.* Chapel Hill: University of North Carolina Press, 2007.

Contributors

Esra Akcan is an associate professor in the Department of Architecture at Cornell University. She is the author of *Landfill Istanbul: Twelve Scenarios for a Global City* (124/3, 2004); *Architecture in Translation: Germany, Turkey and the Modern House* (Duke University Press, 2012); *Open Architecture: Migration, Citizenship and Urban Renewal of Berlin-Kreuzberg by IBA 1984/87* (Birkhäuser-De Gruyter, 2018); and coeditor, with Sibel Bozdoğan, of *Turkey: Modern Architectures in History* ((Reaktion/University of Chicago Press, 2012).

Adrienne Brown is associate professor of English at the University of Chicago. Along with various articles journals and essays in books, she is the co-editor, with Valerie Smith, of *Race and Real Estate* (Oxford University Press, 2016) and *The Black Skyscraper: Architecture and the Perception of Race* (Johns Hopkins University Press, 2017).

Luis E. Carranza is professor of architecture at Roger Williams University and an adjunct associate professor at the Graduate School of Architecture, Planning and Preservation at Columbia University. His research and published work focuses primarily on modern art and architecture in Latin America (with an emphasis on Mexico). He is the author of *Architecture as Revolution: Episodes in the History of Modern Mexico* (University of Texas Press, 2010) and coauthor, with Fernando Lara, of *Modern Architecture in Latin America: Art, Technology, Utopia* (University of Texas Press, 2015).

Jiat-Hwee Chang is associate professor of architecture at the National University of Singapore. He is the author of *A Genealogy of Tropical Architecture* (CRC Press, 2016) which was the winner of the International Planning History Society's book prize in 2018. He is also the coeditor of *Southeast Asia's Modern Architecture* (University of Chicago Press, 2019) and *Non West Modernist Past* (World Scientific, 2011). Chang is currently working on a book on everyday modernism in Singapore and another book on air-conditioning complexes and climate change in urban Asia.

Irene Cheng is associate professor of architecture at the California College of the Arts, where she directs the Experimental History Project. She is the coeditor, with Bernard Tschumi, of *The State of Architecture at the Beginning of the 21st Century* (Monacelli Press, 2003). Her forthcoming book *The Shape of Utopia* (University of Minnesota Press) explores the relationship between architecture and politics in nineteenth-century American utopias.

Mark Crinson is professor of architectural history at Birkbeck, University of London. His most recent books include *Rebuilding Babel: Modern Architecture and Internationalism* (Bloomsbury, 2017) and *The Architecture of Art History* with Richard J. Williams (Bloomsbury, 2019). He is currently working on a book about the first industrial city, Manchester. He is president of the European Architectural History Network, and he directs the Architecture Space and Society Centre at Birkbeck.

Kenny Cupers is associate professor of history and theory of architecture and urbanism at the University of Basel, where he cofounded and leads its new division of Urban Studies. He is an architectural and urban historian with expertise in nineteenth- and twentieth-century Europe and its relationship with the transatlantic world and postcolonial Africa. His publications include The Social Project: Housing Postwar France (University of Minnesota Press, 2014), *Use Matters: An Alternative History of Architecture* (Routledge, 2013), and *Spaces of Uncertainty: Berlin Revisited* (2018). His forthcoming book, *The Earth that Modernism Built*, explores the colonial roots of the modernist belief that we can design the world we live in.

Charles L. Davis II is an assistant professor of architectural history and criticism at the University at Buffalo, State University of New York. His research examines the integrations of race and style theory in paradigms of "architectural organicism," or design movements that emulated natural principles of development to produce a "living architecture." His book *Building Character: The Racial Politics of Modern Architectural Style* (University of Pittsburgh Press, 2019) was supported by grants from the Graham Foundation and the Canadian Center for Architecture.

Addison Godel is a PhD candidate in architectural history at Columbia University, where his research explores infrastructural building types (telephone exchanges, wholesale markets, sewage treatment plants, and port facilities) as a window into the contestation of ownership of American urban space after World War II. His writing has appeared in *Grey Room* and *CLOG*, and together with Jacqueline Gargus and Evan Chakroff, he is the coauthor of *China: Architectural Guide* (2016).

Dianne Harris is an architectural historian and a senior program officer at the Andrew W. Mellon Foundation. Her scholarship of the past twenty-five years has focused on the history of suburban housing, and on "race and space" studies. She is the author of *Little White Houses: How the Postwar Home Constructed Race in America* (University of Minnesota Press, 2013), and of many other scholarly publications.

Andrew Herscher is a cofounding member of a series of militant research collaboratives including the We the People of Detroit Community Research Collective, Detroit Resists, and the Settler Colonial City Project. In his own writing, he works across a range of global sites to explore the architecture of political violence, displacement and migration, and self-determination and resistance. Among his books are *Violence Taking Place: The Architecture of the Kosovo Conflict* (Stanford University Press, 2010), *The Unreal Estate Guide to Detroit* (University of Michigan Press, 2012), and *Displacements: Architecture and Refugee* (Sternberg Press, 2017). He teaches in the architecture program at the University of Michigan.

Reinhold Martin is professor of architecture in the Graduate School of Architecture, Planning, and Preservation at Columbia University, where he directs the Temple Hoyne Buell Center for the Study of American Architecture. At Columbia, Martin also chairs the Society of Fellows in the Humanities and is a member of the Center for Comparative Media. A founding coeditor of the journal *Grey Room*, Martin's books include *The Organizational Complex: Architecture, Media, and Corporate Space* (MIT, 2003), *Utopia's Ghost: Architecture and Postmodernism, Again* (University of Minnesota Press, 2010), and *The Urban Apparatus: Mediapolitics and the City* (University of Minnesota Press, 2016). His new book, *Knowledge Worlds: A Media History of the Modern University*, is forthcoming from Columbia University Press.

Brian L. McLaren is an associate professor and chair in the Department of Architecture at the University of Washington, where he teaches history and theory seminars and design studios. His teaching and scholarship draw upon contemporary critical theory as well as postcolonial studies, with a particular interest in architecture and politics during the interwar period. He is the author of *Architecture and Tourism in Italian Colonia Libya: An Ambivalent Modernism* (University of Washington Press, 2006) His most recent scholarship examines the relationship between modern architecture, empire, and race in Italy during the late Fascist era. He is also working on a new book project that studies the idea of mobility in Italy's African empire.

Joanna Merwood-Salisbury is professor of architecture at Victoria University of Wellington, New Zealand. She has taught at Parsons School of Design, the University of Illinois Chicago, Bard and Barnard Colleges, and the Pratt Institute. Her research focuses on nineteenth-century architecture and urbanism, with special emphasis on issues of race and labor. Her publications include *Design for the Crowd: Patriotism and Protest in Union Square* (University of Chicago Press, 2019); *After Taste: Expanded Practice in Interior Design*, coedited with Kent Kleinman and Lois Weinthal (Princeton Architectural Press, 2012); and *Chicago 1890: The Skyscraper and the Modern City* (University of Chicago Press, 2009).

Peter Minosh is a historian of architecture, urbanism, and landscape with a focus on the relationship between politics and the built environment. His research considers architecture's modernity within the parallel phenomena of expanding global capital and the emergence of revolutionary political movements from the eighteenth century to the present. His current project examines architecture, slavery, and colonial revolution in the eighteenth-century Atlantic world. He received his PhD in architectural history and theory from Columbia University and is a lecturer in architectural and landscape history at the University of Toronto.

Adedoyin Teriba is assistant professor of art and urban studies at Vassar College. His research interests include the built environment in anglophone and francophone West Africa from the eighteenth century to the present day. He received his PhD from Princeton University and has worked as an architect in New York, New Jersey, and Lagos, Nigeria. His most recent publication is "'The House That Makes You Lose Your Cap when Admiring its Height': Creating 'Home' in the Lagos Colony (1913)" in the exhibition catalogue *Histórias Afro-Atlânticas* (Museu de Arte de São Paulo Assis Chateaubriand, 2018).

Lisa Uddin is associate professor in the Department of Art History and Visual Culture Studies and Paul Garrett Fellow at Whitman College. Her work on race brings visual culture into conversation with US urbanism and the environmental humanities. She is the author of *Zoo Renewal: White Flight and the Animal Ghetto* (University of Minnesota Press, 2015), and coeditor of Black One Shot, an art criticism series devoted to black visual and expressive culture on *ASAP/J*. Her current research considers formations of black humanity in relation to California architecture and urban planning since the 1960s.

Mabel O. Wilson is the Nancy and George E. Rupp Professor in Architecture and a professor in African American and African diasporic studies at Columbia University. She is the associate director of the Institute for Research in African American Studies and codirector of Global Africa Lab. She has authored *Begin with the Past: Building the National Museum of African American History and Culture* (Smithsonian Books, 2017) and *Negro Building: African Americans in the World of Fairs and Museums* (University of California Press, 2012).

Index

Note: Page numbers in *italics* refer to figures.

Baier, Lothar, 325
Baker, Josephine, 203–4
Balasingamchow, Yu-Mei, 246
Balibar, Étienne, 337
Banham, Reyner, 312
Barbé-Marbois, François, 35
Bauer, Catherine, 74–75
Beaux-Arts, 163–64
Bellows, Henry, 129–30
Bellows, Henry Whitney, 123
Berger, Martin A., 11, 101, 127
Berlin, Germany, 18, 333–34; discriminatory
    housing laws, 327–29; immigrants in,
    324–27
Berlin Conference (1884-1885), 196
Berlin Wall, 332, 334
Bindman, David, 91
Bing, Dave, 303
Bini, Alberto Calza, 177
biological determinism, 260
biopolitics, 174–75, 186
Black Loyalists, in Sierra Leone, 45–48
Black Metropolis (Drake and Cayton), 301–2
black nationalism, 75
blackness, 37, 42
blacks, 42, 293; inferiority, 37, 65, 119; job
    restrictions on, 203, 312, 377n2;
    mutilation and murder of, 224–26*See
    also* African Americans
Blessing, Hedrich, 218, 220, *223,* 226, 229,
    233–38
blight, 299, 307; causes of, 299, 301–2;
    definitions of, 294, 296–97, 302; effects
    of, 293, 301–3; evolution of concept,
    294–95; removal of, 297, 302–4; studies
    of, 18, 292
Blumenbach, Johann Friedrich, 90, 135–36,
    349n5
Blyden, Edward, 282–83, 397n35
Boas, Franz, 156, 369n3, 369n12
bodies, stereotypes of black female, 119–20
Bottai, Giuseppe, 176, 179
Boullée, Étienne-Louis, 65, *65*
Breath of Fresh Air, 317, *318*
Britain, 92, 275, 286; Chinese ideas in
    vogue in, 85–87, *86*; colonialism of,
    243–44, 280; Granville Town in Sierra
    Leone and, 45–48; Lagos and, 279–80;
    landownership granted to, 281–82;
    Malaya and, 243–48, 255–56; revolts
    against, 243–44, 261
Brown, Elspeth, 221
Buchanan, James, 30
Buffon, Comte de (Georges-Louis
    Leclerc), 36, 135–36

builders, 28–30, 226, 283; architects and,
    227–28
building materials, 103, 173, 197, 218, 254;
    Italian autarchy in, 178, 182–84; publicity
    photos in, 236–37; Shitta-Bey Mosque,
    283–84; use of scrap, 216–17
building methods, 173, 197
built environment, and race, 204–5
Burgess, Ernest, 298–99
Burnham, Daniel, 210

Camper, Pieter, 7
canonicity, 12
capitalism, 5, 215–16, 293
capitols, slave labor in, 14
Carothers, J. C., 260–61
Cayton, Horace R., 301–2
Centurión, Manuel, 166, *167,* 169
Chadowiecki, Daniel, 91
Chambers, William, 86–90, 95
character, 100, 108–9
Cheever, George B., 129
Cheng, Anne Anlin, 11, 206, 379n16
Chen Voon Fee, 252
Cheyenne, Wyoming, railroad station, *105,*
    111–12, *112*
Chicago School, 297–99, *298*
Childe, Cromwell, 215
China, 248; as ahistorical, 92–94; Europe
    and, 80, 92, 94, 196; Europeans'
    perceptions of, 79, 81, 87, 92–95;
    Forbidden City of, 82, *82*; inferiority of,
    92, 95; interest in, 85–87, *86,* 86–87;
    Jesuit reports on, 80–81; monumental
    architecture of, 81–82*See also* gardens,
    Chinese
Chinese, 89, *91*; clothing, *88*; as manipula-
    tors of nature, 90–91; otherness of, 84,
    87, 91–92
Chinese architecture, 81–82, 85
Chinese traditional revival architecture,
    248–49
churches, 123, 129
citizenship, 338, 409n42; exclusion from, 37,
    40, 337; race and, 324–25, 337
civilization, 62–63, 78, 119; American, 73,
    104; definitions of, 64, 71; technology's
    influence on, 72–73, 75–76
*Civilization in the United States: An Inquiry
    by Thirty Americans* (Stearns), 73–75
Civil War, 116, 128, 133
class, social, 75, 129, 143, 221, 232–33, 274,
    282
classicism, 7, 136–37

Montmusard (Dijon, France), 54, 348n39
monuments, 81–82, 99
Morado, José Chavez, 170
Morgan, Graham, 227
Morrison, Toni, 12
Morton, Patricia, 179
mosques, 286. *See also* Shitta-Bey Mosque
Moten, Fred, 37–38
Mould, Jacob Wrey, 122–23
Mumford, Lewis, 73–77
Museum of Modern Art, 75, 152
Mussolini, Benito, 174, 179, 182
Muzim Negara, 247–48, 250, 256

Nair, Devan, 252
Namibia, under German colonialism,
    196–98
Namibian architecture, 196–97
Nanyang University Library, 248, *249, 250*
nation, and race, 87
National Academy of Design, 15, *118,* 130;
    exhibitions of, 116, 118–21; history of,
    122–23
National Academy of Design building,
    116–17, 118, 119, 122, 124, 133; decorative
    carvings on, 121, *125,* 130–31; as Gothic
    Revival, 123–26, 128; symbolism in,
    130–31; by Wight, 121, *124*
nationalism, 152, 155, 158–59, 190, 193;
    cultural, 19, 99–100, 102, 107, 115; race
    in, 77–78
nationality, 108–9, 193
Native Americans, 65, 100, 210–11. *See also*
    indigenous people
nativists, 128
natural history, 135
naturalism, 15, 117, 119–20, 122, 126, 131
natural philosophy, 36
nature, 90–91, 101–3, 108
Nazis, 60, 192
neoclassical style, 5–6, 76, 86, 117; *Africa* as,
    119–20; of Virginia Statehouse and U.S.
    Capitol, 14–15, 23, 30, 43, 52
neo-colonial architecture, 164
Neutra, Rochard, 314
Newton, Isaac, 65, *65*
New York City, 128–30
Ng Keng Siang, 248
Ngũgĩ wa Thiong'o, 265–66
Nichols, J. C., 296
Niemeyer, Oscar, 251
Nieuhof, Johan, 82–84
Nigeria, 17–18, 281. *See also* Lagos
Niggers Ain't Never Ever Be Nothin'
    (Purifoy), 320–21, *321*

Nijku village, *263*
nonwhite, 28

Oasis Model House (LA), 311–12
O'Gorman, James F., 110
O'Gorman, Juan, *155*
Ògúnfúnminire, King, 279–81
Olówógbówó, 279, 281
Omi, Michael, 13
open architecture, 18, 338
Opium Wars, 92, 94
Oppo, Cipriano Esfio, 180
organicism, architectural, 100, *112,* 126, 133
Orientalism, 13, 90
ornamentation, 148, 216, 256; global
    differences in, 138–39, *139*; rejection of,
    150–51, 268; vernacular, 254–55, *255*
orthography, 49–51, 56
òyìnbó, 396n24
òyìnbó *dúdú* (white-black), 279, 283, 286

Pagano, Giuseppe, 177, 183
Palace of Public Education (Mexico),
    165–66
Palace of the Fascist Party (Italy), 177
Pearse, Samuel, 280
Pensabene, Giuseppe, 175–76
people of color, 311; dispossession of, 294,
    302, 304; restricted to blighted
    neighborhoods, 299–301 *See also* African
    Americans; blacks
photography, 16–17; of Emmett Till's body,
    224, *225,* 226; in marketing, 220–22,
    222–23; power of, 230–32; in production
    of meaning, 223, 233–34; in USG
    publicity, 227–28, *229, 231,* 233–38,
    235–37
physiognomy, 7, 92; Chinese, 91–93;
    differences of, 85, 139–41, *140*
Piacentini, Marcello, 172, 177–78, 181, 183
Piazza w gli edifici delle Forze Armate
    (Piazza and buildings of the Armed
    Forces, Italy), 173, 178–81
Pierson, William H., Jr., 9
plantation systems, 46–47
Poland, 193
politics, 57, 100
Pollini, Gino, 173, 180–84, *181, 185*
polygenesis, 37–38
Pomfret, B. George, 227
Pöppelmann, Mattha:s Daniel, 82
Porter, David, 86, 90
positivism, 162
Potter, Janet Greenstein, 111
poverty, 319–20

Powell, Judson, 308, 316, 320
pre-Hispanic traditions, in Mexican
    culture, 159, 161, 163, 170
primitivism, modernist, 148
property ownership, 230, 280, 294
property value, 296–97, 299–300
Prussian Settlement Commission, 193–94
public architecture, 121
public housing, 314, 329
public participation, in urban renewal,
    329–30
Purifoy, Noah, 18, 320; background of,
    311–12; community arts work of, 312,
    314, *315*; exhibits by, 308, 316–17, 319–22;
    furniture design by, 312, *313*; junk
    modernism of, 310–11, 318–19; teaching
    by, 313–15

Quadremère de Quincy, Antoine-
    Chrysostome, 137–41
Quilliam, Abdullah, 277–78

race, 40, 62, 106, 141, 245, 294, 311;
    architecture appropriate to, 142, 164, 251;
    art and, 116–17, 166, *167–68*, 176; as
    biologically determined, 27, 92; blight
    and, 232–33, 292, 307; built environment
    and, 204–5; citizenship and, 324–25, 329,
    337; effects of, 27, 198; evolution of, 13,
    15–16, 27, 121, 143; influence of, 11, 80,
    135–36, 164; interchangeability with
    other identity markers, 87, 326, 330; in
    marketing, 221, 232; meanings of, 60–61,
    159; in Mexico, 156, 166, *167–68*; in
    nationalism, 77–78; of skyscraper
    builders, 211, 215; in spatial planning,
    212–75; transformation of, 174; as
    "variety," 37–38, 90, 349n5; Viollet-le-
    Duc's typology of, 139
race mixing: control of, 169–70, 271; effects
    of, 143–44, 159, 169; in Maragua, Kenya,
    272–74; in *mestizaje* identity, 156,
    161–63 *See also* miscegenation
race organizations, du Bois calling for,
    61–62, 64
race relations, 35, 129–30, 271–73
race science, 135–36, 364n4
racial attributionism, 138, 143
racial differences, 9–10, 26, 60–61, 92, 120,
    136, 146, 211–12, 260; of physiognomy of,
    139–41, *140*
racial hierarchy, 28, 38, 71–73, 156, 349n4
racial historicism, 150–51
racial ideologies, 58, 60, 135, 137, 142, 174

racialism, 15, 134–36, 143, 150–51
racialization, 92, 94, 137–38, 175
racial naturalism, 150–51
racial policies/laws: in Italy, 174–76, 178,
    182–83; "sundown" laws, 221, 227
racial purity/impurity, 16, 176, 179, 182
racial taxonomies, Jefferson's, 35
racism, 63, 302, 330; effects of, 186, 259–60,
    301–2; in Germany, 325, 334–36; in
    responses to junk art exhibit, 318–19;
    state/scientific, 60–61, 77, 174–75, 179;
    unacceptability of, 10, 143
railroads: effects of, 104–5; in Gilpin's
    global proposal, 106–7; stations designed
    by Van Brunt, 102–3, *105,* 111–14
Ramée, Daniel, 142
Ranke, Leopold von, 93
rationalism, 142, 177–78, 184
Rava, Carlo Enrico, 183
real estate development, 296–97, 300–302
realism, 120, 175, 178
reason, 28, 42, 63, 92
religions, 129, 279, 281–83
Renwick, James, 123
Republican Party, US, 130–32
Richardson, Henry Hobson, 110–14
Richardson Romanesque, 110–11
Richmond, Virginia, 23–24, *24, 29*
Riehl, Wilhelm Heinrich, 190–92
rituals, around Gïküyü huts, 264–66
Robertson, Jaquelin, 330
Robinson, Geroidy Tanquary, 73–74
Roediger, David, 132
Romanesque, Richardson's, 110–11
Root, John, 210
Roth, Lorna, 234
rural ideal, in Germany, 190
Ruskin, John, 117, 127–28, 130–31, 268
Rydell, Charles, 179

Saavedra, Gustavo, *155*
Said, Edward, 13
Saldanha, Arun, 311
Sancho, Ignatius, 38
Sandler, H. F., 227
Sàró (Sierra Leonean immigrants), 279,
    281–83, 286–87, 394n11
Savage, Kirk, 116–17
Schönbrunn Palace, 82
Schultze-Naumburg, Paul, 189–91
Schwindrazheim, Oscar, 190
scientism, 60
Scott, George Gilbert, 142
secular rationalism, 35–36

urban renewal, 302; of Kreuzberg, *326, 326–30, 331, 335*

U.S. Capitol, 14–15, 23; designs for, 51–56, 347n33; site for, 52–53; Thornton's design for, 43, *52–55, 52–64,* 347n30

U.S. Gypsum Research Village (Illinois), 218–20, *219,* 220–21; architects and builders of, 227–28; effects of photos of, 222–24; as photographic project, 220–21; publicity for, 218, *219,* 220–22, *222–24, 229,* 229–30, 233; publicity photos for, 226–27, *229,* 229–38, *231, 235–37;* target audience for, 227, 229–30, *231,* 232–33

Van Brunt, Henry, 15, 107; on frontier culture, 101–2; on nationality and character, 108–9; railroad stations designed by, 102–3, *105,* 111–14, *112;* relocating to Midwest, 100, 114; Richardson Romanesque style of, 100, 110–11; Richardson's influence on, 112–13

Vasconcelos, José, 159, 164, 166–67, 169–70

Vedder, Elihu, 121

Venetian Gothic, 128

vernacular architecture, 251, 270, 388n43; high *vs.,* 268–69; in Southeast Asia, 247, 254–55, 389n56; uses of term, 266–68

vernacular culture, Midwest, 107–9, 114

villagization, 262–63, *263,* 264–67, 269, 391n12

Viollet-le-Duc, Eugène-Emmanuel, 3, 11, 102, 139, 142, 144; design theories of, 163–64; on race and style, 173–74

Virginia, 29, 35; cultivation of people of, 33–34; demographics of, 29, 40; Latrobe's paintings of, 24–25, *25;* state government of, 23, 29–30

Virginia Capitol, 14, 26, *34;* construction of, 30, 41–42; design of, 23, 25, 30, *31–32,* 33

Vlach, John Michael, 10

Vohel, Hans-Jochen, 324

Wai, William Lim Siew, 252

Wailly, Charles de, 54, 348n39

Washington, Booker T., 62–63

Washington, George, 52, 56

Watts, Los Angeles, 317, 322; isolation of, 312–13; poor conditions in, 313–14; poverty in, 310, 313

Watts rebellion, 315–16, 319; effects of, 308–9; junk from, 316–17, 319

Wee Chwee Heng, 251

Wehileye, Alexander, 310

Welch, Sue, 322

West Indies, 45, 48, 57–58

Wheatley, Phillis, 38, *39*

whiteness, 101, 132–33, 230; in photos of USG Village, 223, *223–24,* 229–30; qualities attributed to, 100, 142–43

whiteness discourses, in Enlightenment, 19

white supremacy, 12–14, 60, 297

Whitfield, Lela, 291, 305, *306,* 307

Whitney, Anne, 116–19, *117,* 131, 360n8

Wight, Peter B., 15, 120; Gothic Revival of, 117–18, 133; National Academy of Design building by, 117–18, 121, *124*

Williams, Frank B., 296

Williams, Paul R., 314

Wilson, Edmund, 207

Wilson, William, 321

Winant, Howard, 13

Winckelmann, Johann Joachim, 7

Wok, Othman, 252

Wolseley, Garnet, 94–95, 357n43

Wong, Alfred, 250, 388n46

Woodward, Benjamin, 131

workers, 17, 41, 185, 204; in skyscraper construction, 210–12, *212–14,* 215–16, 380n38

world's fairs, 11, 172

World War I, 152

World War II, 184–86, 332, 334

Wright, Henry, 299, *300*

Wynter, Sylvia, 27

Yeap, Kee, 242

Yuanmingyuan garden complex, 84, 92, 94–95

Zea, Leopoldo, 162

Zenobia in Chains (Hosmer), 120–21

zoning, segregation through, 295–96, 300–301